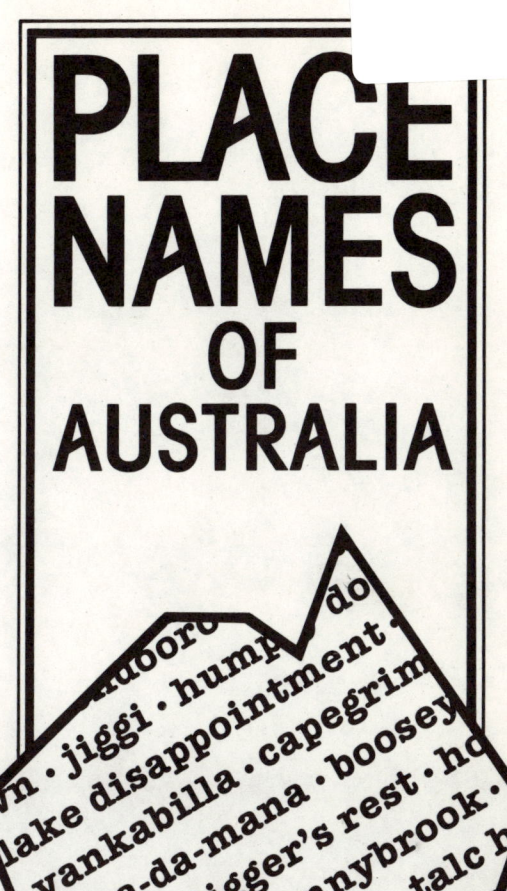

PLACE NAMES OF AUSTRALIA

...jiggi · hump...
lake disappointment ·
yankabilla · capegrim
cobba-da-mana · boosey
...ydney · digger's rest · h...
...long · donnybrook ·
...etland · talc h...
...burgoone...
· you...

A. W. REED

PLACE NAMES OF AUSTRALIA

A. W. REED

First Published 1973
Reprinted 1974
         1979
         1984
         1987

REED BOOKS PTY LTD
2 Aquatic Drive
Frenchs Forest NSW 2086

© A.W. REED

All rights reserved. No part of this publicaiton may be reproduced, stored in a retrieval system, or transmitted in any form or by any means electronic, mechanical, photocopying, recording or otherwise, without the prior written permission of the publishers.

National Library of Australia
Cataloguing-in-Publication data
Reed, Alexander, Wyclif, 1908-1979
   Place names of Australia.
   Index
   First published, Sydney: Reed, 1973
   Bibliography
   ISBN 0 7301 0051 0
   1. Names, Geographical—Australia, I. Title.
919.4

Printed in Hong Kong for Imago Productions (F.E.) Pte. Ltd.

CONTENTS

Introduction 7
Place Names of Australia 9
Personalities 237
Superseded Place Names 261
Aboriginal Names 267
Bibliography 271

INTRODUCTION

EVEN THE MOST CASUAL GLANCE through the place names in this book reveals that Australia owes its nomenclature to a variety of sources. In the earliest days of European contact, Dutch navigators bestowed names on coastal features, several names having survived to the present day. After them came British explorers, notably Captain Cook, who gave a large number of names to features on the eastern coast. Amongst the earliest surveyors of the coastal regions were Matthew Flinders and Philip Parker King. These explorers of British extraction chose names of eminent British personalities, shipmates, and friends, as well as descriptive terms.

Then came the explorers of the inland regions who followed the same practice as the seafarers, and frequently honoured their companions, other explorers, early governors, and officials in this manner. As settlers followed in the footsteps of the explorers, their own names began to appear on the map, as well as those imported from the homeland. Fortunately the heritage of Aboriginal names was not forgotten. The richness and variety has been increased by such names, many of which appear puzzling to visitors and even to Australians.

Some names have been changed or lost in the course of time. One of the several features of the present work is an appendix containing a list of 'lost names', together with their later replacements. Personalities are also indexed, not only when their names have been given to localities, but also where they have some connection with other places. In this way the great name-givers of Australian history are immediately recognisable by the number of entries following their names.

One of the difficulties facing the compiler of a book such as this is that of selection. In this case the names that have been selected are of places that appear in *The Readers Digest Atlas of Australia* and in the *Australian Encyclopaedia,* published by the Grolier Society, together with other lesser known places where the name is of historic or other interest. It is inevitable that some names must be omitted for lack of information. In such cases the compiler will welcome information from readers, especially if it is accompanied by the authority quoted.

In such a popular work, reference to authorities would add to the size and complexity of a book designed for popular use, but it should be noted that wherever possible the meaning and origin has been checked with reference to other sources, and the most authoritative of these being taken.

Many of the more important entries that appear in *Place Names of New South Wales* by the same compiler appear in the present volume, but places of lesser importance and size have been omitted.

The information that is recorded here comes from many sources — books of local and wider interest, periodicals, and communications from private individuals who are interested in the subject. Acknowledgement must also be made to the several books by A. E. Martin, published by the New South Wales Bookstall Company in the 1940s. An indefatigable collector, the late Mr Martin has added much to our knowledge of the subject.

A. W. REED

PLACE NAMES OF AUSTRALIA

ABC Range SA   Reputedly named because of a theory that there are as many separate hills as letters of the alphabet.

Aberdeen NSW   Named after Lord Aberdeen (George Hamilton-Gordon) who was Prime Minister of Britain at the beginning of the Crimean War; or after the Scottish city. Aboriginal name Moonbil, the Greenhead ant.

Aberfeldy V   After Aberfeldy in Scotland.

Abernethy NSW   After a small township in Scotland.

Abrolhos Islands WA   See Houtman's Abrolhos Islands.

Abundance, Mount Q   After T. L. Mitchell's expedition left Boree, near Orange, in December 1845, promising country was found in the Maranoa region. The discovery was celebrated by the naming of Mount Abundance.

Abyssinia T   See under Jericho.

Adaminaby NSW   Aboriginal. Camping place, or Place for resting. The pastoral station established by Cosgrove and York in 1848 was named Adaminaby. A town site was formed in 1885 and given the name Seymour, but was changed to the present form the following year. In 1957 the site was covered by the rising waters of Lake Eucumbene, formed by a large dam in the Snowy River Scheme. The present township is six miles away from the original site. Unusual names often provide a challenge to ingenuity. An apocryphal story relates how a German gave a mine to his wife Ada, and said: 'Ada's mine it be'.

Adavale Q   Originally Ada's Veil, the name recalling an incident when Mrs E. J. Stevens, who was travelling with her husband to Tintinchella in 1870, lost her veil during the crossing of Blackwater Creek. When the railway reached the township the name was changed to Adavale.

Adcock River WA   Discovered and named in 1903 by Frank H. Hann.

Adelaide SA   After Queen Adelaide, consort of William IV, who requested that the Queen's name should be conferred upon the future capital. She left part of her library to the city. The main thoroughfare was called King William Street. Aboriginal name: Tandarnya or Tandarynga.

Adelaide River NT   Discovered by L. R. Fitzmaurice and C. Keys of HMS *Beagle* in 1839, and named in honour of Queen Adelaide, who was dowager queen at the time.

Adelong NSW   Aboriginal. River on a plain. Adelong Creek station was established by David Johnston in 1848.

Adieux, Cape SA   The point at which Nicholas Baudin completed his charting of the coast.

9

Adventure Bay T   On 15 March 1773, Tobias Furneaux wrote: 'Having compleated our wood and water, sailed from Adventure bay, intending to coast it up alongshore as high 'til we fell in with the Land seen by Captain Cook and discover whether Van Diemen's Land joins with New Holland.' Furneaux had accompanied Cook on his second voyage, being in command of the *Adventure*. The *Resolution* and *Adventure* became separated in New Zealand waters. Furneaux set off for Van Diemen's Land and took shelter on 12 March 1773 in the bay he named Adventure Bay. As he says in his narrative, Furneaux then sailed north until the land trended to the west. He surmised that it was a deep bay, unaware of the existence of a strait, and headed for his rendezvous with Cook at Queen Charlotte Sound in New Zealand. Cook accepted Furneaux's report that Van Diemen's Land was part of New Holland, and set sail for Tahiti. On his third voyage he anchored the *Resolution* and *Discovery* in Adventure Bay on 27 January 1777, and remained there for two days. Tasman had attempted to enter the bay in 1642, but was driven out to sea. Other early callers included Bligh and d'Entrecasteaux.

Afghan Rocks WA   Probably named because of the Afghans whose religion prohibited the use of alcohol. They were therefore in demand as carriers of liquor to prospectors.

Afterlea NSW   Formerly known as Cob o' Corn.

Agnes V   After the daughter of John Gellions, a local publican, in the 1850s.

Ainslie, Mount NSW   After a British army officer of this name who arrived in New South Wales about 1823 and managed a sheep run in the Canberra district. While on the summit of the hill with some friends he accepted a wager that he could gallop down the steepest part. The horse missed its footing and Ainslie fell and broke his neck. He was buried on the spot where he died.

Airey's Inlet V   After G. S. Airey, a soldier who fought in the Crimean War.

Airly V   After the Earl of Airly.

Albacutya, Lake V   Aboriginal. Sour quandong.

Albany WA   In November 1826 a detachment of 44 soldiers and convicts were dispatched from New South Wales under the command of Major Edmund Lockyer. Governor Darling feared that the French might claim the western part of the continent, and ordered Lockyer to take possession of it. Lockyer's expedition arrived in the brig *Amity* on 26 December 1826. Unaware of the earlier visit of Captain Vancouver (see under King George Sound), Lockyer named the settlement Frederickstown in honour of Frederick, Duke of York and Albany, Commander in Chief of the British Army, and brother of King George IV. Lockyer was apparently the only one to use the name, for it never became popular, and was replaced in official documents on 1 January 1832 by the name of one of the Duchies.

Albany Island Q   Named by Lieut York of HMS *Rattlesnake*. It was originally intended to use this name for Somerset, q.v.

Albatross Bay Q   After a patrol vessel that cruised in the vicinity of Cape York Peninsula. The *Duyfken* passed across the mouth of Albatross Bay in 1606, and the captain recorded the name Vliege Baij (Fly Bay) on his chart.

Albatross Island T   Matthew Flinders wrote in his journal on 9 December 1798: 'Although we kept to the wind off and on the island while waiting for the boat, yet the tide had drifted us considerably to leeward before she got on board, and when we had unloaded her of the seals and albatrosses, and gotten the boat in and stowed, the island which [I] call Albatross Island bore N. 77° E. 5 or 6 miles.'

Albert NSW   The first station here, well endowed with water holes, was owned by a Mr Albert.

Albert, Lake SA   Discovered by William J. S. Pullen (who later became a Vice-Admiral) in 1840, and named by Governor Gawler in honour of Prince Albert, the Consort of Queen Victoria. Aboriginal name: Yarli.

Albert River Q   The larger of the two rivers of this name in Queensland flows into the Gulf of Carpentaria. It was discovered in 1841 by Captain J. Lort Stokes in the *Beagle*, and named after Prince Albert, consort of Queen Victoria.

Albert River V   Discovered and named by W. A. Brodribb in 1841, doubtless after Prince Albert.

Alberton V   Named in 1842, again after Prince Albert.

Albion NSW   Governor Phillip had some intention of giving this name to the first settlement, but it was not proceeded with, and Sydney Cove and finally Sydney came into use.

Albury NSW   The Aboriginal name was Bungambrewatha, and when the township was surveyed in 1839 it was given this name. As it was unmanageable, it was changed to Aldbury, probably after Aldbury in Hertfordshire. Later the 'd' was dropped and it became Albury. Aldbury means 'Old fort'.

Aldinga SA   A corruption of the Aboriginal Aldingga, Much water.

Aleck, Mount SA   After Alexander Lang Elder, an Adelaide businessman.

Alectown; Alectown West NSW   Originally known as Alec's Flat, the district was named after the three men who first prospected here — Alexander Cameron, Alexander Patton, and Alexander Whitelaw.

Alexandra V   A gold-mining township in the 1870s, it was first known as Red Gate, but later changed to Alexandra in honour of Queen Alexandra, then Princess Alexandra, wife of the Prince of Wales who on his accession to the throne became King Edward VII. She was the mother of King George V.

Alexandrina, Lake SA Named after Princess Alexandrina, later Queen Victoria, by Sturt in 1830. He crossed the lake by whaleboat at the conclusion of his journey down the Murray River and wrote: 'I was influenced by feelings of loyalty when I named this lake, when it was doubtful whether I would ever again see the face of civilised man.' Aboriginal names: Parnka, Kayinga, and Mungkuli.

Alford SA After Henry Alford of the South Australian police. He conducted gold escorts between Adelaide and the Victoria diggings.

Alford, Mount NSW Discovered and named by Allan Cunningham in 1828. The Aboriginal name was Gilladin, meaning Moon setting behind the mountain.

Alfred and Marie Range WA On his epoch-making but unsuccessful expedition in 1873, Ernest Giles sighted the range some 40 km distant. As he was distant some 160 km from the nearest water supply he was forced to turn back, but before doing so named the distant range in honour of the then Duke and Duchess of Edinburgh. On his later expedition from Perth in 1876 he succeeded in crossing the range.

Algebuckina SA Aboriginal, Water hole. The name was confirmed by Governor Buxton in 1898.

Alice Springs NT After Lady Alice Todd, wife of Sir Charles Heavitree Todd, Postmaster-General and Government Astronomer. In 1871 John Ross chose the Heavitree Gap for the route of the Overland Telegraph Line where it lay across the MacDonnell Ranges. The springs, which are a water hole in the Todd River, were used as a watering place by the telegraph staff. They were named in honour of the wife of Todd, who was responsible for the construction of the line. The telegraph repeater station, built in 1872, was also known as Alice Springs. The site was not suitable for the town, which was surveyed and gazetted in 1888 as Stuart, doubtless after J. McDouall Stuart, who passed within about 50 or 60 km of the springs in 1860. The name of the explorer was not perpetuated, for when the original telegraph station was transferred to the town, the name of Stuart was officially replaced by Alice Springs. 'The Alice' is sometimes called 'the capital of the Centre'. Aboriginal: Tjauritji.

Allambee V Aboriginal: Quiet resting place.

Allan Cunningham NSW The botanist-explorer arrived at Sydney Cove in 1816, and went on many botanising and exploring expeditions in various parts of Australia. He accompanied John Oxley on his 1817 expedition through the Blue Mountains. His longest journey was in 1827, when he discovered the Darling Downs and Cunningham's Gap, which was named after him. He became Colonial Botanist in New South Wales in 1837, but resigned shortly afterwards, mainly because he objected to having to grow cabbages for the Governor. The botanical names of many Australian trees perpetuate his name and that of his brother Richard, who preceded him as Colonial Botanist.

Allawah NSW   Aboriginal. Remain here.

Allen Island Q   Discovered and named by Matthew Flinders after John Allen, who was a miner by occupation, and was a member of the crew of the *Investigator*. It is likely that he employed his time gathering rocks for the scientists on board the vessel.

Alligator River NT   Named by Philip Parker King during his survey of Van Diemen's Gulf in 1820, in the belief that the crocodiles that infested the marshes were alligators. Three separate perennial streams were erroneously named the West, South, and East Alligator River. The area was traversed by Leichhardt on his expedition to Port Essington.

Allora Q   Aboriginal. A corruption of Gnallarah, Place of Swamps.

Alma SA   Named in 1856 after the Battle of Alma, which was fought in 1854.

Almaden Q   Aboriginal. Mine (noun).

Almurta V   Aboriginal. Mistletoe.

Alpha Q   The first letter of the Greek alphabet, probably conferred on the locality by the first settler.

Alonnah T   See under Lunawanna.

Alstonville NSW   After the Hon. J. Perry's wife, whose maiden name was Alston. Perry, who owned a great deal of land in the district, conferred the name, changing it from Duck Creek Mountain.

Althorpe Islands SA   This rocky group of islands off Cape Spencer was discovered by Matthew Flinders in the *Investigator*, and named after an heir of Earl Spencer.

Alum Mountains NSW   The range of mountains contains vast deposits of the mineral alutine, or alum rock, some of which is of unusual purity and is burnt with limestone to produce fertiliser. The Aboriginal name was Minni-Minni.

Alvie V   After the birthplace of James MacPherson Grant.

Amadeus, Lake NT   After King Amadeus of Spain. Ernest Giles, who discovered the lake in 1872, wished to confer the name of his patron, Ferdinand von Mueller, but Mueller insisted that the lake and nearby mountain be named 'in honour of two enlightened royal patrons of science', King Amadeus and Queen Olga of Spain; Giles described the lake as an 'infernal lake of mud and brine', so perhaps the Baron was fortunate in insisting that it should be named after the royal personage.

Amaroo NSW   After the pastoral station of this name. Several translations have been given for the Aboriginal name: Beautiful place; Red mud; Rain. It was believed to be the meeting-place of the Macquarie and Lachlan tribes.

13

American River SA   Long before the settlement of South Australia an American sealer, Captain Pendleton, had heard of Kangaroo Island from Nicolas Baudin. He visited it and built a 30-tonne vessel named the *Independence* at the Pelican Lagoon. Later sealers named the river on account of Pendleton's building of the ship.

Anakie V   Aboriginal. Twin hills.

Angaston SA   After George Fife Angas, financier and philanthropist, who has been called the Father of South Australia. The site of the town was selected in 1841 by Flaxman, Angas's agent, and named Angas Town by the surveyors A. Forster and James Smith. Angas was averse to any place being named after him, but in this case either he agreed or was forced to accede to popular opinion. In his later years he lived in Angastown and it is here that he is buried. An earlier name for the site was Gerham Pass.

Anglesea Point WA   After the vessel *Marquis of Anglesea*, which was wrecked at Swan River in 1827.

Annandale NSW   After Annandale in Dumfriesshire, Scotland, the birthplace of George Johnston. In 1793 he was granted 100 acres on the road to Parramatta, and gave the name which is retained for this Sydney suburb, but which was at one time called Johnston's Bush. Johnston was reputed to be the first man to have landed at Port Jackson in 1788, but this distinction is also claimed by James Ruse and Henry Kable. In 1808 Johnston led the troops that arrested Governor Bligh, and he assumed the office of Lieutenant-Governor. He had a stormy career, but was awarded a total of over 4,000 acres for his services. He was buried at Annandale Farm.

Anna's Reservoir NT   Two water holes were discovered by J. McDouall Stuart on 18 April 1860, in the Reynolds Range. One of these, which he regarded as a permanent supply and therefore useful on the return journey, he named after James Chambers's youngest daughter, Anna. As water was such a problem on these arduous exploratory journeys a water hole 'thirty yards in diameter and 100 in circumference' was sufficiently important to justify a name.

Anne, Mount T   Named by Surveyor-General George Frankland in 1835.

Anson Bay NT   After Lord George Anson, the famous English admiral who circumnavigated the world. In 1740, during the war with Spain, he became Commodore of the South American squadron.

Antiene NSW   Named after County Antrim in Ireland. Originally known by its Aboriginal name, Toowong, meaning Rich, or Fertile. It was frequently confused with the Brisbane suburb of that name. On the application of Mr R. D. Wallace, the Postal Department approved a change to Antrim, the birthplace of his father. Unfortunately his hand-writing was not legible, and the authorities read it as Antiene.

Anxious Bay SA   Named on 11 February 1802 by Matthew Flinders. The *Investigator* had been trapped on a lee shore between a headland and a group of islands. Captain and crew passed an anxious night, but next morning a change of wind enabled them to reach an anchorage behind Waldegrave Island.

Anzac Hill NT   On the top of the hill at Alice Springs there is a monument to soldiers of Australia and New Zealand who were killed in World Wars I and II. The name as well as the monument remain as a memorial to the fallen.

Appila SA   The full Aboriginal name is Appila-Yarowie, meaning Kangaroo hunting ground. Founded in 1872, it was originally known as Yarowie, but was changed to Appila in 1941.

Apsley NSW and V   This was the name of the house of a New South Wales resident, R. T. V. Gaden, who was influenced by the fact that it was near the town of Wellington, q.v. Apsley House, a mansion close to Hyde Park in London, was built by Baron Apsley, Lord Bathurst. In 1820 it was purchased by the British Government and presented to the Duke of Wellington. Apsley in Victoria had the same origin.

Apsley Strait NT   Discovered by P. P. King in the *Mermaid*, and named after Baron Apsley, Lord Bathurst.

Aquarius Peak Q   Named in 1846 by Thomas L. Mitchell because of a much needed supply of water discovered here.

Arafura Sea   Believed to be derived from the Portuguese word Alfours or Arafuras, meaning Free men, probably because it was originally given to the inland tribes of the Aroe Islands who remained isolated from the coastal settlements.

Aramac; Aramac Range Q   After Sir Robert Ramsay Mackenzie, Premier of Queensland. According to a well-known tradition, Mr Mackenzie, as he then was, carved the letters R. R. Mac on a tree trunk while searching for pastoral land in the area in the 1850s. Subsequently the explorer Landsborough applied the abbreviated name in the form Aramac to a creek in the vicinity. It was later used for the range, and the town that grew up nearby.

Arapiles, Mount V   Named by T. L. Mitchell in 1836 after the village in Spain where the Battle of Salamanca was fought. Mitchell was with the Duke of Wellington on that occasion, and as the day he discovered the mountain, from which he obtained a view of the western districts of Victoria, happened to be the anniversary of the battle, and the peak resembled an artillery strongpoint at Salamanca, he conferred the name of the village.

Ararat; Mount Ararat V   A pioneer settler, Horatio Spencer Wills, recorded the reason for the name in his journal in 1840 or 1841: '... like the Ark, we rested there'. Wills had been inspired by the reports of T. L. Mitchell's exploration to leave his Burra Burra station at Gundagai and, with his wife and son, his shepherds and their families, and all his livestock, to move to the Grampian Range region. He settled at a place later known as Lexington, and while surveying the region, conferred the name Ararat on his viewpoint. The Aboriginal name for Ararat was Butingitch, and of Mount Ararat, Gorambeep Barak.

Archer River Q   Named by Frank Jardine after Thomas Archer and family of Gracemere, Rockhampton, who took a prominent part in opening up central Queensland. The river was crossed by Jardine and his party on 5 January 1865. It may well have been the river discovered by the men of the *Pera* on 8 May 1623 and named after the Dutch Governor-General, Coen, by Jans Carstensz.

Ardglen NSW   A Scottish name. Once known as Doughboy Hollow.

Ardlethan NSW   High, or Hilly, in the Gaelic original; named after a place in Scotland.

Ardrossan SA   Named by Governor Fergusson about 1870 after Ardrossan (which he represented in Parliament after serving in the Crimea War) in Ayrshire, Scotland.

Argylla Ranges Q   A corruption of the Aboriginal name Yamamillah. It was coined by Ernest Henry who discovered the mineral field at Cloncurry in 1866. Aborigines guided him to the spot by the offer of clothes and a tomahawk if they would take him to where 'big fella copper sit down'. This was at Yamamillah, and the distorted name is still used for the ranges near Cloncurry.

Ariah Park NSW   A portion of the Wellman estate, which was purchased by Sam Harrison and named by him.

Arkaba SA   Aboriginal. Hidden or underground water. There are more springs about here than elsewhere in the North Flinders ranges. The word Arkaba is probably a corruption of Arkapa.

Arkaroola SA   Aboriginal. The place of Arkaroo, a great legendary Dreamtime snake. It drank Lake Frome dry, carved out the Arkaroola creek, and filled it by making water.

Armidale NSW   Properly Armadale, a town of Linlithgowshire in Scotland, the birthplace of G. J. Macdonald, Commissioner of Crown Lands for the New England district, who in 1839 established his station on the property first taken up by William Dumaresq about four years earlier. It seems that Macdonald called it Armadale, but this was corrupted to Armidale.

Arnhem Cape NT   The master of the *Arnhem* sighted the north-east cape of Arnhem Land and recorded it on his chart as De Caep Hollandie. See Arnhem Land.

Arnhem Land NT   The name was given by Matthew Flinders in honour of the Dutch vessel that skirted the coast of the Northern Territory in 1623. In January of that year Jan Carstensz in the yacht *Pera*, accompanied by a smaller vessel, the *Arnhem* (or *Aernem*), followed the course taken by the *Duyfken* in 1606. The *Arnhem* became separated from the *Pera,* and discovered the north-east coast of Arnhem Land. Shortly afterwards a landing was made on the coast of New Guinea where the master and ten of the crew were killed by the natives.

Aroona SA   Aboriginal, a condensation of Alcaroona, meaning Running water (though another translation has been given as Place of frogs). It was Samuel Parry, a surveyor, who named the valley, and who omitted the first syllable of the name that is applied to the creek, valley, and mountain.

Arrowsmith River WA   Discovered and named by George Grey in 1839.

Artarmon NSW   An Irish name, the ancestral home of the Gore family. In 1810 William Gore, Provost-Marshal of NSW, was given a land grant of 150 acres, which he called Artarmon. It has been suggested that it is a corruption of the Greek surname Artemon. There were five Greeks of this name in ancient times, all of whom had some literary interests, as writers or editors of books — such as the Letters of Aristotle, bibliographical treatises, writings on the collection and use of books, commentaries, a book on dreams and another entitled *Famous Exploits of Women.* It is a coincidence that this suburb of Sydney is now the home of a number of publishing houses and book wholesalers.

Arthur, Mount NSW   Named by John Oxley in honour of Arthur Wellesley, first Duke of Wellington.

Arthur, Mount T   After Sir George Arthur who was Lieut-Governor of Tasmania from 1824 to 1837. Though a controversial figure, he has been described as 'unselfish, of inviolable integrity, and a pre-eminently able administrator'. His name is kept alive by three other mountains of the same name, and also in the Arthur Range and Port Arthur, q.v.

Arthur River T   Also after Sir George Arthur (see above). Fossey and Goldie reached the river in 1826 but did not recognise it as a new discovery. A year later it was rediscovered by Henry Hellyer, surveyor for the Van Diemen's Land Company, who realised that it joined the Hellyer River in its lower reaches and named it after the Lieut-Governor.

Ashbourne SA   After the Parish in Derbyshire where Thomas Moore wrote *Lalla Rookh.* It was earlier named Finnis, after Colonel Boyle Finniss.

Ashburton River WA   Discovered in 1861 by F. T. Gregory and named by him in honour of Lord Ashburton, President of the Royal Geographical Society.

Ashville SA   After George Ash, who was in partnership with the South Australian statesman Charles Cameron Kingston.

Ashley NSW   After the English home of Mr Hassall, MP for Moree in the State Parliament.

Arthur's Creek V   After Henry Arthur, an early settler, and nephew of Sir George Arthur, Lieut-Governor of Van Diemen's Land.

Atherton; Atherton Tableland Q   John Atherton was a pioneer pastoralist. He was the first to take stock overland from Rockhampton and to settle in the district, at the Emerald End station, and the first to find tin in northern Queensland. The Atherton Range was also named after him.

Attack Creek NT   On his courageous attempt to cross Australia from south to north, J. McDouall Stuart and his two companions were attacked here by Aborigines. As the men were exhausted, the horses starving, and their provisions nearly all gone, the hostility of the Aborigines convinced Stuart of the need to give up the attempt at that time. The date was 26 June 1860. The indomitable explorer vowed to return. Less than a year later he succeeded in returning to the creek (which he then named), and penetrated a further 160 km north.

Attunga NSW   Aboriginal. High place.

Attunga Peak SA   When the Adelaide Bushwalkers produced a map of Wilpena Pound and vicinity in the late 1950s, they were anxious to use Aboriginal names wherever possible, but the local names had long been lost. For the bluff they chose Attunga, High place, chosen from H. M. Cooper's *Australian Aboriginal Words*.

Augustus, Mount WA   F. T. Gregory and James Roe were the first to climb the mountain, on 3 June 1858. Gregory named it after his brother, Augustus Charles Gregory, who later became Surveyor-General of Queensland.

Auld's Chain of Ponds NT   Discovered in 1862 by J. McDouall Stuart and named by him for William Patrick Auld. Auld was usually known as Pat, but Stuart referred to him as William. He was born in 1840, his father being Patrick Auld of Auldana Vineyards. The younger Patrick became a Cadet in the South Australian Survey Department and spent some time working for Goyder, the Surveyor-General, in the Lake Eyre region.

Austin, Lake WA   Named after Robert Austin, the surveyor who discovered the lake in 1854. Austin had been commissioned to search for gold. Though he found none, he predicted that the region would eventually prove to be one of the richest gold fields in the world.

Australia   At the time of first settlement there was no thought of naming the great island continent Australia. The terms New Holland, New South Wales, and even Botany Bay were used for its identification. It is primarily to Matthew Flinders that we owe the name Australia for collecting the regions of the mainland and Tasmania under one identifying name.

The origins of the term, however, go back to the Latin word Australis, meaning Southern, which was in use in various forms long before Flinders's time. As early as 1531 the French cartographer Oronce Fine placed an imaginary continent in the southern portion of his world map, and named it Terra Australis. In 1569 Mercator, and in 1570 Ortelius, used the terms Continens Australis or Australis Continens for the supposed southern land.

In 1605 Pedro Fernandez de Quiros led an expedition from Callao in Peru in search of Terra Australis. On 1 May 1606 he believed he had discovered it and named the island he had found Austrialia del Espiritu Santo, the Southern Land of the Holy Spirit. It was later proved to be simply an island in the New Hebrides, but the form Austrialia lingered for many years. de Quiros's *Memorial* contains the world Australia Incognita in the title.

An English translation of a remarkable book by Gabriel d'Foigny, probably the most famous of the fictitious accounts of the southern continent that was so eagerly sought by men of different nationalities, was published in 1693. John Dunstan, its translator and publisher, treated the French name Terre Australe as Australia, and referred to the inhabitants as Australians. A century later, in the *Zoology and Botany of New Holland and the Isles Adjacent*, by George Shaw and James Edward Smith (London 1793-4), the name Australia is used for the continent.

The accepted genesis of the present name can be ascribed to 17 July 1814, the day when Matthew Flinders's *Voyage to Terra Australis* was published. In a footnote he wrote: 'Had I permitted myself any innovation upon the original term (Terra Australis) it would have been to convert it into Australia, as being more agreeable to the ear...' It was in fact his wish to include 'Australia' in the title, but his old patron, Sir Joseph Banks, objected. In 1817 Governor Macquarie, who had read Flinders's footnote, recommended that the name Australia should be adopted, and used it in official correspondence. The term New Holland, however, was used occasionally until the middle of the 19th century.

The earlier name of New Holland was conferred because of the discoveries made by Dutch navigators in the seventeenth century.

Australind WA   A combination of the names Australia and India, originating in the abortive settlement scheme of 1841 by the Western Australia Land Company. As horses were bred here for consignment to India, it may possibly account for the 'India' portion of the name.

Avoca River V   From the 'sweet vale of Avoca', the poem by Thomas Moore. The river was originally called the Loddon by T. L. Mitchell, who reserved the name Avoca for another stream, now known as the Avon.

Avoid Bay SA   Writing on 17 February 1802 of the point and bay close to the easternmost of Whidbey's Islands, Flinders said '... there are rocks and breakers on each side of the entrance; on which account, and from its being exposed to the dangerous southern winds, I named it *Avoid Bay*'.

Avon River V   Named by Angus McMillan about 1840. It was first called the Avoca (see above).

Awk Point T   It has been conjectured that the name of this coastal prominence may have been a sailor's spelling of Hawk.

Axedale V   This and the Axe Creek were named after the Axe River in Dorset.

Ayers Rock NT   Named by William Gosse in honour of Sir Henry Ayers, Premier of South Australia, in 1873. Gosse was not the discoverer, but was the first to visit the rock. The previous year Ernest Giles had sighted it from the northern side of Lake Amadeus. He reached the rock in 1873, shortly after Gosse had departed. Aboriginal name, Uluru or Oolra.

Ayr Q   The first settlers arrived in the 1870s, but the town was surveyed in 1881, and named after the birthplace in Scotland of the Premier of Queensland, Sir Thomas McIlwraith.

Baan Baa NSW   Aboriginal. Swim away. Named after a local estate.

Babbage, Mount SA   After B. G. Babbage. Babbage first named it Mount Hopeful in 1857 as an antidote to E. J. Eyre's Mount Hopeless, which was 32 km distant. The Assistant Surveyor-General G. W. Goyder renamed it the following year.

Babinda Q   Aboriginal. From Bunda: Mountain.

Bacchus Marsh V   The town was founded in 1839 by Captain W. H. Bacchus. It was gazetted as a shire in 1856.

Backstairs Passage SA   Matthew Flinders discovered the strait in the *Investigator* in 1802 and wrote: 'It forms a private entrance, as it were, to the two gulphs (Gulf St Vincent and Investigator Strait) and I named it Backstairs Passage.' This portion of Investigator Strait is about seven miles across at its narrowest part.

Baddaginnie V   A Cingalese word meaning Hungry belly. The surveyor J. G. Wilmot gave the name when he came to his camp and found that his men were short of food.

Bagdad T   See under Jericho.

Bagshot V   Named after the Bagshot Beds of Berkshire, where there are beds of sand over a clay foundation.

Baines, Mount NT   Named by A. C. Gregory in 1855 after Thomas Baines, a member of his party. The expedition was organised to investigate the land adjacent to the Victoria River.

Baines River NT   The stream was discovered by Thomas Baines while in search of horses that had escaped from A. C. Gregory's party, mentioned in the previous entry. Gregory named it the Baines. The geologist J. S. Wilson was of the opinion that it should be named after Norton Shaw, the secretary of the Royal Geographical Society. The Society kept the peace by including both names on the maps.

Bairnsdale V   First called Bernisdale by an early settler who so named his selection after his village in Scotland. The name was later changed to Bairnsdale, the town being proclaimed in 1861. The Aboriginal name was Wy Wung.

Balaklava SA   Derived from Balaklava on the Crimea Peninsula.

Balladoran NSW   Aboriginal. Platypus. The name was first given to an estate by James Morris.

Ballan V   Named by von Steiglitz after his birthplace in Ireland.

Ballarat V   Aboriginal, from Ballaarat, Camping place or Resting place. The nearby swamp, now Lake Wendourie, was a favourite camping place for the Aborigines. The original form Ballaarat is still used in official circles.

Balldale NSW   At the time the railway station was named, R. T. Ball was MLA for the district.

Ballendella V   Named after the son of an Aboriginal who accompanied T. L. Mitchell on his 1836 expedition.

Balliang V   Named after a local Aboriginal.

Ballina NSW   A corruption of an Aboriginal name that had been recorded variously as Ballena, Balluna, Bull-na, Bulluna, and Bullina. James Ainsworth, who settled on the banks of the Richmond River in 1847, said that the name was Bullenah, and had some connection with fish or with oysters. The interpretations given are as varied as the spellings: Place of dying; Place where the wounded lay after a fight; Fighting ground or place where a battle was fought; Blood running from a wound. There seems to be some affinity with Bullenbullen, to fight. Further conjectures are that it was the name of a Richmond River tribe or that it was named by an early surveyor after Ballina, the seaport in counties Mayo and Sligo, Ireland.

Balmain NSW   After William Balmain, surgeon and landholder. As assistant Surgeon he arrived at Port Jackson in 1788, subsequently being transferred to Norfolk Island. In 1796 he was appointed Principal Surgeon in New South Wales. He was granted a total of 975 acres of land and purchased further allotments. One of his grants is now part of the Balmain suburb of Sydney.

Balmattum V   Aboriginal. Man lying on his back.

Balmoral V   After the royal residence in Scotland. The Aboriginal name was Daarangurt.

Balonne River Q   Aboriginal. There are two possible meanings. 1: Balonne or Ballon is said to mean Pelican. 2: Baloon is the local term for Stone axe. The river was discovered in April 1846 by Sir Thomas Mitchell, who used what he believed to be the Aboriginal name. One account, however, states that when he asked local blacks for the name of the river he pointed to it with a stone tomahawk which he proposed to offer as a gift, and that in return he was given the word for a tomahawk. On the other hand it seems unlikely that he would be in the possession of such a primitive implement.

Balook V   Aboriginal. Scrub country.

Bambra V   Aboriginal. Mushroom.

Bandiana V   E. J. Martin says that the name came from a bandy-legged Aboriginal woman named Anna — but it sounds a very tall story.

Bangalow NSW   A corruption of the Aboriginal name Bangalla, Low hill; or, as another version has it, because of the palm tree *Archontophoenix cunninghamiana*, a tall graceful tree with fernlike foliage, that grows in the vicinity.

Bangaroo NSW   Aboriginal. Native bear.

Banks, Cape NSW   The North Head of Botany Bay, named by Captain Cook after Sir Joseph Banks. Banks accompanied Cook on the *Endeavour* on Cook's first voyage. As a young man with a considerable fortune he devoted himself to botanical pursuits and was elected a Fellow of the Royal Society at the unusually early age of twenty-three. Banks bore all the expenses of the botanical equipment and scientific personnel of the Cook expedition, amounting to at least $20,000. His journals and the drawings of the artists provide an invaluable addition to the natural history observations made by Cook. Subsequently Banks took a great interest in the development of the first settlement and gave practical encouragement to Matthew Flinders, who added greatly to the knowledge of the Australian coast. Banks has been called the 'Father of Australia'. From 1778 until his death, he was President of the Royal Society. An obelisk was erected to his memory at Kurnell in 1914.

Banks, Cape SA   Named after the famous botanist (see above), on 3 December 1800, by Lieut James Grant, who was in command of the *Lady Nelson*. In 1801 Matthew Flinders added West to the name 'to distinguish it from Cape Banks on the East Coast, named by Captain Cook'.

Banks Strait T   Also named after Sir Joseph Banks.

Bannockburn V   After the Scottish town which is the scene of the famous battle.

Baradine NSW   Aboriginal. Red wallaby.

Baranduda V   Aboriginal. Swamp.

Barcaldyne Q   After Barcaldine in Ayrshire, Scotland. Donald Charles Cameron, a pioneer pastoralist, had visited relatives in Ayrshire, and named his station Barcaldine Downs, from which the town took its name.

Barcoo River Q   The Aboriginal name for the upper part of Cooper Creek (a name which also appears on maps). The meaning is not known. In 1846 T. L. Mitchell was anxious to find a river flowing to the north. On 15 September the discovery of a river flowing in a north-easterly direction delighted him — 'the realisation of my long-cherished hopes', he wrote, and named it after Queen Victoria (unadvisedly so, for he was aware that J. L. Stokes had already bestowed this name on a river in the Northern Territory). Mitchell's 'reward from heaven', as he described it proved singularly unrewarding, for when E. B. Kennedy, who was deputy leader of Mitchell's expedition, was sent back in the following year to trace the course of the river, he found that it turned west and flowed into the Thomson River. He wisely reversed his superior's decision, and adopted the Aboriginal name, which is used alternatively with Cooper Creek, for the river is in fact the upper waters of the Cooper, q.v.

Bardoc WA   Aboriginal. Wild man.

Barellan NSW   Aboriginal. Meeting of the waters, or possibly, Bowels. It was the name of a local sheep station.

Bargo NSW   A corruption of the Aboriginal name Barago, Thick scrub, or Brushwood. It was sometimes called Bargo Brush.

Baringhup East V   Aboriginal. Grassy place.

Barker, Mount SA   When Charles Sturt first sighted this mountain in 1830 from Lake Alexandrina he mistook it for Mount Lofty. The mistake was corrected by Captain Collet Barker, an explorer who came to Australia in 1828. He was Commandant of the British stations at Raffles Bay and Albany. In 1831 he was on an expedition that was endeavouring to discover a connection between Lake Alexandrina and Encounter Bay. He climbed Mount Lofty and saw Sturt's mountain from the summit, thus proving that it was not, as Sturt had surmised, Mount Lofty. Sturt insisted that Barker's name should be conferred on the mountain. A monument has been erected on the summit in memory of Barker, who lost his life shortly afterwards. He became separated from his companions, swam across the mouth of the Murray River and disappeared among the sandhills on 30 April 1831. This was the last that was seen of him. It is thought he met his death at the spear of an Aboriginal. The Aboriginal name of the mountain is Woma- (or Womma-) mu-kurta, or Yaktanga.

Barker, Mount WA   The mountain near the town was named in 1839 by a naval surgeon, T. B. Wilson, after Collet Barker (see above). The town of Mount Barker was proclaimed in 1899.

Barker's Creek V   After Dr Edward Barker who made an early journey from Melbourne to Gippsland.

Barkly Tableland NT and Q   This area of 140,000 sq km was discovered by William Landsborough in 1861 when in search of the Burke and Wills expedition, and named by him after Sir Henry Barkly who was then Governor of Victoria.

Barlee, Lake WA   Named by John Forrest on his first expedition in 1869.

Barmera SA   Aboriginal. The name was once applied to Lake Bonney, q.v. as well as to the settlement on its shore. It is a corruption of Barmeedjie, the tribal name of the local Aborigines.

Barn Hill SA   Named by Matthew Flinders who wrote in his journal on 8 March 1802: '. . . an elevated part, called *Barn Hill* from the form of its top'.

Barossa Valley SA   By a curious coincidence Col William Light named the Valley after the famous wine-growing district in Spain, though in actual fact it was because his friend Thomas Graham (Baron Lyndoch) had served in the Peninsula War. Light, who was South Australia's first Surveyor-General, visited the district in 1837. A few years later the German geologist Johann Menge reported that the valley would prove a good locality for vine grapes.

Barmedman NSW   After a small village in Scotland, which was the name given to a sheep station near here.

Barnawather V   Aboriginal. A corruption of Barna-woodther, Deaf and dumb.

Barney, Mount NSW   Named by Allan Cunningham in 1828. The Aboriginal name was Boogarah Boogarah, meaning Keep away! Keep away! The local tribe lived in fear of the spirits that inhabited the steep slopes and were supposed to have killed several who had the temerity to climb the mountain.

Barongarook V   Aboriginal. Running water.

Barraba NSW   The name of a station owned by J. Joskins in 1838. The Aboriginal name was Taengarrah Warrawarildi, Place of yellow-jacket trees.

Barrallier NSW   After Francis Barrallier, engineer and explorer. In 1802 he was ordered by Governor King to find a passage across the mountains beyond the Nepean. This was the first serious attempt to cross the Blue Mountains, and was a notable feat, for the explorer traversed nearly 250 km of difficult country in seven weeks, reaching a point 'towards the head of Christy's Creek, about fifteen or sixteen miles in a direct line southerly from Jenolan Caves'.

Barrenjoey Head NSW   Aboriginal. Young kangaroo.

Barrier Range SA   On leaving Adelaide to commence his crossing of the continent from south to north, Charles Sturt headed north-east to avoid the desolate salt lakes. Presently he sighted a range of hills 'rising like islands out of a vast sheet of water'. The lake was a mirage, but the hills were real. Sturt named them the Barrier Range for obvious reasons.

Barron River Q   Named by the police inspectors R. A. Johnstone and A. Douglas in 1876 in honour of their friend T. H. Barron who was a clerk in the Queensland police department. The river had been discovered a year earlier by J. V. Mulligan, who was under the impression that it was the Mitchell River.

Barrow Creek NT   Discovered by J. McDouall Stuart in 1860, and named for the South Australian journalist and politician John Henry Barrow.

Barrow Island WA   Discovered by P. P. King in June 1818 and named after John Barrow, one of the Secretaries of the Admiralty.

Bartle Frere Q   While George A. F. E. Dalrymple was exploring rivers and inlets north of Cardwell, he named Mount Bartle Frere after Sir Henry

Bartle Frere, at one time Governor of Bombay, and President of the Royal Geographical Society.

Barton SA   This station on the Transcontinental railway was named after Sir Edmund Barton, first Commonwealth Prime Minister.

Barwite V   Named after a local Aboriginal.

Barwon River NSW and V   The Aboriginal name for the river has attracted several interpretations: Wide river, Awful river, Wide awful river, and River of muddy water. A refreshingly different interpretation is Good water, because it was allegedly good to drink. The word is probably a corruption of Bawon or Bawum. Between the Macintyre and Gwydir Rivers the stream is known as the Barwon, while between Gwydir and Culgoa Rivers it is either the Darling or the Barwon. Barwon is a place name found in three different counties, each place having some legend or superstition to account for it. Another Aboriginal name for the river was Karaula.

Bass Hill NSW   After George Bass, naval surgeon and explorer who, with Matthew Flinders, made a number of notable journeys. In his *Voyage to Terra Australis,* Flinders wrote of Bass: 'I had the happiness to find a man whose ardour for discovery was not to be repressed by any obstacles nor deterred by any danger, and with this friend a determination was formed of completing the examination of the east coast of New South Wales, by all such opportunities as the duty of the ship and procurable means could admit.' Some of the discoveries were made in an eight-foot boat christened *Tom Thumb.* Bass's most notable voyage was made in 1837 and 1838 when he covered 1,200 miles in an open whaleboat.

Bass Point NSW   Named by Matthew Flinders in honour of George Bass, who is mentioned in the preceding entry. The two men explored the south coast of New South Wales. Flinders described the point as 'a long, sloping, projection which I have called Pt Bass'.

Bass Strait T   For many years it was believed that Tasmania was part of the mainland. Neither Tasman, Cook, Flinders or other early navigators had been able to prove the existence or non-existence of a strait, though Furneaux had convinced Cook that the island was part of the mainland (see Adventure Bay). Bass's claim to fame is his strong conjecture that a strait did exist. In 1798 he sailed along the south coast of present-day Victoria as far as Westernport and returned to Sydney. On observing that the tide ebbed to the east, and from the swell to the south-west he conjectured that 'whenever it shall be decided that the opening between this and Van Dieman's Land is a Strait, this rapidity of tide, and that long S.W. swell that seems to be continually rolling in upon the coast to the westward, will then be accounted for'.

Governor Hunter had himself observed the same phenomena when, as second captain of the *Sirius,* he had passed the eastern end, and thought that they might well prove the existence of the strait. He therefore accepted Bass's theory and named the Strait in honour of Bass. Later in the year 1798 George Bass and his friend Matthew Flinders finally proved the theory by sailing through the strait from east to west in the sloop *Norfolk*, and then circumnavigated the island.

Batavia River Q   See under Wenlock River.

Bateman's Bay NSW   The bay originally appeared on Captain Cook's chart, being discovered on 21 April 1770 and named after Nathaniel Bateman, Captain of the *Northumberland*, on which Cook had sailed as Master.

Bathurst NSW   After Henry, third Earl Bathurst, Secretary for the Colonies from 1812 to 1827. The name was given by G. W. Evans who reached the plains to the west of the main range in 1813 and set up his camp on the present site of Bathurst. The next day he wrote: 'I call the Plain last passed over Bathurst Plain.' When Governor Macquarie traversed the road built over the Blue Mountains some eighteen months later he recorded the name of the future town officially as Bathurst.

Bathurst Harbour T   Discovered in 1815 by Captain James Kelly and named in honour of Earl Bathurst.

Bathurst Island NT   In 1819 P. P. King proved that Bathurst and Melville Islands were separated from each other (they had been seen in 1644 by Tasman who thought they were a part of the mainland). King named the smaller one after Earl Bathurst.

Bathurst, Lake NSW   Also named after Earl Bathurst. The lake was discovered by Hamilton Hume and James Meehan in 1818.

Batman's Hill V   John Batman, the founder of Melbourne, who arrived at Port Phillip in April 1836, lived in a small house on this hill.

Battle Camp Range Q   Named after the scene of a fight nearby between prospectors who were on their way to the Palmer gold fields and a number of Aborigines.

Bauer, Cape SA   Named by Matthew Flinders in January 1802 in honour of the Austrian, Ferdinand Bauer, the natural history painter on the *Investigator*, whose drawings of plants are of outstanding merit.

Baxter V   After an early Melbourne postmaster.

Baxter Range SA   Named by E. J. Eyre after his overseer, John Baxter, whom he sent to examine a low range of hills. On his return to the camp, Baxter reported that he had failed to find water anywhere in the vicinity. At a later date he was killed by Aborigines.

Bay of Rest WA   During one of his survey expeditions, on which he was accompanied by Flinders in the *Investigator*, Philip Parker King anchored off North-west Cape in the cutter *Mermaid* on 10 February 1818. Stormy weather caused the cable to part. A day or two later the fluke of a second anchor broke. After three days of tense and dangerous battling against wind and sea, the *Mermaid* came to a safe anchorage in the bay that King thankfully named the Bay of Rest.

Bayswater V The name was given by J. J. Miller who was born in Bayswater, London.

Beabula NSW Aboriginal. Two black cockatoos.

Beachport SA Beachport in Rivoli Bay was surveyed and named by Sir Samuel Way in honour of Sir M. E. Hicks-Beach, who was Secretary of State for the Colonies. Aboriginal name Wirmalngrang, Owl's cave.

Beaconsfield V After Benjamin Disraeli, Earl of Beaconsfield, the famous statesman.

Beaconsfield T Also named by F. A. Weld, Governor of Tasmania, in honour of the Earl of Beaconsfield. When Lieut Col Paterson established a settlement at Port Dalrymple, the site of Beaconsfield was known as Cabbage Tree Hill. When gold was discovered it was renamed Brandy Creek, and did not receive its present name until 1879.

Beagle Bay WA After HMS *Beagle*. The bay was discovered on 24 January 1838 while the *Beagle*, commanded by J. C. Wickham, was surveying the north-west coast. John Lort Stokes who was aboard at the time wrote somewhat ponderously that the bay was 'named Beagle Bay, and may serve hereafter to remind the seamen who benefit by the survey in which the vessel bore so conspicuous a part, of the amount of his obligations to the Government that sent her forth, the skill and energy that directed her course, and the patient discipline by which, during her long period of active service, so much was done for the extension of our maritime knowledge'.

Bealiba V Aboriginal. Flood red gum creek.

Beames Brook Q Named by Leichhardt after Walter Beames of Sydney.

Beardy Plains; Beardy River; Beardy Waters NSW Colonel Dumaresq, the owner of Tilbuster station some five miles from Armidale, employed two stockmen named Duval and Chandler in the 1830s. They both had an intimate knowledge of the region round about, and were notable for their long black beards. Newcomers to the region who were searching for suitable locations to establish their stations were usually advised to consult the 'beardies'. The nickname was eventually given to the district, and also to the two rivers named Beardy River and Beardy Waters. There is also a Beardy Street in Armidale. In more serious mood Mount Duval, Chandler River, and Chandler's Peak provide a permanent memorial to these two notable stockmen.

Beatrice Hill NT Named by William Greig Evans after his daughter Madge Evans.

Beatrice River Q After Mrs Beatrice Boulter, the wife of C. C. Boulter who conducted surveys in Arnhem Land.

Beaudesert Q From an early stock station, originally owned by Edward Hawkins, and known in 1842 as Beau Desert, the name being taken from Beau Desert Park in Staffordshire where Hawkins was born.

Beaufort V   Named after Rear-Admiral Sir Francis Beaufort. The Beaufort scale used for wind velocities was introduced by him. The place was known at one time as Fiery Creek, on account of a raging bush fire. The Aboriginal name of the town site was Yarram Yarram.

Beckom NSW   A corruption of Beckham, the maiden name of the wife of Wellman, the squatter who named his farm Ariah Park.

Beeac V   After a local Aboriginal.

Beechworth V   Named after the English home of one of the Government surveyors who laid out the town in the 1850s. The site was passed by Hume and Hovell in 1824, but the first settler in the valley did not arrive until 1839. When gold was found at Woolshed Creek, the shanty town was known first as May Day Hills or Ovens Diggings.

Beelbangera NSW   Aboriginal. Native companion.

Beenac V   Aboriginal. Bag or Basket.

Beenleigh Q   Aboriginal name Wobbumarjoo, Boggy clay.

Beerbarrum Q   Aboriginal. Parrot, or Sound of parrots' wings.

Beerwah Q   Aboriginal. Up in the sky.

Bega; Bega River NSW   Aboriginal. Beautiful, or Large camping ground. On an early plan it appears as Bika. It appeared as Biggah in 1839, when the first licence was taken out for the station. By 1848 the licence was held by Dr George Imlay in the form of Bega, which was finally adopted for the town.

Belaringar NSW   Aboriginal. Freshwater crayfish.

Belgrave V   Named by E. W. Benson after Belgrave in Leicestershire, meaning Marten grove.

Bell NSW   After Archibald Bell, who discovered the route over the Blue Mountains by way of Richmond. The route was later known as Bell's Line, and the township also was named after him.

Bell Q   After Joshua Peter Bell, a squatter, owner of the Jimbour station, member of Parliament, and President of the Legislative Council. He was noted for his race-horses, and won several international prizes for wool.

Bell Point SA   Named by Flinders in January 1802 after Hugh Bell, surgeon on the *Investigator*. In a letter to his wife Flinders wrote of him: 'Mr Bell is misanthropic and pleases nobody.'

Bellarine V   Aboriginal. Elbow.

Bellarwi NSW   Aboriginal. River oak.

Bellata NSW   Aboriginal. Kangaroo.

Bellbird NSW   Probably the name of the original coalmine.

Bellender-Ker Range Q   Named on 22 June 1819 by P. P. King at the request of Allan Cunningham after John Bellender-Ker, a man of Scottish descent. The mountains were frequently referred to as the Wooroonooran Range, this name still being used on occasion.

Bellerive T   The name of a village on the shore of Lake Geneva, which George Frankland, who became Surveyor-General of Tasmania, conferred on the Hobart suburb.

Bellevue Hill NSW   First called Vinegar Hill (not to be confused with the hill of the same name which later became Rouse Hill). The name offended Governor Macquarie, who in 1820 ordered 'a finger board . . . to be painted with the name "Belle Vue" and fixed on the centre of a circle or mound on top of the hill vulgarly called "Vinegar Hill".'

Belmont NSW   From Belmont Farm, which was established in the early 1860s, Belmont House being built by the middle of the decade.

Beltana SA   Aboriginal. Probably Running water, or Place of running water, though it has been suggested that the word is a corruption of Peltana, meaning Opossum skin. It was at first known as Mount Deception. In 1840 E. J. Eyre set out on an exploratory trip which took him first to Lake Torrens, whence he struck out to the east, following the Flinders Range. The outlook was confined to salt, mud, arid desert wastes and rocky outcrops. To two of the prominent peaks he therefore gave the names Hopeless and Deception, and from the latter the site of Beltana took its earlier name.

Belubula River NSW   Aboriginal. Stony river.

Ben Bullen NSW   Aboriginal. Two meanings have been given: High quiet place, and Lyre bird. On the other hand Henry Lawson stated that Ben Bullen was a bullock driver who prospered by selling potatoes at the time of the gold rush at Mudgee.

Ben Lomond NSW   After the Scottish mountain. The New England town is on the western slope of the mountain that bears the same name.

Ben Lomond T   First sighted by Flinders, the mountain was later named by Col William Paterson, doubtless after the Scottish mountain, when he founded the first settlement in northern Tasmania in 1804. The Aboriginal name was Toorbunna.

Ben, Mount NT   Named in 1860 by J.'McDouall Stuart after Benjamin Head, who was a member of his expedition.

Benalla V   From the Aboriginal word Benalta meaning either Musk duck, or Crossing place. T. L. Mitchell crossed Broken River and discovered the site that was taken up as a sheep run by Rev Joseph Docker in 1838 and named Benalta. When the township was surveyed in 1846 the name was changed to Benalla.

Benayeo V   Aboriginal. To throw.

Bendick Murrell NSW   Aboriginal. Plain. The name was first given to Major Stewart's station and to the surrounding parish.

Bendigo V   The name originated indirectly from the famous English prize-fighter William 'Abednego' Thompson, popularly known as Bendigo. In 1850 he was Champion of All England. He had a colourful career. On his retirement he became a drunkard, was converted, and toured England with General William Booth as an evangelist.

Bendigo, or Bendigo's Creek was known as early as 1840, when the first sheep run in the district was taken up by Charles Sherratt (or Sherrard) at Ravenswood, eleven years before the gold rush began. One of the Ravenswood shepherds had a reputation as a prize-fighter and was nicknamed Bendigo after his British counterpart. A Ravenswood outstation was first known as Castleton and then as Sandhurst, but was always referred to locally as Bendigo, even when Sandhurst was officially recognised. In the long run officialdom had to bow to popular opinion and in 1891 Bendigo at last had the blessing of authority.

Benerembah NSW   Aboriginal. Man eloping with a woman — a very dangerous practice amongst the Aborigines. The name was that of a pastoral holding.

Bennelong Point NSW   The site of the Sydney Opera House commemorates one of the first Aborigines to be introduced to European society. As early as 1789 Governor Phillip captured a young man named Bennelong, who gradually became accustomed to the food and clothing of his white captors. The Governor gave him a house on the eastern point of Sydney Cove (once known as Cattle Point), on which his name was later conferred. He lived there with his wife Barangaroo. His life was an uneasy one, halfway between two cultures. In 1792 he accompanied Governor Phillip to England and was presented to King George III. On his return his second wife Gooroobarrooboollo rejected him. It is thought that he was born in 1764 and was killed in a tribal fight in 1813.

Bennett Springs SA   Has the distinction of being named after a horse. The springs were named by J. McDouall Stuart in February 1861 after one of his horses which died. It had been with him on an earlier expedition and was described as one he 'could depend on for a hard punch'.

Bentinck Island Q   Discovered on 19 November 1802 by Matthew Flinders and named in honour of Lord Bentinck, Governor-General of India, whose term of office was notable for the suppression of the practice of *suttee* and the *thug* cult.

Bentley NSW   After a homestead belonging to R. V. Dawson.

Bermagui NSW   Aboriginal. Canoe with paddles. It has also been spelled Bermaguee, while an early plan was Permageua.

Berri SA   Aboriginal. The name of a bush found growing freely in the district. Early settlers referred to the township as Beri-Beri.

Berrigan NSW   Aboriginal. A common bush, *Eremophila longifolia*. It is possible that the word may be a corruption of Beereegan, Place of quails.

Berrima NSW   Aboriginal. Southward.

Berriwillock V   Aboriginal. Birds eating berries.

Berry; Berry's Bay NSW   After Alexander Berry, who arrived at Sydney in 1819 and became the first settler in the district now known as Berry, in 1822. The place was earlier known as Broughton Creek, and only received its present name in 1888. Together with his brother-in-law Edward Wollstonecraft, Berry set up in business as a general merchant. The partners' vessels frequently moored in the bay that took its name from Berry.

Bessiebelle V   Named by J. G. Wilmot after Bessie Cameron.

Beta Q   The second letter of the Greek alphabet. See under Alpha.

Bethungra NSW   Aboriginal. Black mountain. The name was originally given to Frank Cowley's pastoral station.

Beulah V   An appropriate name from Isaiah 62:4: 'Thou shalt no more be termed Forsaken; neither shall thy land any more be termed Desolate: but thou shalt be called Hephzi-bah, and thy land Beulah; for the Lord delighteth in thee, and thy land shall be married.'

Beveridge V   After Peter Beveridge, an early settler. Aboriginal name, Tipa.

Beverley WA   Probably after the town in England, close to York, and named by Sir James Stirling. A loyal Yorkshireman in the first group of settlers in 1830 said that the scenery reminded him of his native Yorkshire, and so the principal town was later named York. Beverley comes from an old English word meaning Beaver stream.

Bexhill NSW   After Bexhill in Surrey. The name means Boxwood hill.

Bibbenluke NSW   Aboriginal. Big look-out, or Place of birds.

Biboohra Q   Aboriginal. First known as Barron Falls, it then reverted to the original name.

Bicheno T   After James Ebenezer Bicheno, who was Colonial Secretary. The settlement was first called Wauba Debar, after an Aboriginal woman.

Billabong; Billabong Creek NSW   Aboriginal. Stream, or Pool. Billabong or Billabung was a common Aboriginal place-name in the counties of Clarendon, Goulburn, Hume, Townsend, and Waljiers. The term has been defined as 'an effluent from a river, sometimes returning to it and sometimes ending in the sand'. In *Austral English,* Edward E. Morris stated that in 'the Wiradhury dialect of the centre of NSW, East coast, *billa* means a river and *bung* dead . . . *Billabong* is often regarded as a synonym for *Anabranch;* but there is a distinction. From the original idea, the *Anabranch* implies rejoining a river; whilst the *Billabong* implies continued separation from it; though what are called *Billabongs* often do rejoin'. The latter condition would probably occur most frequently in time of flood.

Billagoe NSW   Aboriginal. Sandpiper. Possibly a corruption of Biligow or Billegoe.

Billeroy NSW   Aboriginal. Running creek.

Billiatt Springs NT   Named by J. McDouall Stuart in 1862 after John W. Billiatt 'in token of my approbation of his thoughtful, generous and unselfish conduct throughout the expedition'. Billiatt was a young man of 21 at the time. He had not been selected as a member of Stuart's expedition, but had purchased an outfit and joined it voluntarily. It has been recorded that he was motivated by the fact that he had fallen in love with a young woman whose brother, Stephen King, was a member of the party and 'conceived the romantic idea that he must look after his sweetheart's brother'.

Billimari NSW   Local legend has it that this was the name of an old Aboriginal who was well known in the district.

Billy Blue's Point NSW   After Billy Balloo, an Aboriginal. Legend says that Billy Balloo discovered rich deposits of gold, which he sold. The location of his find was never discovered, but there were rumours that it was at the point that is named after him.

Bimbi NSW   Aboriginal. Place of many birds. An abbreviated form of Bimbimbi.

Binalong NSW   Aboriginal. Two contradictory suggestions have been offered: Towards a high place; or, that it was the name of a well-known Aboriginal named Bennelong who came from another part of the country. (It has not been suggested that this was Bennelong of Bennelong Point, q.v.). The same authority says that the local residents objected to Bennelong because it was not euphonious, and that they preferred to change it to Binalong.

Binda NSW   Aboriginal. Deep water.

Bindi V   Aboriginal. Stomach.

Bingara NSW   Aboriginal. Creek.

Biniguy NSW   Aboriginal. Large expanse of open country. It was first the name of a homestead in the district.

Binnaway NSW   Aboriginal. Ear thrown away. (Binna, ear; wai, to throw away.) The name was given as a result of an incident when one Aboriginal cut off another's ear and threw it away.

Binnum SA   Aboriginal. Many she-oaks.

Binya NSW   Aboriginal. Large mountain, or Cutting in a hillside.

Birchip V   An abbreviation of the Aboriginal name Wirrembirchip.

Birdsville Q   The name was probably first given by Robert Frew of Pandie Pandie station because of the many birds to be seen there, including seagulls that came from the salt lakes a thousand miles away. When the town was laid out in 1885 by F. A. Hartnell he confirmed the name officially. Prior to this it was known as the Diamantina Crossing.

Birregurra V   Aboriginal. Kangaroo Camp. It was known as Buntingdale, the site of the first Aboriginal mission in Victoria, and also as Bowden's Point. The true Aboriginal name was Morone or Murroon.

Birriwa NSW   Aboriginal. Plain or Bustard turkey.

Bischoff, Mount T   After James Bischoff, Chairman of the Van Dieman's Land Company.

Bittern V   It seems apparent that the site was named after the swamp bird.

Black Dog Creek V   A black dog was shot near the stream by Joseph Hawdon.

Black Rock SA   A descriptive name given by Surveyor-General Frome in 1843. Aboriginal name Mitchylee or Mitehylie.

Black Stump NSW   'This side of the Black Stump' and 'the other side of the Black Stump' are colloquial expressions for a place at a great distance. As Colin Sinclair says in *Tall Bronzed and Handsome,* 'It is generally conceded that no Australians live on the other side of the Black Stump — but other people might.'

Through the courtesy of Mr R. Cameron, Shire Clerk of Coolah, we are permitted to quote from an interesting leaflet published by the Shire. 'There is evidence that several wayside inns existed in the Coolah Shire area. These were needed for travellers along the long road routes. The best known was the Black Stump Wine Saloon situated near the Gunnedah road, six miles north of Coolah. It was the staging post for north-western New South Wales. The importance of this inn resulted from its position at the junction of the old coach roads. It was also a resting place on the old Sydney stock route before passengers entered the rough country on the last leg of the journey.

'The position of the inn is clearly marked on old New South Wales Lands Department maps and like many a pub before and since, it became the hub from which men dated their journeys and gauged their distances . . . The saloon was named after the nearby Black Stump Run and Black Stump Creek, both of which derived their names from the local saying of "beyond the Black Stump".

'In 1826 Governor Darling proclaimed "limits of location" or boundaries "beyond which land was neither sold nor let" nor "settlers allowed". This boundary was located in 1829 as being the northern side of the Manning River up to its source in the Mount Royal Range, then by that range and the Liverpool Range westerly to the source of the Coolaburragundy River, then along the approximate location of the Black Stump Run, then in a south-westerly direction to Wellington.

'Land north of this location was referred to as land "beyond" and the use of the word "beyond" can be found in the Government Gazette of 19th January, 1837.'

'However, settlers did not strictly adhere to the Governor's proclaimed boundaries and often let their stock graze "beyond". Thus in the Coolah area, to avoid detection by officialdom, the location of these pastures was vaguely described as being "beyond the Black Stump" . . .

'It is understood that the Black Stump Wine Saloon was erected in the 1860s. The centre was then a small settlement possessing its own racetrack. The saloon was destroyed by fire in 1908.'

Black Springs NSW   At one time a small stream ran through black soil near the site of the present station.

Blackall; Blackall Range Q   The town was surveyed in 1868 and this and the range were named after Samuel Wensley Blackall, Governor of Queensland. The hills were known to the Aborigines as Bonyi, the place where the bunya pine grew and provided nuts that were regarded by them as a great delicacy.

Blackheath NSW   After visiting Bathurst in 1815, and while on his return journey to Sydney, Governor Macquarie camped on the site of the future town. He wrote in his Journal on 15 May: 'This place having a black, wild appearance I have this day named it *Black-Heath*. It affords however plenty of good water for man and beast and tolerable good feed for the latter.' Major Antill was somewhat critical of the Governor's choice. While Macquarie was recording his decision, Antill wrote: 'From the appearance of this station, it being a kind of heath, but a very wild and dreary scenery, the Governor gave it the name of Blackheath, though to my eye very unlike its namesake.' It was scarcely a fair comment, for Macquarie does not seem to have had the London common and suburb in mind.

Blackman Bay T   Originally named Frederick Henricx Bay by Tasman on 7 December 1642 after it had been explored by pilot-major Visscher. He landed on the shore and heard the Aborigines in the bush. The bay was next named Baie du Nord by d'Entrecasteaux. In 1798 Flinders wrote: '. . . as I apprehended this is the place that Tasman called Frederick Henry or Hendrick's Bay more than a century ago, I have prefixed that name to it in the chart'.

Blacktown NSW   In the early days of settlement the Aborigines were commonly referred to as 'blacks', and by even less complimentary names. Governor Macquarie was mindful of their welfare and established a 'Native Institution' for them at Parramatta in 1814. In 1823 land for cultivation was set aside and huts were built for the 'blacks' in the locality first known as Black Town, or Black's Town, Blacktown Road, and later Blacktown. The Institution was designed to inculcate the rudiments of 'civilisation', and it is said that Mrs Macquarie herself taught the Aboriginal children sewing and singing.

Blackwood V   After Captain Henry Blackwood. See below.

Blackwood River WA   Named by Sir James Stirling after Captain Henry

Blackwood. Stirling had served in the *Warspite* under the captain from 1808 to 1810. At the Battle of Trafalgar Nelson said to Blackwood: 'God bless you, Blackwood — I shall never see you again.'

Blair Athol Q   After a parish in Scotland, in the vicinity of the Pass of Killiecrankie.

Blanche, Lake SA   After Lady Blanche Skurray MacDonnell, wife of the Governor of South Australia. The lake, which is usually dry but occasionally has a few inches of water, was first sighted by E. J. Eyre in 1840, and visited by Charles Sturt in 1845. Both explorers believed it to be part of Lake Torrens, but this was disproved by A. C. Gregory during his search for Leichhardt. The name was given later, apparently in association with Blanchewater Plains, q.v.

Blanche Town SA   A township was laid out in 1855 on the site passed by Sturt on his Murray River voyage in 1830, and named after the wife of the Governor.

Blancheport SA   Named by Governor MacDonnell in honour of his wife, Lady Blanche MacDonnell.

Blanchewater Plains SA   Named by Benjamin H. Babbage in honour of Lady Blanche MacDonnell. See also MacDonnell Creek.

Blaxland NSW   After Gregory Blaxland, one of the members of the first expedition to cross the Blue Mountains, in 1813. He is known as a successful grazier and explorer, and the pioneer in wine-making in Australia. Blaxland was first named Wascoes, after John Outrim Wascoe, proprietor of the Old Pilgrim's Inn on Lapstone Hill.

Blaxland, Mount NSW   Named after Gregory Blaxland. It was the last stopping place of the Blaxland, Lawson, Wentworth expedition of 1813. On 26 November of the same year W. G. Evans, who completed the crossing of the Blue Mountains, recorded in his Journal: 'I stopped this evening near the foot of a very handsome Mount, which I took the liberty to call *Mount Blaxland*.'

Blaxland's River NSW   Named by Allan Cunningham on his 1823 expedition from Bathurst to the Liverpool Plains. His journey north of the Wemyss River was bedevilled by the almost impassable mountains. On his return towards Goulburn he named Blaxland's River on 21 April, doubtless after Gregory Blaxland.

Blayney NSW   The origin of the name has not been traced, but the plan of a 'village at King's Plains . . . to be called Blaney' was approved by Governor Gipps in 1843.

Blenheim Q   After Blenheim Park in Oxfordshire, which was named in celebration of the victory of Blenheim in 1704.

Blinman Q   After 'Pegleg' Robert Blinman, a shepherd with a wooden leg who was employed on the Angorichina run. According to legend his favourite resting place was on a hilltop. One day, somewhere about 1859, he broke off a piece of rock and found traces of copper, and from this chance discovery came the rich peacock ore which led to the establishment of the copper-mining town that was surveyed in 1859.

Black, Mount T   Discovered and named by Henry Hellyer and Joseph Fossey in November 1828.

Bloomsbury Q   After the London suburb, which was earlier called Blemondsbury, after William de Blemont, first Lord of the Manor.

Blue Lake SA   This mysterious lake, the most beautiful of all the lakes in the crater of Mount Gambier, owes its name to its colour, which changes strikingly from grey in winter to a brilliant blue in summer. It was seen by S. G. Henty of Portland, the first white man to visit it. As the district became settled it was generally known as the Devil's Inkbottle, then Lake Power, after the wife of David Power who owned property in the neighbourhood. In 1856 Governor MacDonnell and his wife were the first people to venture out on to the lake in a boat, and from this incident it was renamed Lady Blanche Lake until the descriptive name superseded the earlier ones. The Aboriginal name was Waaor or Waawor.

Blue Mountains NSW   In 1793 David Collins wrote that the mountains were commonly known as Blue Mountains 'from the appearance which land so high and distant generally wears'. The name was adopted by popular consent (though the reason advanced by Collins seems scarcely sufficient). But this was not their first name. They were seen as early as April 1788 by Governor Phillip, who named the northern portion Carmarthen Hills after the Marquess of Carmarthen, and the southern portion Lansdowne Hills after the Marquess of Lansdowne. The Governor viewed them from somewhere in the neighbourhood of the Pennant Hills, and wrote: '. . . a very fine view of the mountains inland, and northermost of which I named Carmarthen Hills, and the southernmost Lansdowne Hills'. These early names did not survive. The name 'Blue Mountains' was first recorded by Captain Paterson in a despatch on his unsuccessful attempt to cross them by way of the Grose River in 1793. For twenty years the barrier remained uncrossed, until the Blaxland and Lawson expedition of 1813. By 1815 a road was completed and Governor Macquarie travelled to the site of Bathurst.

The 'City of the Blue Mountains', covering an area of hundreds of square miles, was founded in 1947 to co-ordinate the work of a number of local councils.

The blue haze seen on distant hills is a phenomenon known as 'Rayleigh scattering' after Rayleigh, the scientist who first investigated it. It is caused by light reflected from dust particles and droplets of water scattering in various directions, these reflections resulting in the wavelength that appears blue to the eye of the observer. Professor Messell believes that minute droplets of oil from the eucalypt trees are the cause of the pronounced colouring to be seen in the Blue Mountains.

Blue Nob NSW   A corruption of the Aboriginal name Boolool Nahl, Dark side of a mountain.

Blue's Point NSW   After Billy Blue, a West Indian who was granted land here. He operated a ferry to Jack the Miller's Point. He became a popular character and was affectionately known as the 'Old Commodore'. He died at the age of ninety-seven. The Aboriginal name for the point was Warungarea. At one time it was called Billy Blue's.

Blyth SA   After Sir Arthur Blyth, Premier, and Agent-General for South Australia, who came to Australia in 1830 as a lad of 16.

Bodalla NSW   Aboriginal. Tossing a child up and down in the arms. Possibly a corruption of the word Bowdall. At one time the name was amusingly rendered as Boat Alley.

Boga, Lake V   Named by T. L. Mitchell after the Boga tribe.

Bogan Gate NSW   Aboriginal. The name Bogan has several times been translated Birthplace of a king, or Birthplace of a great king. As any concept of royalty was foreign to Aboriginal mentality, it would seem that the name is proper tribute to a man with extraordinary capacity for leadership.

Bogan River NSW   The name has the same origin as Bogan Gate in the preceding entry. On 1 January 1829 it was named New Year's Creek, but this name, given by Charles Sturt when he discovered it, did not persist. In December 1828 Captain Sturt and Hamilton Hume began to explore the western course of the Macquarie. Their progress was blocked by swamps which led them to another creek which they named after the day of its discovery.

Boggabilla NSW   Aboriginal. Great chief born here. See Bogan Gate.

Boggabri NSW   Aboriginal. Place of creeks. Other forms of the Aboriginal word that have been recorded are: Bukkiberai, Bukkibera, and Bukkabri. An unusual and less likely theory is that the word was Boorgaburrie: Emu, or Young.

Boigbeat V   Aboriginal. Broken tree.

Boisdale V   Probably after a place in the Hebrides.

Bolga V   Aboriginal. High hill.

Bolwarrah V   Aboriginal. Laurel tree.

Bombala NSW   Aboriginal. Meeting of the water.

Bonaparte Archipelago WA   Named in honour of Napoleon Bonaparte by Baudin, who wrote: '. . . after the august patron of our expedition'.

Bondi NSW   Aboriginal. Corruption of the word Boondi, Sound of waves breaking on the beach, or Noise of tumbling waters — an appropriate name for a beach that is famous for its surf.

Bonegilla V   Aboriginal. Windy place, or Large swamp.

Bonney, Lake SA   There are two lakes of this name in South Australia. Lake Bonney, about 24 km from Renmark was discovered and named in 1838 by Joseph Hawdon who with Charles Bonney was driving stock overland for the first time from New South Wales to South Australia. The name was later changed to Barmera, q.v., because of confusion with the other Lake Bonney in the south-east of the state, near Mount Gambier. When the older name emerged again, the settlement was called Barmera. The second lake, also named after Charles Bonney, had the Aboriginal name Nookamba. In 1839 it was proposed to name certain territory Bonneia, but this did not eventuate.

Bonnie Doon V   Named by Thomas Nixon, after the famous stream in Scotland.

Booborowie SA   Aboriginal. Round water hole.

Booby Island Q   On 23 August 1770 Captain Cook wrote in his Journal: 'Being now near the Island, and having but little wind, Mr Banks and I landed upon it, and found it to be mostly a barren rock frequented by Birds, such as Boobies, a few of which we shott, and occasioned my giving it the name of Booby Island.' Apparently unaware of this, Captain Bligh later recorded in his Journal: 'A small island was seen bearing W. and found it was only a rock where boobies resort, for which reason it is called Booby Island'.

Bookabie SA   Aboriginal. Brackish water.

Boolarra V   Aboriginal. Plenty.

Booleroo Central SA   Aboriginal. Plenty, or Soft mud or clay. The word Centre was added because it was the centre of the Hundred of Booleroo.

Boomahnoomoonah V   From the Aboriginal word Boonah, Large kangaroo.

Boolgun SA   Aboriginal. Plenty.

Booligal NSW   Aboriginal. Windy place, or Large swamp.

Boomi NSW   This may be a form of the name of the Creator Spirit, usually rendered Biami or Baiamai, of the Kamilaroi tribe. Another supposition is that it is an Aboriginal word meaning dark brackish water.

Boona, Mount NSW   Aboriginal. From Boonah, Swamp country.

Boonah Q   Aboriginal. From Buna, Bloodwood tree. First known as Blumbergville, after an early storekeeper.

Booral NSW   Aboriginal. Large.

Boorhaman V   This appears to be an Indian word meaning Ragged beggar.

Boorowa NSW   Aboriginal. Plain or bustard turkey, or Fish-hawk. The 'Burrua run of water' was settled in 1830.

Boort V   Aboriginal. Smoke.

Boorthanna SA   Aboriginal. A contraction of Boortheboorthanna, Plain covered with bushes. The full name was in use until its inevitable simplification.

Boosey V   Aboriginal. A corruption of Boosi, Gum tree. See also under Katamatite.

Booyong NSW   Aboriginal. Ironwood trees. They grew plentifully here.

Borambil NSW   Aboriginal. A name derived from the bora ceremony at which young men were initiated as a prelude to recognition as full-grown men. The bora ring is the sacred ground where the initiation rites are observed.

Borambula NSW   Aboriginal. Another form of Borambil, q.v.

Borda, Cape SA   Named by the navigator Nicolas Baudin after Jean Charles Borda, French mathematician and astronomer.

Bordertown SA   The name is now a misnomer, for it is 19 km west of the actual border, which at one time was in dispute. In 1851 Alexander Tolmer was responsible for the escort of gold between the Mount Alexander diggings in Victoria and Adelaide, and a depot was set up in this locality. When a township was surveyed the following year Tolmer felt aggrieved when his name was not given to it.

Boree Creek NSW   Aboriginal. Weeping myall tree.

Borenore NSW   Aboriginal. Bora rock. (See also under Borambil.)

Borika SA   Aboriginal. Hut built for strangers.

Boston Bay SA   Discovered by Matthew Flinders and named by him on 25 February 1802 in memory of Boston in Lincolnshire, the place where he grew up. It is a busy market town in the Fens and the place from which the Pilgrim Fathers left. The American city of Boston also took its name from the English town. Boston Island and Boston Point have a similar origin. In this case the Christian tradition spreads over many centuries, for the English Boston probably got its name from a stone cross at which St Botulf preached to the Middle Anglians in the Seventh Century AD.

Botany Bay NSW   On 28 April 1770 Captain Cook wrote in his Journal: 'At daylight in the morning we discovered a Bay which appeared to be tolerably well sheltered from all winds, into which I resolved to go with the Ship, and with this in view sent the Master in the Pinnace to sound the entrance.' On 6 May he wrote: 'In the evening the Yawl return'd from fishing, having caught two sting rays weighing near 600 pounds. The great quantity of New Plants &ca. Mr Banks and Dr Solander found in this place occasioned my giving it the name of Botany Bay.'

It seems almost certain that the name was not decided on while the *Endeavour* was in the harbour. The first names conferred were Sting-Ray Harbour, Sting-Rays Harbour, and Stingrays Bay. Cook altered the name first to Botanist Bay and then to Botany Bay when he realised how much plant material the scientists had gathered. While there was for a considerable time some doubt of the facts of the naming, the discovery of Banks's and Cook's journals in their own handwriting has provided a final answer. Cook deleted Sting-Rays Harbour and then Botanist Bay and inserted the words Botany Bay, while the log entry remained as Sting-ray Harbour. The conclusion is that Cook made the changes later in the voyage, while Banks's first use of the name Botany Bay was in his summary, which was written after the ship left the Australian coast.

Cook's first landing in Australia was on the Kurnell Peninsula, off which the *Endeavour* lay from 29 April to 7 May 1770. It is interesting to note that in 1840 a writer (T. L. McQueen) stated that 'the term Botany Bay is used to represent a country co-equal in extent with all Europe united'. For some time it was a term in general use for Sydney as well as for the harbour to the south of Port Jackson.

Bothwell T   Named by Governor Macquarie after Bothwell in Scotland. Many of the first settlers here were Scots. Originally known as Fat Doe River.

Bottle Hill SA   In August 1855 Dr W. J. Browne, who was leading an exploratory expedition in South Australia, wrote: 'We named . . . a conspicuous small hill, after its shape, Bottle Hill.'

Boulder City WA   In *The Mile that Midas Touched**, Gavin Casey and Ted Mayman tell the story of the name-giving: 'In 1893 in Dashwood's Gully in South Australia, four men discussed the future of a local mining lease, The Boulder. Its main features were large sandstone boulders in which were found some small wiry stringers of gold. W. G. Brookman and Charles de Rose had been working the lease without much success, and George Brookman, a businessman who was backing them, had gone to Dashwood's Gully with an experienced prospector, Sam Pearce, to discuss the matter . . . George (later Sir George) Brookman told them he might be able to raise funds in Adelaide to send a small party to Coolgardie, and later the Adelaide Prospecting Company was formed . . . W. G. Brookman and Sam Pearce left Adelaide on 7 June 1893. On the last stage of their journey they walked beside their cart and two horses for 300 miles to Coolgardie. Sam Pearce had a good knowledge of geology and he and Brookman moved their camp to the Ivanhoe Hill. While Brookman was away at Coolgardie applying for 20 acres, Pearce discovered a rich lead a few chains away and in August they registered another lease. With memories of their Dashwood's Gully lease, they called it the Great Boulder.

'Boulder City is now merged with Kalgoorlie . . . Horse cabs used to ply for hire between Kalgoorlie and the Boulder Rock, the terminus of the road to the mines and close to the Great Boulder lease. The cab

* Rigby Ltd, Adelaide. 1964

drivers attracted fares by shouting, "Right away to the Boulder" – and from this great mine the town of Boulder City took its name.'
Boulder City (official title) was generally spoken of as 'The Boulder'. The Post Office described the address of most of the mines of Kalgoorlie and Boulder City as Finniston, but 'Boulder Block' was the popular name and the one that stuck. In the locality you just say 'the Block' and everyone knows what you mean.

Bountiful Island Q   Named by Matthew Flinders in December 1872 when his men captured 46 green turtles of an average weight of 135 kilos. It was a welcome occasion, for fresh food was desperately needed to supplement a year-old diet of salt pork and ship's biscuit on the *Investigator*.

Bourke NSW   After Sir Richard Bourke who was Governor from 1831 to 1837. The name was first conferred by the explorer T. L. Mitchell in the form Fort Bourke, for it was here, at the Eight Miles Lagoon, that he built a stockade as a protection against possible attacks by hostile Aborigines. The town, which was laid out in 1862, is seven miles from the site of the fort. The Aboriginal name has been rendered as Nulta Nulta, and also as Wertie Mertie or Wurtamurtah, meaning High ground.

Bowden Q   After a man named Bowden who, with another named Dickie, accompanied the prospector William Lakeland in 1887 when he discovered wolfram between the Pascoe River and Canoe Creek.

Bowen Q   After Sir George Ferguson Bowen, first Governor of Queensland, and afterwards Governor of Victoria. George A. F. E. Dalrymple formed a settlement here in 1861 and named it after the Governor, who had been appointed in 1859. The township was surveyed in 1863. One of the settlers who saw the bearded Dalrymple with a belt full of revolvers described him as 'the most fearsome-looking chief I ever saw'.

Bowen Strait NT   Discovered on 16 April 1818 by P. P. King, who wrote: 'It was named after my friend James Bowen, esq., one of the Commissioners of the Navy.'

Bowenfels NSW   After G. M. C. Bowen, the police magistrate at Berrima. The place was first named Bowen Falls.

Bowenvale V   After Sir George Ferguson Bowen, Governor of Victoria from 1872 to 1879.

Bowning NSW   Aboriginal. Large hill.

Bower SA   After a Commissioner of Public Works in South Australia.

Bowman River V   Named by Angus McMillan about 1840.

Bowmans SA   After E. and C. Bowman, who were pastoralists.

Bowral NSW   Aboriginal. In 1829 T. L. Mitchell referred to a 'hill on the north of Mr Oxley's station . . . called by the natives Bowral'. The meaning has been given either as High, or. as Two, the latter referring to the two hills with an intervening gap. From 1816 John Oxley grazed stock in the district. Stockmen referred to the place at Gibraltar, which became shortened to The Gib. The settlement of the present name was formed in 1862.

Boyd River Q   Named by Leichhardt on his first expedition, on 27 November 1844, probably after a member of his party.

Boyd Town NSW   After Benjamin (usually referred to as Ben) Boyd, founder of the firm of Boyd and Co. He spent a great deal of money to found the twin townships of Boyd Town and East Boyd at Twofold Bay in 1843, the headquarters of his whaling fleet. On his return from the Californian goldfields he landed on Guadalcanal with the intention of blackbirding natives from Wanderer Bay, named after his yacht, which foundered on the New South Wales coast on its return.

Boyne River Q   Discovered and named in 1823 by John Oxley, who was then Surveyor-General of New South Wales.

Boys' Town NSW   Named after and planned for the same purpose as Boys' Town in the United States, to rehabilitate neglected and delinquent boys. It was founded in 1939 by Father T. V. Dunlea.

Brachina Gorge SA   Aboriginal. River red gums beside running water.

Bradfield NSW   After John Job Crew Bradfield, designer of the Sydney Harbour Bridge. The bridge was completed in 1932. Bradfield Highway was named after him. Later, both the suburb and the federal district were named in his honour. At an earlier date he was the proposer of Sydney's underground railway, and was appointed engineer-in-charge.

Bradley's Head NSW   After Lieutenant William Bradley, who arrived in Sydney in 1788 as first lieutenant of HMS *Sirius*. He was engaged in the survey of Port Jackson and Broken Bay. More than twenty years later he reached the rank of rear-admiral, but after being superannuated was accused of theft and sentenced to transportation for life. The Aboriginal name was Burroggy, or Burra-gy.

Braefield NSW   A Scottish settler, John McKee, gave his holding this name.

Braidwood NSW   Two explanations of the origin of the name have been given: 1. After Dr Thomas Braidwood, a pioneer settler. 2. After Braidwood Wilson, a surgeon in the Royal Navy. The former explanation appears to be the more likely.

Branxton NSW   The township, formed in 1848, was given the same name as the parish in which it lay. Formerly it was known as Black Creek. The English Branxton means Branoc's town.

Brawlin NSW   Aboriginal. Native companion. The name was first given to a pastoral holding here.

Breadalbane NSW   Possibly named by James Chisholm after a district in

Scotland. Olaf Ruhen points out that Chisholm's property was named Kippilaw, after the district in Scotland from which his wife came, and that the name Breadalbane antedated him.

Breaksea Island WA Named by Captain George Vancouver because the waves break unceasingly on the shores. Vancouver discovered King George Sound in September 1791, and gave names to all the prominent features.

Breaksea Spit Q Named by Captain Cook on 21 May 1770: 'This Shoal I called Break Sea Spit, because now we had smooth water, whereas upon the whole Coast to the Southward of it we had always a high Sea or swell from the S.E.'

Breeza NSW Aboriginal. A corruption of Biridja, Flea. Another interpretation is One hill.

Bremer Range WA This group of low hills overlooking the salt lakes was discovered in November 1848 by J. S. Roe, Surveyor-General of Western Australia, and named after Sir James Gordon Bremer. He was sent to establish a colony on the north-west coast, and took possession at Port Essington on 20 September 1824. On 26 September he visited Melville Island, where he formed a settlement, and Bathurst Island. Mount Gordon in the range was also named after him.

Brentwood SA Named after the birthplace in Essex of one of the early settlers. The name means Burnt wood.

Brewarrina NSW Aboriginal. Two different meanings have been given: 1. The fisheries, or Fishing. Fish traps were built on the river by the Aborigines, and in support of this explanation it should be noted that in the 1870s the place was known as 'the fishing village'. 2. The place where the birie grows. Birie, Burie, or Bre is the native gooseberry; Warrina, the place of.

Briagolong V Aboriginal. Swamp plain, a resort for native companions.

Bribie Island Q Said to be named after an early convict. Matthew Flinders landed here in 1799 and made contact with the Bribie Islanders, who are now extinct.

Bridgetown WA It seems likely that the township received its name because it was close to the only bridge across the Blackwood River. Local residents spoke of going to 'bridge town' and so the name came into use when the town site was declared on 4 June 1868. Another explanation is that it was named after the first ship to land cargo at Bunbury.

Bridgewater SA John Dunn established a water-mill here in 1852 and named it Bridgewater. The auctioneer who sold blocks of land in the same year advertised it as the place 'where a hot wind has never been known'. An earlier name was Cox's Creek.

Bridgewater, Cape V Named by Lieut James Grant in the *Lady Nelson* in December 1800. He wrote: 'I named it Bridgewater, in honour of the Duke of that title.'

Brigalow Q   Aboriginal. Brigalow scrub, a form of acacia.

Bright V   Named after John Bright, the English orator and statesman of the 19th century. It was proclaimed a shire in 1866.

Brim Brim V   Aboriginal. Spring of water.

Bringagee NSW   Aboriginal. Standing breast to breast.

Bringelly NSW   After an estate in Wales owned by Judge-Advocate Ellis Bent, the first practising barrister-at-law to reach the colony (in 1809).

Brinkworth SA   After George Brinkworth, the original owner of the site of the town.

Brisbane; Brisbane River Q   Named in honour of Sir Thomas Macdougall Brisbane who succeeded Macquarie as Governor of New South Wales in 1821. It is the only state capital to be named after a Governor. Brisbane had served in the Peninsula War, where the Duke of Wellington said that he 'kept the time for the army'. Brisbane was an amateur astronomer. When his appointment was announced Lord Bathurst remarked that he wanted a man to govern the earth, not the heavens.

The Brisbane River was discovered or re-discovered during Brisbane's term of office. It was discovered on 2 December 1823 by John Oxley who had been ordered to find a suitable locality for the establishment of another penal colony. During October and November Oxley explored Port Curtis and inspected Moreton Bay, where he met a white man who was living there with the Aborigines. He went up the river for about 50 miles, was greatly impressed by it and named it after the Governor.

In company with Lieut Miller, a detachment of soldiers and a number of convicts, Oxley landed at Redcliffe in September 1824, but recommended the present site of Brisbane as a more suitable locality. In December of that year the site was inspected by the Chief Justice, Sir Francis Forbes, who suggested the name Edinglassie. The penal settlement was finally established in 1825, and the name Brisbane, which had been proposed by John Oxley, prevailed.

Brisbane Water NSW   Named in 1825 in honour of Governor Brisbane. As a result of his founding of an observatory at Parramatta he was called the founder of Australian science by Sir William Herschel. Brisbane Water was earlier known as North East Arm.

Brit Brit V   Aboriginal. Plovers.

Brixton Q   After Brixton in Devonshire, Beortsige's Town.

Broad Sound Q   Named by Captain Cook on 1 June 1770. 'The Western Inlet . . ., known in the Chart by the Name of Broad Sound, we had now all open. It is at least 9 or 10 Leagues wide at the Entrance . . .'

Broadwater NSW   A descriptive name. At one time it was known as The Wallaby Ground. The Aboriginal name was Keirbarban, White ants' nest.

Brocklesby NSW   The name of an estate owned by Charles Cropper, and also of the parish.

Brocks Creek NT   After one of the Overland Telegraph workers.

Brodribb River V   After William Adams Brodribb, an explorer and pastoralist who took up land first at Monaro and then adjacent to the Murrumbidgee River near the present town of Gundagai. He claimed to be the first to mark the road from Sydney to Port Phillip when he took a mob of cattle through. He discovered several rivers and took up a political career in 1861.

Broke NSW   After Sir Charles Broke Vere, named by the explorer T. L. Mitchell, who was acquainted with him.

Broken Bay NSW   Sighted by Captain Cook on 7 May 1770. In his Journal he wrote: 'At sunset the Northernmost land in sight bore N26° East, and some broken land that appear'd to form a Bay bore N40° West distant 4 Leagues, this bay I named *Broken Bay,* Latitude 33° 36′ s.' In *Journals of Captain James Cook,* Vol 1, page 313, Dr J. C. Beaglehole states there is a marginal note by Cook: 'Bay in Lat 33° 42″ but: 'This is not the present Broken Bay, a few miles further north, which Cook missed during the succeeding night, but the land in the neighbourhood of the Narrabeen Lagoon. This is seven or eight miles north of Port Jackson . . . . Flinders was the first to note the discrepancy.'

Broken Hill NSW   In September 1883 a boundary rider pegged out forty acres of the 'broken hill' which he believed to be a source of tin but which proved to be an outcrop of ironstone. The Broken Hill Proprietary Company was floated two years later. The Aboriginal name was Willyama, Hill with a broken contour, and even in 1886 a Mines Department report said that this was the official name of the township. Eventually the European name survived, which seems a pity, especially as it has the same meaning as the Aboriginal name.

Brooklyn NSW   After Brooklyn, New York.

Broome WA   The well-known pearling port (known as the Port of Pearls) was named after Sir Frederick Napier Broome, Governor of Western Australia. The township was founded in 1883.

Broughton Islands NSW   Named by Captain Cook on 11 May 1770 after Captain Broughton of the *Providence*. The entry in the Journal reads: '. . . on the Main near the shore are some high round hills that make at a distance like Islands'.

Broughton River SA   Discovered and named by E. J. Eyre after the Anglican Bishop of Australia.

Brown, Mount SA   Mt Brown has the distinction of being climbed by and named after a world-famous botanist. Robert Brown was the naturalist on the *Investigator,* and spent more than three years on Flinders's exploratory voyages. During this time he collected 3,400 plant specimens,

2,000 of which were new to science. One of the tragedies of those early days was that when Flinders commenced his voyage back to England the *Porpoise* which he commanded was wrecked and most of Brown's collection lost.

It was 10 March 1802 that a trio of young men, Robert Brown the botanist, Ferdinand Bauer the natural history painter, and William Westall, the landscape painter, accompanied by several of the crew of the *Investigator*, went ashore with the intention of climbing a mountain a few miles away, which Flinders had described as a remarkable peak. On their return Flinders named the peak after Brown.

Many tributes have been paid to the scientist who remained in Australia until 1805, and achieved fame in his chosen field in England. It was said of him, that 'No naturalist ever taught so much by writing so little, or made so few statements that had to be recalled, or even recast.' This was certainly true of his great work *Prodromus Florae Novae Hollandiae*, published in 1810, which Hooker described as 'the greatest botanical work that has ever appeared'. The Aboriginal name was Wetiarto.

Browne, Mount NSW   After a member of Sturt's 1845 expedition.

Bruce, Mount WA   Named by F. T. Gregory in 1861 after Lieut Col John Bruce.

Bruny Island T   The French Admiral Bruni (or Bruny) d'Entrecasteaux gave his Christian name to the island in 1792, while engaged in charting the channel between the island and the mainland. It had previously been discovered by Abel Tasman. D'Entrecasteaux paid a second visit in 1794. Two months after he had left, Commodore Sir John Hayes, who knew nothing of d'Entrecasteaux's visit, gave the name William Pitt's Island after the British statesman. This was later corrected when the facts were known (see under Derwent River). The Aboriginal name was Lunawannaalonna, which has been preserved in the towns Lunawanna and Alonnah.

Bruthen V   Aboriginal. Evil spirit.

Bryan, Mount SA   After Guy Bryan, who was lost in the bush near North-west Bend on the Murray River.

Buccaneer Archipelago WA   Named by P. P. King from the fact that William Dampier had landed in the vicinity. On his fourth and last voyage King continued his survey of the north-west coast in the *Bathurst*, and in June 1821 found Cape Leveque to be the point of land that sheltered Dampier in 1868. It was then that he gave the name Buccaneer Archipelago to the islands fronting Cygnet Bay, which in turn had been named after Dampier's vessel.

Dampier was indeed a swash-buckling buccaneer. In 1686 he embarked on the *Cygnet* bound for Guam. Dampier led a mutiny, put Captain Swan and 36 loyal crew members ashore at Mindinao and set off on further adventures. The *Cygnet* arrived at the islands off the coast of Australia on 4 January 1688 and spent 10 weeks there while the vessel was scraped and repaired. (See also Dampier Bay.)

Buccleuch SA   After the Duke of Buccleuch.

Buchan V   Aboriginal. A corruption of Buk Kan, meaning Dilly-bag.

Buchanan Hills NT   Discovered by Nathaniel Buchanan and named after him. Buchanan was a pioneer pastoralist as well as an explorer. About 1896 he was provided with camels by the South Australian Government and set out to seek a practicable stock route from South Australia to Queensland. His route from Oodnadatta went past Tennant and Sturt's Creek. Some 60 km from Hooker's Creek he came in sight of the mountains that were named after him. He was not successful in his quest but his report on his journey proved useful to the Government.

Buchanan's Creek NT   Also named after Nathaniel Buchanan (see above). On this occasion, in October 1877, he had discovered the creek and watering place in company with S. Croker.

Buckland Tableland Q   Named by T. L. Mitchell in 1846 after the English geologist William Buckland. The plateau has been called 'Home of the Rivers' for it is the source of the Barcoo, Belyando, Comet, Dawson, Maranoa, Nogoa, and Warrego rivers.

Buderim Q   Aboriginal. A corruption of Butharum, the name of a species of Banksia or honeysuckle tree among the Kabi tribespeople.

Buffalo, Mount V   A descriptive name given by the explorers Hume and Hovell in 1824, for the humped granite mass of the mountain reminded them of a buffalo.

Buffon, Cape SA   Named after the French naturalist Comte Buffon.

Bugaldie NSW   Aboriginal. Blossoms damaged by possums (probably apple or gum tree blossoms). The Aboriginal word was Bugaldi, the 'e' being added after the Second World War to commemorate soldiers who lost their lives, the pronunciation being 'bugle die'.

Bugilbone NSW   Aboriginal. Place of the death-adder. It has sometimes been written as Bucklebone.

Bukkulla NSW   Aboriginal. Tall black stump.

Bulahdelah NSW   Aboriginal. Meeting of the waters.

Bulart V   Going grey (of hair).

Bulga NSW   Aboriginal. Single peak, or one mountain.

Bulgandry NSW   Aboriginal. Boomerang in the hand. The full name may have been Bulgandramine, from Bulgang, boomerang; Derra, hand; Mine, Aboriginal man.

Bulla V   Aboriginal. Two.

Bulla Bulla V   Aboriginal. Four (twice two).

Buller, Mount V   Named by T. L. Mitchell in 1835 after a friend in the Colonial Office. Aboriginal name, Marrang.

Buller River WA   Discovered in 1839 and named by George Grey.

Bulli NSW   Aboriginal. The original Aboriginal name was Bulla or Bulla Bulla, meaning Two mountains (Mounts Kembla and Keira). As early as 1823 reference was made to a small landholding at 'Bull Eye'. Other more fanciful meanings for Bulli have been given, e.g. White grubs, and Place where the mooki (Christmas bush) grows.

Bulloo River Q   Aboriginal. Slow.

Bullumwaal V   Aboriginal. Two spears.

Buloke, Lake V   Aboriginal. Place of frogs. (Not to be confused with the tree bull oak which is sometimes spelt buloke).

Bumbaldry NSW   Aboriginal. An onomatopoeic word to imitate the sound of people jumping into the water.

Bunbury WA   The district was discovered by Lieut Henry Williams St Pierre Bunbury of the Scots Fusiliers in 1829 while making an overland journey from Perth to the Vasse River settlement (Busselton). Governor Stirling proposed to establish a military outpost in charge of Bunbury and named the place after him. The scheme was not put into effect but eventually a township was laid out in 1836.

Bunda Plateau SA   The Aboriginal name of the cliffs about the head of the Great Australian Bight was Bunda, and from this the plateau on the borders of the Nullarbor Plain takes its name.

Bundaberg Q   One of the first surveyors in the district was admired by the local Aborigines. They 'adopted' him (so goes the tale) and gave him their own tribal name, Bunda. From this the township took its name with the addition of 'berg'.

Bundaleer SA   Aboriginal. Among the hills. The local name was adopted in 1841 by John Bristow Hughes when he took up land here. It was some of the best land north of Adelaide, and the run gradually covered an area of about 800 sq kms, and included the site of present-day Jamestown.

Bundalong V   Aboriginal. Married, or joined together.

Bundanoon NSW   Aboriginal. Big or deep gullies.

Bundarra NSW   Aboriginal. Big kangaroo.

Bungaree V   The name of one of the Aborigines who signed the document conveying land at Melbourne to John Batman.

Bungeet V   Aboriginal. Swamp.

Bungulla NSW   Aboriginal. Black bream. Formerly known as Jump Up.

Bungunyah Q   Aboriginal. Deserted hut.

Bungwahl NSW   Aboriginal. Swamp in which bulbous-rooted reeds grow. They were eaten by the Aborigines when other food was in short supply.

Buninyong, Mount V   Aboriginal. Discovered in 1837 by T. L. Learmonth. He was accompanied by a party of young Scottish squatters. They climbed to the top and from there saw the future site of Ballarat. The proper Aboriginal name was Bonan Yowang, which is thought to mean Man lying on his back with his knees up, and probably refers to the shape of the mountain.

Bunya Mountains Q   Aboriginal. The name of a species of pine that is plentiful in the mountains. They were an important gathering place for Aboriginal tribes from a great distance, as the edible nuts of the pine were valued as a food supply.

Bunyah NSW   Aboriginal. Possum, or White mahogany tree.

Bunyip V   Aboriginal. The legendary monster of lakes and swamps, of which grim and unusual tales are told. The hollow booming so often heard from the margin of reedy swamps, more hollow and louder by night than by day, was the voice of the bunyip – even though sceptical white men might ascribe it to the lonely bittern. The Aborigines' belief in such powerful spirit beings as the Rainbow Serpent, which dwelt in water holes and rivers, may be the basis of legends of the bunyip.

Buralyang NSW   Aboriginal. Bluck duck.

Burdekin River Q   Discovered on 2 April 1845 by Leichhardt on his first expedition and named in honour of Mrs Mary Ann Burdekin, who was one of his financial backers. Mrs Burdekin was the wife of Thomas Burdekin, a prominent Sydney merchant.

Burges, Mount WA   Named in 1863 by H. M. Lefroy, an explorer, who was also a Superintendent of convicts in Western Australia, after an old friend.

Burgooney NSW   Aboriginal. Ant that makes a hole in sandy ground, or Ant tunnelling in sandy soil.

Burketown Q   After Robert O'Hara Burke, leader of the ill-fated Burke and Wills expedition.

Burleigh Heads Q   Little Burleigh had the Aboriginal name Jellurgul, Big Burleigh, Jabbribillum.

Burley Griffin, Lake ACT   After Walter Burley Griffin, a Chicago architect, who won a worldwide competition for the design of the Federal Capital City. The lake is artificial.

Burnett River Q   Named after James Charles Burnett, the surveyor who discovered it in 1847. Burnett was a clerk under Sir Thomas Mitchell. He rose to be surveyor in charge of the department in Queensland and explored the Mary and Burnett rivers. The Aboriginal name for the upper reaches was Borrallborrall, and of the lower, Birrabirra.

Burnie T   After William Burnie. The Van Diemen's Land Company purchased 50,000 acres of land round Emu Bay in 1826. The Chief

Surveyor of the Colony, Henry Hellyer, explored the north-west of the island in 1827, and in 1829 a village was established at the mouth of the river and named after William Burnie, a director of the company.

Burning Mountain NSW   A common name for Mount Wingen, the Aboriginal name which means fire. Mount Wingen is one of the natural curiosities of Australia. There is a seam of coal within the mountain which has been burning slowly probably for thousands of years, causing smoke to rise through fissures in the ground. There are also sulphur deposits which cover the hot rocks with a yellow coating. Since the phenomenon was first observed in 1828 (and again by T. L. Mitchell in 1831) the burning area has crept less than a hundred yards up the slope. The slow rate of combustion is due to the lack of oxygen deep under the surface.

Burr Creek; Burr Mountain SA   Named by E. J. Eyre after Thomas Burr, Deputy Surveyor-General of South Australia.

Burra SA   There is some uncertainty whether this is an Aboriginal or an Indian word. The town certainly takes its name from the nearby Burra Burra Creek, which is said to mean Large or Great. If an Indian word it was probably introduced by Indian shepherds who were employed here at one time. The place was also known by its true Aboriginal name Kooringa.

Burraga NSW   Aboriginal. Bitter swamp. Another conjectural meaning is Bandicoot.

Burragorang, Lake NSW   Aboriginal. To hunt a small animal. (Booroon, small animal; gong, going to hunt.) It may be a tribal name, which Tyrrell translates as Tribe that wore a nose-pin.

Burrapine NSW   Aboriginal. Yellow.

Burrawang NSW   Aboriginal. Zamia palm. It grew abundantly here. The tree has a cone containing large seeds with a pungent flavour. The Aborigines crushed it to powder, mixed it with water, and baked it as cakes, which were a favourite food.

Burren Junction NSW   Aboriginal. Boomerang, or Big creek.

Burringbar NSW   Aboriginal. Place of a boomerang. The burring was a swordlike boomerang used as a striking implement, and not for throwing.

Burrinjuck NSW   Aboriginal. Precipitous or rugged-topped mountain.

Burrowye V   Aboriginal. Eastwards.

Burrumbeet V   Aboriginal. Muddy water.

Burrumbuttock NSW   Aboriginal name of obscure and tantalising origin, originally adopted for T. F. Gibson's station, and then used for the parish.

Burungule SA   Aboriginal name of a legendary hero who in tribal lore overcame an evil spirit.

Busselton WA   Named after a pioneer family who settled at the Vasse or Busselton River. Thirty years after Baudin's visit to Geographe Bay (see

Busselton River), John Garrett Bussell took up a run at Augusta on Flinders Bay. One day, some of their cattle strayed and were found a few miles further north in better pasture on the banks of what was then known as the Vasse River. The family was attracted to the spot and moved there in 1832. They named the new run Cattle Chosen. The district then became known by several names — The Vasse, Cattle Chosen, and Bussell Town, but when the site was declared a town in June 1837 the name became stabilised as Busselton. The Bussells arrived in 1830. Grace Bussell has been termed the Grace Darling of Australia, for when the *Georgette* was wrecked in Geographe Bay in 1876 she plunged into the breakers on horseback and rescued 48 people over a period of four hours.

Busselton River WA   Formerly known as the Vasse River. When Nicolas Baudin was leaving Geographe Bay in 1801 one of the sailors, Vasse by name, was thought to have been drowned, and Baudin named the river after him. According to later reports, however, Vasse may have struggled ashore, and continued to live in the district for several years. (See also under Busselton.)

Bustard Bay Q   Named by Captain Cook on 23 May 1770. His Journal reveals that: 'All, or most of the same sort, of Land and Water fowl as we saw at Botany Harbour we saw here; besides these we saw some Bustards, such as we have in England, one of which we kill'd that weighed 17½ pounds, which occasioned my giving this place the Name of Bustard Bay.' The bay was the first place at which Cook landed in the present state of Queensland, and is marked by a memorial.

Bute SA   After an island in the Firth of Forth, noted for its excellent climate.

Butler SA   After Sir Richard Butler, Premier of South Australia in 1905, and a prominent Minister in several Governments.

Butler Dome NT   Also after Sir Richard Butler, named by the explorer L. A. Wells.

Buxton V   After Buxton in Derbyshire, meaning Rocking stone.

Byaduk V   Aboriginal. Stone axe.

Bygalorie NSW   Aboriginal. Red kangaroo. The name was first used by Europeans for a pastoral station.

Bynoe Harbour; Bynoe Range NT   Named in 1839 by Captain J. C. Wickham of the *Beagle* after Benjamin Bynoe, the ship's surgeon.

Bynoe River Q   Also named after Benjamin Bynoe, by J. L. Stokes who succeeded J. C. Wickham as commander of the *Beagle*.

Byrock NSW   The name given to a pastoral station in the proximity of an outcrop of rock. At one time it was spelt Byerock.

Byron NSW   After Lord Byron, the poet, who was at the height of his popularity at the time the district was settled.

Byron Bay; Cape Byron NSW   Named by Captain Cook after Captain John Byron, grandfather of the subject of the preceding entry. Captain Byron circumnavigated the globe in 1764-66 and thus preceded Cook in the Pacific. He was in command of HMS *Dolphin.* On 15 May 1770, Cook wrote: 'A Tolerable high point of land bore N.W. by W., distant 3 Miles; this point I named Cape Byron.' The bay was also named at this time. Cape Byron is the most easterly point of the continent.

Caboolture Q   Aboriginal. A corruption of Cabul-tur, Carpet snake.

Cadell SA   Named after Francis Cadell, one of Australia's most adventurous and exciting personalities. He arrived in Australia in 1851 at the age of 29, and two years later set out to win the reward of £2,000 offered by the South Australian government for the first person to navigate the Murray River in a steam vessel. A contest developed between Cadell and W. R. Randell. Cadell won the 'race', but did not collect the reward, for the Government had specified an iron vessel. Randell, who piloted the *Mary Ann,* was awarded the cash, but it has been said that Cadell was given a candalabrum worth £900 for his pioneer voyage in the *Lady Augusta.* He later obtained two boats, the *Albury* and the *Gundagai* and used them to form the River Murray Navigation Company, and maintained a regular service until 1864. He then went to New Zealand to give advice on navigation on the Waikato River, which was used to supply troops and ammunition at the time of the Maori wars. His adventurous spirit next took him to a life of exploration and pearl-fishing. He was arrested for kidnapping Aborigines from Queensland and was finally killed by the crew of his fishing vessel.

Cadibarrawirracanna, Lake SA   Aboriginal. The longest recognised place name in Australia. Its claim could be challenged by Mirranpongapongunna, and, doubtless the longest of all, Cardivillawarracurracurracurrieappalarndoo (The reflection of the stars in the lake water) — but who could possibly tolerate such an address?

Cairns Q   After William Wellington Cairns, Governor of Queensland from 1875 to 1877. The inlet on which the town was built in Trinity Bay was visited by beche-de-mer fishermen who cut mangroves for firewood to smoke their catches. It was not until 1876 that William Smith went to the Hodgkinson Goldfield and brought back 40 miners that the town was established and named Cairns. Prior to that it was known as Thornton after the Queensland Collector of Customs, and then Dickson, after the Colonial Treasurer.

Caldermeade V   After the Scottish town of Calder.

Caledon Bay; Caledon, Mount NT   Named by Matthew Flinders, who camped there in 1803, 'as a mark of respect to the worthy gentleman, late the Governor of the Cape of Good Hope'. It had been visited by Dutch explorers long before this, and the bay marked on their charts as a 'river-like opening'.

Caley Hills; Caley's Repulse NSW   After George Caley, botanist and explorer. According to one account, a cairn on the hilltop was erected in 1789 by a party of explorers who had reached this point in the Blue Mountains and were forced to turn back because of the deep, almost impassable ravines they encountered. The cairn was later named by Governor Macquarie. The *Australian Encyclopaedia* states that the cairn, named by Macquarie, may possibly have been built by Caley during his unsuccessful attempt to cross the Blue Mountains in 1804.

Callabonna, Lake SA   Originally thought to be part of the 'horseshoe' configuration of Lake Torrens. This was disproved by A. C. Gregory in 1858 when he passed between Lake Callabonna and Lake Blanche. Lake Callabonna was first known as Mulligan, a corruption of the Aboriginal name Mullachan.

Callanna SA   Aboriginal. Although the meaning is not known, it has reference to a legendary kangaroo that came to the water hole to drink. The first sheep station, owned by C. C. Dutton, was called the Callanna.

Callignee V   Aboriginal. Water.

Callington SA   After a town in Cornwall, meaning 'village by a grove of trees'.

Calliope; Calliope River Q   Named after HMS *Calliope,* noted as being the only naval vessel to escape from Apia, Western Samoa, in 1889 at the height of a hurricane. The feat was ascribed to the good quality of the coal that fired the furnaces, having come from Westport on the west coast of the South Island of New Zealand. The river was once known as the Liffey.

Caloundra Q   Aboriginal. A corruption of Callandra. Beautiful.

Caltowie SA   Aboriginal. Water hole of the sleeping lizard. Known at one time as Red Banks.

Calvert River NT   Named by Ludwig Leichhardt on 28 June 1845, after a young member of his expedition to Port Essington. James Snowden Calvert arrived in Sydney in 1842 at the age of 17. Leichhardt made his acquaintance on board ship and was glad to take the young botanist with him in spite of his delicate constitution. While in the Mitchell River district the party was attacked by Aborigines and Calvert was severely wounded. Leichhardt promptly named a peak and the plain as well as the river after his young friend.

Cam River T   The river was discovered during surveys undertaken by the Van Diemen's Land Company in 1826 and 1827, and named after the English river. Cam is an English river-name, probably related to the Welsh word Cam meaning 'crooked'. It was first named Emu River by Henry Hellyer when he found emu tracks leading down to the river.

Cambewarra NSW   Aboriginal. Fire hill. (From cambe, fire; warra, hill.) There was a legend current amongst the Aborigines of the Nowra district that fire and smoke issued from the mountain. It was found that in fact there had been a seam of coal that had ignited at some time before the coming of white men and eventually burnt itself out. At one time the township was known as Good Dog.

Cambridge Gulf WA   Named by Philip Parker King in 1819 after the Duke of Cambridge, seventh son of King George II.

Camden NSW   After Lord Camden, Secretary of State, the name Camden Park being first given by John Macarthur when the grant of two properties in the district was authorised by Lord Camden. The Aboriginal name was Benhennie, meaning Dry land.

Camooweal Q   Aboriginal. Strong wind. Camooweal was proclaimed a town in 1884.

Campaspe River V   Discovered and named by T. L. Mitchell in October 1836. From a classical source.

Campbell Town T   The settlement was established in 1811 by Governor Macquarie after his second wife, whose maiden name was Elizabeth Campbell. As the river is called the Elizabeth it seems probable that it, too, was named after his wife.

Campbell's Creek V   After a pioneer settler, William Campbell.

Campbelltown NSW   After Lady Macquarie. Governor Macquarie first named it Airds in 1810 'to be called Airds in honour of my dear good Elizabeth's family estate'. He later changed his mind, and when revisiting the site in 1820 he wrote: 'I name the new township Campbelltown in honour of Mrs Macquarie's maiden name.' She had been Miss Henrietta Elizabeth Campbell.

Camperdown NSW   After the English naval victory over the Dutch fleet in 1797. The battle was fought off the Dutch coast near the village of Camperdown.

Camperdown V   The district was pioneered by John and Peter Manifold in 1838, and a village grew up round their property in 1850. It was then named Camperdown (see above) by Governor La Trobe. Earlier it was known as Duncan, after Lord Duncan, who commanded the British fleet at the Battle of Camperdown. The Aboriginal name was Karlk.

Campsie NSW   After a range of hills in Stirlingshire, Scotland.

Canberra ACT   Aboriginal. Possibly Woman's breasts, so named because of the peaks of Mount Ainslie and the Black Hill. This information was provided by Canon Champion, a local authority, and prompted Bill Beatty to write in *Unique to Australia:* 'It seems singularly appropriate for the site chosen as the mother city of the Australian Commonwealth.' This meaning cannot, however, be accepted with complete confidence. Another possibility is that it comes from the Aboriginal Nganbirra, Meeting-place, which would be equally appropriate in view of Canberra's being the

Federal capital. The area was once known as Limestone Plains, so named because of its outcrops of limestone. An early visitor, Brigade-Major John Ovens, was the first to use this name.

Cannawigara Q   Aboriginal. Path made of sticks laid on soft ground.

Cannie V   Aboriginal. Snake.

Canning River WA   Named by Captain James Stirling in 1827 after George Canning, the British Prime Minister.

Canning Stock Route WA   The route, which gave an outlet for cattle from the Kimberleys to the railway at Wiluna, was discovered by the surveyor Alfred Wernham Canning in 1906, and also pioneered by H. S. Trotman from 1907 to 1910. The 1,400 km long route is negotiable only in good years. It was used during World War II, but has since fallen into disuse. Canning was also notable for his survey for Western Australia's first rabbit-proof fence.

Canobolas, Mount NSW   Aboriginal. Two shoulders. (coona, shoulder; booloo, two.) The two shoulders are the twin peaks of Old Man and Young Man Canobolas. Booloo is a variation of Bulli, q.v.

Canowindra NSW   Aboriginal. Home, or Camping-place.

Cape River Q   Named by Leichhardt on his first expedition, on 27 March 1845, after Captain Cape of the *Sovereign*. The vessel was wrecked on a voyage from Moreton Bay to Port Jackson. Forty-four lives were lost, but local Aborigines came to the rescue and saved ten of the people aboard.

Capertee NSW   A corruption of the name of a holding owned by Sir John Jamieson, who had named it Capita.

Capricorn, Cape Q   Named by Captain Cook on 25 May 1770: 'I found this point to lay directly under the Tropic of Capricorn, and for that reason called it by that Name.'

Caragabal NSW   Aboriginal. To spit (probably a corruption of Karagbilliko, which has this meaning). It was earlier the name of a creek, and of the property of one of the earliest settlers, F. F. Gibson.

Carboor V   Aboriginal. Koala.

Carcoar NSW   Aboriginal. Probably Kookaburra. The syllables imitate the laughing cry – cah-co-ah. It is just possible that it may instead (or in addition) be a rendering of the voice of the frog or of the crow, both speculations having been made in the past.

Cardinia V   Aboriginal. Sunrise.

Cardwell Q   After Viscount Cardwell, Minister for the Colonies. The port was established in 1864 by George A. F. E. Dalrymple to provide an outlet for produce from the Upper Burdekin region.

Cargelligo, Lake NSW   In *The Man Who Sold His Dreaming* Ronald Robinson writes that the Aboriginal Fred Biggs of the Ngeamba tribe told

55

him that the name was the nearest the white man got to saying Kartjellakoo (kartjell, coolamon; akoo, he had). The name therefore means 'He had a coolamon.' It was first named Regent's Lake by the discoverer, John Oxley, in 1817, after the Prince Regent (George IV). The name has suffered many changes. A pastoral run here was called Gagellaga by Francis Oakes in 1842, and given its present spelling by D. and S. O'Sullivan in 1848. T. L. Mitchell superseded Oxley's choice of name in 1836 when he called it Cudjallagong. Other forms are Cudgellico and Cudgelligo. The town on the borders of the lake has the same name, Lake Cargelligo.

Carina V   An Aboriginal word connected with water.

Carisbrook V   In remembrance of a daughter of an early settler; the name is really a condensed version of Caroline's Brook.

Carlsruhe V   Named by Charles Elden after a town in Germany.

Carlton Hill Q   Named after the Edinburgh suburb.

Carlwood NSW   Named after Carl W. R. Johnson, a local politician.

Carnarvon WA   Named after Lord Carnarvon, Secretary of State for the Colonies from 1866 to 1874. The town site was surveyed in 1883 and proclaimed in 1886.

Caroline, Mount WA   Named by Robert Dale in 1830.

Caroline Range WA   Discovered and named by Frank H. Hann.

Carpentaria, Gulf of NT, Q   In March 1623 Jan Carstensz sailed southwards from the coast of New Guinea in the *Pera*. On 12 April the northern coast of Australia was sighted near the present Port Musgrave on Cape York Peninsula. He called the gulf Carpentaria after Pieter de Carpentier, Governor-General of the Dutch East Indies. Carstensz had been preceded by Willem Jansz in the *Duyfken* when it touched on the west coast of the Cape York Peninsula in 1605-1606.

Carrajung V   Aboriginal. Fishing line.

Carrathool NSW   Aboriginal. Native companion.

Carrieton SA   Named after Carrie, daughter of Governor Jervois.

Carrington NSW   Charles Robert Wynn-Carrington, first Marquis of Lincolnshire and first Earl Carrington, was Governor of New South Wales 1885-90. It was said that he was the 'Champagne Charlie' of the popular song of the day. It is possible that the suburb of Newcastle was named after his grandfather, the first Baron. In the 1830s James Backhouse said he 'arrived at the little village of Carrington'. It is curious, however, that a very early record has the name Carreabean, and that in 1824 it was recorded as Caribean, both of which have a resemblance to the present name.

Carrington Heights NSW   Once known popularly and amusingly as Bilacote Hills, because it was a favourite grazing ground for billygoats.

Carron River Q   Probably named after one of the three survivors of E. B. Kennedy's expedition, which left Rockingham Bay for Cape York in 1848. The others were killed by the Aborigines.

Carrum Downs V   Aboriginal. Yesterday.

Carwarp V   Aboriginal. River bend.

Cascade Bay WA   J. L. Stokes of the *Acheron* made the following entry on 23 March 1838: 'After passing the N.W. point of the mainland, seen from the ship, we discovered a deep bay, which once reached, would afford safe anchorage for a fleet. Near its northern point a large stream of water fell into the sea in a glittering cascade.'

Casino NSW   After Cassino, the Italian monastery-city, which came into such prominence in World War II. The station was established in the 1840s by Clarke Irving, and was named Cassino either by him or by Clay and Stapleton. The modern spelling is corrupt.

Cassowary Q   Named after the bird.

Casterton V   This area was taken up for settlement in 1837 and named, probably by one of the Henty brothers, from the town of this name in Westmoreland. The name means Camp.

Castle, Mount NSW   Discovered and named by Allan Cunningham in 1828. The Aboriginal name was Butcha, a hero of the Ugarapul tribe who died while defending his people against the warriors of Baluchi. His recumbent figure can be seen in the profile of the mountain.

Castlemaine V   Named by the chief gold fields Commissioner, Captain W. Wright, after his uncle, Viscount Castlemaine. The area was crossed by T. L. Mitchell in 1836 and settled shortly afterwards. In 1851 gold was discovered at Specimen Valley. There was a sudden influx of miners to the diggings first called both Forest Creek and Mount Alexander, the latter name still remaining in the Mount Alexander Koala Park, eight miles from Castlemaine. The township was gazetted a borough in 1855.

Castlereagh; Castlereagh River NSW   On 6 December 1810 Governor Macquarie noted in his Journal: 'The township for the Evan or Nepean District I have named *Castlereagh* in honour of Lord Castlereagh.' The site first chosen by Macquarie is three miles from the present settlement. The Governor founded five towns in the district (Aboriginal name Mulgoa): Castlereagh, Windsor, Richmond, Wilberforce, and Pitt Town.

The Castlereagh River was discovered by G. W. Evans during Oxley's expedition in 1818, and was also named after Lord Castlereagh, Secretary of State for the Colonies, as was Castlereagh Street in Sydney.

Castlereagh Bay NT   Named by Philip Parker King in honour of Lord Castlereagh.

Casuarina, Mount WA   This is the botanical name for the she-oak.

Catastrophe, Cape SA   The nomenclature of this and other natural features in the vicinity of the entrance to Spencer Gulf was chosen by Matthew Flinders to commemorate the tragedy when eight of his crew were drowned on the evening of 21 February 1802. The *Investigator* passed Cape Wiles. Flinders sent a cutter ahead to seek a safe anchorage for the vessel. The sailing master, or mate, John Thistle, was in command, together with William Taylor, midshipman, and a crew of six. On its return the cutter was sighted and then disappeared in a sudden squall. A search proved in vain. The following day broken pieces of the boat and a cask which had been filled with fresh water were found, but there was no trace of the bodies.

'I proceeded to the southern extremity of the main land, which was now named Cape Catastrophe,' wrote Flinders. He called the inlet where the party had been ashore for water Memory Cove, and named islands in the vicinity after the men who were drowned.

Cathcart NSW   After Major Cathcart, who was responsible for the erection of military barracks here. The Aboriginal name was Togranong.

Caulfield V   After John Caulfield, a committee member of the Mechanics Institute in Melbourne in 1839.

Cave River WA   Discovered and named by Harry Whittall Venn, probably in the 1860s.

Cavendish V   After Lord Frederick Cavendish, Secretary to the British Treasury.

Ceduna SA   Aboriginal. A corruption of Chedoona, Resting place. The present name was chosen in 1915, but the place was known more than a hundred years before. Baudin named it Murat Bay in 1802, and this name was used when it was proclaimed a township in 1901. Although the village was not founded until 1896, a whaling station was in existence on St Peter's Island, off Cape Thevenard, as early as 1850.

Cemetery Plain NT   The thirty-mile wide area sprinkled with 'magnetic' ant hills that lie due north and south is popularly known as Cemetery Plain. The ant hills, which are only found here and in the Cape York Peninsula stand up like monuments in a cemetery.

Central Australia Q, SA, WA   This area existed for only five years, from 1926, to 1931, as a legal and administrative territory. Today 'The Centre' is regarded as the whole area within a radius of about 700 to 800 km from Alice Springs, and is so named for obvious reasons.

Central Mount Stuart NT   On 23 April 1860, John McDouall Stuart climbed this hill, about 160 km north of Alice Springs, built a stone pyramid or cone, planted the British flag, and named it Central Mount Sturt after Charles Sturt. On the 22nd he wrote in his Journal: 'Today I bid from my observation of the .LL III 00′ 30″ that I am now camped in the Centre of Australia. I have marked a tree and planted the British flag in the centre; there is a high mount about two miles to the N.N.E. which I hoped would be in the centre but on it tomorrow I will raise a cone of stones and plant the flag there and will name it Mount Sturt after my excellent and esteemed commander of the expedition in 1844 and 45, Captain Sturt, as a mark of gratitude for the great kindness I received from him on that journey.'

Stuart was fully justified in his use of the word Central, for he was within 30 minutes of the centre of longitude of the continent, and midway along a line between Arnhem Land and the Great Australian Bight.

There is no doubt of the name first conferred on it by Stuart, not only because of the Journal entry recorded above, but also because he recorded the fact that he and his men gave 'three hearty cheers and one more for Mrs Sturt and family'.

Some mystery attaches to the change to Central Mount Stuart. Stuart continued to use 'Sturt' during the remainder of his fourth expedition, but on his fifth journey in 1861 he himself used the form Central Mount Stuart. By that time it had come into popular use. Two Adelaide newspapers had published a letter he had written to his sponsor, Mr Chambers, and it is agreed either that a genuine mistake was made or that Chambers had requested that the central point be named after its discoverer.

Central Mount Wedge NT   The peak, a few miles from Central Mount Stuart, q.v., was discovered by Major Egerton Warburton in 1873, on his journey from Alice Springs to Roebourne in Western Australia.

Ceratodus Q   This railway station bears the scientific name of the Queensland lungfish, which is regarded as a living fossil.

Ceres NSW   Probably after the ancient Roman corn-goddess, who was identified with Demeter, the Greek goddess.

Cessnock NSW   After Cessnock Castle in Scotland, and named by John Campbell, who was given a land grant here in 1826.

Chace Range SA   Popularly and probably rightly believed to be named after William Chace, a teamster employed by Browne. He had been asked to explore the hinterland and so discovered Wilpena Pound and the Arkaba and Aroona creeks in the Flinders Ranges. The name is sometimes misspelt Chase.

Chakola NSW   Aboriginal. Lyre Bird.

Chalkerup WA   Sir Henry Somerset, when writing to the compiler in 1968, and discussing Western Australian names ending in 'up' (which always refers to water or a water hole), stated: 'I am always looking for new "up" names and was delighted to find, on the map, a defunct mining town with a derelict hotel – "Chalkerup" it said. No doubt the last attempt by the publican to remain solvent.'

Chambers Bay NT   This was the northern terminal of J. McDouall Stuart's successful crossing of the continent from south to north in 1861-62. He buried an air-tight tin with the following message: 'SOUTH

AUSTRALIAN GREAT NORTHERN EXPLORING EXPEDITION. The exploring party, under the command of John McDouall Stuart, arrived at this spot on the 25th day of July, 1862, having crossed the entire Continent of Australia from the Southern to the Indian Ocean, passing through the centre. They left the City of Adelaide on the 26th [25th] day of October, 1861, and the most northern station of the colony on 21st day of January 1862. To commemorate this happy event, they raised this flag, bearing his name. All well. God save the Queen!' Stuart and the members of his party all signed the document.

'As this bay has not been named,' Stuart wrote, 'I have taken this opportunity of naming it in honour of Miss Chambers, who kindly presented me with the flag I have planted this day.'

The incident may conceal this strange, shy, indomitable man's love for the daughter of his supporter and well-wisher, James Chambers. She had made the flag (a Union Jack) and sewed his name on it. In his pencil journal he had entered her Christian name Elizabeth. It has been conjectured that he altered it to her surname for he felt it would be presumptuous to indulge in the intimacy of recording her Christian name in this way. Tradition also says that he was engaged to Elizabeth, or to her sister Katherine, and that, on account of ill-health resulting from his arduous journeys, he broke it off after his return.

Chambers, Mount SA   The name was probably conferred by J. McDouall Stuart who was at the time engaged in surveying. In 1858 the Surveyor-General, Frome, who triangulated the area, recorded the name Frome's Eagle Nest — 'a pretty name and ought to be retained by the hill being now well-known as Mt Chambers. I must against my will retain Chambers.' Stuart doubtless named it after the brothers James and John Chambers.

Chambers Pillar SA   Once again J. McDouall Stuart honoured his supporter in the following note, written on 6 April 1860: 'It is a pillar of sandstone, standing on a hill upwards of 100 feet in height. From the base to the top of the pillar it is 105 feet, twenty feet wide by ten feet deep, and quite perpendicular, with two peaks on the top. This I have named Chambers's (sic) Pillar, after James Chambers, Esq, of Adelaide, one of the promoters of all my expeditions.'

The Aboriginal name was Idracowra or Etikaura.

Chandler River; Chandler Peak NSW   After the celebrated stockman Chandler. See under Beardy Plains.

Channel Country, The Q   So named because of the channels that are formed by 'gutter floods' after summer rains in the upper catchment areas of the Balloo, Cooper, Diamantina, Georgina, and Mulligan rivers. The area is that of the flood plains of these rivers. Alternative names are Kidman Country and Corner Company.

Chappell, Mount T   Matthew Flinders married Annette Chappelle in 1801 in England. He named the mountain and the nearby Chappell Islands after her, and possibly also for her sisters.

Charles Creek NT   J. McDouall Stuart's Journal of 24 July 1862 gives the reason for the name: 'This creek I named "Charles Creek", after the eldest son of John Chambers, Esq.'

Charleville Q   Named by William Alcock Tully, who surveyed the site in 1868, after his boyhood town in Ireland. The Irish name was in turn derived from Charleville in France.

Charlotte Waters NT   Lady Charlotte Bacon was the daughter of the sixth Earl of Oxford. The surveyors R. B. Knuckey and A. T. Woods, surveyors engaged by the Overland Telegraph promoters, were equally responsible for the choice. They had been reading Byron's *Childe Harold*, which had been dedicated to her as Ianthe. Knuckey wrote: 'We solemnly filled our pannikins and I named the "waters" Charlotte after Lady Charlotte Bacon, daughter of the Earl of Oxford.'

Charlton V   Named after Charlton near London; meaning Town of the free peasants.

Charnley River WA   Discovered and named by Frank H. Hann in 1903.

Charters Towers Q   A composite name, bestowed on the gold field by Hugh Mossman, one of the original discoverers – Charters after a local gold warden, Tors because of similarity with the Dartmoor tors in England, which consist of granite hills strewn with boulders. Eventually Tors became corrupted to Towers by those who did not recognise the appropriateness of the original name.

Chasm Island NT   A name that is descriptive of the fissures in the cliffs at the end of Groote Eylandt. The caves with which the cliffs are honeycombed contain magnificent specimens of Aboriginal art.

Chatham, Cape WA   Named by George Vancouver on 26 September 1791 after his own vessel. Ten years later it was sighted by Flinders, on 7 December 1801, who described it as 'the land first made upon this coast by Captain Vancouver'.

Chatswood NSW   After 'Chat' or 'Chatty', the second wife of Richard Harnette, who operated the first ferry from Mosman to Circular Quay and was a pioneer in the district.

Chermside Q   The Brisbane suburb was named after Sir Herbert Charles Chermside, Governor of Queensland from 1902 to 1904.

Chetwynd V   Named in memory of G. Chetwynd Stapylton, the deputy leader of T. L. Mitchell's journey from Sydney to Port Phillip in 1835 and 1836.

Cheyne Island WA   The number of natural features that bear the name of George McCartney Cheyne are as varied as the occupations he adopted. He arrived at Fremantle in 1831 and was successively a farmer, whaling promoter, timber-man, merchant, ship's chandler, and grazier. The features named after him include an inlet, point of land, creek, ledge, head, and beach.

Chifley SA   After Joseph Benedict Chifley, the railways shopboy, cleaner, fireman, locomotive driver, who rose to the position of President of Federal Labor in New South Wales and, from 1945 to 1949, Prime Minister of Australia.

Childers Q, V   After Hugh Culling Eardley Childers. He was a tally-clerk on the Melbourne wharves, and had a meteoric career. He became a school inspector and then entered politics, and was appointed Agent-General for Victoria, in England. After this his Australian connections ceased, and he achieved the distinction of becoming First Lord of the Admiralty, Chancellor of the Duchy of Lancaster, Secretary of War, Chancellor of the Exchequer, and Home Secretary. Formerly Isis Scrub.

Chillagoe Q   The Chillagoe station was named and owned by a son of John Atherton.

Chillingollah V   A. E. Martin states that this Aboriginal-sounding name was in fact a corruption of Chillianwallah, a battle between the British and Indian forces on 13 January 1849.

Chiltern V   After Chiltern in England, famous on account of the Chiltern Hundreds. It was first called New Ballarat. The Aboriginal name was Doma Mungi.

Chinchilla Q   Aboriginal. A corruption of Jinchilla, Cypress pine.

Chiswick NSW   After Chiswick in Middlesex, on the bank of the River Thames. In *The History and Description of Sydney Harbour**, P. R. Stephensen wrote: 'At about the same time, other names of vicinities on the banks of the Thames were officially applied to districts on the banks of the Parramatta River, among them "Greenwich", "Woolwich", "Henley", "Putney", and "Mortlake"; but whether this was sentimental nostalgia of exiles, imperialistic propaganda, or an example of the Australian sense of humour — after Ted Trickett won the World's Sculling Championship on the Thames — has not been ascertained.'

Chowilla SA   Aboriginal. Land of spirits.

Christmas Island   Although the island was discovered by Richard Rowe of the *Thomas* in February 1615, it was not named until 1653, when the Dutch Captain William Mynors sighted it on Christmas day.

Church Point NSW   Mrs Oliver, whose husband William Oliver donated land for the first Wesleyan church in Pittwater, told Bible stories to her children at the Church Point. It is said that she had a musket by her side as she related the stories, to deter any hostile Aborigines. It is also said that the name came from an old church that has almost disappeared.

Churchill Island V   Named by James Grant of the *Lady Nelson* after

---

* Rigby Ltd, Adelaide, 1966, p.256.

Thomas Churchill. The first seed plantings in what is now Victoria were made here when Grant planted wheat, vegetables, seeds of apples, plums, peaches, and a little rice and coffee, all of which had been supplied to him in England by Churchill.

Circular Head T   A descriptive name applied by Bass and Flinders who sailed past it in December 1789. It has given its name to the surrounding district. The mass of rock is known locally as The Nut.

City of Gold Coast Q   A name which appears designed to encourage a flourishing holiday and tourist industry, but was given when land values increased spectacularly. It was formerly known as South Coast Town. The local government area embraces the towns of Coolangatta and Southport, and part of the shire of Nerang. The name was proclaimed on 14 May 1959.

Clare SA   There is an old eucalypt tree growing in the town. According to the tablet affixed to it, E. J. Eyre was the first visitor to the district in 1839, followed by Edward B. Gleeson and John Maynard who camped under the tree and settled there in 1842. Gleeson had the town site surveyed and named it after his birthplace, County Clare in Ireland. Aboriginal name, Kyneetchya.

Claremont Isles Q   Named by Philip Parker King.

Clarence River NSW   The discovery and naming of this river are somewhat involved. Matthew Flinders anchored at the mouth in 1799 and named it Shoal Bay, but the river was first discovered when it was crossed by four escaped convicts in 1825. For some time it was known simply as the Big River. John Oxley had discovered and named the Tweed River, but when Captain H. J. Rous of the *Rainbow* sailed into the Tweed in 1828 he believed that he was the discoverer and named it the Clarence, after the Duke of Clarence. When it later became clear that he was not the discoverer of this river, the name Clarence was transferred to what was previously known as the Big River. The Aboriginal name of the Clarence was Booroogarrabowyra-neyand, head of the tide (booroogarra, salt water; bowyra, head of a creek; neyand, top).

Clarence Strait NT   Surveyed and named by P. P. King in May 1818 and named by him in honour of the Duke of Clarence who later became William IV.

Clarendon SA   Named by Sir John Morphett after the Earl of Clarendon, British Foreign Minister during the Crimean War.

Clarke Island T   After the super-cargo of the wrecked *Sydney Cove*. See under Preservation Island.

Clarke River Q   The name was conferred by Leichhardt on 22 April 1845, probably after a member of his party.

Claudie River Q   Discovered by William Lakeland while on a prospecting trip, and named after his son Claude.

Clear, Cape V   In a compilation such as this, 'Cape Clear' provides a little light relief. In *A Treasury of Australian Folk Tales**, Bill Beatty says that a teamster's wagon was bogged here. Before going off for assistance the teamster, who appears to be of Irish descent, put up a notice warning others that the ground was soft, or to warn them from touching his wagon, and spelt the words Keep Clear as Kape Klear.

Cleland Hills NT   After a Government medical officer.

Clermont Q   After the birthplace in France of Oscar de Satge, the pioneer pastoralist in this district, who later represented Clermont in the Queensland Parliament. The name was bestowed by A. C. Gregory when he surveyed the site in 1862.

Cleve SA   After the home in England of Thomas Snow, Governor Jervois's aide-de-camp. The English name has the meaning Cliff or Hill.

Cleveland; Cleveland Bay and Cape   Named by Captain Cook on 6 June 1770, probably after Henry, second Duke of Cleveland, but possibly for John Cleveland, Secretary to the Admiralty from 1751 to 1763. The Aboriginal name of the cape was Nandeebie.

Clifton, Mount WA   Discovered and named by Frank H. Hann in 1903.

Clinton Centre SA   Named in 1862 by Governor Daly after Clinton in Canada, where he had previously been Chief Secretary. The locality was in the centre of the Clinton Hundred.

Cloncurry Q   During their expedition in 1861, Burke and Wills travelled down the Corella River to another which Burke named the Cloncurry after his cousin, Lady Elizabeth Cloncurry of Castle Hackett, County Galway, Ireland. The town was subsequently named after the river.

Clonmel Island V   The scene of the wreck of the *Clonmel,* the first ship to provide a regular service between Melbourne and Sydney. The wreck occurred on 3 February 1841.

Clontarf Q   Doubtless after the town on the Bay of Dublin, or of the county.

Clunes NSW   Probably after Major Archibald Clunes Innes, soldier and pastoralist. The *Australian Dictionary of Biography* says of him: 'In a time and place when much existence was drab and bitter the doings and the mode of Archibald Clunes Innes wore a cheering brightness.'

Clunes V   When William Campbell discovered gold in March 1850 he named the site Clunes after a farm in Inverness-shire, Scotland.

Clyde NSW, V   After the Clyde River in Scotland. C. M. G. Eddy, Railway Commissioner, wrote of the New South Wales Clyde: 'New Glasgow is close by, and as Old Glasgow is watered by the Clyde (to which the Duck River may be likened), perhaps "Clyde" would not be unacceptable.'

*   Ure Smith, 1960.

Clyde River NSW   Also named after the Scottish River. Discovered by Lieutenant Robert Johnston in the *Snapper* in December 1821. The river was named either by Lieutenant Johnston or Alexander Berry, a merchant who accompanied Johnston to the river a year later and explored it. The Aboriginal name was Bindoo.

Clyde River T   Named in 1820 by Lieut-Governor Sorrell because of the large proportion of Scottish settlers.

Coal River T   When John Bowen explored the region in 1803 he discovered the river, and named it when he found deposits of coal, but these proved to be of little importance.

Coal and Candle Creek NSW   The origin of this name will probably never be known. Two versions are current: 1. That it is a corruption of Colin Campbell (Sir Colin Campbell, later Lord Clyde), who commanded the Highland Brigade in the Crimean War, and who later suppressed the Indian Mutiny. 2. That it is a corruption of the Aboriginal name, Kolaan Kandahl. The latter theory is probably correct, the former the more romantic.

Coalcliff NSW   Three survivors of a wreck in 1797 set out to walk to Sydney, more than 300 miles away. At this point they discovered coal and lit a fire to warm themselves. After they were rescued they reported the presence of coal, and Governor Hunter sent George Bass to investigate. Bass found several seams that extended for some distance and conjectured that they might extend throughout the range. This was the origin of the name.

Cobar NSW   Probably Aboriginal, from Coburra, the reddish-coloured burnt earth used by Aborigines in body-painting in preparation for corroborees. The fact that Cobar is a mining centre may also have been cause for the conjecture that it was an Aboriginal attempt to pronounce the word 'copper'.

Cobargo NSW   Aboriginal. Grandfather.

Cobba-da-mana Q   Aboriginal. Caught by the head. The name refers to an incident in which an Aboriginal woman suffered an accident when giving birth to her child.

Cobbler, The SA   The name was given by shearers travelling south along the Strzelecki River. The Cobbler was the last of the sandhills and the most difficult to cross, just as a 'cobbler' is the most difficult sheep to shear.

Cobden V   Named after the British statesman, Richard Cobden, noted for his campaign for Free Trade.

Cobdogla SA   A mysterious and intriguing name. The story is that when the first settlers arrived, one of them made a sketch of the Murray River and the surrounding terrain on the tailboard of their cart. A lubra was looking on. When the drawing was finished she exclaimed, 'Cobdogla!' — but to this day no one knows whether it was an expression of approval or criticism.

Cobourg Peninsula NT   P. P. King named the peninsula in 1818 during his survey of the northern coast after Prince Leopold of Saxe-Cobourg, son-in-law of George IV, and uncle of Queen Victoria. He later became King of Belgium.

Cobram V   Aboriginal. Head.

Coburgh V   Named shortly after the visit of the Duke of Edinburgh, who was also Duke of Saxe-Cobourg. Earlier known as Pentridge.

Cocamba V   Aboriginal. Kookaburra.

Cockaleechie SA   Named after the soup of that name. The student is free to make his own version of the naming.

Cockatoo V   Named on account of the profusion of these birds.

Cockatoo Island NSW   A translation of the Aboriginal word Biloela, which was the name given to the industrial school for girls established on the island in 1871. The name Cockatoo Island, however, was in use by 1800, as well as Banks Island. It is therefore more likely that Biloela was taken as an alternative to Cockatoo for the school. It is said that the original Aboriginal name for the island was Warrieubah.

Cockburn SA   After Sir John Cockburn who was a doctor at Jamestown. He later entered Parliament and was appointed Agent-General for South Australia.

Cockburn, Mount NT   Named by P. P. King in September 1818 in honour of Vice-Admiral Sir George Cockburn, an Admiralty Commissioner at the time.

Cockburn Sound WA   Also named after Admiral Cockburn. See above.

Codrington V   After the captain of the *Orion*.

Coen River Q   See under Archer River.

Coffin Bay SA   Named by Flinders in February 1802: 'The large piece of water . . . I named Coffin's Bay, in compliment to the present Vice-Admiral Sir Isaac Coffin, Bart.' Coffin was resident naval commissioner at Sheerness, and assisted Flinders in fitting out the *Investigator*.

Coffin, Mount SA   Named after a bullock driver by J. McDouall Stuart.

Coff's Harbour NSW   Named, rather distortedly, after John Korff who is reputed to have been the discoverer.

Cohuna V   Aboriginal. Native companion, or Camping place.

Colac V   Possibly a corruption of the Aboriginal Coladjin, the name of a local tribe.

Colebrook T   Once known as Jerusalem. See under Jericho.

Coledale NSW   Previously spelt Coaldale, the name refers to coal deposits in the locality.

Coleraine V   Named by the surveyor Bryant after the town in Northern Ireland. The meaning of the Gaelic name is Land covered with fern.

Collarenebri NSW   Aboriginal. Place of many flowers. In 1867 the town was gazetted as Collarindabri, and is still sometimes spelt Colarendabri, but is known locally as Colly.

Collaroy NSW   Two entirely different versions of the origin of the name are current: 1. Aboriginal word meaning either Junction of creeks or Large swamp reed. This was the name of an adjacent sheep station. 2. The paddle-steamer *Collaroy*, which traded between Sydney and Newcastle for many years, was wrecked here and refloated two years later, rigged as a three-masted schooner, and eventually cast away on the Californian coast four years later.

Collector NSW   It was recorded in T. L. Mitchell's records that the Aboriginal name was Colegdar; the present modification to the English word can readily be understood.

Collier NSW   Aboriginal. Water. The word was usually applied to lagoons and large waterholes, and in this form, and as Colly, appears in many Aboriginal place-names.

Collie; Collie River WA   Named after Alexander Collie, naval surgeon and naturalist on HMS *Sulphur*, which reached Fremantle in 1829. Collie and Lieut William Preston set out to explore the country round Perth. On 17 November the two men left to make a reconnaissance of the southwest coast, and discovered two rivers, one of which was named the Collie and the other the Preston.

Collinsville Q   After Charles Collins, the member for Bowen for many years in the Queensland Parliament.

Colton SA   After Sir John Colton, who arrived in Australia in 1839 and became Premier of South Australia in 1876.

Combara NSW   Aboriginal. Tomorrow, or Yesterday, i.e. one day away.

Comboyne NSW   Aboriginal. Female kangaroo.

Come-by-chance NSW   The name was given by George and William Colless when, in 1862, they found to their surprise that they were able to purchase a sheep station in this district. The *Australian Encyclopaedia* relates how Banjo Paterson was reading a postal guide, and wove the name into one of his ballads:
> But my languid mood forsook me when I found a name that took me;
> Quite by chance I came across it – 'Come-by-chance' was what I read;
> No location was assigned it, nor a thing to help one find it,
> Just an N which stood for northward and the rest was all unsaid.

Comet; Comet River Q   The river was discovered by Leichhardt, who gave the name because he observed a comet there on 28 December 1844.

Compton SA   After the owner of a local factory.

Compton Downs NSW   Probably after a place in England. The word means Village in a narrow valley.

Condobolin NSW   Aboriginal. Hop bush, a species of *Dodonaea*. There were two pastoral runs of this name in the district, owned respectively by Benjamin Boyd and William Lee.

Condowie SA   Aboriginal. Good water.

Conmurra SA   Aboriginal. Stony hill.

Conner, Mount NT   Named by W. C. Gosse, the explorer and surveyor, in 1873 after M. L. Conner, a South Australian Member of Parliament. The Aboriginal name has been spelt Artula, Artilla, and Atula, and may have some connection with the legend of the terrible ice-men who control cold weather.

Connewarra V   Aboriginal. A corruption of Koonoowarra, Black swan.

Connewirricoo V   Aboriginal. Tea tree, or Forehead.

Connors Range Q   After Daniel Connor, who settled here in the 1860s.

Constitution Hill T   In searching for some explanation of this name, an imaginative mind has suggested that it arose from the remark of some person unknown, and doubtless non-existent: 'You need a damn good constitution to get to the top of that hill.'

Conway, Cape Q   Named by Captain Cook on 3 June 1770 after Henry Seymour Conway, Secretary of State from 1765 to 1768.

Coober Pedy SA   Aboriginal. 'White fellow's hole in the ground' – in reference to the underground dwellings of the opal seekers. The popular belief is that the dugouts were constructed to enable the prospectors to escape the heat, but the fact remains that there is no timber in the neighbourhood, and excavation is the simplest way to provide shelter. Temperatures at Coober Pedy may reach 130° during the day, the nights are cold, and gales not infrequent. Dugouts are, from every point of view, the answer to the problems of the opal gougers. Most of the 'dwellings' have a hole about two metres high and one metre wide as an entrance, with shafts for ventilation. The number of rooms, which may contain a fireplace, a chimney, table, chairs, shelves and furniture of all kinds, depends on the size of the family.

Coobowie SA   Aboriginal. Plenty of water.

Coogee NSW   Aboriginal. Rotting seaweed, Stinking place, or Smell of seaweed. The original word may have been Koojah.

Cook SA   This station on the Transcontinental Line that crosses the Nullarbor Plain was named after a former Prime Minister.

Cook, Mount Q   Named after the famous navigator by P. P. King on 27 June 1819.

Cook, Point V . After John M. Cooke, mate of HMS *Rattlesnake* when Captain William Hobson charted parts of Port Phillip in November 1836. The 'e' has been dropped from the name.

Cooke's Plains SA   After Archibald Cooke, a pastoralist.

Cook's Passage Q   The passage just north of Lizard Island, where Cook's *Endeavour* finally escaped from the perils of the Barrier Reef.

Cook's River NSW   After Captain James Cook, for it was here that he made his first landing in 'New Holland' on 29 April 1770. The first record of the name is on a chart of the NSW settlement dated 10 January 1798.

Cooktown Q   The town that has risen on the banks of the Endeavour River, where Cook beached the *Endeavour* after the vessel had been holed on the Barrier Reef, was named in honour of the captain. The crew remained there for 45 days, from 18 June to 4 August repairing the vessel and gathering food and water.

Coolabah NSW   Aboriginal. The well-known box tree, a species of eucalypt, *Eucalyptus microtheca.* Perpetuated by Paterson's jolly swagman in *Waltzing Matilda*, who reclined 'under the shade of a coolabah tree'.

Coolac NSW   Aboriginal. Native bear.

Coolah NSW   Aboriginal. Two meanings have been given: 1. Junction, possibly a contraction of Coolaburagundi. 2. Angry, or Bad temper.

Coolalie NSW   Aboriginal. South wind.

Coolamon NSW   Aboriginal. Wooden vessel. The shallow dish used by Aborigines for many domestic purposes, such as holding water, grain, etc. The area was first a stock station, owned and named by J. Atkinson in 1848, in the form of Cooleman.

Coolangatta Q   Named by early cedar-cutters after the *Coolangatta,* a small vessel owned by Alexander Berry, that was wrecked here on 18 August 1846. The Aboriginal meaning is Look-out. Other and similar renderings are: Splendid look-out; Highest land; View; Good look-out; Elbow hill; Large hill; Good view. The original word may have been Cooloongatta.

Coolgardie WA   Aboriginal. A corruption of Koolgoor-biddie, Mulga tree growing in a hollow. The name was first recorded by the gold field warden, John Michael Finnerty, when he asked an Aboriginal what a nearby water hole was called and, according to the record, received the reply: 'Golgardie country belonga this feller.' The present name was in use early in the history of the gold fields, but was also known at times as Bayley's Find, Fly Flat, and the Old Camp.

Coolum, Mount Q   The name of an Aboriginal man of ancient legend. Old man Nindherry (after whom Mount Nindherry is named) was jealous of young Coolum. He threw a large stone at him and knocked off his head, which is now Mudjimba Island.

Cooma NSW   Aboriginal. A contraction of Coombah, Big lake, or Open country. Other meanings assigned to it are Swamp, and Junction of two streams.

Coomandook SA   Aboriginal. Named by Aborigines who lived at a distance, and called the place Coom-an-duk, Country where the enemy lives.

Coombah, Lake NSW   Aboriginal. Male baby.

Coombe SA   Named after the Member of Parliament, E. H. Coombe.

Coomera Q   Aboriginal. From Kumera kumera, a species of fern that grows there. The Coomera River was first known as the Arrowsmith.

Coonabarabran NSW   Aboriginal. Inquisitive person. In the form Coolabaraban, it was the name of the station owned by James Weston in 1848. The local contraction is 'The Bran'.

Coonalpyn Downs SA   Aboriginal. Barren woman. Earlier called the Ninety Mile Desert.

Coonamble NSW   Aboriginal. Bullock dung, or Human excrement. This was the name of the station held by James Walker in 1847.

Coonawarra SA   Aboriginal. Honeysuckle growing on a hillside.

Coondambo SA   Aboriginal. Small kangaroo rat.

Coonong NSW   Aboriginal. Dirty water. The name of a pastoral holding.

Coopernook NSW   Aboriginal. Elbow. Probably referring to a bend in a stream.

Cooper Creek Q, SA   The naming of Cooper Creek (which has now supplanted Cooper's Creek) has long been a matter of controversy. It was discovered by Charles Sturt. He found that the Strzelecki Creek flowed from another river and, in the course of his return from his second expedition from Fort Grey towards the northern regions in October and November 1845, he followed the stream until he came to a point where it diverged into many channels, and was forced back. On 9 November 1845 he wrote: 'I gave the name Cooper's Creek to the water-course we had so anxiously traced, as a proof of my respect for Mr Cooper.' Mr Cooper, later Sir Charles Cooper, was the first Chief Justice of South Australia. Sturt encountered incredible hardships in his struggle to reach the central regions of the continent and those further north.

Shortly afterwards T. L. Mitchell, accompanied by E. B. Kennedy, made a further attempt to reach Sturt's goal but on reaching Queensland he turned back and to his delight discovered the Barcoo River (q.v.), which semeed to be flowing northwards. Kennedy later found that the Barcoo gradually turned southwards and that in fact it was the upper reaches of the Cooper.

In 1848 A. C. Gregory proved that the Barcoo, the stream named the Victoria by Mitchell, and the Cooper were one river, and that as Sturt's discovery preceded that of Mitchell, the Victoria was again named the Cooper. By 1860 the Secretary of State for the colonies ruled that the whole length of the river should be known as the Barcoo, and this name, together with that of the Cooper as an alternative, was recorded on the map. After many years it was tacitly agreed that the name Barcoo should be confined to the part of the river above its junction with the Thomson.

The term 'creek' has also been called in question, for bushmen have a saying that the streams are unique. 'It takes two rivers (the Thomson and the Barcoo),' they say, 'to make one creek.'

Coorabin NSW   Aboriginal. Curlew.

Cooran Q   Aboriginal. Moreton Bay ash.

Coorong, The SA   Aboriginal. The name of the salt water lagoon and the surrounding country is a corruption of Kurangh, Neck.

Cootamundra NSW   Aboriginal. Turtles, Swamp, or Low-lying. One authority says that the original Aboriginal word was Gooramundra. In the form Cootamondra, it was a stock station owned by John Hurley in the 1830s. Later it was known as the 'Village of Cootamundry'.

Coot-tha, Mount Q   Aboriginal. Place of wild honey. When the hill was cleared of heavy bush in the early days of settlement, to provide a look-out above Brisbane, one tree was left standing, and for this reason the hill was known for many years as One Tree Hill.

Cope Cope V   Aboriginal. A. E. Martin states that the proper term was Gope Gope, that it had something to do with drainage, and that an Aboriginal phrased it: 'You take one big fellow bottle and two three little fellow bottle. You put water out of little fellows into big fellow bottle; then big fellow same as gope gope.'

Copperfield Q   Derived from the mineral development to which the growth of the town was due. The site was developed by the Peak Downs Copper Mining Company.

Cora Lynn Q   A corruption of the Gaelic word for Cauldron.

Coraki NSW   Aboriginal. A corruption of Gurrigai, Blowing up the mountain. Other renderings are: Plain turkey, or from Kurrachee, Mouth of river.

Corangamite, Lake V   Aboriginal. Bitter.

Cordeaux; Mount Cordeaux NSW   After William Cordeaux, an early resident and Land Commissioner. The Aboriginal name for the mountain was Niamboyoo.

Coreen NSW   Aboriginal. End of the hill.

Corio; Corio Bay V   Aboriginal. The meaning is obscure, but it may be noted that for a time the settlement of Geelong q.v. was also known as Coraiya, and that this evolved into Corio. One explanation of the word is Sandy.

71

Corner Country Q   See Channel Country.

Corner Inlet V   In 1798 George Bass wrote of Wilson Promontory (which he named Furneaux Land) that it was 'a corner-stone of this great island, New Holland'. Flinders followed up this imaginative concept later in the year by naming Corner Inlet.

Corny Point SA   'A remarkable point, which I named Corny Point,' wrote Flinders on 19 March 1802, as the *Investigator* lay at anchor under the shelter of the headland.

Coromby V   The Aboriginal name of a swamp in the vicinity.

Corowa NSW   Aboriginal. Corowa or Currawa is the Curra pine which yielded gum used by the Aborigines to fasten the heads of spears to the shafts. Another translation is Rocky River.

Corrimal NSW   The Aboriginal name of the adjacent hill was Kori-mul.

Corunna NSW   After Corunna in Spain, where the English army defeated the French on 16 January 1809, and Sir John Moore was killed.

Cosgrove V   The name of an early settler, P. Cosgrove.

Costerfield V   There were two miners, Coster and Field, whose names were incorporated to form Costerfield.

Cotton Vale Q   Named after a local orchardist.

Coulta SA   Aboriginal. From Koolto, the name of a nearby spring, meaning unknown.

Cowan, Lake WA   Discovered by the surveyor C. C. Hunt in 1864 and named after John Cowan, a member of the survey team.

Coward Springs SA   Discovered by P. E. Warburton in 1858 and named after Corporal Thomas Coward, a member of his party.

Cowcowing Lakes WA   Aboriginal. Discovered by Robert Austin, Assistant Surveyor of Western Australia, who used the name of a nearby spring known to the Aborigines as Cowcow.

Cowes V   Named after the well-known port on the Isle of Wight, the home of the Royal Yacht Squadron.

Cowpastures, The NSW   The district of which Camden is the centre gained the name of Cow Pasture Plains, subsequently shortened to The Cowpastures as early as 1796. Governor Phillip had brought several cattle from the Cape of Good Hope when the First Fleet arrived in 1788. The convicts who were given charge of them allowed most to escape. In June 1788 four cows, according to White, 'the only animals of the kind in the colony' and two bulls were missed. They were lost in the bush. In 1795 the Governor sent out a search party, for he had heard reports of the missing beasts from Aborigines. To his 'great surprise and satisfaction' the little herd had increased tenfold during the seven years by the time they were found beyond the Nepean River on 22 November. By 1806 it was estimated that there were 3,000 head of cattle in The Cowpastures. It is said that this was the reason for John Macarthur's choice of a land grant at Camden.

Cowper NSW   After a well-known family in NSW. The eldest son of the pioneer, William Cowper, colonial chaplain under Marsden, became Premier of NSW in 1857, and a younger son became Archdeacon and Dean of Sydney.

Cowra NSW   Aboriginal. Rocks. The first station there, owned by the Rev. Henry Fulton, made the meaning doubly clear, being named Cowra Rocks.

Cox's Pass; Cox's River NSW   After William Cox, who was appointed Superintendent of Works in 1814, and made history by constructing 160 km of road over the Blue Mountains in six months. Governor Macquarie, who traversed the road in April and May 1815, expressed his approval by naming the pass over Mount York and the river beyond the summit (where Divine Service was held) after the celebrated roadmaker.

Crab Island Q   When the *Duyfken* passed this tiny coastal island, the name Moent was recorded on the chart.

Cradle, Mount T   So named from a fancied resemblance to a miner's cradle.

Cranbourne Q   After Viscount Cranbourne, the son of Lord Salisbury.

Craven NSW   The name is believed to embody a play on words. The area was first known as Craven Flat, after a shepherd known as 'Old Craven Jack' because of his ceaseless 'cravin' for higher wages and a change of scene.

Creighton Creek V   Named after W. A. Creighton, a successful and well-known farmer.

Cremorne; Cremorne Point NSW   Formerly a picnic place, Cremorne took its name from Cremorne Gardens on the bank of the Thames, where nineteenth-century Londoners enjoyed themselves at fetes and entertainments on summer evenings. The point was first known as Careening Point, for obvious reasons, and then as Robertson's Point. The Aboriginal name was Wulworra-jeung.

Cressy V   A Frenchman named Duverney and his wife kept an inn here and a French name was therefore given by the settlers. The Aboriginal name was Bitup.

Creswick V   After John and Henry Creswick, two early settlers in the district. The township was first known as Creswick Creek. The Aboriginal name was Collum-been.

Crib Point V   So named because two of the first settlers built a crib or hut here.

Croajingalong V   Aboriginal. Go east. There is no actual place of this name; it is applied to the State of Victoria east of the Snowy River. Due to its lilting nature it became popular in bush ballads.

Cronulla NSW   Aboriginal. There are two current explanations: 1. A contraction of Kurranulla, Small pink shells. 2. Aboriginal pronunciation of Connell. John Connell was an early settler who received several land grants in the district. The original Aboriginal name for the place was Gunnamatta, Beach and sandhills.

Crookwell; Crookwell River NSW   When land was reserved here in the 1830s it was called Kiama or Kiamma, a common name meaning Good fishing ground. The town site was surveyed in 1860, and the name changed to that of the river, which had been known by this name for many years.

Crowlands V   After the old abbey town in Lincolnshire, meaning Bend in the river.

Crow's Nest NSW   Edward Wollstonecraft was granted 500 acres of land here. He built a cottage called Crow's Nest, and this is the origin of the name of the suburb.

Croydon NSW   After Croydon, Kent, the site of London's first civil airport. It was a very ancient English town with a proud history, appearing in the Doomsday Book as Croindene, but earlier still was Craydene, meaning chalk hill. The New South Wales Croydon, so named in 1878, was chosen because there was a racecourse at Homebush, and the English Croydon had a similar amenity close at hand.

Croydon V   Similar origin to Croydon in New South Wales.

Croydon Q   The Croydon goldfield was discovered by W. C. Brown, manager of the Croydon Downs station, from which the name is taken, in November 1885.

Crystal Brook SA   Discovered in 1840 by E. J. Eyre while on his third expedition and named because of the clarity of the water.

Cudal NSW   Aboriginal. Flat.

Cudgee V   Aboriginal. Kangaroo skin.

Cudgegong NSW   Aboriginal. Red hill, noted for the red clay used by the Aborigines in body decoration.

Cudgen NSW   Aboriginal. Red clay.

Cudgewa V   Aboriginal. Kangaroo skin.

Cue WA   After Thomas Cue, a local resident.

Culcairn NSW   The name was given by James Balfour, who was responsible for arranging for the town to be laid out. He named it after the property of the Balfour family in England.

Culgoa River V   Aboriginal. Leatherhead, or Friar-bird. The name of these honey-eaters comes from the absence of feathers on the head.

Cullen Bullen NSW   Aboriginal. Place where many waters meet, or Lyre bird. The name was taken from the property of Mrs Dalhunty.

Cumberland NSW   The name chosen for the county that embraced Sydney and its environs. The name was conferred by Governor Phillip in honour of Ernest Augustus, Duke of Cumberland, later King of Hanover, at a gathering to celebrate the birthday of his father, King George III, on 4 June 1788.

Cumberland Islands Q   Named by Cook on 4 June 1770 'in honour of His Royal Highness the Duke of Cumberland'. Henry Frederick, Duke of Cumberland, was a younger brother of George III.

Cummins SA   After W. P. Cummins, a Member of Parliament.

Cumnock NSW   After the old Scottish town in Ayrshire, the home of an early settler named Straborn.

Cundletown NSW   Mixed Aboriginal and English. Cundle is a native plant, the fruit of which resembles carrot.

Cunnamulla Q   Aboriginal. The Cunnamulla station was established on the east side of the Warrego River by Cobb & Co.

Cunningham Q   Named after Allan Cunningham, the well-known botanist and explorer.

Cunningham Islands NT   Named by Matthew Flinders in 1803 in honour of Captain Charles Cunningham of the Royal Navy.

Cunningham's Gap Q   The pass on the Great Dividing Range between Toowoomba and the New South Wales border is named after Allan Cunningham who crossed it on 25 August 1828. Cunningham had previously discovered the Darling Downs from the south. On this journey from Moreton Bay he approached them from the east. The Aboriginal name was Cappoong.

Curban NSW   Aboriginal. Large crack in the ground, or Stuck between two trees.

Curdimurka SA   Aboriginal. The name of a legendary snake that lurked in Lake Eyre. Its Aboriginal name was Kuddimuckra, from which Curdimurka is derived, and perpetuated in the railway station.

Curlewis NSW   The meaning of this name has not been discovered, but apparently it was suggested by W. C. Brown, MLA, in 1880.

Curlewis V   After a man who settled here in the 1830s.

Currabubula NSW   Aboriginal. Two forked trees, or Place where two ranges meet. The name was recorded by the explorer T. L. Mitchell as Carrabobila, which his men promptly dubbed 'Terrible Billy'.

Curramulka SA   Aboriginal. Currie: emu; Mulka: deep water. Emus reputedly came to drink at the water hole, and were killed there by the Aborigines.

Currency Creek SA Named after the *Currency,* the first boat to sail into it. The Aboriginal name was Bungung.

Currumbin Q Aboriginal. A species of pine tree.

Curtis Island Q Matthew Flinders discovered and named Port Curtis and Curtis Island in August 1802 and named them after Admiral Sir Roger Curtis who had been of assistance to him when he was at the Cape of Good Hope.

Custon SA After a son-in-law of Governor Jervois.

Cygnet T When d'Entrecasteaux discovered the port in 1793 he named it Port des Cygnes on account of the large number of swans in the water.

Cygnet Bay WA Named after the *Cygnet.* The crew mutinied, marooned the captain and later sighted the shore of New Holland on 4 January, 1688. On 5 January the vessel was anchored near King Sound and was careened and overhauled. William Dampier was among the mutineers but left the ship at Nicobar later in the voyage.

Daguilar Range Q Named after Sir George S. D'Aguilar, a British army officer. The name was probably conferred by T. L. Mitchell. The D'Aguilar Range in Tasmania is also doubtless named for him.

Daintree, Mount Q Named by William Hann who led the Northern Expedition Party of 1872, after Richard Daintree. Hann and his brother Frank H. were partners with Daintree at Maryvale Station on the Clarke River from 1864. Daintree worked as a geologist and petrologist in Victoria. In 1869 he was appointed Government Geologist for Northern Queensland, and then became Agent-General in London.

Daintree River Q Discovered by G. A. F. E. Dalrymple in 1873 and named after Richard Daintree.

Dalby Q Originally known as Myall Creek, the township was proclaimed on 13 March 1854 and named after Dalby on the Isle of Man.

Dalrymple; Dalrymple, Mount Q Named after George Augustus Frederick Elphinstone Dalrymple, explorer and pastoralist. Both the mountain west of Mackay and that in the Ravenswood district were named for him. Dalrymple was a member of Queensland's second Parliament, the Colonial Secretary for a short period, and police magistrate and Government Resident at Somerset. Dalrymple Heights and Dalrymple Creek were also named after him.

Daly River NT Named by B. T. Finniss in 1865 after the Governor of South Australia, Sir Dominick Daly.

Daly Waters NT   Discovered by J. McDouall Stuart in 1862 and named after Governor Daly.

Dampier Archipelago WA   Named by P. P. King after William Dampier who joined the buccaneer crew of the *Cygnet* in 1684. In January 1688 the north-west coast of New Holland was sighted in the vicinity of Buccaneer Islands, q.v., and the *Cygnet* was careened and overhauled. After further adventures Dampier returned to England. When *A New Voyage Round the World* was published in 1697, Dampier rose to fame. He was placed in command of the naval vessel *Roebuck* and sent to make further explorations around New Holland. The voyage began in January 1699. The west coast was sighted on 30 July. In August the *Roebuck* was anchored near the islands which P. P. King, who was there in 1821, named the Dampier Archipelago.

Dampier Bay WA   When Dampier anchored the *Roebuck* here and went ashore he found the land to be more fertile than he had anticipated, but no fresh water was available.

Dandarragan WA   Aboriginal. Good country.

Dandenong; Dandenong Ranges V   Aboriginal. A corruption of Tanjenong, Lofty.

Danger, Point NSW, V   Named by Captain Cook on 16 May 1770. As there were breakers on the shoals, he wrote in his Journal: 'The point of which these shoals lay I have named Point Danger.'

Danyo V   Aboriginal. Young mallee bush.

Dapto NSW   Aboriginal. Lame person.

Dargo V   Aboriginal. High hills.

Darke Peak SA   Named after John Charles Darke, an explorer who died here. Darke led an expedition north-west of Port Lincoln in 1844, and wrote in his report that 'no land existed beyond the Gawler Ranges available to the Port Lincoln settlers'. On 23 October, on his return journey he was wounded by the spears of hostile Aborigines, and died on the night of the 24th at the place now known as Darke Peak. An obelisk was erected over his grave by the South Australian Government in 1910. The Aboriginal name was Carrappee.

Darling Downs Q   Discovered by Allan Cunningham in 1827, on his second attempt. Leaving Liverpool Plains, he crossed the Namoi River, and then the Dumaresq. The land offered little promise, but Cunningham was undeterred and finally found rich fertile land which he named after the Governor of New South Wales, Sir Ralph Darling, who held office from 1825 to 1831.

Darling Range WA   First named General Darling's Range after the Governor of New South Wales, in 1827 by James Stirling. It was quickly shortened to Darling Range.

Darling River NSW   After Sir Ralph Darling. The river was discovered by Charles Sturt, who had set out to find what happened to the rivers that flowed westward. The Macquarie River was followed, and great excitement was engendered by the discovery of a larger stream — balanced by disappointment when it was found that its waters were salt. (The saltness was caused by the river flowing over beds of salt deposited by an ancient inland sea.) Sturt, who had received much encouragement from the Governor, conferred his name on the newly discovered river on 2 January 1829.

It should be noted that in its upper course it has several names — these usually being accepted in sequence as the Severn, Dumaresq, Macintyre, and Barwon. As the Darling it runs from its junction with the Culgoa to its meeting with the waters of the Murray.

Darnum V   Possibly the corruption of an Aboriginal word for Parrot. Another somewhat startling explanation is that it was an expression frequently used by the Premier of Victoria, Thomas Bent.

Dartmoor V   After Dartmoor in Devonshire, the site of the well-known prison. The Aboriginal name was Pokar, Big place.

Dartmouth Q   After Dartmouth in Devon.

Darwin NT   The harbour (Port Darwin) was discovered in 1839 by Captain J. C. Wickham of the *Beagle*, who named it after the famous naturalist who had been on the *Beagle* in an earlier voyage. In 1864 it was thought by some of the officials of the Escape Cliffs settlement, q.v., about 58 km distant, that the site of Darwin might be more suitable, but this was not followed up. Further consideration was given to the proposal in 1866, but it was not until 1869 that G. W. Goyder, Surveyor-General for South Australia, arrived on the coast and surveyed the site, and the name Palmerston was transferred from Escape Cliffs, the settlement there having been withdrawn. By September 1869 Goyder had completed the survey, thereby earning the nickname 'Little Energy'. The name Palmerston had been given in honour of Viscount Palmerston, and remained as the official designation until 1911, when control of the Northern Territory was transferred from South Australia to Commonwealth administration, and it reverted to the original name Darwin. See also Port Darwin.

Darwin, Mount T   Named in 1862 by Charles Gould, who was the Government Geologist at the time, in honour of Charles Darwin.

Dawson Range; Dawson River Q   Discovered by Ludwig Leichhardt on 5 November 1844 and named after Robert Barrington Dawson, who had given considerable assistance to Leichhardt's expedition.

Daylesford V   When a town was surveyed and gazetted on the Jim Crow gold fields (so named from a popular song) it received the name of Daylesford in Worcester, the home of Warren Hastings.

Daymar Q   Aboriginal. Red ridge.

De Grey River WA   Discovered in 1861 by F. T. Gregory and named in honour of the President of the Royal Geographical Society, the third Earl de Grey, Earl (and later Marquis) of Ripon.

De Witt Island T   It was sighted by Tasman in 1642 and named after a member of the Dutch Council of India.

De Witt's Land WA   The name was given to an area of land (not strictly defined) which appeared on early Dutch maps as De Witt's Landt after Gerrit Frederickszoon de Witt, in command of the *Vyanen*. was driven south from Java and came unexpectedly in sight of land. The ship ran aground but was refloated and skirted the coast in the vicinity of Roebourne for about 300 km.

Dead Heart of Australia   The arid area in the vicinity of Lake Curdamurka and the Simpson Desert was so designated by the geologist John Simpson in 1901, and has attained some popularity.

Dead Man Crossing Q   This dangerous ford near Windorah has been the site of five drownings. The first was that of a young man who was swept off his feet and drowned while his mother looked on helplessly. He was buried on an adjacent sandhill. The grave is sometimes covered with flood water or sand storms, but legend says it always reappears and that a light has been seen to flicker over it at night. The legend is recorded in Bill Beatty's *A Treasury of Australian Folk Tales and Traditions**.

Dead Secret, The NSW   One of the romantic stories of the gold days. The legend is that there came to Dubbo a prospector who had dug up some nuggets of exceptional size. He refused to reveal the location of his find, but local curiosity. and cupidity were roused, and shortly after he left he was followed. His dead body was found, but no sign of the gold, the whereabouts of which thereafter remained a 'dead secret'.

Deakin WA   Named after Alfred Deakin, the second Premier of Australia, and the outstanding political leader of the first years of Federation.

Deception, Mount SA   Named by E. J. Eyre in 1840 on his third expedition to express his frustration at being unable to find promising land beyond Lake Torrens. He had ascended the mountain in the hope that from this vantage point he would be able to see fertile plains. The view proved extensive, but disappointing, and so the name was conferred on the hill.

Dederang V   Aboriginal. Hail.

Dee River T   Named by Lieut-Governor Sorell after the Scottish river.

Dee Why NSW   There are three popular explanations of the origin of the name, the first of which scarcely stands up to investigation, the second seeming to provide a reasonable explanation, and the romantic third which was favoured by Bill Beatty, who makes this interesting suggestion in *A Treasury of Australian Folk Tales and Traditions*.

* Ure Smith, 1960.

1. That the lagoon bears a resemblance to the shape of the letters D and Y. 2. From the Aboriginal word Diwai, the name of a bird that frequented the lagoon. 3. That the Spanish galleon *Dona Ysabel* was wrecked here, and that a survivor carved its initial letters on a rock. The name was first used by James Meehan, the surveyor, on 27 September 1818, who recorded 'Dy Beach — marked a honeysuckle near beach'. Meehan had difficulty in getting through swamps and brush in the locality. It has been further suggested that he wrote 'Dy' as an abbreviation of the Greek word *dyspropositos* — 'difficult to reach'.

Deepwater NSW   Aboriginal name was Dulgambone, Hard, dry earth.

Deer Park V   Deer were kept here by the Melbourne Hunt Club.

Degilbo Q   Aboriginal. In the Wakka language the word means standing stone, derived from Dugie: Stone; Bu, an abbreviation of bubai: standing, and was applied to a rock wall in the creek. At various times the theory has been pointed out that the name is 'obliged' spelt backwards, but the Place Names Committee of the University of Queensland concluded that this was purely a coincidence.

Delegate NSW   Apparently a corruption of an Aboriginal word the meaning of which has not been discovered. On an early plan it appeared as Dilligat, and a local station was named Deligat.

Deloraine T   The site was surveyed in 1831, while the area was leased to the Van Diemen's Land Company, by Thomas Scott, who was related to Sir Walter Scott. He named it after Deloraine in the latter's *Lay of the Last Minstrel*. The Scottish Deloraine is in Selkirkshire.

Delungra NSW   Aboriginal. A water weed.

Denial Bay SA   In January 1802 Matthew Flinders referred to Point Peter and Denial Bay and named them 'as well in allusion to St Peter as to the deceptive hope we had found of penetrating by it (the inlet) some distance into the interior country'. The place has been described as a graveyard of hopes to explorers by sea, whose expectations of finding a waterway into the interior met with disappointment. The Aboriginal name was Nadia.

Deniliquin NSW   Aboriginal. Wrestling ground; or, in the form Denilicoon or Denilakoon, the name of a local Aboriginal who achieved fame for his wrestling exploits. In 1843 Benjamin Boyd acquired land here, to which he gave this name. Previously it had been known as The Sandhills.

Denison V   After Sir William Denison, Governor of Tasmania from 1847 to 1855, and of New South Wales from 1855 to 1861.

Denmark WA   Named after the river, which was discovered in December 1929 by Surgeon T. B. Wilson, who perpetuated the name of a naval colleague, Surgeon Denmark.

Dennington V   After Dennington in Suffolk, the birthplace of Sir Charles Hotham.

D'Entrecasteaux Channel T   The channel was discovered by Lieut de Cretin and Lieut de Saint-Aigan of the *Recherche* and *Esperance* on 1 and 18 May 1872. They named it after Admiral d'Entrecasteaux. Prior to this the channel was thought to be a bay, but the Admiral's systematic survey revealed that Furneaux's Adventure Bay, q.v., was in fact part of an island separated from the mainland, and d'Entrecasteaux was able to sail through it at the conclusion of his survey.

Rear-Admiral Joseph Antoine de Bruni d'Entrecasteaux's hydrographical engineer was C. F. Beautemps-Beaupre, the father of French hydrography. He was the first hydrographical engineer on the *Recherche,* his charts being published as an *Atlas du Voyage de Bruny-Dentrecasteaux* in 1807.

D'Entrecasteaux Point WA   The point was sighted by and named after Admiral d'Entrecasteaux on 6 December 1792 during the French expedition sent in search of La Perouse. The discovery of the point was celebrated with such enthusiasm that the smith on board the *Recherche,* Jean-Marie Marbadour, was seized with an apoplectic fit the following day and died.

D'Entrecasteaux Reef SA   It was here that the Admiral was forced to leave the coast and head for Van Diemen's Land, as he had not been able to replenish food and water for the ship's company as he sailed along the coast of the Great Australian Bight.

Derby V   After the English Derby, which means Village of wild beasts.

Derby WA   The site was surveyed in 1883 and named after Lord Derby who was Secretary of State for the Colonies in 1882.

Derriwong NSW   Aboriginal. Place of magpies.

Derwent River T   In 1793 Captain John Hayes, in command of the *Duke of Clarence* and the *Duchess,* left Calcutta on a trading voyage to New Guinea. He was forced as far south as New Holland by strong gales and eventually reached Van Diemen's Land. On 25 April the ships attempted to anchor in Adventure Bay. Failing in this attempt they penetrated D'Entrecasteaux Channel, recently discovered during the French Admiral's survey, and anchored in North-west Bay.

Hayes was unaware of the French discoveries in this area or, for that matter, of Bligh's visit in the *Providence* and *Assistant* a little over a year earlier, and set out to make a careful survey. The ships' boats recorded many points of interest, to which Hayes appended names of many of the officials of the East India Company. Several weeks were spent in this way. Meanwhile the ships were moved into the northern river, which d'Entrecasteaux had already named Riviere du Nord, and further explorations were made for several kms from the mouth.

Owing to the earlier nomenclature of d'Entrecasteaux and other explorers, few of Hayes's names were retained, but the Derwent survived on account of the thorough exploration of the upper reaches made by Hayes – the first penetration, in fact, of the interior of the island. Hayes, who later in life was knighted, called it Derwent or Derwentwater after the English river of that name. The Aboriginal name was Teemtoomelemenennye.

Desire, Mount SA Named by Samuel Parry in 1859, who told the Surveyor-General that it was symbolic of his desire to return home after more than a year of continuous survey work in the north. The place was earlier named Crown Hill by Sinnett.

Destruction, Mount WA Named by Ernest Giles in 1873 because it was here that his horses and all his hopes for success in his expedition were destroyed. In an attempt to find a practical route to the west, he left his companions and went on alone, establishing a camp called Fort McKellar. Then he pushed on westward; but the ranges seen in the distance sank into insignificance. There was nothing but sandhills. He turned to the north-west where he could see a mountain in the distance, but when he reached it he found nothing but barren slopes with no trace of water.

He was forced to return. On that terrible 140 km journey across waterless desert, desperately trying to get back to camp before it was too late, he pushed his horses to the limit, several of them dying on the way.

'I called this vial mountain which had caused this disaster Mount Destruction,' he wrote, 'for a visit to it had destroyed my horses and my hope.'

Tietkins, one of his party, also recorded the event: 'At dawn next day, three horses lay dead. We collected the rest with all speed and started for the water. It was a day that threatened to destroy every living thing. Four horses dropped before we reached our destination. When we arrived at Fort McKellar, we drank as only thirsty horses and men will drink. We hurried back with kegs of water to try to save the poor beasts that had dropped. We were only 2 hours but they were all dead. That terrible journey cost us 8 of our best horses and was a very near thing for ourselves.'

Devil's Marbles NT So named on account of the granite boulders, varying in size from 20 cm to 6 m in diameter, found about 100 km south of Tennant Creek.

Devonport T After one of the chief naval and military stations in England, at the head of Plymouth Sound.

Diamantina River Q, SA While in search of the Burke and Wills Expedition in 1862 John McKinlay located a river on 8 April, which he called the Mueller in honour of Ferdinand Von Mueller. The stream was rediscovered in 1866 by William Landsborough, who renamed it the Diamantina after Diamantina Roma Bowen, the wife of Sir George Ferguson Bowen, the first Governor of Queensland. The Aboriginal name of the lower Diamantina was Tooma-thoo-gamie.

Diamond Creek V So named because it was thought that diamonds were found here, but they proved to be zircons.

Diggers' Rest V Named after the huts built for diggers in gold mining days.

Diggora V A corruption of Diggory's hut.

Dilkoon NSW Aboriginal. Running water.

Dimboola V   A mis-spelling of the Cingalese word 'dimula', meaning Land of figs. The name was given by J. G. Wilmot who had been a Government surveyor in India.

Dingee V   Aboriginal. Star.

Dingo Mountain Q   Aboriginal, but not necessarily named by Aborigines, Wild dog.

Dinosaur Point SA   Fossilised footsteps of a dinosaur have been found at the foot of the cliffs. Dr E. H. Colbert of the American Museum of Natural History has stated that they were made by a carnivorous type of dinosaur, about 8 m long and 2 m tall. Dr Colbert and Duncan Merrilees decided it was a theropod dinosaur and intended to name it as a new species and a new genus. A full description of the footsteps is contained in *Nature Walkabout* by Vincent Serventy*.

Dipwood, Mount T   When Henry Hellyer journeyed south-east from Circular Head, he came upon swampy land which he named Dipwood Marsh, and from this the mountain probably received its name.

Direction Hill Q   A survey party in 1843 had difficulty in making observations owing to interference from the Aborigines. Dr Jukes diverted their attention by dancing, and while they were watching, the observations were completed. It was from this incident that the hill received its name.

Dirk Hartog Island WA   The west coast of New Holland was first discovered and landed on by Dirck Hartog, skipper of the *Eendracht*. He set up a metal plate recording his visit on the northernmost point of the island (see Cape Inscription) on 25 October 1616.

Dirrung NSW   Aboriginal. Red.

Disappointment, Lake WA   F. H. Hann gave the name in 1897 to recall his disappointment at finding no water there. L. A. Wells and his men had crossed the southern end of the dry, salt lake in August 1896 without naming it.

Disappointment, Mount NSW   Named by Hume and Hovell, who had hoped to see the ocean when they ascended the Plenty Range in 1824.

Discovery Bay V, SA   Although the bay was sighted in December 1800 by Lieut James Grant in the *Lady Nelson*, and charted by Nicolas Baudin in April 1802, it was not named until 1836, when T. L. Mitchell sailed down the lower reaches of the Glenelg River. On 20 August 1836 he found that the river 'terminated in a shallow basin . . . choked up with the sands of the beach . . . so our hopes of finding a port at the mouth of this fine river were at an end.'

Docker V   After the Rev Joseph Docker who left New South Wales and established the Boutherambo run.

* Reed, 1967.

Doctor's Creek Q   This stream in the Goombunge district was named after a horse. It had been purchased from a horse doctor and was called Doctor. The animal became stuck in the mud and died. The creek, then unnamed, was subsequently referred to as the creek where Doctor died, and was eventually recognised officially as Doctor's Creek.

Donald V   When the shire, from which the town is named, was proclaimed in 1864, it commemorated an early pioneer, W. Donald.

Doncaster V   After Doncaster in England, where the St Leger is held, and so named by John Robert, racing fan.

Donington SA   Named by Matthew Flinders on 25 February 1802 after his birthplace, where there is now a tablet to his memory in the parish church. The name means Dwellers on a hill.

Donna Buang, Mount V   It is generally believed that this is the Aboriginal name of the mountain. It has also been suggested that it may be a corruption of Toole-le-wong, Place of the mist. This was the name they applied to the range in the same locality, and is now given to a mountain a few km south-west of Donna Buang.

Donnybrook V, WA   A number of Irishmen, led by George Nash and James Bessonet settled in Western Australia for a short time in 1842, and named their settlement on the Preston River after Donnybrook in Ireland. The Victorian Donnybrook doubtless has the same origin.

Doo Town T   Pamela Davis, in *People*, 22 February 1967, wrote that the town was founded about 1937 by the tradespeople of Hobart. Each of them named his house Doo — Doo Us, Doo I, Doo Me, followed by Av Ta Doo, Thistle Doo, Doo Nix, Digeridoo, How Doo U Doo, Doo Us 2, etc. A sign was erected: 'Welcome Doo Town Doo Drive Slowly.'

Dooen V   Aboriginal. Perimeter of a circle.

Dookie V   Named by J. G. Wilmot, from the Indian word Dooky, meaning Lament, because the woman he met while on a survey was lamenting the loss of part of her property.

Dorrigo NSW   Aboriginal. Stringy-bark. A contraction of the word Dondorrigo.

Double Bay NSW   So named because it contains two beaches separated by a headland.

Dowling Ville SA   Named by G. P. D. and J. T. Whitaker after the maiden name of their mother.

Dr George Mount NSW   After Dr George Imlay. After leaving his home at Bega, q.v., at the end of 1846, he disappeared and his body was not found by his brother until 30 December. He had shot himself on the hill-top now known as Dr George Mountain.

Drayton Q   So named from the large number of drays there, or so it is said. An earlier name was The Springs.

Drik Drik V   Aboriginal. Limestone.

Dripstone NSW   On a hilltop there is or was a stone over which water trickled and dripped to the ground. In an early period the district was known as The Springs, because there were so many of them.

Dromana V   After a town in Ireland.

Dromedary, Cape; Mount NSW   On 21 April 1770 Captain Cook wrote in his Journal: 'At 6, we were abreast of a pretty high Mountain laying near the Shore, which, on account of its figure, I named Mount Dromedary . . . . The shore under the foot of the Mountain forms a point, which I have named Cape Dromedary, over which is a peaked hillock.'

Drouin V   Both alluvial and quartz mining were carried out here, and the name was given in honour of the Frenchman who invented the chlorination process for the extraction of metals from ore. At one time it was called Whisky Creek, because bullock drivers had camped there and broached a cask of whisky.

Drummond V   After James Drummond, the naturalist.

Dryander, Mount Q   Discovered on 24 July 1820 by P. P. King and named by him after Jonas Dryander, the Swedish botanist. He was Sir Joseph Banks's librarian, and later librarian of the Royal Society.

Drysdale V   After Miss Drysdale who established a station here with a woman friend.

Drysdale River WA   Named by the surveyor and explorer C. A. Burrowes in 1886, probably after a local settler.

Dubbo NSW   Aboriginal. Head covering, or skull-cap. Probably from Tubbo. Headgear of this kind was made of several kinds of material such as netted headbands or possum fur. There is reason to believe that the particular kind referred to in this name was made from the skin of an eagle with the down adhering to it. The name was given to the stock station owned by R. V. Dulhunty in the early 1830s.

Dugandan Q   Aboriginal. Reeds suitable for making dilly bags.

Dulhunty; Dulhunty Plains; Dulhunty River Q   After the Dulhunty family, founded in Australia by John Dulhunty, a surgeon who was appointed Superintendent of Police in 1827. Two of the sons, John and Robert, were well-known pastoralists.

Dumaresq River NSW, Q   The river was discovered by Allan Cunningham in 1827, who named it 'in honour of the family with which His Excellency, the Governor, is so intimately connected'. Henry Dumaresq was Governor Darling's brother-in-law. The river, and subsequently the township, were probably named after Lady Darling.

Dumbalk V   Aboriginal. Cold.

Dumosa V   The botanical name of the mallee, *Eucalyptus dumosa.*

Dunbible NSW   Aboriginal. Probably from Tunbible, meaning either a Tree, or a Creek at the foot of a high mountain. A local version, too good to be true but quite irresistible, is that on one occasion the creek was crossed by an itinerant preacher, accompanied by an Aboriginal convert. The preacher having accidentally dropped his Bible into the flooded stream, his companion cried out, 'Mister! Done Bible!'

Dundas Strait NT   After Henry Dundas, Viscount Melville.

Dundee NSW   After Dundee on the shore of the Firth of Tay, Scotland.

Dunedoo NSW   Aboriginal. Swan.

Dungog NSW   Aboriginal. Clear or bare hill. Also the name of a local tribe.

Dunk Island Q   Cook recorded in his Journal on 8 June 1770: '. . . a Tolerable high Island, known in the Chart by the Name of Dunk Isle'. Halifax Bay, Dunk Island, Mount Hinchinbrook, and Sandwich Bay in this vicinity were all named in honour of George Montagu Dunk, First Lord of the Admiralty, who was Cook's patron. Dunk was both Earl of Halifax and Earl of Sandwich. His estate was named Hinchinbrook. The Aboriginal name is Coonanglebah.

Dunkeld V   After the town in Perthshire, Scotland, which derived its name from a Culdee Church founded in 815 by Constantin, King of the Picts.

Dunolly V   Named by Archibald C. McDougall in 1845 after Dunolly Castle in Scotland.

Dunoon NSW   Either Aboriginal, meaning Ridge; or from Dunoon, a seaside resort in Argyllshire.

Duntroon ACT   The military college takes its name from the property (or the house) owned by Robert Campbell, who received a grant of 5,000 acres in 1834. One account says that he was related to the Campbells of Duntroon Castle, Argyllshire; another that it probably originated with the sailing vessel *Duntroon,* a picture of which is to be seen in the Commandant's room at Duntroon House.

Durack River WA   Named after the Durack family who pioneered the cattle country of western Queensland, and later opened up grazing land in the Kimberley district.

Duri NSW   Aboriginal. Hollow from which issues a cloud of smoke.

Dutton, Lake SA   The lake was first named after S. T. Gill, by John A. Horrocks in 1846. Gill was the artist in his party. Twelve years later B. H. Babbage rediscovered the lake but did not realise that it was Horrocks's Lake Gill, and renamed it in honour of Charles Christian

Dutton, the unfortunate pastoralist who was forced to abandon the Pillaworta station in 1842 on account of attacks by the Aborigines. He was lost and never found again while on his way to the head of Spencer Gulf. This is one of the infrequent cases where a name has been retained in spite of an earlier discovery and naming.

Duyfken Point Q   On 8 November 1802 Matthew Flinders named the point in commemoration of the Dutch vessel *Duyfken* or *Duyfhen*. While Torres was threading the strait between Australia and New Guinea in 1606, Willem Jansz sailed into the Gulf of Carpentaria and down the west coast of Cape York Peninsula. The *Duyfken* (Little Dove) anchored in what afterwards was called Albatross Bay, not far from the point named by Flinders. Jansz's crew went ashore, and were the first Europeans, so far as we are aware, ever to set foot in Australia. They were attacked by Aborigines, but the sailors killed several of them and drove the others away. The landing site was named Cabo Keer-weer or Turn Again. The Dutchmen gave an unfavourable report of the inhospitable country they had visited.

Eacham, Lake Q   Aboriginal. A corruption of Yeetcham.

Ebor NSW   After Eboracum, a Roman town in England which eventually became the city of York.

Echo Lake T   A descriptive name which was applied when the echo was first heard. At one time known as Jones Lake.

Echuca V   Aboriginal. Meeting of the waters — an appropriate name, for it is located at the junction of the Murray, Campaspe, and Goulburn rivers. It was originally known as Hopwood's Ferry after Henry Hopwood, the successor to Isaac White's punt service established in 1847. In the 1850s Echuca was the busiest inland port in Australia and was sometimes known as New Chicago.

Echunga SA   Aboriginal. Close.

Eclipse Island Q   On 12 December 1871 a party of scientists endeavoured to observe an eclipse of the sun on this island in the Claremont Group, but failed owing to bad weather.

Eclipse Islands WA   George Vancouver observed an eclipse of the sun on 25 September 1791, when he sighted the islands from HMS *Discovery*.

Eddington V   After Captain John Eddington. The Aboriginal name was Nyarritch.

Edel Land WA   An old name that appeared on early Dutch charts. When the *Dordrecht* and *Amsterdam* sighted the coast in 1619, the name of the supercargo was given to the coast.

87

Eddystone T   There are two rocks of this name in Tasmania. One was sighted by Furneaux in command of the *Adventure*, in 1773, and appears on his chart.

The other was seen by Cook on 24 January 1777. He wrote: 'About a league to the eastward of Swilly is another elevated rock, that is not taken notice of by Captain Furneaux. I called it the Eddystone, from its very resemblance to that lighthouse. Nature seems to have left these two rocks here for the same purpose that the Eddystone lighthouse was built by man, viz., to give navigators notice of the dangers around them: for they are the conspicuous summits of a ledge of rocks under water, on which the sea in many places breaks very high. Their surface is white with the dung of sea-fowls, so that they may be seen at some distance, even in the night.'

Eden NSW   After the family name of Baron Auckland, Secretary for the Colonies at the time the town was planned in 1842.

Eden Valley SA   It is said that the early surveyors found the word Eden carved in the bark of a tree, and adopted it for the future township.

Edeowie SA   Aboriginal. Ethie or Ithie is the name of the chestnut-eared finch; Owie is Water.

Edgcumbe Bay Q   Named by Captain Cook on 4 June 1770 almost certainly after Lord Edgcumbe, who became the Earl of Mount Edgcumbe. When Cook was serving in the Fleet in North America in 1758 Captain G. Edgcumbe, as he then was, commanded the *Lancaster*. It is possible that the bay was named after John Edgecumbe, sergeant of marines on the *Endeavour*, but unlikely, for during June of 1770 Cook was perpetuating the names of the English aristocracy.

Edgeroi NSW   Aboriginal. Creek. It was the name of a local sheep station.

Edi V   Aboriginal. Cold wind.

Edillilie SA   Aboriginal. Two adjacent springs.

Edithburg SA   Named after the wife of Governor Fergusson.

Edkins Range WA   Discovered and named by Frank H. Hann, probably after R. E. Edkins with whom Hann was in partnership at the Lawn Hill Station in the Gulf of Carpentaria in 1875.

Eendracht Land WA   When the *Eendracht* under the command of Dirck Hartog arrived on the coast of Western Australia in 1616, on its way to Batavia, the name of the ship was given to this part of the coast.

Ehrenberg Range NT   Discovered and named by Ernest Giles in his 1872 expedition westward from the Overland Telegraph line.

Eidsvold Q   After a village in Norway. It was earlier known as Rose, or Mount Rose Township.

Eighty Mile Beach WA   Long known as Ninety Mile Beach, the name was changed in 1946 because of the confusion with the Ninety Mile Beach in Gippsland.

El Arish Q   After El Arish in Egypt, the scene of an engagement in which Australian soldiers were involved during World War I.

Eildon Weir V   So named after Eildon Hills in Scotland.

Elaine V   After Elaine the fair, of Tennyson's poem.

Elbow Hill SA   Discovered on 8 March 1802 by Matthew Flinders who wrote: '...the ridge of hills turns suddenly from the shore, and sweeps round at the back of the lagoon, into which the waters running off the ridge appeared to be received. The corner hill, where the direction of the hill is changed, was called Elbow Hill.'

Elder Range SA   After Alexander Lang Elder, a successful pastoralist who was also associated with the establishment of Port Augusta. The Aboriginal name was Woodnawolpena, Great mountain.

Eliza, Lake SA   Discovered by the Governor, George Grey, who named it after his wife.

Elizabeth SA   Named in honour of Queen Elizabeth II. It was planned as a satellite town four miles from Salisbury in the 1950s. By the 1960s it had outgrown Salisbury.

Elizabeth Town T   Named after Elizabeth Macquarie, Lachlan Macquarie's second wife.

Ellam V   Possibly Mallee spelt backwards and abbreviated.

Ellendale T   After Ellen Brown, the wife of Nicholas Brown, Speaker of the House of Assembly. Formerly Monto's Marsh.

Ellery, Mount V   The mountain was named about 1869 after R. L. J. Ellery, a Victorian astronomer and one of the founders of the Royal Society of Victoria. The mountain is topped by a monolith 25 m in height, which had the Aboriginal name Goon-gerah, Egg rock.

Ellinbank V   A settler, John Hardie, named his property after his wife.

Elphinstone V   After Montstuart Elphinstone, a British administrator in India. The locality was first known as Sawpit Gully.

Elphinstone Creek Q   Named after G. A. F. E. Dalrymple.

Elsey Creek NT   Discovered and named by A. C. Gregory after Joseph Ravenscroft Elsey who was the surgeon and naturalist on the expedition that Gregory led in search of Ludwig Leichhardt in 1856.

Eltham NSW V   After a town in Kent, meaning Elta's village.

Embley Range; Embley River Q   After J. T. Embley, a surveyor who was at work in the 1880s.

Emerald Q   After the old Emerald Downs station.

Emerald Hill NSW   A stockman is said to have made a find of emeralds here.

Emu Park Q   The Aboriginal name was Woolpal.

Emu Plains NSW   So named, as early as 1808, because there were so many emus there. The name originated with Captain Tench, but in the form Emu Island. In 1814 Governor Macquarie referred to 'Emu Plains (hitherto erroneously called Emu Island)'.

Encounter Bay SA   A name that celebrates the encounter between Flinders and Baudin. Flinders sailed from England in the *Investigator*. After leaving Kangaroo Island, he sailed through Backstairs Passage and, on 8 April 1802, was astounded to sight another vessel. The French ensign was hoisted to the masthead. England was at war with France, and though the French commander might well respect Flinders's ship, Flinders took every precaution and prepared for a fight. The tension eased suddenly, when it was seen that Nicolas Baudin was prepared to meet Flinders peacefully. *Le Geographe* had left France nine months earlier, equipped for scientific and exploratory work, and with the French Government's orders to investigate the possibility of French claims to part of New Holland. The two captains met amicably, the memory of their encounter being preserved in the name of the bay.

Endeavour Reef Q   It was on 11 June 1770 that the *Endeavour* struck a coral reef, a little north of Weary Bay, that is known as Endeavour Reef. The name is of some importance in Australian history, for shipwreck might well have delayed the discovery of the fertile east coast of New Holland for many years, and even prevented British possession. It seems appropriate, therefore, to allow Captain Cook to tell the dramatic story, from 10.00 p.m. on 11 June 1770 to the afternoon of 13 June.

'Before 10 o'Clock we had 20 and 21 fathoms, and Continued in that depth until a few minutes before 11, when we had 17, and before the Man at the Lead could have another cast, the Ship Struck and stuck fast. Immediately upon this we took in all our Sails, hoisted out the Boats and Sounded round the Ship, and found that we had got upon the S.E. Edge of Coral Rocks, having in some places round the Ship 3 and 4 fathoms Water, and in other places not quite as many feet, and about a Ship's length from us on the starboard side (the Ship laying with her Head to the N. E.) were 8, 10, and 12 fathoms. As soon as the Long boat was out we struck Yards and Topmast, and carried out the Stream Anchor on our Starboard bow, got the coasting Anchor and Cable into the Boat, and were going to carry it out in the same way; but upon my sounding the 2nd time round the Ship I found the most water a Stern, and therefore had this Anchor carried out upon the Starboard Quarter, and hove upon it a very great Strain; which was to no purpose, the Ship being quite fast, upon which we went to work to lighten her as fast as possible, which seem'd to be the only means we had left to get her off. As we went ashore about the Top of High Water we not only started water, but threw overboard our Guns, Iron and Stone Ballast, Casks, Hoop Staves, Oil Jarrs, decay'd Stores, etc.; many of these last Articles lay in the way at coming at Heavier. All this time the Ship made little or no Water. At 11 a.m., being high Water as we thought, we try'd to heave her off without Success, she not being afloat by a foot or more, notwithstanding by this time we had thrown overboard 40 or 50 Tuns weight. As this was not found sufficient we continued to Lighten her by every method we could think off; as the Tide fell the ship began to make Water as much as two pumps could free; at Noon she lay with 3 or 4 Streakes heel to Starboard; Lat. observed 15° 45′ S.

'*Tuesday, 12th.* – Fortunately we had little wind, fine weather, and a smooth Sea, all this 24 Hours, which in the P.M. gave us an opportunity to carry out the 2 Bower Anchors, one on the Starboard Quarter, and the other right a Stern, got Blocks and Tackles upon the Cables, brought the falls in abaft and hove taught. By this time it was 5 o'Clock in the p.m.; the tide we observed now begun to rise, and the leak increased upon us, which obliged us to set the 3rd Pump to work, as we should have done the 4th also, but could not make it work. At 9 the Ship righted, and the Leak gain'd upon the Pumps considerably. This was an alarming and, I may say, terrible circumstances, and threatened immediate destruction to us. However, I resolv'd to risque all, and heave her off in case it was practical, and accordingly turn'd as many hands to the Capstan and Windlass as could be spared from the Pumps; and about 20 Minutes past 10 o'Clock the Ship floated, and we hove her into Deep Water, having at this time 3 feet 9 Inches Water in the hold. This done I sent the Long boat to take up the Stream Anchor, got the Anchor, but lost the Cable among the Rocks; after this turn'd all hands to the Pumps, the Leak increasing upon us.

'A mistake soon after hapned, which for the first time caused fear to approach upon every man in the Ship. The man that attended the well took the Depth of water above the Ceiling; he, being relieved by another who did not know in what manner the former had sounded, took the Depth of water from the outside plank, the difference being 16 or 18 inches, and made it appear that the leak had gained this upon the pumps in a short time. This mistake was no sooner cleared up than it acted upon every man like a Charm; they redoubled their vigour, insomuch that before 8 o'clock in the morning they gained considerably upon the leak. We now hove up the Best Bower, but found it impossible to save the small Bower, so cut it away at a whole Cable; got up the Fore topmast and Foreyard, warped the Ship to the S.E., and at 11 got under sail, and stood in for the land, with a light breeze at E.S.E. Some hands employ'd sewing Oakham, Wool, etc., into a Lower Steering sail to fother the Ship; others employ'd at the Pumps, which still gain'd upon the Leak.

'*Wednesday, 13th.* – In the P.M. had light Airs at E.S.E., with which we kept edging in for the Land. Got up the Maintopmast and Mainyard, and having got the Sail ready for fothering of the Ship, we put it over under the Starboard Fore Chains, where we suspected the Ship had suffer'd most, and soon after the Leak decreased, so as to be keept clear with one Pump with ease; this fortunate circumstance gave new life to every one board.

'It is much easier to conceive than to discribe the satisfaction felt by everybody on this occasion. But a few minutes before our utmost Wishes were to get hold of some place upon the Main, or an island, to run the Ship ashore, where out of her Materials we might build a Vessel to carry us to the East Indies; no sooner were we made sencible that the outward application to the Ship's bottom had taken effect, than the field of every Man's hopes inlarged so that we thought of nothing but ranging along Shore in search of a Harbour, when we could repair the Damages we had sustained. In justice to the Ship's Company, I must say that no men ever behaved better than they have done on this occasion; animated by the behaviour of every Gentleman on board, every man seem'd to have a just sence of the Danger we were in, and exerted himself to the very utmost.'

Endeavour River Q   On 18 June 1770 the *Endeavour,* having been successful warped off the reef (see above), reached a river at the present sight of Cooktown. It was lightened by removing everything possible and hauled ashore. Work on the vessel continued until 20 July. On account of unfavourable weather, Cook was unable to leave the shelter of the river until 4 August, on which day he wrote an interesting description of the natural life of the region. 'I shall now give a Short description of the Harbour, or River, we have been in, which I have named after the Ship, Endeavour River.' It was the only river in Australia named by Cook.

Endeavour Strait Q   It was with much difficulty that the *Endeavour* threaded its way between islands and reefs at the tip of the Cape York Peninsula, but at last a clear passage was found, and on 23 August 1770, Cook wrote: 'This passage, which I have named Endeavour Straits, after the Name of the Ship . . .'

English Company's Islands NT   Matthew Flinders named the islands in February 1803 in acknowledgement of the support given to his expedition by the East India Company. They had first been sighted from the *Arnhem* in 1623. Flinders saw a number of Malay proas there and named one of the islands after Pobasso, the captain of a Malay vessel. The remainder of the islands were named 'mostly after gentlemen in the East India directory; and in compliment to that respectable body of men, whose liberal attention to this voyage was useful to us and honourable to them, the whole concern is named the English Company's Islands'.

In a letter to Sir Joseph Banks he also remarked: 'I should be inclined to think that if the East India Company have had any intention of making a settlement on New Holland, the good harbours in Cape Arnhem, the wild nutmegs, and perhaps the trepang which seem to bring the Malays a good many thousand dollars annually from the Chinese, might be additional inducements.'

Enmore NSW   The name was taken from Captain Sylvester Browne's residence at Newtown.

Epping V   After the town of Epping or the famous nearby Epping Forest in Essex. Epping means People on the upland.

Epsom V   After Epsom in England, meaning Ebbe's village.

Ernabella SA   Aboriginal. Creek with water holes. The Ernabella Creek and Gorge were discovered by Ernest Giles in 1873. The creek he named

Ferdinand, after his patron, Ferdinand von Mueller, but during the anti-German hysteria of the first World War, the Aboriginal name was reinstated. The Ernabella mission was established near the creek in 1937.

Escape Cliffs NT   So named because of the narrow escape of two officers of the *Beagle* in 1829 when they were pursued by Aborigines. When South Australia annexed Northern Territory in 1863, preparations were made to establish a settlement on the northern coast. In August 1864 Colonel B. T. Finniss led the hopeful settlers in a fleet of three vessels and chose a site at Escape Cliffs in Adam Bay. But dissensions occurred, and the settlement was a failure. The Aboriginal name of the cliffs was Pater-purrer.

Esk Q   Named by early settlers Alexander and Gideon Scott after the Esk River in Scotland.

Esperance; Esperance Bay WA   Huon de Kermadec, an officer of Admiral d'Entrecasteaux's squadron, in command of the frigate *L'Esperance*, visited the bay in 1792. The Aboriginal name was Gabie Kylie, Place where the water lies like a boomerang.

Essendon V   From the village in Hertfordshire, meaning the Valley of Elsa's people.

Etheridge Goldfield; Etheridge River Q   Named after Donald Etheridge, an employee of Robert Towns.

Eton Q   After the town of Eton in Buckinghamshire. The famous English name means Town on the River Thames.

Ettalong NSW   Probably an Aboriginal name. Formerly known as Bar Swamp and then as Gittins Lagoon.

Ettamogah NSW   Aboriginal. Let us have a drink. This was the name of a local vineyard.

Euchareena NSW   A resident, Mrs Leslie Smith, so named her property after an Aboriginal worker on a Queensland estate. It is said that the meaning of the Aboriginal word is Young dingo.

Eucla SA   Aboriginal. When E. J. Eyre discovered this site on his pioneer route overland round the Great Australian Bight, he named it after the Aboriginal word for the bluff, which has been rendered as Yeergilie, Yercoloya, and Yirculyer, thus demonstrating the varied spellings of Aboriginal names. The word, whatever its form, means Bright fire, and is descriptive of the planet Venus, which from the track rises over the sandhills and thus shows the sight of the only permanent water holes within 200 km in one direction and 100 km in the other. The actual town site was known to the Aborigines as Chiniala.

Eumungerie NSW   Aboriginal. Tree. After a pastoral station.

Eungai NSW   Aboriginal. Singing creek.

Eungella National Park Q   Aboriginal. Land of clouds. The area was officially proclaimed a park in 1941.

Eurabba NSW   Aboriginal. Swampy creek.

Euratha NSW   Aboriginal. Cones of the uri bush. The name of an adjacent estate.

Eurelia SA   Doubtless an Aboriginal word. There is a tale that could even be true. A traveller who arrived at the station heard two porters shouting the name. One said, 'You're a liar,' while the other said, 'You really are'. The latter is the correct pronunciation.

Euroa V   Aboriginal. The correct form is Yera-o, meaning Joyful, or Joyful place.

Eurobin V   Aboriginal. Lagoon at the foot of the mountain.

Evans Island SA   Named by Flinders in 1802, after Thomas Evans, a midshipman on the *Investigator,* of whom he said, 'a fine lad, but he does not grow . . .'.

Evans, Mount NSW   G. W. Evans wrote in his Journal in 1813: '. . .a remarkable Sugar Loaf Hill having a stone on the Peak of it, which I have named after myself'.

Everard, Cape V   See Point Hicks Hill.

Everard Range SA   Discovered by W. C. Gosse in 1873, and named after William Everard, who was Commissioner of Crown Lands. The lake and mountain were also named after him.

Exeter NSW   After the county town in Devonshire, an important railway centre, and noted for its cathedral. Exeter means the Roman military station on the Exe River.

Exford V   The Werribee River was known at one time as the Exe, from which this locality got its name.

Exmouth Gulf WA   'The inlet was named Exmouth Gulf, in compliment to the noble and gallant Viscount,' wrote P. P. King in February 1818, while conducting a survey of the coast in the *Mermaid.* King had served under Exmouth in the Royal Navy.

Exhibition Range Q   Discovered and named by Leichhardt on his first expedition which set out with the object of reaching the settlement at Port Essington. They left the Darling Downs on 1 October 1844, crossing several rivers and ranges, chief of which were the Dawson and Exhibition Ranges, the latter being reached in November.

Eyre Creek Q   Named after E. J. Eyre by Charles Sturt in 1845, but the name has since been supplanted by Mulligan River.

Eyre, Lake SA   The largest of the great salt lakes of South Australia bears the name of its discoverer, Edward John Eyre. It was on his third expedition, in 1840, that Eyre passed beyond Lake Torrens, without realising that he had done so, and reached the lake that was to be named after him some years later. G. W. Goyder mapped the area between the two lakes in 1860, and followed a newspaper suggestion that '... it would be a graceful and well-merited compliment to affix to the principal lake of the chain discovered by Eyre the name of the discoverer'. Governor MacDonnell approved Goyder's choice, and officially named it Lake Eyre in a dispatch dated 26 October 1860. The Aboriginal name was Katitanda.

Eyre, Mount SA   Shortly after E. J. Eyre's arrival at Adelaide on 29 June 1839, at the conclusion of his first expedition, Governor Gawler conferred his name on the mountain at the most northerly point of his journey.

Eyre Peninsula SA   On his second expedition, in 1839, Eyre crossed the peninsula which had first been seen by Flinders in 1802. Governor Gawler wrote to him: 'I have felt it proper to call after your name, the Peninsula of which you have been the first investigator'. A still-born proposal was made to name it Eyria.

Faraday, Mount Q   Faraday Peak was named by T. L. Mitchell in 1846, after Sir Michael Faraday, the British scientist.

Farina SA   A name chosen by Governor Jervois because it meant Flour. Originally called Government Gums, because there were a number of gum trees at Leigh Creek and a Government reserve and well, the township was laid out in 1878. It was hoped that the place would become 'the granary of the north'. A newspaper correspondent, who thought little of the Governor's choice, suggested that the next two towns to be surveyed should be called Bran and Pollard respectively.

Farm Cove NSW   An experimental farm was laid out in this part of what are now the Botanical Gardens in Sydney. Plants and seeds obtained at Rio de Janeiro and the Cape of Good Hope were planted, but with poor results, probably because the first plantings by the Governor's house were made in February. There was only one farmer in the First Fleet, and the sandstone soil in the bay on the eastern side of Sydney Cove, near the Governor's house, was not suitable for the purpose. It was only when cultivation was commenced at Parramatta that satisfactory results were obtained.

Farnham NSW   After Farnham in Surrey, derived from a word meaning Thornbush.

Farrell Flat SA   After Dean Farrell, the second Colonial Chaplain of South Australia.

Fawkner V   After John Pascoe Fawkner.

Field Island NT   After Judge Barron Field.

Figtree NSW   The giant figtree growing at this place gave rise to the name of the township. It was at the junction of two important roads, and when

95

travellers were being directed to or from Sydney in the early days, the best way of describing the route was to tell them to 'turn off at the figtree'. The tree has been preserved and is still an historic landmark. Observing it from the summit of Mount Kembla, A. G. Hamilton said that it resembled the shadow of a cloud projected on the ground.

Finch Hatton Q   Named after George William Finch-Hatton, Earl of Winchelsea.

Fine Flower NSW   The Aboriginal name was Mungungboora or Mungungcoora, Bulrush.

Finke, Mount; Finke, River NT   When on his 1860 expedition, J. McDouall Stuart made the notable discovery of a river lined with gum trees. He wrote on 4 April 1860: 'The creek I have named the Finke, after my sincere friend William Finke of Adelaide — one of the liberal promoters of the different expeditions I have had the honour to lead.' Mount Finke was also named by Stuart, in August 1858. The Aboriginal name of the Finke River was Larapinta or Lirambenda, Creek with permanent water. Baldwin Spencer called the whole river system south-east of the Macdonnell Range Larapinta Land.

Finley NSW   After F. G. Finley, who surveyed the district in the 1860s. The Aboriginal name was Carawatha, Place of pines.

Finniss; Finniss River; Finniss Springs SA   After Colonel Boyle Travers Finniss, who arrived in South Australia with Colonel Light. The springs were named by Major Warburton.

Fish Creek V   So named because of the plentiful supply of blackfish.

Fish River NSW   After Blaxland's crossing of the Blue Mountains in 1813, Governor Macquarie sent G. W. Evans to extend the discoveries westward if possible. He pressed on through the mountainous terrain of the Great Dividing Range until he reached the watershed, at the end of November in the same year. The first stream that flowed westward down a gentle and fertile valley convinced Evans and his companions that they had reached their goal. The river was then given its name because of the many fish to be seen in it.

Fisher SA   After Andrew Fisher, the Labor Prime Minister.

Fisher's Ghost Creek NSW   A name that preserves a true ghost story. In *A Treasury of Australian Folk Tales and Traditions,* Bill Beatty tells how John Farley saw a ghost at Campbelltown in 1826. He recognised it as Fred Fisher, but no one would believe him, for Fisher had left the district some time before. Farley insisted that the ghost had been pointing at the creek, and this was where the police eventually found Fisher's body. A man named Warrell was tried for the murder, and was executed.

Fitzmaurice River NT   'This river was named Fitzmaurice after its discoverer,' wrote J. Lort Stokes on 20 October 1839. L. R. Fitzmaurice served on the *Beagle* under Stokes.

Fitzroy Downs Q   Discovered and named by T. L. Mitchell after Governor Sir Charles Fitzroy.

Fitzroy Gardens V   After Sir Charles Fitzroy.

Fitzroy Island Q   Named by Captain Cook on 9 June 1770 after Augustus Henry Fitzroy, third Duke of Grafton and Prime Minister at the time of Cook's departure.

Fitzroy River Q   Discovered and named by Charles and William Archer in 1753 after Governor Fitzroy.

Fitzroy River V   Also named after Governor Fitzroy.

Fitzroy River WA   The river was explored by J. L. Stokes of the *Beagle*. In February 1838 he wrote: 'Our success afforded me a welcome opportunity of testifying to Captain Fitz-Roy my grateful recognition of his personal kindness; and I determined, with Captain Wickham's permission, to call this new river after his name.' The *Beagle* was formerly commanded by Captain Robert FitzRoy. John Clements Wickham was appointed to the command of the *Beagle* in 1837.

Five Dock NSW   'The place is called Five Dock Point for you see those five rocky docks or inlets from which the Point and Bay received their name.' This was recorded by an early writer of a name that was current as early as 1797. The 500-acre grant owned by John Harris was called Five Dock Farm.

Flattery, Cape Q   After leaving the Endeavour River, Captain Cook was in difficulty, being 'surrounded on every side with Dangers'. On 10 August 1770 he wrote. 'We now judged ourselves to be clear of all Danger, having, as we thought, a Clear, open Sea before us; but this we soon found otherwise, and occasioned my calling the Headland above mentioned Cape Flattery.'

Flemington V   Named after Robert Fleming, who was an early importer of cattle and supplied meat for consumption at the race meetings.

Fleurieu Bay V   See Oyster Bay.

Flinders V   Named after the famous explorer Matthew Flinders who conferred so many names on the coastline of Australia, but on no occasion did he ever give his own name to any of his discoveries.

Flinders Bay WA   As above.

Flinders Chase SA   Set apart in 1919 and named after Matthew Flinders who discovered the island in 1802.

Flinders Group Q   On 13 February 1802 the *Investigator* sheltered behind a large island which Matthew Flinders named after his brother, Samuel Ward Flinders. The name is also applied to the group of five islands, of which Flinders Island is the largest.

Flinders Island T   Named by Governor P. G. King after Matthew Flinders who circumnavigated Van Diemen's Land in 1798.

Flinders Passage SA   In 1802 Matthew Flinders had the difficult task of surveying Torres Strait and the west coast of the Cape York Peninsula. The *Investigator* was at first accompanied by the *Lady Nelson,* but on 18 October he ordered Lieut John Murray to take her back to Sydney and went on alone. On 28 October he negotiated the passage through the Barrier that was subsequently named after him.

Flinders Ranges SA   First sighted by Flinders in 1802, but the ranges were not named until 1839 when E. J. Eyre made his report on the range he had seen when on his first expedition north. Flinders marked the range on his map and described it as 'a ridge of high, rocky, and barren mountains'. When it was discovered that there were further ranges in the same system, the plural form was used.

Flinders River Q   Discovered in July 1841 by J. Lort Stokes of the *Beagle* and named after Matthew Flinders. The mountain in the vicinity is also named Flinders Peak.

Flynn V   After a resident police constable.

Forbes NSW   After Sir Francis Forbes, first Chief Justice of New South Wales. John Oxley, the explorer, was the first to reach the site, and named Camp Hill, now the main residential district of the town.

Forrest WA   Named after Sir John Forrest, the forcible first Premier of Western Australia under responsible government. He was a tireless explorer as well as politician, and on 13 April 1874 reached the Overland Telegraph line with his brother Alexander, having covered about 3,000 km in 166 days. Forrest Lakes, Mount Forrest, and the Forrest River also perpetuate his name.

Fort Dundas NT   The name of a vanished settlement that was established in 1824 with the double object of forestalling Dutch interest in the northern coast and promoting trade with the Far East. Captain Maurice Barlow hoisted the colours over the fort on 21 October 1824 and named it after the First Lord of the Admiralty.

Fortescue River WA   After C. S. P. Fortescue (later Lord Carlingford), Under Secretary of State for the Colonies. The river was discovered by A. C. and F. T. Gregory while exploring the Hamersleys in 1861, and named by F. T. Gregory in recognition of the assistance that Fortescue had given them.

Forth T   Named after the barque *Forth* in 1823.

Forth River T   Discovered by surveyors of the Van Diemen's Land Company in 1826-1827 and named after the English river.

Foster V   After John F. Foster. During a short term as Acting Governor in 1854 he passed the Act that conferred responsible government on Victoria. Later in life he changed his name to Fitzgerald under the terms of his uncle's (Lord Fitzgerald) will. The town was first called Stockyard Creek.

Fowler Bay; Fowler Point SA   Named by Flinders in 1802 after the 1st Lieutenant on the *Investigator*, Robert Fowler, who later in life rose to the rank of Admiral. The bay and point were seen by Peter Nuijts in 1827. A town site was dedicated in 1890 and given the Aboriginal name Yalata, meaning Shellfish, but it reverted to Fowler Bay in 1840.

Frances SA   Named by Governor Fergusson after the wife of D. O. Jones, the owner of Binnum Station, who had entertained him there on one occasion.

Frankland Beach T   The Surveyor-General of Tasmania, George Frankland, named the beach after himself in 1828. He was a noted explorer, botanist, and artist.

Frankland, Mount WA   In a survey in 1838 T. B. Wilson wrote that he had seen 'three mountains conspicuous for their superior attitude, and as they will be leading points in a trigonometrical survey of the country we named them after the Surveyors-General of Australia'. The mountains so named were Frankland, Mitchell, and Roe. Frankland's name was later given to the river and the township.

Franklin T   Named after Sir John Franklin, Lieut-Governor of Tasmania, who had a notable career and is a world-famous figure, not only for his humane rule in Tasmania, but for his polar explorations and his discovery of the North-west Passage.

Franklin Harbour SA   After Sir John Franklin.

Franklin Island SA   Named by Flinders while Franklin was a midshipman on the *Investigator*. On 31 May 1802 he wrote: 'He is capable of learning everything we can show him, and but for a little carelessness, I would not wish to have a son otherwise than he is.'

Franklin River T   Named the King River by George Frankland in 1835, but later renamed after the Lieut-Governor.

Fraser Island Q   The largest island off the Queensland coast was named after Captain James Fraser of the *Stirling Castle*. His vessel struck on Swains Reef off Rockhampton in May 1836. Some of the crew together with Fraser and his wife landed on the island (which had been named Great Sandy Island by Cook on 20 May 1770 and still retains the name together with Fraser Island). Fraser and several other members of the shipwrecked party were killed by the Aborigines. Mrs Fraser and several others eventually managed to escape.

Freeling SA   Named by J. McDouall Stuart after Sir A. H. Freeling, a Commissioner in early Adelaide.

Fremantle WA   When Captain James Stirling, RN, took the first settlers to the new settlement on the Swan River, in order to forestall any possible claims by the French or the Americans, Captain Fremantle was sent ahead to take possession as quickly as possible. Stirling arrived on 25 April 1829 and hoisted the flag on the present sight of Fremantle on 2 May. Eventually the settlement was established at Perth, but the port was named in honour of Captain Fremantle, commander of the *Challenger*. Eventually Charles How Fremantle was knighted.

French Island V   So named because of the visit of the French scientific visits led by Baudin at the beginning of the 19th century.

French's Forest NSW   After James French, Crown lands ranger, who had a grant of 200 acres here. He established his home in the 'forest' in order to keep an eye on timber-workers in the locality.

Frew River NT   Named by J. McDouall Stuart after James Frew, the youngest member of his party on his 1842 expedition. On 14 April a water hole was also found and named Frew's Ironstone Pond 'in token of my approbation of his care and attention to the horses'.

Freycinet Peninsula T   First explored by Pierre Faure of Baudin's expedition, and named after Louis Claude de Saulces de Freycinet. Tasman had named the peninsula Vanderlyn Island.

Frome Creek SA   Named in 1840 by E. J. Eyre while on his third expedition, after the Surveyor-General, E. C. Frome.

Frome, Lake SA   In 1840 E. J. Eyre saw part of the lake which he supposed to be part of Lake Torrens. Eyre believed that Lake Torrens curved round in a great horseshoe bend, blocking further progress. In 1843 E. C. Frome, the second Surveyor-General of South Australia, tried to by-pass the lake that offered such a barrier to exploration. When he came across the lake that bears his name he, like Eyre, believed it to be part of Lake Torrens. Finding it was quite dry, he wrote: 'All our dreams of discovery of a large, fresh-water lake now vanished, and we turned with disgust from this dreary spot and made the best of our way back.'
  The puzzle of the horseshoe lake was solved a few years afterwards, and the lake seen by Frome named after him.

Frome, Mount NSW   After a town in Somerset. It was a river name meaning Fast running.

Furneaux Group T   Named by Captain Cook after Tobias Furneaux, who was in command of the *Adventure*. After becoming separated from Cook's *Resolution* in New Zealand waters in 1773, Furneaux visited Van Diemen's Land and sailed past these islands off the northern coast.

Furner; Furner, Mount SA   After Luke Furner, a Parliamentarian.

Fyansford V   Named after Foster Fyan, soldier, magistrate, Protector of Aborigines, and Commissioner of Crown Lands. He was responsible for the erection of a dam on the Barwon River, the site being called Fyansford.

Gabo Island V   Named by Captain Cook on 20 April 1770. There is a story, probably apocryphal, that when asked the name of the locality, the Aborigines replied, 'Gabo' (we don't understand).

Gairdner, Lake SA   Discovered about the same time in 1857 by separate expeditions led by Stephen Hack and P. E. Warburton, the lake was named by Governor Macdonnell after Gordon Gairdner, the chief clerk in the Australian Department of the Colonial Office in recognition of his long and faithful services.

Galah V   Aboriginal. Rose-breasted Cockatoo. Known at one time as Anderson's Plains, after a stockman.

Galaquil V   Aboriginal. Rushes.

Galga SA   Aboriginal. Hunger.

Galilee, Lake Q   After the famous lake in Palestine.

Galong NSW   Aboriginal. Swampy plain.

Gama V   Aboriginal. Large cockatoo.

Gambier Islands SA   Flinders wrote in his Journal on 24 February 1802 that the group was named 'Gambier's Isles in honour of the worthy admiral (now Lord Gambier) who had a seat at the Admiralty board when the *Investigator* was ordered to be fitted'. Admiral James Gambier was in command of the British fleet at the Battle of Copenhagen.

Gambier, Mount SA   Named by Lieut James Grant of the *Lady Nelson*, and sighted by him on 3 December 1800 (see Gambier Islands). At first Grant believed he had sighted four islands, but when he grew closer discovered they were all on the mainland. He named them Cape Banks, Mount Gambier, Cape Northumberland, and Mount Schank. This was the first part of South Australia to be named. The town of Mount Gambier was founded as a private venture by Hastings Cunningham in 1854. He called it Gambier Town, but Mount Gambier survived as a name, and is popularly known as The Mount. The Aboriginal name was Erengbalam, Place of the eaglehawk.

Ganmain NSW   Aboriginal. Tattooed man is the explanation normally given, but tattooing was a form of decoration not known to the Aborigines; the more probable meaning is Man decorated with scars. The name was given to the holding of N. Devlin.

Gannawarra V   Aboriginal. Geese.

Garrah NSW   Aboriginal. Far away, or Long distance.

Garden Island Q   The Aboriginal name was Dundeppa, Lookout place.

Garden Island WA   Named by Captain James Stirling on 9 June 1829. The settlers landed here on 1 June. On a previous visit in 1827 Stirling had planted seeds on the island, but they came to nothing. The island has been described as a sandy waste blasted by bleak winter winds. The island was soon deserted when the new settlement was located at the present site of Perth.

In June 1801 Captain Hamelin of the *Naturaliste* had called it Isle Buache after the French hydrographer Jean Nicolas Buache, but this name was superseded in 1829.

Gardiner's Creek V   After John Gardiner, the celebrated overlander, who took up a run along the creek from Toorak to the Dandenongs.

Garema NSW   Aboriginal. Camping place.

Garfield V   After the President of the United States, James Abram Garfield.

Garland NSW   After Charles Garland, an MP for the district.

Garoolgan NSW   Aboriginal. One man going to fight.

Gascoyne River WA   Discovered by George Grey in 1839 and named by him 'in compliment to my friend, Captain J. Gascoyne'. The region called the Gascoyne includes the Minilya, Wooramel, Gascoyne, and Lyndon rivers and the districts of Gascoyne-Minilya and Upper Gascoyne.

Gatton Q   Probably after Gatton Park in Surrey. Gatton means Place where goats are kept.

Gawler SA   Named by Governor Gawler after himself, although William Light, who had been in the district in 1837 and 1839 felt that the township should have been named for himself. George Gawler was appointed Governor of South Australia in 1838 and recalled in 1841. The Aboriginal name was Kaleeya or Kaleteeya.

Gawler Ranges SA   First seen in 1838 by E. J. Eyre and explored by Stephen Hack and P. E. Warburton in 1857. Named after the Governor by Eyre.

Gawler River SA   Strangways and Blunden, the discoverers, wrote: 'We struck a fine, running river, deep and strong...We named it Gawler after His Excellency.' The Aboriginal name was Moole Yerke Perre.

Gayndah Q   Though undoubtedly of Aboriginal origin, there is some uncertainty about the name. It comes either from Gu-in-dah (or Gi-un-dah), Thunder, or from Ngainta, Place of scrub. It was called Norton's Camp at one time, after a local carrier.

Geelong V   The Aboriginal name was Jillong, Place of the native companions, and was actually in current use when the Deed was signed by John Batman and eight leading Aboriginals in 1835, and also in 1838 when the town was surveyed and proclaimed. For some time the settlement was also known as Coraiya, which in turn was corrupted to Corio and is still used for the bay on which the town is built.

Gellibrand V   After Joseph Tice Gellibrand, who drew up the deed of purchase for the site of Melbourne at the time of Batman's purchase. The Aboriginal name was Walar Walar.

Geelvink Bay WA   The bay and the channel between Houtman Abrolhos Islands and the mainland were named by Willem de Vlamingh after his vessel, the *Geelvink,* in 1705.

Geeveston T   The town site was first settled in 1849 by William Geeves who, with his family, took up land in Lightwood Bottom, as it was then known. It was named Geeves Town in 1861 and then changed to Geeveston.

Gembrook V   So named because of the finding of topaz, sapphires, and garnets by the Rev Dr Bleesdale.

Genoa V   The name commemorates a visit by the Duke of Genoa in 1873.

Geographe Bay WA   'We discovered a very large bay open to the northwest, which was given the name Geographe Bay', wrote Lieut de Freycinet who was on the *Naturaliste* at the time. It was on 30 May 1801 that Captain Nicolas Baudin anchored *Le Geographe* in the bay during his scientific expedition, and lost contact with the *Naturaliste.*

George, Lake NSW   Discovered by Joseph Wild in August 1820 and named after King George IV three months later by Governor Macquarie. The Aboriginal name was Werriwa, which is now applied to a Federal Electoral Division.

George, Lake SA   After Sir George Grey.

George Gill Range NT   Discovered and named by Ernest Giles.

George's River NSW   After King George III. It was explored and named by Flinders and Bass in their tiny boat *Tom Thumb* in 1795.

Georgetown Q   After H. St George, Assistant Gold Commissioner at Gilberton in 1870.

Georgetown SA   Surveyed in 1869 and named after George Fisher, the original owner of the Bundaleer station on which the town is built.

Georgina River Q   Named after Georgina Kennedy, daughter of Sir Arthur Kennedy, Governor of Queensland from 1877 to 1883. During his search for Burke and Wills in 1861, William Landsborough discovered the river and named it the Herbert after the first Premier of Queensland. The name was later changed when it was found that it had already been given to a river on the east coast.

Geraldton WA   Named after the Governor, Charles FitzGerald when the town site was surveyed in 1850. Lead was discovered on the Murchison River by a party under A. C. Gregory in 1848, the mine that was established also being named for the Governor. The town was at first called Gerald Town.

Geranium SA   So named because of the profusion of these flowers.

Gerogary NSW   Aboriginal. Magpie-lark.

Gerringong NSW   Aboriginal. The popular explanation is that the word means Fearful, or I fear myself — exclamations uttered by the Aborigines when they first saw the sails of the *Endeavour* in 1770; but in view of the lack of interest displayed by the Aborigines with whom Cook came in contact, the theory is not convincing. A somewhat more realistic version is that the word is a corruption of Jerrungarugh, Ambush, referring to an incident of tribal warfare here or, possibly, Place where water is found.

Gibbo V   Aboriginal. High mountains, or Bold.

Gibson Desert WA   Named by Ernest Giles after Alfred Gibson, a member of his second expedition. On 1 May 1874 their water was exhausted. Giles lent Gibson his best horse, the Fair Maid of Perth, and instructed him to return to a cache that had been established a little while before and bring back a fresh supply to the camp in the Rawlinson Range. When he did not return Giles set out in search of him. Following the track of the horse he came to the conclusion that it had followed some lost pack horses. With some difficulty Giles returned to the camp and with two companions continued the search for Gibson, but without success.

Gidley NSW   After Philip Gidley King, the third Governor of New South Wales. His name came from the King family estate, Gidleigh, in Devonshire.

Gilbert Range; **Gilbert River** Q   Named by Leichhardt on 12 July 1845, while on his first expedition from Darling Downs to Port Essington, in memory of John Gilbert who was killed on the night of 28 June, Gilbert was a naturalist employed by John Gould, the ornithologist and bird painter. The expedition ran into an ambush of Aborigines who resented the invasion of their tribal hunting grounds. Roper and Calvert were wounded and John Gilbert was killed. There is a possibility that the river was the Staten, q.v.

Gilberton Q   Also named after John Gilbert. See above.

Giles, Lake WA   After the well-known explorer, Ernest Giles.

Gilgandra NSW   Aboriginal. Long water hole.

Gilles Plains SA   Named after Osmond Gilles, who was involved in the formation of the South Australian Company, and first Colonial Treasurer of South Australia.

Gilles Highway Q   After the premier who was in office when the highway was begun.

Gin Gin Q   Aboriginal. A corruption of Jinjinburra, the name of the tribe in this locality.

Gippsland V   On 19 May 1840 Paul Edmund de Strzelecki completed a journey overland to Melbourne, and wrote: 'On account of the cheering prospect which this country holds out to future settlers, and which it was my lot to discover, I took the liberty of naming it in honour of His Excellency the Governor, Gipps Land.' The Governor was Sir George Gipps.

Strzelecki's claim to be the discoverer cannot be sustained. Angus Macmillan had explored it thoroughly a year earlier and had conferred several names on the natural features of the region. As a loyal Scot he wished to name it Caledonia Australis, or New South Caledonia, but local loyalties prevailed.

Girilambone NSW   Aboriginal. Place of a star, or Place of many stars. There is a theory that the name was given on account of the many meteorites found here.

Girral NSW   Aboriginal. Star.

Gisborne V   Named by Governor Latrobe after Henry Fyshe Gisborne, the first Commissioner of Crown Lands in the Port Phillip district.

Gladstone Q   Named after William Ewart Gladstone, who, as Colonial Secretary, insisted on the establishment of a settlement for certain classes of convicts, and to colonize Northern Australia (another name for the 'colony' was Northern Australia). Lieut Col George Barney was placed in charge, and on 15 September 1842 he chose a spot at Port Curtis for the experiment. It was not successful, and when Earl Grey succeeded Gladstone in 1846 the settlement was abandoned. As the land round about was fertile the town of Gladstone was founded on the site of the abandoned penal colony.

Gladstone V   Also named after W. E. Gladstone. In 1871 two land owners, W. Moorhouse and O. Horner, with adjoining properties decided to lay out a township, which they proposed to name after the British statesman. In 1875 the Government, which had no liking for privately owned towns, commenced a survey on H. B. Hughes's run adjacent to Gladstone, and adopted the Aboriginal name Booyoolie. As the double township grew it gradually merged into one, under the name Gladstone. Booyoolie was not officially dropped until 1940. Mrs H. B. Hughes advanced the ingenious explanation that the true origin of the name was Beau-ewe-lea, Beautiful sheep country. But there is little doubt that it is an Aboriginal name meaning Boiling up of a smoke cloud.

Glasshouse Mountains Q   'These hills lay but a little way inland,' wrote Cook on 17 May 1770, 'and not far from Each other; they are very remarkable on account of their singular form of Elivation, which very much resembles Glass Houses, which occasioned my giving them that Name.'

Cook was referring to the glass furnaces of his native Yorkshire. He remarked on only three of these remarkable peaks (though he noted other lesser ones), but in fact there are eleven main peaks.

Glen Innes NSW   After Archibald Clunes Innes, soldier and pioneer, who was granted more than 2,500 acres when he was appointed police magistrate at Port Macquarie. By means of convict labour he transformed a wilderness into the best pastoral property north of Sydney, and named it Lake Innes. He owned many properties, including Furracabad, the site of Glen Innes, which was named by him, though he never lived there. The Aboriginal name was Kindaitchin, meaning Plenty of stones.

Glen Osmond SA   After Osmand Gilles who took up land near Adelaide on his retirement as Colonial Treasurer.

Glenbrook NSW   A place that has suffered many changes of name, being successively called Watertank, Wascoe's Siding, Brookdale, and finally Glenbrook. Brookdale was chosen as a name by Alfred Stephens, because the place was well watered, a factor that no doubt affected the final choice of name.

Glencoe NSW   After the gloomy valley in Argyllshire, Scotland, where mountains rise almost perpendicularly from the valley floor.

Glencoe SA   Named by Edward and Robert Leakes, also after the Scottish Glencoe.

Glenelg River V   Discovered by T. L. Mitchell in 1836 and named in honour of Lord Glenelg, Secretary of State for the Colonies.

Glenelg River WA   Also named for Lord Glenelg, by the discoverer George Grey, in 1838.

Glennies Creek NSW   After James Glennie, an early settler.

Glenora T   An elided name which came from Norah, the wife of a pioneer settler.

Glenorchy SA   Alexander Campbell, one of the early pioneers of the district, built a house here for his parents and named it after their Scottish home.

Glenorchy V   Also named after the Scottish Glenorchy. At one time it was called Four Posts Inn. The Aboriginal name was Janukin.

Glenreagh NSW   After Glenreagh in Scotland, the name meaning Valley surrounded by hills.

Glenrowan V   Named by two brothers named Rowan.

Gloucester NSW   The town takes its name from the Gloucester Estate which was owned by the Australian Agricultural Company in the late 1890s. The obvious origin is in the cathedral city of Gloucester in the county of Gloucestershire (from OE word meaning Bright, Splendid place, and the Latin word for camp or fort).

Gloucester Island Q   The island, cape, and passage were named by Captain Cook on 4 June 1770 after William Henry, Duke of Gloucester and Edinburgh, a younger brother of George III.

Gobondery NSW   Aboriginal name of a native tree.

Goddard, Mount WA   The mountain and a creek bear the name of W. P. Goddard who examined this part of the country in 1890.

Gogeldrie NSW   Aboriginal. Canoe fashioned from a hollow tree.

Gold Coast, City of Q   See City of Gold Coast.

Good Island Q First named Good's Island by Flinders on 2 November 1802 after the 'botanical gardener' on the *Investigator*. The name was subsequently misspelt Goode, but in 1948 the Admiralty changed it back to Good. The Aboriginal name was Palilug.

Goodnight SA This peculiar name was derived from an incident when the captain of a river steamer on the Murray heard a voice calling from the bank, 'Goodnight!' Ever afterwards he called that particular spot 'the place where the bloke said "goodnight".'

Goolwa SA Aboriginal. Elbow. It was formerly known as Port Pullen, after Captain Pullen, Colonel Light's second-in-command who later became an Arctic explorer.

Goodooloo SA Aboriginal. The stars of the Southern Cross.

Goondah NSW Aboriginal. Dark, Night, Rain, or Cloud.

Goondiwindi Aboriginal. Droppings of ducks or shags, Place of wild ducks, or Water running over rocks.

Goonoo Goonoo NSW Aboriginal. Green tree, or Plenty of water, or Poor game land.

Goorawin NSW Aboriginal. Flowers.

Gooray Q Aboriginal. Cypress pine ridge.

Goorong V Aboriginal. The name of a plant.

Goose Island WA Flinders's men killed 65 Cape Barren geese here in January 1802.

Gordon SA Surveyed in 1879 and named by Governor Jervois after his brother. Formerly Wirreanda Siding.

Gordon, Mount WA Named by J. S. Roe after Sir James Gordon Bremer.

Gordon River T Discovered by James Kelly in 1815 during an exploratory voyage in a whaleboat lent to him by the Pittwater magistrate James Gordon, after whom Kelly named the river.

Gordonvale Q Named in 1812 after one of the pioneer settlers, John Gordon. Earlier names were Mulgrave and Nelson.

Gore Q After the Parliamentarian St George Gore.

Gormanston T After Governor Jenico William Joseph Preston, 14th Viscount Gormanston.

Goroke V Aboriginal. Magpie.

Gosford NSW Probably after the second Earl of Gosford. Named by Governor Gipps in 1839, who was acquainted with the Earl. The English village of Gosford is in Oxfordshire.

Gosse Range NT Named after William Christie Gosse, appointed

Deputy Surveyor-General of South Australia in 1875.

Goulburn; Goulburn Plains; Goulburn River; Goulburn Valley NSW James Meehan and Hamilton Hume reached the Goulburn Plains, named by the former, in 1818, after Henry Goulburn, Secretary of State for the Colonies. The Goulburn River was discovered and named by William Lawson in the early 1820s. The town of Goulburn was gazetted in March 1833, but was earlier known as Strathallen, the Aboriginal name being Burbong. There were other localities of the same name, one of them being named after Henry Goulburn's brother Frederick, Colonial Secretary in Sydney. The *Australian Encyclopaedia* quotes a verse by the Rev J. D. Lang, who was an advocate of the preservation of Aboriginal names:
> *I hate your Goulburn Downs and Goulburn Plains,*
> *And Goulburn River and Goulburn Range,*
> *And Mount Goulburn and Goulburn Vale; one's brains*
> *Are turned with Goulburns. Pitiful this mange*
> *For immortality! Had I the reins*
> *Of Government for a fortnight, I would change*
> *The Government appellatives and give*
> *The country names that should deserve to live.*

Goulburn Islands NT   Named by P. P. King in March 1818 in honour of Henry Goulburn.

Goulburn River V   The Goulburn was crossed by Hamilton Hume and Henry Hovell in 1824 and named the Hovell, but was later renamed in honour of Frederick Goulburn. In 1836 T. L. Mitchell complained that the name Hovell had not been retained as there was already a Goulburn River in New South Wales. The Aboriginal name was Bayunga.

Gould V   Probably named after John Gould, the famous painter of birds.

Goyder Lagoon NT   This large swamp is named after George Woodroffe Goyder, Deputy Surveyor-General of South Australia. Goyder's Line of Rainfall was an important pronouncement, for it showed the limits where wheat could be grown. It was drawn in 1865 when he was sent to survey the country after a disastrous drought.

Goyura V   Aboriginal. Mountain of light.

Gracemere Q   Named by the discoverers, Charles and William Archer in May 1853 as a compliment to Mrs Grace Lindsay Morison. The lagoon was first called Farris.

Grafton NSW   After Augustus Henry Fitzroy, Third Duke of Grafton, Prime Minister from 1767-70. He was notable for his conciliatory policy to America, and his opposition to the duty on tea exported to America contributed to his unpopularity in England.

Grafton, Cape Q   Named by Captain Cook after the Duke of Grafton on 9 June 1770.

Graman NSW   Aboriginal. A corruption of Gooraman, Long plain, or Glade.

Grampians, The V   In July 1833 T. L. Mitchell came in sight of the mountains and named them after their Scottish counterpart. Aboriginal names for the range were Cowa and Narram Narram.

Grange Burn V   Also named by T. L. Mitchell, in 1836.

Grant Island NT   P. P. King named the island in memory of his old commander Captain Charles Grant, RN.

Grantville V   After Lieut James Grant, captain of the *Lady Nelson*.

Gravesend NSW   After the river port and market town in Kent, on the banks of the River Thames. It is an ancient borough and appears in the Doomsday Book as Graves-ham.

Graysholme Q   After William Gray, a teamster who took heavy loads across the range to Warwick.

Great Australian Bight SA, WA   Although the first European to sail along the coast was Pieter Nuijts in the *Gulden Zeepaert* in 1627, and later by d'Entrecasteaux in 1792, the name was not given until 1802, when Matthew Flinders referred to it as 'the great bight or gulph of New Holland', and in his *A Voyage to Terra Australis* as the Great Australian Bight.

Great Dividing Range NSW, Q, V   The eastern highlands of Australia which extend from Cape York Peninsula through New South Wales to Victoria. 'The title,' states the *Australian Encyclopaedia,* 'is an unfortunate one, as the divide is nowhere "great" in comparison with the world's big ranges, and it is not a range in the accepted meaning of the word.' See also Australian Alps.

Great Sandy Island Q   Sandy Cape was named by Cook on 20 May 1770 'on account of 2 very large white Patches of Sand upon it'. He did not realise it was an island with sandhills rising to a height of 250m. It is also known as Fraser Island, q.v., both names still being used.

Great Victoria Desert SA, WA   Crossed from east to west by Ernest Giles in 1874, he travelled nearly 500 km without finding water until he reached a supply which he named the Great Victoria Spring. The desert was given the same name, doubtless after Queen Victoria.

Great Western V   There is uncertainty whether the name was bestowed on account of the geographical position or not.

Gredgwin V   Aboriginal. Muddy water.

Greenly Islands; Greenly, Mount SA   Named by Flinders in honour of the fiancee of Sir Isaac Coffin. On 16 February 1802 Flinders wrote; 'Our course was then directed to the south-west, towards two high pieces of land, which appeared in the offing, and obtained the name of *Greenly's Isles* . . . The highest of these hills I call Mount Greenly.'

Greenock SA   Named by George Fife Angas's Secretary, James Smith, after Greenock on the Clyde River.

Greenough River WA   Discovered and named by George Grey in 1839 after George Bellas Greenough, President of the Royal Geographical Society.

Greensborough V   After an early settler.

Greenthorpe NSW   After G. H. Greene, MLC, who owned property in the district.

Gregory, Lake SA   When B. H. Babbage identified the lake, later known as Lake Eyre, as being separate from Lake Torrens, he gave it the name Gregory, but Governor MacDonnell refused to accept this. He insisted on calling it Lake Eyre. Subsequently Babbage's choice was transferred to a smaller lake east of Lake Eyre.

Gregory River Q   William Landsborough went by sea in 1861 to the Gulf of Carpentaria to commence his search for the Burke and Wills expedition. He discovered this river and named it for the explorer A. C. Gregory.

Grenfell NSW   After T. G. Grenfell, Gold Commissioner for the district, who was killed by bushrangers at Narromine in 1866.

Greta NSW   Long before coal was discovered here, a village was surveyed at Anvil Creek in 1842 and named Greta by the Governor-in-Council after a small river in Cumberland, England. This is probably adjacent to Greta Hall in Keswick, where there were two houses under one roof. The poets Coleridge and Southey lived one in each house.

Greta V   The origin of the name is as above.

Griffith NSW   After Arthur Griffith, a former Minister of Public Works. The town was designed by Walter Burley Griffin in 1914.

Grim, Cape T   On 9 December 1798 Flinders and Bass in the *Norfolk* sailed along the northern coast of Van Diemen's Land, prior to sailing round the island. They noticed that the coast was turning southwards and realised that the long swell was coming through a strait, which had not been proved up till this time. The appearance of the headland caused them to name it Cape Grim. The Aboriginal name was Kennaook.

Grong Grong NSW   Aboriginal. Bad camping ground, or Very bad camping ground. The name of a pastoral holding.

Groongal NSW   Aboriginal. Long grass, a corruption of Kooroongal, a name used by the Aborigines for a bend in the river about ten miles distant, and adopted for a nearby property owned by the Learmonth family.

Grose River; Grose Vale; Grose Wold NSW   After Lieut-Governor Francis Grose, who followed after Governor Phillip. The name was conferred by William Paterson, who explored the Blue Mountains with George Johnston, John Palmer, and Edward Laing in 1793. They travelled by boat from the Hawkesbury River. Paterson's objective was to discover a way across the mountains (in which he failed) and to gather botanical specimens for Sir Joseph Banks. His entry was made through the Grose Valley. After Paterson's death his widow married Grose.

Groote Eylandt NT   The island was noted in 1623 from the *Arnhem* and again in 1644 by Tasman, who gave the name, which means Great Island.

Guichen Bay SA   Named by Nicolas Baudin in 1802 after the Dutch Admiral Guichen.

Guildford V   After Guildford in Surrey, meaning Ford where tolls are collected.

Gular NSW   Aboriginal name that comes from Gulargambone, Plenty of galahs. It first bore its correct name of Gulargambone, but as it could be confused with Girilambone there was a proposal to call it Galah. It was pointed out this was likely to result in further confusion because of the similar-sounding name Garah. The obvious solution was the shortened form Gular.

Gulf of Carpentaria   See Carpentaria, Gulf of.

Gulgong NSW   Aboriginal. Deep water hole.

Gulnare SA   John Horrocks named the plains in 1841 after his dog which had kept his party well supplied with food. It killed seven emus in four days.

Gumbowie SA   Aboriginal. Water.

Gunbower V   Aboriginal. A corruption of Gundowringha, meaning Camping place.

Gundagai NSW   Coming from the Aboriginal Gundabandoobingee, it is locally shortened to Gundy. The full word means Cut with tomahawk at the back of the knee (Gunda: sinews at back of knee; bingee: cut with a tomahawk). Or, Going upstream.

Gunedah NSW   Aboriginal. From the root word Guni, meaning White stone. This accounts for the usual explanation, Place of the white stone, or, Place of many white stones. Another conjecture is Place of the destitute.

Gunning NSW   Aboriginal. Probably a corruption of Goong, swamp mahogany, a tree which has branches of small white flowers and a hard reddish wood resembling Spanish mahogany.

Gunson, Mount SA   After Dr Gunson, a member of the first Council of the University of Adelaide.

Gunyah V   Aboriginal. The common term for hut. An early description (1845): 'Their only habitation . . . is formed by two sheets of bark stripped from the nearest tree, at the first appearance of a storm, and joined together at an angle of 45 degrees. This, which they call a gunnya, is cut up for firewood when the storm is passed.' (J. O. Balfour, *Sketch of New South Wales.*)

Gurley NSW   Aboriginal. Creek; or a tree that is common in the district. It was also the name of a pastoral station nearby, and a creek.

Gurrai SA   Aboriginal. Food.

Guyra NSW   Aboriginal. Fish can be caught. A pastoral run of this name was held by Charles W. Marsh in 1848. By 1866 there were two properties Guyra East and Guyra West, but the locality was not proclaimed a village until 1885.

Gwydir River NSW   Although there have been several conjectures on the meaning of this so-called Aboriginal word, the matter was settled for all time by an entry in Allan Cunningham's diary made when he crossed this river in 1827: 'I named the river after Lord Gwydir.'

Gymbowen V   Aboriginal. A long time ago.

Gympie Q   Aboriginal. From Gympi Gympi or Gimpi Gimpi, Stinging tree. In 1867 it was called Nashville when James Nash found gold there and started a gold rush, but in 1868 it reverted to its Aboriginal name.

Hahndorf SA   In December 1838 Captain D. M. Hahn arrived in South Australia on the Danish vessel *Zebra* with 187 German Lutheran immigrants. They settled on 150 acres of land in the Mount Lofty Ranges and called their village Hahndorf after their leader. At the time of anti-German prejudice during the first World War the name was changed to Ambleside, but restored to Hahndorf in 1935. The Aboriginal name was Bukartilla, Swimming place.

Halbury SA   The Hundred of Hall was named after George Hall, Governor Gawler's Secretary and son-in-law, and Halbury so named because it was in the Hundred.

Halidon SA   After Halidon Hill.

Halifax Bay; Halifax Island Q   Named by Captain Cook on 8 June 770 after the Earl of Halifax, who was Secretary of State from 1763 to 1765. It seems apparent that the present Halifax Bay was first named Rockingham Bay in Cook's Journal, and that subsequently the position of the two names was reversed.

Halifax Bay, Dunk Island, Mount Hinchinbrook, and Sandwich Bay in this vicinity were all named in honour of George Montagu Dunk, First Lord of the Admiralty, who was Cook's patron. Dunk was both Earl of Halifax and Earl of Sandwich. His estate was named Hinchinbrook.

Hallett SA   Named after the owner of Wandilla station. The Aboriginal name was Willogoleeche.

Hall's Creek WA   Charles Hall and Jack Slettery struck gold in the Kimberleys in 1885 at the place that became known as Hall's Creek. It quickly developed into a typical gold fields town and was at its peak in 1886, but then faded away. The present day Hall's Creek on the Broome-Darwin section of the Great Northern Highway is 15 km away from the old shanty township.

Hamersley Range WA   Discovered by F. T. Gregory in June 1861 and named after a generous supporter of his exploratory work, Edward Hamersley.

Hamilton V   The origin of the name has not yet been discovered. T. L. Mitchell traversed the district in 1836. The present location of the town was a corroboree ground called Mulleratong. Mitchell named the river Grange Burn. The first settlers called the township The Grange, but in 1851 the name was changed to Hamilton.

Hamley Bridge SA   After Lieut-Colonel Hamley, the acting Governor, who performed the official opening ceremony of the bridge.

Hammond SA   Named in 1879 after Hammond Jervois, the son of Governor Jervois.

Hann, Mount; Hann River WA   The mountain was discovered by Frank H. Hann in 1889. He named it Mount William, but the Surveyor-General changed it to Mount Hann. The Hann Range and Hann Tabletop, further to the south, were also discovered by Hann from 1896 to 1898. The Hann River was called the Phillips by Hann, but this too was changed by the Surveyor-General.

Hannah's Bridge NSW   After William Hannah, the owner of a nearby property.

Hanson SA   After Sir Richard Hanson, Premier of South Australia and Chief Justice.

Harcourt V   After Sir William Harcourt, a prominent Cabinet Minister and Leader of the Opposition in England.

Harefield NSW   Supposedly after Harefield in Middlesex. Probably meaning Field of the people.

Hargraves NSW   After Edward Hammond Hargraves, the discoverer of gold at Ophir in 1851. He was later appointed Commissioner of Crown Lands and given grants by the Governments of New South Wales and Victoria.

Harrington NSW   Named after the Earl of Harrington by John Oxley.

Harris, Mount NT   In April 1861, J. McDouall Stuart reached the mountain. The printed version of his Journal states: 'I ascended the hill, which I have named Mount Harris after Peter Harris Esq of Adelaide.' In his MS journal however, the name Mount Sullivan appears, so named after one of his companions on his journey.

Harrow V   After the English Harrow.

Harry, Lake SA   Named by G. W. Goyder after Harry Franklin, a member of his survey expedition in 1860.

Hart SA   After Captain John Hart, an early settler.

Hartley; Little Hartley; Hartley Vale NSW   Governor Macquarie named this 'beautiful extensive vale of five miles' the Vale of Clwydd, in 1815. The township was formed and named in 1838 after a place in Northumberland. The name means Stag hill.

Harvey WA   The Harvey River, after which the town was named, was explored in 1834 by Major Harvey. The Aboriginal name was Korijekup.

Hastings Point; Hastings River NSW   The Hastings River was discovered and named by John Oxley in 1818. The point is known locally as Cudgera Head, from the Aboriginal word Kudgeree, Raw flesh. It was named after Warren Hastings, Governor-General of India, by John Oxley in 1823. It has, however, been suggested that as Mrs Oxley came from Hastings in England, this may have influenced his choice of the name.

Hawke, Cape NSW   After Admiral Sir Edward Hawke, First Lord of the Admiralty. The name was given by Captain Cook, who wrote in his Journal on 11 May 1770: 'At 8 we were abreast of a high point of Land, which made in 2 Hillocks; this point I called Cape Hawke.' Admiral Hawke fought against the appointment of Alexander Dalrymple as commander of the Pacific exploration voyage, and settled for the comparatively unknown James Cook.

Hawker SA   After George Charles Hawker, pioneer settler of Bungaree, who achieved a reputation as a breeder and wool grower, and became Speaker of the South Australian Parliament.

Hawkesbury River NSW   After Charles Jenkinson, first Earl of Liverpool, Baron Hawkesbury, who was President of the Council of Trade. For some time it was not realised that Broken Bay was the estuary of a river, but in June 1789 Governor Phillip was rowed up it for some miles and bestowed the name. Captain Watkin Tench shortly afterwards discovered a river 'nearly as broad as the Thames at Putney', which Governor Phillip named the Nepean, q.v. When Tench revisited the district two years later he realised that the Nepean and the Hawkesbury were in fact the same river. From the junction of the Hawkesbury and the Warragamba as far as the confluence with the Grose, the Hawkesbury is known as the Nepean. The Aboriginal name was Deerabubbin.

Hay NSW   After Sir John Hay, the local Member of Parliament for Murrumbidgee, who became Speaker of the Assembly in 1982. An earlier name was Lang's Crossing, called a crossing because it was a ford on the Murrumbidgee River for cattle bound for Victoria.

Hayes T   After Captain Sir John Hayes, commander of the *Duke of Clarence*, who named the Derwent River.

Haystack, Mount V   Angus McMillan crossed from New South Wales into Victoria and in May 1839 climbed a mountain he named McLeod and saw a distant view of the sea. The mountain was subsequently named Haystack, probably on account of its shape.

Head, Range NT   Named by J. McDouall Stuart in 1860 after Benjamin Head, a member of his expedition.

Healesville V   After Sir Richard Heales, Premier of Victoria.

Heathcote NSW   Probably after Heathcote in Derbyshire. Meaning, Cottage or Sheep-fold on a heath.

Heathcote V   When gold was first discovered in 1852 it was known as the McIvor diggings. The name Heathcote was conferred on the town in 1870, probably on account of the flowering heath in the vicinity.

Heavitree Gap NT   After Sir Charles Heavitree Todd. See under Alice Springs.

Hedley V   After a local doctor in the 1850s.

Hellyer River T   Originally named the Don River by the Van Diemen's Land Company in 1827, it was later renamed for its discoverer, Henry Hellyer.

Henty NSW   After Henry Henty who owned property there.

Hepburn V   After Captain Hepburn who was among the first overlanders who brought cattle from Sydney to Port Phillip. The Aboriginal name was Morrekyle.

Herbert NT   After Herbert Hughes, owner of the Booyoolee station. The Aboriginal name was Booyooarto, Booyoolee's hill.

Herbert River; Herbert Range Q   Discovered by G. A. F. E. Dalrymple in 1864, and named by A. C. Gregory, the Surveyor-General, after Sir Wyndham Herbert, the first Premier of Queensland.

Herberton Q   The town on the Herbert River is also named for Sir Wyndham Herbert.

Hermannsburg NT   The mission station was founded by two German missionaries, Kempe and Schwarz who left from Bethany in South Australia in October 1875 and, with their livestock, reached their destination 19 months later. The Lutheran mission station was named after Hermannsburg in Germany. It is notable for the work of the Rev C. Strehlow, the story of whose labours and tragic death has been told so graphically and sympathetically in T. G. H. Strehlow's *Journey to Horseshoe Bend**.

Hervey Bay Q   Observed by Captain Cook on 21 May 1770 and named by him after Captain Augustus John Hervey, who later became third Earl of Bristol and was promoted to Admiral.

* Angus and Robertson, 1969.

Hexham NSW After the market town in Northumberland, on the River Tyne. Meaning, The Lagustald's stream.

Hey River Q Named after Rev Nicholas Hey, a Bavarian missionary who named the Mission River and established missions at Mapoon and Weipa in the 1890s.

Hicks Hill; Point Hicks V See Point Hicks Hill.

Hillgrove NSW Formerly known as Cara, a name chosen by Sir Maurice O'Connell.

Hillston NSW After William Hill, who built and owned a hotel there. The locality was first known as Redbank, and by the Aboriginal name Melnunni, Red soil.

Hinchinbrook Island Q Named by Captain Cook on 8 June 1770. See under Halifax Bay. Cook noted the island as Mount Hinchinbrook for he was not aware of the channel that separated it from the mainland. Its insularity was recognised by P. P. King in 1819.

Hindmarsh SA The island at the mouth of the Murray River was seen and landed on by Charles Sturt in 1830, but not named until 1837. Y. B. Hutchinson and T. B. Strangways made a closer inspection in 1837 and named it after the Governor, Sir John Hindmarsh, the first Governor of South Australia. The Aboriginal name was Korra-condungga.

Hindmarsh, Lake V Discovered by E. J. Eyre in 1838 while on his way from Port Phillip to Adelaide and also named in honour of Sir John Hindmarsh. The Aboriginal name was Gooro.

Hobart T Named after Robert Hobart, fourth Earl of Buckinghamshire, Secretary of State for War and the Colonies from 1801 to 1804. Lieut John Bowen had formed a settlement at Risdon Cove, but Lieut-Governor David Collins considered the site unsuitable, and shifted it to Sullivan Cove, taking possession on 19 February 1804. Bowen had already called the Risdon Cove settlement Hobart, a dispatch to the Governor of New South Wales, dated 27 September 1803, bearing this address. Collins transferred the name as well as the settlement to Sullivan Cove. Early forms of the name were Hobart Town, Hobarton, and Hobarttown. In 1813 Lieut-Governor Davey tried to have Hobart Town shortened to Hobart, but official approval was not given until 1881.

Hodgkinson River Q On his third expedition in 1874 J. V. Mulligan crossed the Mitchell River and discovered another which he named after William Oswald Hodgkinson, who had been a member of McKinlay's expedition in search of Burke and Wills in 1862. See also Mulligan River.

Hodgson Q The Hodgson Creek was named after Christopher Pemberton Hodgson by Leichhardt in 1864. Hodgson had joined the Leichhardt expedition to Port Essington, but left after some weeks, probably through a disagreement with the leader; but when Leichhardt disappeared, Hodgson joined in the search.

Holbrook NSW   After Lieutenant Norman Holbrook, RN, who was awarded the Victoria Cross in World War I for taking his submarine underneath mines to torpedo the Turkish battleship *Messudiyeh*. The first name, given in 1858, was Ten Mile Creek. This was replaced by Germanton in 1875, in honour of one of the first settlers, John Pabst. During the First World War, when anything of German origin was suspect, the present name was substituted.

Holder SA   After Sir Frederick Holder, whom Alfred Deakin described: 'No Speaker more gentle, patient, or equitable, has ever presided.'

Holmwood NSW   After a place in Surrey, meaning Wood in low-lying river land, or Holly wood.

Home Hill Q   After Colonel Home, an officer who served in the Crimean War.

Hookina SA   Aboriginal. A corruption of Wonoka, which may be the name of a tree with edible roots.

Hope Islands Q   After the *Endeavour* struck the reef, having survived the disaster, and was in search of a place to careen the vessel, which was taking in water at the rate of 15 inches an hour, Cook wrote (on 13 June 1770): 'At 9 we past close without 2 small low Islands . . . I have named them Hope Islands, because we were always in hopes of being able to reach these Islands.'

Hopeless, Mount SA   The place where E. J. Eyre was finally convinced that his search for good, fertile country was hopeless. This was in 1840 on his third expedition. Even before climbing it he was resolved 'to waste no more time or energy on so desolate and forbidding a reason'.

Hopkins River V   Discovered and named by T. L. Mitchell in 1836, after Sir John Paul Hopkins.

Hopping Dick Creek WA   A humorous name bestowed because of the affliction of a gentleman named Richard Wood. Another name with the same origin was Limpinwood.

Horeb, Mount NSW   After the peak in the Sinai Peninsula which Moses ascended to receive the tablets containing the Ten Commandments. The name was first given to a nearby sheep and cattle station.

Horn Island Q   The island takes its name from Horned Hill which Flinders described in 1803 as 'forming something like two horns at the top'. Aboriginal name Narupai.

Horrocks, Mount; Horrocks Pass SA   John Ainsworth Horrocks was a young man with an adventurous disposition and great strength and powers of endurance. In his search for land in the vicinity of the Hutt and Wakefield rivers, he earned the title of 'King of the North'. He was the first person in Australia to use camels in his explorations, as early as the 1840s. At the time of his centenary memorial plaques were erected at

Penwortham, the small settlement he formed, and at Georgetown, Woocalla, and Horrocks Pass. When he negotiated the pass in 1846 his two drays capsized, the camel tore holes in the flour bags and bolted, leaving his possessions scattered all over the pass.

Horsham V   Named by the first settler, James Monckton Darlot, from his home town in Sussex, after he had established himself here in the 1840s. A Post Office and store began operations in 1849 and the town was surveyed in 1854. The Aboriginal name was Bongambilor, meaning Place of flowers.

Hotham, Mount V   The district was explored, and the mountain where the alpine village of Hotham Heights is situated, named by von Mueller in 1854 after Sir Charles Hotham, Governor of Victoria.

Hotspur V   Named by T. L. Mitchell after Sir Henry Percy.

Howe, Cape V   In his Journal, 20 April 1770, Captain Cook wrote: 'This point I have named Cape Howe.' This, the south-east limit of the mainland, was therefore named after Admiral Richard Howe, the first Earl Howe, who was Treasurer of the Royal Navy at that time.

Houtman's Abrolhos Islands WA   Abrolhos is derived from a Portuguese expression 'Abre olhos', meaning 'Look out!' or 'Be careful!' It was in 1619 that Frederick de Houtman, in command of the vessels *Dordrecht* and *Amsterdam,* sailed from Holland bound for the Spice Islands. In July the west coast of New Holland was sighted and on 30 July, he found his ships among the reefs and islands, to which he gave the Portuguese name, probably after recalling the similarly named rocks off the coast of Brazil. The implied warning was timely but in spite of this the *Pelsaert* was wrecked here in 1629, and the *Vergule Draeck* in 1656. The name appeared on Gerritz's chart published in 1622.

Howlong NSW   Aboriginal. A corruption of Oolong, Place of native companions.

Howqua V   According to A. E. Martin, the name came from a term for 'improvised tea'.

Hugel, Mount T   Named by George Frankland in 1835.

Hughenden Q   The town was built on the Hughenden station owned by Ernest Henry, and established by him in 1864. It was named after Hughenden Manor, the home of his maternal grandfather, in Buckinghamshire. As Henry had been accompanied by his friend Hugh Devlin in opening up a trail to Western Queensland, a year before he settled on the station, it may be conjectured that his friend's name was regarded as part of the name and possibly influenced his choice.

Hughes SA   After the Prime Minister, William Morris Hughes.

Hume Dam; Hume Highway; Hume Reservoir NSW, V   The Murray River was first named the Hume, in 1824, by W. H. Hovell after Andrew

Hamilton Hume, though there has been a suggestion that Hume named it after his father. Hovell was a retired sea captain who accompanied Hamilton Hume on an expedition from Lake George to Westernport in southern Victoria. They came to a wide river which, in spite of the name that was then conferred on it, became known as the Murray River. The dam, reservoir, and highway still preserve the explorer's name.

Humpty Doo Q   According to Bill Beatty in *Unique to Australia**, the first white settler made occasional trips to Darwin and when asked how he was getting on, replied, 'Everything's humpty doo.'

Hunt, Mount WA   After C. C. Hunt who set up a series of watering points between Kalgoorlie and Coolgardie.

Hunter Group T   Discovered by Flinders and Bass in December 1898, and named after Governor Hunter. From Flinders's Journal, 9 December: 'I have denominated them Hunter's Isles after His Excellency Captain Hunter, by whose orders this little voyage of discovery was made.'

Hunter River NSW   After Governor (and Admiral) John Hunter, named by Lieutenant T. G. Shortland in 1797. It had previously been discovered by a party of escaped convicts, in search of whom Shortland had been dispatched by the Governor. A fishing party had found coal at Newcastle, and Shortland made a similar find at the river, which for some years was known as Coal River. The Aboriginal name was either Coonanbarra or Gognon (or both).

Huon V   The name of Charles and Paul Huon who were pioneer settlers.

Huon River T   The river (and the peninsula) were named by d'Entrecasteaux in honour of his second-in-command, Huon de Kermadec, when he surveyed the channel between the mainland and Bruny Island, in 1792. It has been said that for the most part d'Entrecasteaux was intent on commemorating himself, but at least he accorded this honour to his lieutenant.

Huonville T   The town that arose on the banks of the Huon River was also named after de Kermadec.

Hurst Bridge V   The name of an early settler.

Hutt River SA   Named after Sir William Hutt, the British politician who took a practical interest in E. G. Wakefield's colonisation schemes. His name is perpetuated in New Zealand as well as in Australia.

Huxley, Mount T   Named by Charles Gould, the geologist, after the great British biologist, T. H. Huxley. Huxley was assistant surgeon on HMS *Rattlesnake* as a young man, and spent three years in Australian waters.

* Ure Smith, 1965.

119

Ida, Mount T   This classical Grecian name was applied by George Frankland in 1835.

Ilfracombe Q   After Ilfracombe in Devon, meaning Alfred's narrow valley.

Illabo NSW   A contraction of the familiar word Billabong. To avoid confusion with another place of the same name, q.v., the first and last two letters were deleted.

Illabrook V   Aboriginal. A corruption of Ilburro. Formerly Bulldog Creek.

Illaburra V   Aboriginal. A corruption of Ilburro.

Illawarra NSW   An adaptation of an Aboriginal word Elouera, Eloura, or Allowrie, variously translated as Pleasant place near the sea, or High place near the sea, or White clay mountain. Wurra or Warra probably means Mountain, and Illa may be White clay. George Bass and Matthew Flinders were the first to visit the district. Flinders recorded the fact that it 'was called Alowrie by the natives'. It was first known as Five Islands, but the name of the group of five islands off Red Point was transferred to part of the coastal district fifty miles south of Sydney, later known by the Aboriginal name of Illawarra. It was in use in 1806. In 1817 Governor Macquarie wrote of 'part of the coast known generally by the name of the Five Islands, but called by the natives Illawarra'.

Illawarra, Lake NSW   George Bass, Matthew Flinders, and the loblolly boy William Martin landed near the lake in their tiny 8-foot craft, the *Tom Thumb*, in March 1796, while in search of a reported river, and named the lake Tom Thumb's Lagoon. It was also known for a while as Big Tom Lagoon. The name Lake Illawarra was finally adopted and the name Tom Thumb's Lagoon was given to a stretch of water at Port Kembla.

Illbillee SA   Aboriginal. The meaning is not known, but someone once said that 'when the Aborigines named it they must have left their aspirates behind'.

Illilliwa NSW   Aboriginal. Setting sun, or West.

Iluka NSW   Aboriginal. Near the sea.

Imlay, Mount NSW   After the Imlay brothers, Alexander, Peter, and George, who came to New South Wales in 1829, 1830, and 1833 respectively. They were the pioneers of the Bega district.

Indooroopilly Q   Aboriginal. It may be a corruption of Windurripilly, Running water; but A. E. Martin gives the meaning as Gully of leeches.

Ingham Q   First settled in 1864, but the name was given on account of William Bairstow Ingham, an engineer, who settled here in 1873 and established the first successful sugar cane plantation in the district. An early name was Lower Herbert.

Ingleburn NSW   After Ingleburn in England.

Inglewood Q   First known as Brown's Inn, from a hotel on the Darling Downs, and then changed to Inglewood, a pleasing English place name. When a railway station was built the authorities wished to revert to the Aboriginal name, Parrieagana, but met with such opposition that when the Governor arrived for the opening ceremony the sign was discreetly removed.

Innamincka SA   Aboriginal. A corruption of Yidniminkani, 'You go into the hole there'. This commemorated an event when a totemic ancestor commanded a rainbow snake to disappear into a hole. The town site was named Hopetoun, but local preference for the Aboriginal name won the day.

Innisfail Q   First known as Nind's Camp, after an early settler, P. N. Nind; subsequent names centred round Thomas Henry Fitzgerald who commenced sugar cane cultivation in Queensland. It was so successful that the industry boomed and the town was renamed Geraldton in honour of Fitzgerald. This, however, led to confusion with Geraldton in Western Australia, and in 1911 it was changed to Innisfail, after Fitzgerald's property Innisfail, a Gaelic name meaning Isle of Destiny. A. E. Martin mentions that the final change was made when a consignment of goods arrived from the United States, addressed to a firm that was not known in Geraldton. It was then found that the correct destination was thousands of miles away on the other side of the continent.

Inscription, Cape WA   The captain of the *Eendracht*, Dirck Hartog, was the first European to set foot on the west coast of Australia. He landed on Dirk Hartog island in 1616, and set up a pewter plate with an inscription giving particulars of his visit. The cape was named in 1801 when Captain Hamelin of the French vessel *Naturaliste* visited the island. He found that another Dutch voyager, Willem de Vlamingh, had called at the island in 1697, and had replaced Hartog's plate with another to commemorate the same event.

Investigator Group SA   Named by Matthew Flinders in February 1802, on his voyage out from England in the *Investigator*.

Investigator Strait SA   The strait between Kangaroo Island and the mainland was named by Flinders, again after his vessel, on 26 March 1802. Shortly afterwards Nicolas Baudin passed that way and called it Détroit de Lacépède, being unaware of Flinders's earlier name. The French name did not survive.

Ipswich Q   Named Ipswich after the town in Suffolk, meaning Wide river mouth, by Governor Brisbane in 1843. The settlement was known as Limestone up till then. Captain Patrick Logan, who commanded the penal settlement at Moreton Bay, discovered calcareous hummocks which he first named Limestone Hills in 1827. The lime was transported to Brisbane in whaleboats by the convicts. The Aboriginal name was Tulmur.

Iron Knob SA   So named from the rich deposits of iron ore in this hill and the adjacent Iron Monarch. The towns were built when the Broken Hill Pty began the manufacture of steel in 1911.

Iron Monarch SA   See Iron Knob.

Ironstone, Mount T   In September 1836 Jorgen Jorgensen was sent by the Van Diemen's Land Company to try to find a practical route from the Shannon River to Circular Head. Mount Ironstone probably marks the limit of travel of his arduous task, and was so named because of its effect on the explorer's compass.

Irwin River WA   Discovered in 1839 by George Grey and named for Frederick Chidley Irwin, the commander of a detachment of soldiers assigned to the duty of protecting the Swan River settlement. For about 18 months he held the office of Governor of the Colony.

Isa, Mount Q   John Campbell Miles, a bushman and prospector, made an accidental discovery of a rich silver lead ore, and named the site Mount Isa after his sister Isabella. The mining centre, which is rich in silver-lead, copper, and uranium ores has since developed spectacularly.

Isaac River Q   Discovered on 12 February 1845 by Leichhardt, who named it after Frederick Neville Isaac, a squatter on the Darling Downs, who had helped with the organisation of Leichhardt's expedition.

Isdell River WA   Discovered and named by Frank H. Hann in 1903.

Isle of Condemned T   The worst of the convicts from Sydney were sent to a small island close to Settlement Island in Macquarie Harbour, and so this sinister name came into current use.

Ivanhoe NSW   Adopted from Sir Walter Scott's novel.

Jacky Jacky Q   The faithful Aboriginal companion of E. B. C. Kennedy who lost his life on Cape York Peninsula in November 1848, See under Kennedy Bay and River. He was given a silver breastplate bearing testimony to his courage and fidelity by the Governor. Jacky Jacky Creek is also named after him.

Jaffa, Cape SA   Named in 1802 by Nicolas Baudin after the port of Jaffa in Palestine, rendered Joppa in the Biblical narrative.

Jameroo NSW   Aboriginal. Track. A corruption of Jambaroo.

Jamestown SA   The town was laid out in 1871 and named after the Governor, Sir James Fergusson. The Main street was called Ayr after his birthplace, and others after towns in the County of Ayr. The Aboriginal name was Belalie, which has been retained for a stream, and for the township Belalie North.

Jamieson V   After a family of early settlers.

Jardine River Q   When John Jardine of Rockhampton was appointed to the command of the settlement at Somerset, on Cape York Peninsula, his two sons Francis Lascelles, and Alexander Jardine, aged 22 and 20 respectively, went ahead with the cattle to find a way to the site. They had much difficulty in avoiding the tortuous bends of a river which they supposed was the Escape. It is now known as the Jardine after the elder brother, Frank. They were also in constant danger from Aboriginal tribesmen. It is said by A. E. Martin that on their return they were met by Aboriginal employees of their father's, who greeted them with the words, 'Alicko! Franko! Tobacco!' so that they would not be taken for hostile tribesmen.

Jarvisfield Q   After Jane Jarvis, Governor Macquarie's first wife, whom he married in Bombay in 1793. She was the daughter of Thomas Jarvis, a former Chief Justice of Antigua. She died of consumption in 1792 at the age of twenty-four. Formerly called Picton.

Jeerabung NSW   Aboriginal. Corruption of Jerrabung, meaning Old man.

Jeetho V   Aboriginal. Send away.

Jenolan Caves NSW   Jenolan, or Geonowlan, was the Aboriginal name of a nearby mountain, with the possible meaning of Foot. It was officially adopted for the caves in 1884. At first they were known as McKeown's Caves, after a bushranger called McKeown or McEwan who, according to tradition, reported his discovery to Charles Whalan. However, no authentic record of such a bushranger has been found, though the stream that flows through the Devil's Coach House still bears his name. Charles Whalan's brother James may have been the discoverer of the caves. Another version of the story is that the bushranger was named White and that he camped in the Devil's Coach House. Later the caves were known as the Fish River Caves. There is an apocryphal account which ascribes the origin of the name to a supposed surveyor, J. E. Nolan. Aboriginal name, Binoomea or Benomera, Holes in a hill.

Jeparit V   Aboriginal. Home of small birds.

Jericho Q   After the Biblical town.

Jericho T   During the years from 1804 to 1809 Hugh Germaine, a private of Marines and two convicts ranged widely through the hinterland of Hobart Town, shooting kangaroos which provided food for the settlement. Germaine was reputed to have two books in his saddlebag, the *Bible* and the *Arabian Nights*, and these constant companions suggested names such as Jericho, Jerusalem (now Colebrook), River Jordan, Lake Tiberias, Bagdad, Abyssinia etc.

Jerilderie NSW   Aboriginal. Reedy place. Possibly derived from Jereeldrie. There is an amusing legend which has no basis in fact, that the wife of an early settler called her husband 'Gerald dearie' and, so the settlement received its name.

Jerrara NSW   Aboriginal. Place where the eels lie down, or Sleep. Originally the name was given to a sheep station.

Jerrawa NSW   Aboriginal. Goanna.

Jerseyville NSW   The Aboriginal name was Cussrunghi, Place of the white gum tree with the bark peeling off.

Jervis Bay NSW   The bay was first sighted by Captain Cook on 25 April 1770. He wrote: 'About 2 Leagues to the Northward of Cape St George the Shore seems to form a bay, which appear'd to be shelter'd from the N.E. winds; but as we had the wind it was not in my power to look into it, and the appearance was not favourable enough to induce me to loose time in beating up to it. The N. point of this bay, on account of its Figure, I nam'd Long Nose.' The bay was first entered by the transport *Atlantic* in 1791, and named by Lieutenant Richard Bowen, the naval agent aboard, in honour of Admiral Sir John Jervis, afterwards Earl St Vincent, under whom he had served.

Jervis, Cape Q   Named by Flinders on 23 March 1802 after Sir John Jervis.

Jervois Range NT   Named after the Governor of South Australia, Sir William Francis Drummond Jervois.

Jiggi NSW   Aboriginal. Satin bird; or possibly a kind of reed which grew profusely in the swamps near Lismore.

Jindalee NSW   Aboriginal. Bare hill (literally, No skin on bones). This name is applied to Morris Hill, which is bare on top while nearby hills are well timbered.

Jindivik V   Aboriginal. Torn apart.

John, Mount SA   A mountain that, strictly speaking, is still unnamed. The surveyor Sinnett wished to name it after a business partner, Ohlssen-Bagge, but this was never adopted. There is a story that says that a bus driver was often asked the name of the mountain behind the chalet and, not knowing the answer, replied, 'That's Mount John,' thereby saving himself a great deal of discussion.

Johnstone River Q   Discovered in 1872 either by Lieut Sydney Smith of HMS *Basilisk* (commanded by Captain John Moresby after whom Port Moresby is named) or by Robert Arthur Johnstone, Sub-Inspector of Police, when they led a party in search of survivors from the wrecked brig *Maria*. Moresby named the river the Gladys, but a year later G. A. F. E. Dalrymple renamed it the Johnstone, and the name Gladys was transferred to the inlet.

Jordan River T   See under Jericho.

Joseph Bonaparte Gulf WA   Named by Nicolas Baudin in 1803 after the eldest brother of the Emperor Napoleon. The name was removed by P. P. King, but reinstated after World War II.

Judgment Rock T   A curious name which is explained by Flinders's entry: '... two or three rocks, one of which obtained the name of Judgment Rock, from its resemblance to an elevated seat'.

Jukes, Mount Q   So named by G. A. F. E. Dalrymple after the famous geologist Joseph Beete Jukes.

Jukes, Mount T   Also named after the geologist, by Charles Gould.

Julia Creek Q   Named by R. O'H. Burke after an actress, Julia Matthews.

Jundha Q   Aboriginal. Woman.

Jumbuk V   Aboriginal. Cloud, or Sheep. Because of their white fleeces the Aborigines applied the word for clouds to them, and the early settlers adopted the term. In this case, however, the name may mean Conversation.

Jumbunna V   Aboriginal. Talking together, or Conference.

Junee NSW   Aboriginal. Speak to me. An earlier name was Loftus; the present name was first spelt Jewnee.

Jung V   Aboriginal. Mixed up, or In trouble.

Kadina SA   Aboriginal. A corruption of Kaddy-inna, Lizard plain. The township was surveyed in 1861, and named by Governor MacDonnell after the locality so named by the Aborigines.

Kadungle NSW   Aboriginal. A small lizard.

Kalangadoo SA   Aboriginal. Possibly from Kalangbool, Swamp with many red gums, and named after a station established in 1849.

Kalbar Q   Aboriginal. Star. It was earlier known as Engelsburg after Philip Engel, the first storekeeper. The German name was replaced during the first World War.

Kalgoorlie WA   Aboriginal. From Galgurli, a shrub which grew profusely in the locality. When Patrick Hannan found gold there in June 1893, the gold field was called Hannan's Find, but as it developed into a township this was thought unsuitable and as early as 1894 was replaced by its present name. Nevertheless old-timers referred to it affectionately as Hannan's. An early spelling was Kalgurli. To local residents it is Kal.

Kalkee V   Aboriginal. Timber.

Kalimnah V   Aboriginal. Beautiful.

Kalyan SA   Aboriginal. Stay here.

Kamarah NSW   Aboriginal. Sleep. At one time known as By Goo.

Kameruka NSW   Aboriginal. Wait here till I arrive. The original run of this name was taken up by W. and J. Walker.

Kandos NSW   Originally Candos, the name was compiled from the initials of the first six directors of the cement company located here. It became necessary to change it to Kandos because it was sometimes confused with Chandos in South Australia.

Kangaroo Island SA   Matthew Flinders has told the story of the experiences of the crew of the *Investigator* on the island, and the subsequent naming of it, in his Journal dated 22 May 1802:

'After coming to an anchor, some black substances were seen moving about on the Shore, by some of the young gentlemen, and were thought to be animals of some kind, but the wiser ones who thought they were lumps of stone, and that imagination supplied them with motion, laughed at this, asking if they were not elephants.

The 'black substances' turned out to be kangaroos, which had been so hard to identify in the dusk. 'The whole ship's company,' Flinders continued, 'was employed this afternoon, in skinning and cleaning the kanguroos; and a delightful regale they afforded, after four months privation from almost any fresh provisions. Half a hundredweight of heads, fore quarters, and tails were stewed down into soup for dinner on this and the succeeding days: and as much steaks given, moreover, to both officers and men, as they could consume by day and by night. In gratitude for so seasonable a supply I named this southern land Kanguroo Island.'

It is perhaps worthy of mention that Péron named it L'Isle Decreè in spite of Flinders's prior claim, but the French name was never adopted.

The island was not inhabited by any Aboriginal tribe. It was known to them as Karta. They believed that it had been made by Nurrundeeri, a cult-hero who turned his wives into the two small islands now known as The Pages.

Kanni SA   Aboriginal. Frilled lizard.

Kanyaka SA   Aboriginal. The property took its name from a rock 7 m in height which overlooks a water hole in the Kanyaka Creek. The original name was Undenyaka, The place of a stone, and had some religious significance, for those at the point of death lay under its shadow.

Kapunda SA   Aboriginal. A corruption of Kappie-oonda, Water jump out, or possibly Place of smoke.

Kaputar NSW   Aboriginal. A corruption of Kapular, entered by T. L. Mitchell on a sketch map on 3 January 1832.

Karangi NSW   Aboriginal. Duck.

Kardella V   Aboriginal. Possum.

Karkoo SA   Aboriginal. She-oak.

Karoonda SA   Aboriginal. Winter camp.

Karte SA   Aboriginal. Thick scrub.

Karuah; Karuah River NSW   An Aboriginal name which has survived in spite of the fact that when Governor Macquarie visited Port Stephens in 1812 he conferred the name Clyde on the river.

Katamitite V   Aboriginal. A word that refers to a camping ground near a water supply. That indefatigable collector of Australiana, Bill Beatty, has recorded that there was a local legend to the effect that one of the early settlers used to ask his wife, on his return from the local inn, 'Kate, am I tight?' A nearby creek was called Boosey, and Kate would reply, 'No, just half over the Boosey.'

Katanning WA   Aboriginal. A corruption of Kartannin, Big meeting place. A pond that is now in the central park was in fact a regular meeting place. One seemingly improbable explanation of the name is that it was that of an Aboriginal woman Kate Ann, or Anning.

Katherine; Katherine River NT   Leichhardt crossed the source of the river in 1845, but the real discovery was made by J. McDouall Stuart on his 1862 crossing of the continent and named by him after the daughter of James Chambers.

Katoomba NSW   Aboriginal. Falling together of many streams, or Waters tumble over hill. (Said to be derived from Kattatoon-bah.) In 1869 the railway from Wentworth Falls to Mount Victoria was opened. A siding at the 68-mile peg, to serve the quarry which supplied ballast for the line, was called Crushers or Crushings. A station was located there in 1876 and the name changed to Katoomba the following year.

Keer-Weer, Cape Q   Cabo Keerweer (Cape Turnagain) was the first European name bestowed on any part of Australia. The *Duyfken*, under the command of Captain Willem Jansz, and with subcargo Jan Lodewijs van Roosengin, sailed south-east from the coast of New Guinea and in 1606 coasted down the western shore of Cape York Peninsula. Running short of water and provisions, the captain turned back after reaching 'Cape Turnagain'. While surveying the Gulf of Carpentaria in 1802, Flinders confirmed the Dutch name 'from respect to antiquity'.

Keilor V   Aboriginal. Brackish water.

Keira, Mount NSW   Aboriginal. Brush turkey.

Keith SA   After Keith Stirling, the son of Sir Lancelot Stirling, naturalist.

Kellerberrin WA   Aboriginal, unknown. Earlier rendered as Killaburing.

Kelly Bay; Kelly Island T   Named after James Kelly, who sailed round Tasmania in 1815 and 1816. He may have discovered Port Davey and Macquarie Harbour in 1815. A few years later he was appointed harbour master and pilot on the Derwent. Kelly Point, the northern point of Bruny Island, is also named after him.

Kelly Country V   Glenrowan and district are known as 'the Kelly country' because of the activities of Ned Kelly and his gang.

Kempsey NSW   After the Valley of Kempsey on the Severn River in Worcestershire. Probably named by E. W. Rudder because of its likeness to the English valley. Meaning, Cymi's island.

Kempton T   After an early resident, Anthony Fenn Kemp. Formerly Green Ponds, so named because of the ponds in the vicinity.

Kendall NSW   Either named after Henry Kendall, one of the most important poets of the nineteenth century in Australia or, more probably, his uncle, Captain Joseph Kendall, a whaling-master.

Kenilworth Q   The name comes from Sir Walter Scott's novel.

Kenmore NSW   After a village in Perthshire, Scotland.

Kennedy Bay; Kennedy River Q   Named in memory of E. B. C. Kennedy who led an ill-fated expedition to the Northern Territory. They left from Rockingham Bay for Cape York on 30 May 1848. On 9 November Kennedy left most of his men at Weymouth Bay and struggled on towards Cape York, where a vessel was waiting for them, with four of his companions. Further privations decided him to press on with young Jacky Jacky, an Aboriginal boy, but Kennedy was killed. The rescue expedition found that six of the men left at Weymouth Bay had died of starvation. The only survivors of the expedition were the botanist, Carron, Goddard, and Jacky Jacky.

Kent Group T   Discovered by Matthew Flinders, who had been sent to recover the crew and cargo of the *Sydney Cove* that had been wrecked on the Furneaux Islands. In February 1798 he wrote: 'These two clusters were called Kent's Groups, in honour of my friend captain William Kent, then commander of the *Supply*.' Kent was a nephew of Governor Hunter.

Kentish T   Named after Nathaniel Lipscombe Kentish, the surveyor who superintended the construction of the road along the coast from Deloraine to the north-west.

Kentucky NSW   Probably named after the state of Kentucky, USA.

Keppel Bay; Keppel Islands Q   Named by Captain Cook in honour of Viscount Keppel, who later became First Lord of the Admiralty.

Kerang V   Aboriginal. A choice may be made between Moon, Cockatoo, and Parasite, all of which have been offered by way of translation.

Kergunyah V   Aboriginal. Camping ground above flood level. The first settlers were McKenzie and Wild, about 1842.

Kernot V   The name of the Chief Engineer of the Victorian Railways.

Kersbrook SA   Possibly a corruption of Kesbrook, for this was the name of John Bowden's birthplace in Cornwall, and the spelling he used when he painted the name on his bullock wagon in 1838.

Keyneton SA   After Joseph Keynes, one of the first pastoralists in the district.

Kiki SA   Aboriginal. Water hole where worms are found.

Kiacatoo NSW   Aboriginal. Shovel. The name of an early pastoral holding.

Kiama NSW   Aboriginal. A wide variety of translations has been suggested: Where the sea makes a noise; Plenty of food; Place where many fish may be caught; Fish may be caught from the rocks (Kia-ra-mia); or the name of the Creator Spirit, usually known as Baiame (or by similar names) in New South Wales.

Kiamel V   Aboriginal. To squat.

Kiata V   Aboriginal. The heat of summer.

Kidman Country NT   After Sir Sidney Kidman, who was known as the Cattle King of Australia. Also called Channel Country, q.v.

Kidston Q   After William Kidston, a bookseller who in 1906 became Premier of Queensland.

Kielpa SA   Aboriginal. Short distance.

Kiewa V   Aboriginal. Sweet water.

Kilcoy Q   After the Scottish home of Sir Evan McKenzie, the first run-holder in the district.

Kilkerran SA   The name was given by Governor Fergusson in memory of his Scottish home.

Killarney Q   After Killarney in County Kerry. The name is derived from the Celtic Cill Arne, Church of the Sloes.

Killawarra NSW, V   Aboriginal. Scrub.

Kilmore V   Although the district was settled as early as 1837 the present name was not given until 1941 when William Routledge bought a large estate for development and named it after his birthplace in County Cavan, Ireland.

Kimba SA   Aboriginal. Bush on fire.

Kimberley Range WA   Named in honour of the Earl of Kimberley, the British Colonial Secretary.

Kinchela NSW   After John Kinchela, Attorney-General of New South Wales, appointed in 1830, who arrived in Sydney in 1831.

King George, Mount NSW   The mountain was discovered in 1804 by the botanist George Caley, who named it Mount Banks in honour of his patron, Sir Joseph Banks. The name was not recognised and was changed to Mount King George.

King Edward River WA   Named by F. S. Brockman, Chief Surveyor of Western Australia, in honour of King Edward VII.

King George Sound WA   In 1791 Captain George Vancouver, in command of the *Discovery,* together with Lieut W. R. Broughton in the *Chatham,* sighted the west coast of New Holland on 16 August. On 28 August he arrived at the spacious harbour, which he named King George the Third's Sound. 'We took possession of the country,' he wrote, '. . . in the name of his present Majesty for him, his heirs, and successors, giving the port first discovered, the King's name — King George's Sound'. On a second visit a shore party climbed Mount Clarence and sighted Princess Royal Harbour.

King Island T   First discovered in 1798 by Captain Reid of the *Martha*, the island was named in January 1801 by John Black, in command of the brig *Harbinger* (the second vessel to pass through Bass Strait from the west), in honour of the Governor, P. G. King.

King Leopold Range WA   Named by Alexander Forrest, who explored much of the land in the vicinity, after King Leopold II of Belgium.

King Sound WA   Surveyed by J. L. Stokes in the *Beagle* in 1838, and named by him after Captain Philip Parker King, who had been in charge of an earlier survey of the north coast. King had terminated his survey at Disaster Bay on the west coast of the sound named after him.

Kingaroy Q   Aboriginal. Red ant. However there is some uncertainty about the origin of the name, some saying that it is a corruption of the Aboriginal word Kinjerroy, others that it came from an early settler by the name of King. Whatever the actual origin it is generally accepted that the town was named by C. R. Haly, the owner of the Taabinga station, in 1846.

Kinglake V   Named by Lindsay Beale after Alexander William Kinglake, the historian.

Kingoonya SA   Aboriginal. Nardoo seeds.

King's Cross NSW   Queen's Cross was the name given to the intersection of William and Victoria Streets and Darlinghurst and Bayswater Roads by the Municipal Council in 1897. It remained until 1905, when it was changed to the present name to avoid confusion with Queen's Square. Referred to in Sydney as 'The Cross'.

Kingscote SA   As well as being the principal town and port on Kangaroo Island, Kingscote also has the distinction of being the first town site decided on in South Australia. It was first known as Angas, after George Fife Angas, but the modesty of this outstanding citizen prompted him to protest, and it was changed to Kingscote, after Henry Kingscote, a member of the first Board of Directors of the South Australia Land Company. In 1883 the name was officially changed to Queenscliffe as a tribute to Queen Victoria, but the residents wished to retain the older name, which was eventually reinstated.

Kingston SA   Sir George Strickland Kingston, a pioneer surveyor and politician, was honoured by Governor MacDonnell in the naming of the town. In 1840 it had been called Maria Creek, after the brigantine that was wrecked offshore in the vicinity, the survivors all losing their lives at the hands of the Aborigines. Then it was renamed Port Caroline, after the *Caroline* which took shelter there from a gale, and finally changed to the present name at Governor MacDonnell's request.

Kingston T   First settled in 1804, the township was known as Brown's Bay after Robert Brown, the botanist, who was visiting Hobart Town at that time.

Kinnabulla V   The Aboriginal term used when cattle were shot for their meat.

Kirkstall V   After the town of Kirkstall in Yorkshire, meaning Site of a church.

Kissing Point NSW   A name that inevitably invites romantic conjecture, though it may have been suggested by boats 'kissing' the rocks as they came ashore. At least it can be said that picnics were sometimes held here, Lieutenant-Governor Paterson and Governor Hunter both being named as the fortunate recipient, perhaps when either one carried a lady ashore to keep her skirts dry. An even less credible story is that the men of a picnic party fell asleep in the hot sun, and were roused by the kisses of the girls of the party, and that one of them went so far as to suggest that the event should be commemorated by so naming the point. Now part of Ryde.

Kitchener NSW   After Field-Marshal Horatio Herbert Kitchener, Viscount of Khartoum and Aspall, noted for his army career in Egypt and during the First World War. Kitchener in Western Australia has the same origin.

Kittakittaooloo, Lake SA   Aboriginal. The meaning is not known but this and the sister lake Koolkootinnie are, as the *Australian Encyclopaedia* remarks, of perennial interest because of their flowing names.

Klemzig SA   Named after a town in Prussia by the German immigrants of 1838 and 1839, led by Augustus Kavell. The Aboriginal name was Warkowodli-wodli.

Knocker Bay NT   Entered by P. P. King in April 1818 and probably named by him.

Knowsley V   After Knowsley, near Liverpool in England.

Knuckey, Mount NT   The lagoon and doubtless the mountain were named after R. B. Knuckey who was in charge of a section of the Overland Telegraph line during its construction.

Kogarah NSW   Aboriginal. Place where rushes grow. Land was first granted here to John Townson, a soldier and pioneer settler, and first named Townson's Bay.

Koloona NSW   Aboriginal. Young man.

Kongorong SA   Aboriginal, from Koongeronoong, Corner.

Kongwak V Aboriginal. To catch.

Kookabookra NSW Aboriginal. A form of Kookaburra.

Koolywurtie SA Aboriginal. Rocky peninsula.

Koonadan NSW Aboriginal. Canoe

Koonda V Aboriginal. Day.

Koondrook V Aboriginal. Moon.

Koonwarra V Aboriginal. Oysters, or Swan.

Koorawatha NSW Aboriginal. Place of pine trees.

Kooreh V Aboriginal. Old man kangaroo.

Kootingal NSW Aboriginal. Sisters.

Koo-wee-rup V Aboriginal. A corruption of a word meaning Blackfish swimming.

Koppio SA Aboriginal. Oysters.

Korogoro, Cape NSW Aboriginal. Three-pointed headland.

Koroit V Aboriginal. Fire. There is a tradition of volcanic activity here, and vulcanologists believe that an eruption occurred here some 5,000 years ago — the most recent volcanic activity anywhere in the continent. There is now a lake in the crater and a number of lava hillocks in the national park.

Korong, Mount V Aboriginal. Canoe.

Korumburra V Aboriginal. Blowfly. An early name for the district was The Wild Cattle Run.

Korweinguborra V Aboriginal. An onomatopoeic word that imitates the croaking of a frog.

Kosciusko, Mount NSW After Tadeusz Kosciusko, the Polish patriot, and named on 15 February by Paul Edmund Strzelecki during his exploration of the Australian Alps in 1840. He wrote: 'The particular configuration of this eminence struck me so forcibly by the similarity it bears to a tumulus elevated in Krakow over the tomb of the patriot Kosciusko, that, although in a foreign country . . . . but amongst a free people . . . I could not refrain from giving it the- name Mount Kosciusko.' The *Australian Encyclopaedia* points out that Strzelecki's memory was at fault. Kosciusko was in fact buried in Krakow cathedral, but a memorial mound was erected on the outskirts of the city.

There has been much discussion on whether the peak Strzelecki climbed was actually Kosciusko. See Mount Townsend. The Aboriginal name of this part of the Australian Alps was Muniong or Munyong.

Kotupna V Aboriginal. A kind of grass frequently used for making nets.

Koyuga V Aboriginal. Clearing in the bush.

Krambach NSW   Aboriginal. From Krambakh, a species of gum tree. It is equally possible that the name may be of German origin.

Kulpara SA   Aboriginal. Water in head.

Kunama NSW   Aboriginal. Snow.

Kundabung NSW   Aboriginal. Place where apple trees grow.

Kungala NSW   Aboriginal. To shout, or Listen.

Kunlara SA   Aboriginal. Native companion.

Kununurra WA   Aboriginal. Big water.

Kuranda Q   Aboriginal name of a plant.

Ku-ring-gai NSW   Aboriginal. Either the name of a local Aboriginal group or clan which occupied the site of the future capital of New South Wales; or The hunting grounds of the Kuring clan.

Kurnell NSW   Probably a corruption of Aboriginal Kundle or Kundull, the Wild carrot. The name was varied over the years being known at different times as Cunthall, Colonel, Collonell, Kundel, Kundell, and Curnell. It has even been suggested that it was an attempt by the Aborigines to pronounce the surname of John Connell who bought Captain James Birnie's land grant of 700 acres in 1828. The district is notable as the scene of Cook's first landing in Australia, and a reserve and various monuments and plaques have been erected to commemorate Cook, Banks, Solander, and Midshipman (later Rear-Admiral) Isaac Smith, cousin of Mrs Cook, who was the first to set foot on the shore.

Kurrajong NSW   Aboriginal. The well-known tree which provides shade. This quality may be the real meaning of the name given to it by the Aborigines. It is the best fodder tree in Australia, provided bark fibre and edible roots for the Aborigines, and now makes a pleasing ornamental tree.

Kurri Kurri NSW   Aboriginal. Man, or First.

Kurumbul Q   Aboriginal. Scrub maggie.

Kwinana WA   Aboriginal. Pretty girl. The name, however, came from the freighter *Kwinana* of the State Shipping Service that was driven ashore in Cockburn Sound. The Australian Petroleum Refinery Company adopted the name for the site of its $80,000,000 oil refinery.

Kyabram V   Aboriginal. Dense forest.

Kybybolite SA   Aboriginal. Place of ghosts.

Kyneton V   After the English village of Kineton, near Stratford-on-Avon, meaning Royal manor.

Kywong NSW   Aboriginal. Camping place.

La Pérouse NSW   After Jean Francois de Galaup, Comte de la Pérouse, the celebrated French navigator, who camped on the shore of Botany Bay in January 1788. After leaving Botany Bay his ships were lost, and no trace of them was found until thirty years later, when Captain Dillon discovered relics of the expedition on the reef of Vanikoro, one of the islands in the Santa Cruz group. The wrecks were discovered in recent years by Reece Discombe, who lives at Port Vila, New Hebrides. In 1825 the son of Louis de Bougainville arranged for a monument to be erected to the memory of La Pérouse on the site of his camp in Botany Bay. The locality was known as Frenchman's Bay before receiving its present name.

La Pérouse, Mount T   Also named after the Comte de Pérouse.

Laanecoorie V   Aboriginal. Place of kangaroos.

Lacépède Bay SA   Discovered by Nicolas Baudin in 1802 and named by him in honour of Count B. G. E. Delaville de Lacépède, the French naturalist.

Lachlan River NSW   After Governor Lachlan Macquarie. The river was discovered in 1815 by Acting-surveyor G. W. Evans, and explored by John Oxley in 1814. The Aboriginal name was Callara.

Lady Barron T   Named after Lady Barron, wife of Sir Harry Barron, in 1910. Sir Henry was Governor of Tasmania and later of Western Australia.

Lady Julia Percy Island V   Discovered by Lieut James Grant in the *Lady Nelson*, who recorded in his Journal on 6 December 1800: 'I named this island Lady Julia's, in honour of Lady Julia Percy.' The Aboriginal name was Dhinmar.

Lady Nelson's Point; Lady Nelson's Reef NSW   After the *Lady Nelson*, a 16-ton brig which arrived in Australia in 1800 under the command of Lieut James Grant. Although christened 'His Majesty's Tinderbox' when launched, and her safe passage to Australia doubted, she arrived and was used extensively in the early days of the colony.

Ladysmith NSW   After Ladysmith, the town in Natal, which was the centre of the struggle at the beginning of the Boer War in South Africa.

Lakes Entrance V   A descriptive name. The holiday resort and fishing port stands on the east side of the narrow entrance between the ocean and the Gippsland Lakes. The interconnected lakes stretch for 80 km parallel with the Ninety Mile Beach, separated from the sea by a narrow line of sand dunes.

Lal Lal V   Aboriginal. Dashing waters.

Lalbert V   Aboriginal. A corruption of Laal-bit, Knob at the end of a mallee parasite.

Lamb Range Q   Named after E. W. Lamb, Secretary for Public Lands in Queensland in the 1860s.

Lamington Q   After Baron Lamington, the title name of Charles Wallace

Alexander Napier Ross Cochrane-Baillie, Governor of Queensland from 1895 to 1901. Lamington Plateau and Lamington National Park were also named after him.

Landsborough Q   Discovered by William Landsborough and Nathaniel Buchanan in 1860, and named after the former. The Aboriginal name was Waroojra, and the township was at one time known as Woodlands. Landsborough was on board the *Firefly* when she was wrecked on Sir Charles Hardy Island, where he hoped to establish a base for a search for Burke and Wills. Landsborough in Victoria was also named after William Landsborough.

Lang Lang V   While this has the appearance of an Aboriginal word, the place was actually named after an early settler whose name was Lang.

Langhorne Creek SA   After Alfred Langhorne, who brought cattle overland from Sydney in 1841.

Lantree NSW   Named after a surveyor.

Langwarrin V   The name was first used for a pastoral run established in 1853.

Lansdowne NSW   After Lansdowne, a suburb of Bath, Somerset, noted for the race meetings held on Lansdowne Hill. Meaning, Neck of land.

Lara V   Aboriginal. Hut on stony ground. Earlier names were Duck Ponds and Hovell's Creek.

Larpent V   The name of the ship on which many of the first settlers arrived.

Larras Lee Q   An estate in this locality, owned by Mr Lee, was known as Larras Lee.

Lascelles V   After an early settler, E. Lascelles.

Lasseter Country NT   The area in which this adventurous wanderer claimed to have discovered a rich gold-bearing reef. Lewis Harold Bell (Harry or Possum) Lasseter's reported discovery resulted in the setting out of an expedition, equipped with trucks and aircraft, in 1930. Lasseter was guide. After some difference of opinion with others in the party he went on alone, and disappeared. A search party, led by Bob Buck, eventually found his body, buried it, and returned with Lasseter's diaries. Buck was of the opinion that no such reef existed. The diaries were used by Ion L. Idriess as source material for his well-known book *Lasseter's Last Ride*.

Latrobe T   Named in 1861 after Charles Joseph La Trobe who was appointed Administrator for a short period in 1846 and 1847, and later became Lieut-Governor of Victoria.

Latrobe, Mount; Latrobe River V   The river was discovered and named by Angus McMillan in 1840 (though another claimant was W. A. Brodribb) the Glengarry River, later changed to the Latrobe (see previous entry).

Launceston T   David Collins, the first Lieut-Governor of Tasmania, ordered William Collins to make a reconnaissance of the Tamar River. During his search, he discovered the present site of Launceston, on 9 January 1804. A year later it was examined more thoroughly by Colonel William Paterson, who had already established a settlement further down the river, at Yorktown. By 1806 Paterson moved his settlement further up-river, to the site of Collins's discovery. Governor King then proposed to call it Patersonia. Paterson was not enamoured of the proposal, and the name was soon changed to Launceston, the birthplace in Cornwall of Governor King.

Launching Place V   The terminus for boats that plied on the Yarra River.

Laura SA   The town was laid out in 1872 on the property first taken up by J. B. and H. B Hughes in 1843, and named after the wife of H. B. Hughes. The Aboriginal name was Wirramatya, Gum tree flat.

Lauraville V   After Mrs Laura Hardy, the wife of a surveyor.

Lavender Bay NSW   After George Lavender, the bosun of a hulk in which convicts were accommodated before being sent to Norfolk Island. The bay was first known as Hulk Bay. Lavender married Susannah, daughter of Billy Blue, in 1834. The Aboriginal name was Quiberee.

Laverton WA   After a local pioneer, Dr Laver.

Lawley, Mount WA   Named after the popular Governor of Western Australia, in 1901, Sir Arthur Lawley, sixth Baron Wenlock. His term of office was short, for at the conclusion of the South African War he was appointed Lieut-Governor of the Transvaal.

Lawson NSW   After William Lawson, an early official and explorer in New South Wales. In 1813 he accompanied Blaxland and Wentworth in a successful attempt to cross the Blue Mountains, and was the surveyor in the party. Lawson was once known as Blue Mountains.

Leadville NSW   So named because of the silver-lead mines established here.

Learmonth; Learmonth, Lake V   It seems probable that the lake was named after Thomas L. Learmonth, who opened up a large area as emergency grazing during the drought year of 1837. The Learmonth family built the famous Scottish baronial mansion Ercildoun. A. E. Martin, however, says that Learmonth was named after Somerville Livingston Learmonth who explored the Buninyong district and discovered Lake Burrumbeet.

Learmonth WA   Named after Charles Learmonth, a pilot in the Second World War, who was killed when his Beaufort plane crashed. He was able to radio the events leading up to the crash, thus explaining several earlier accidents and helping to eliminate the cause.

Lebrina T   Aboriginal. Hut.

Leeton NSW   After Charles Alfred Lee, Minister for Works when the irrigation area was devleoped.

Leeuwin, Cape WA   One of the earliest names to appear on the map of New Holland. On Hessel Gerritz's chart, published in 1627 there was a note stating that ''t Landt van de Leeuwin' was discovered in March 1622. Nothing more is known save that the *Leeuwin* (Lioness) was dispatched to the East Indies about that time and that she arrived at Batavia in 1622. Her captain is not known. In December 1801 Flinders referred to the cape as 'the southern and most projecting part of Leeuwin's Land'.

Lefroy T   After Sir John Lefroy, Governor of Tasmania for a short period in 1880 and 1881. Formerly Nine Mile Springs.

Lefroy, Lake; Lefroy Mountain WA   The salt lake was discovered by Charles Hunt in 1864, and named after Henry Maxwell Lefroy, who had been engaged in exploratory work in that region a year earlier. Lefroy was assistant superintendent of the Fremantle gaol.

Legerwood T   Named after the parish in Scotland, the birthplace of Assistant-Surveyor James Scott, who explored the district in the Ringarooma, Scottsdale area.

Leichhardt, Mount NT   Named by J. McDouall Stuart, who was in search of Leichhardt, and who, after leaving Central Mount Stuart, wrote: 'I have seen no trace of him.'

Leichhardt River Q   Named in 1856 by A. C. Gregory, who was searching for the lost explorer Ludwig Leichhardt. While leading an expedition from Darling Downs to Port Essington, Leichhardt discovered the river on 6 August 1845. He thought it was the Albert River, so named by J. L. Stokes in 1841, and it was not until Gregory rediscovered it that it received its present name. Leichhardt disappeared in 1848 and the mystery has not yet been solved, although nine fully equipped expeditions and many lesser ones have been mounted over a period of more than a hundred years. Leichhardt Range was also named after the explorer.

Leigh Creek SA   Although E. J. Eyre crossed the creek at an early date, and the first settlers arrived about 1841, the name was not conferred until the arrival of Harry Leigh, who in 1856 took up an extensive area of land in the vicinity.

Leisler, Mount NT   Named after Louis Leisler, a Scotsman who tried unsuccessfully to establish grazing land on the Nullarbor Plain.

Lemana Junction T   Aboriginal. She-oak.

Lennard, Mount; Lennard River WA   Discovered in 1879 by Alexander Forrest, and named by him for his future wife Mary Barrett Lennard.

Leongatha V   Aboriginal. Teeth, or Tooth.

Leopold V   Named after Leopold, the Duke of Albany, son of Queen Victoria.

Leopold Range WA   See under King Leopold Range.

Leschenault Estuary WA   Discovered by de Freycinet in 1803 and named after the botanist on the *Geographe*.

Leslie Peak Q   After Patrick Leslie, the first settler on the Darling Downs, in 1840.

Lethbridge V   After a man who took part in the construction of the railway line. Its first name was Muddy Waterholes.

Leven River T   Discovered during a survey undertaken for the Van Diemen's Land Company and named after the English river.

Levendale T   Named after the river. See above.

Leveque, Cape WA   Sighted and no doubt named by Nicolas Baudin in the *Geographe* in 1801.

Leyburn Q   After Leyburn in Yorkshire, meaning Lylla's stream.

Liddel NSW   Possibly from the Liddel River, Roxburghshire, which gives its name to the Scottish Liddesdale; or after Henry Liddell, a noted professor at Westminster.

Light River SA   Named after Colonel William Light. The Aboriginal name was Yarralinka.

Lightning Ridge NSW   The name arose from an occasion when a flock of sheep were struck by lightning, or by a thunderbolt.

Lillico V   After Andrew Lillico, an early settler.

Lillimur V   Aboriginal. Bone.

Lilliput V   A settler named Gullifer gave the name in 1845, maintaining that he had found the fabulous land brought to life by Dean Swift.

Lilydale V   This was one of the earliest vine-growing areas in Victoria, originally named Yering, after William Ryrie's Yering cattle run. The vines were planted at Yering in 1838, and the town that arose was supposedly called Lily after the wife of Paul de Castella, who has been described as the first and most distinguished viticulturist.

Lima V   The owner of the estate from which the name came had visited Peru, and thus commemorated the occasion.

Limmen Bight NT   Named by Abel Tasman in 1644, after one of his vessels, the *Limmen*. On his chart he wrote 'limmens bocht'.

Lindeman Island Q   The Aboriginal name was Yarkiamba, Place of the red-throated.

Lindenow V   The name was given by a settler after a place he had known in India.

Lindesay, Mount NSW   After Sir Patrick Lindesay, Acting Governor of New South Wales. In 1831 T. L. Mitchell stated his intention of giving Lindesay's name to the range, but evidently did not do so. The range was called Nundewar, Lindesay's name being confined to the peak. It is sometimes misspelled Lindsay. A further complication arises from the fact that in 1827 Allan Cunningham named the peak Mount Hooker after the noted English botanist. Lindesay's name was given to the peak now known as Mount Barney, but a reallocation was made later. The Aboriginal name of the present Mount Lindesay was Talcumbin or Jalgumbun.

Lindesay River SA Named by Sturt during his 1829-1830 expedition, after Patrick Lindesay, an officer in his regiment.

Linga V Aboriginal. A corruption of Lingi, Camp.

Lipson SA After Captain Lipson, the first Harbourmaster at Port Adelaide. The Aboriginal name for Lipson Cove was Budiu.

Lismore NSW So named by William Wilson, an early station-owner, because the scenery resembled that of the Island of Lismore off the mouth of Loch Linnhe, Argyllshire, Scotland. The Aboriginal name was Tuckurimbah, Tuckerimbah, or Tchukarmboli, meaning Glutton, or Junction of two creeks. Lismore South was Pwooyam, Sleeping lizard.

Lismore V After a place in Ireland. Once called Brown's Waterholes. The Aboriginal name was Bongerimennin.

Lithgow NSW After William Lithgow, Auditor-General of New South Wales. The name of the first station was Cooerwull, and the site of the present city was first known as Lithgow Valley.

Liverpool NSW After the second Earl of Liverpool who became Prime Minister of Britain, the name being given by Governor Macquarie in 1810.

Liverpool Plains; Liverpool Range NSW Named by John Oxley in 1818 after the Earl of Liverpool. See preceding entry.

Liverpool River NT On 30 July 1818 P. P. King discovered and named the river, and went some distance up it. It is thought that it is the same river as the Speult that was charted by the captain of the *Arnhem* in 1623.

Lizard Island Q On 12 August 1770 Cook wrote in his Journal: 'The only land Animals we saw here were Lizards, and these seem'd to be pretty Plenty, which occasioned my naming the Island Lizard Island.'

Llanelly V A name given by a number of miners in memory of their home in Wales.

Lobethal SA The name means Valley of praise, or blessing. (See 2 Chronicles 20:26.) The word comes from Luther's translation and was used with high hope by the German Lutheran settlers who arrived in 1841 after fleeing from persecution in their own country. The wave of anti-German feeling in World War I resulted in the town being renamed Tweedvale, but the original choice was restored in 1935.

Loch V After the Governor of Victoria, Henry Broughan Loch, who later became Baron Loch.

139

Lochiel NSW   Named by a Scotsman Ewan Cameron, doubtless after the chief of the clan Cameron and the hero of Thomas Campbell's *Lochiel's Warning.*

Lochinvar NSW   After the hero of the ballad included in the fifth canto of *Marmion* by Sir Walter Scott.

Lockhart NSW   After C. G. N. Lockhart, the district surveyor, and one of the first Commissioners of Crown Lands in New South Wales.

Lockhart River Q   Named by R. Logan Jack after Hugh Lockhart of Edinburgh.

Locksley NSW   Although this place was once known as Locke's Platform, it is said that the present name came from Alfred Lord Tennyson's *Locksley Hall,* published in 1842. The place was first known as Dirty Swamp.

Lockyer Valley Q   Probably named after Edmund Lockyer who was dispatched by Governor Brisbane to explore the Brisbane River in 1825, and then to Western Australia to forestall any possible French occupation of that territory. He arrived at King George Sound on Christmas Day 1826, and declared the territory a British possession.

Loddon River V   First named Yarrayne River (the Aboriginal name), but later renamed the Loddon, which Sir Thomas Mitchell, who discovered it in 1836, transferred from another river, which was then called the Avoca. The name was given 'from its resemblance in some respects to a little stream in England'. Meaning, Muddy river.

Lofty, Mount SA   While Matthew Flinders was examining the St Vincent Gulf in the *Investigator,* he used the words 'a lofty mountain' in his Rough Log on 28 March 1802, and on 1 April, 'Mount Lofty'. The latter date is therefore to be regarded as that on which the name was conferred. A monument on the summit commemorates the sighting and naming. The Aboriginal name was Yure Idla, Place of the ears, or Whelp's ears.

Logan River Q   When Patrick Logan, Commandant of the Moreton Bay convict garrison from 1826 to 1830, discovered the river he named it the Darling after Governor Darling, but Darling changed it in recognition of Logan's discovery. Logan is remembered both for his exploratory journeys and for his brutality as a commander in this difficult position.

Long Nose Point NSW   In his Journal for 25 April 1770, Captain Cook wrote: 'The N. point of this bay [Jervis Bay], on account of its Figure I nam'd Long Nose.' Aboriginal name Yerroulbine, Swift running water.

Longford T   When settlers who had been removed from Norfolk Island in 1807 and 1808 arrived, the district was known as Norfolk Plains. Then for a short time Latour, and finally Longford, possibly through the influence of Roderic O'Connor who took up land here.

Longford V   After Lord Longford.

Longlea V   Named after a pioneer settler, W. J. Long.

Longreach Q   The name is derived from the long reach of the Thomson River.

Longwood V   The town took its name from Napoleon's residence on St Helena.

Lonsdale, Point V   After Captain William Lonsdale, the first Administrator at Port Phillip.

Lookout, Point Q   The conspicuous headland on North Stradbroke Island was named by Cook as he was endeavouring to find a way through the shoals. On 11 August 1770 he wrote: '...the point I am now upon, which I have named Point Lookout...' He gave the same name earlier to a point on the northern side of Moreton Bay.

Lord Howe Island   Named after the British Admiral by the discoverer, Lieut Lidgbird Ball in February 1788. Mount Lidgbird, on the island, is named after him.

Lorne V   First named Loutit Bay after Captain Loutit who called here while on a voyage to London in 1841 with the first consignment of wool from the district. When the township became a seaside resort in 1871 the name was changed to Lorne, after the town in Argyllshire, Scotland.

Lowaldie SA   Aboriginal. Summer.

Lowly, Point SA   Flinders's Journal, 9 March 1802: '...the furthest hummock seen from the anchorage was distant four or five miles; it stands on a projection of low sandy land, and beyond it was another similar projection to which I gave the name *Point Lowly*'.

Lowood Q   So named because of the low brigalow scrub in the vicinity.

Loxton SA   First known as Loxton's Hut, from a hut built by W. C. Loxton, a boundary rider on the Bookpunong station. The town was not proclaimed until 1907 and named Loxton by Governor Le Hunte.

Lucinda; Lucinda Point Q   The name of the point and the settlement came from that of a Government steam yacht.

Lucindale SA   Named after Lady Lucinda Musgrave, wife of Governor Musgrave.

Lucky Bay; Lucky, Mount WA   The *Investigator* was in great danger when off Mondrain Island in Esperance Bay. Flinders consulted with the Master, John Thistle, took the only course left to him, and steered for the mainland where he could see a sandy beach. The decision proved to be the right one, for they were able to enter a sheltered bay and cast anchor. This was the reason Flinders chose the name Lucky on 9 January 1802. While on shore, the botanist, Broome, gathered more than 100 specimens of plants new to naturalists.

Lunawanna T   Lunawanna-alonna was the Aboriginal name for Bruny

Island. It has been preserved in the present name and that of Alonnah, both on Bruny Island.

Lyell, Mount T   Discovered by the Government geologist Charles Gould and named by him after Sir Charles Lyell, the noted British geologist.

Lynd Range; Lynd River Q   The river was discovered by Leichhardt on 22 May 1845 on his first expedition and named by him on 9 June 1845 after one of his strongest supporters, Robert Lynd, who was an army officer and social worker. Leichhardt described him as 'a generous friend... and a splendid adviser when I am feeling restless'. The range as well as the river were named for Lynd.

Lyndhurst NSW, V   Possibly after John Singleton Copley, Baron Lyndhurst, Lord Chancellor.

Lyndhurst SA   Also named in honour of 'the most eloquent Lord Lyndhurst', by Samuel Parry.

Lyndoch SA   Named by Governor Gawler after General Lyndoch, a veteran of the Peninsula War. The Aboriginal name was Putpa or Putrayerta.

Lyons WA   After Joseph Aloysius Lyons, Prime Minister of Australia from 1931 to 1939.

Macalister NSW   After Lachlan Macalister, soldier and pioneer, who was in charge of the mounted police at Goulburn Plains in 1829.

Macalister River V   In 1839 Lachlan Macalister sent Angus McMillan on an exploratory journey from Picton into eastern Victoria, and this and later expeditions resulted in the discovery and settlement of Gippsland. McMillan named the river after his employer.

McArthur River Q   Named on 21 September 1845 by Leichhardt, while on his first expedition, after James and William Macarthur of Camden, who were good supporters. James Macarthur was the fourth son of Captain John Macarthur, and William the fifth son. The name applied to the river was correctly spelt by Leichhardt, but has since been changed.

Macdonald, Lake SA   The lake was discovered and named by Henry Tietkens who was conducting an exploration in the vicinity of Lake Armadeus in honour of A. C. Macdonald, Secretary of the Victorian branch of the Royal Geographical Society of Australasia.

MacDonnell Range NT   Named by J. McDouall Stuart on his fourth continental crossing of the continent from south to north in honour of the Governor of South Australia, Sir Richard Graves MacDonnell. MacDonnell Creek and McDonnell Bay were also named for the Governor.

McIlwraith Range Q   Named by Captain Moresby after Sir Thomas McIlwraith, the Premier of Queensland.

Macintyre River NSW   Named by Allan Cunningham in 1827 after Peter Macintyre, manager of the Segenhoe station on the upper Hunter River. Aboriginal name Karaula.

Mackay Q   In January 1860 Captain John Mackay left Armidale at the head of an expedition which reached Rockhampton. Near the source of the Isaac River there was trouble with hostile Aborigines, after which a river, which they named the Mackay, and its fertile valley, were discovered. On the return journey an Aboriginal lad who had accompanied them died. Mackay fell ill and the members of the expedition were in a desperate case until they met two settlers who were able to assist them. About this time a stream near Rockhampton was named the Mackay by Captain Burnett, and the Mackay River renamed the Pioneer. The Government then sanctioned the name Mackay for the township that arose from the station.

Mackay, Lake NT   The lake was not discovered until 1931 when Donald Mackay was conducting an aerial survey and sighted a sheet of water W.N.W. of Alice Springs, on the border of Western Australia.

Mackenzie River Q   Named on 12 January 1845 by Leichhardt on his first expedition, after Sir Evan Mackenzie who had assisted him in the preparations.

Maclean NSW   After the surveyor who planned the first settlement. Before this it was known as Rocky Mouth.

Macleay, Point; Macleay Range; Macleay River NSW   After Alexander Macleay, scientist and official, who played an important part in the early history of the colony. The Macleay Islands in Moreton Bay, Queensland, were also named after him. The Forest Kingfisher, *Halcyon macleayi*, was also named after him. The Aboriginal name of Macleay Point was Yarrandabby.

McPherson Range Q, NSW   Named in 1828 by Allan Cunningham after Major Duncan McPherson of the 39th Regiment.

Macquarie Fields; Macquarie, Lake; Macquarie Pass; Macquarie River NSW Governor Lachlan Macquarie and his wife have been commemorated in many place-names. The Governor was appointed in 1809 by Lord Castlereagh, Secretary of State for the Colonies. His instructions read: 'The Great Objects of attention are to improve the Morals of the Colonists, to encourage Marriage, to provide for Education, to prohibit the Use of Spirituous Liquors, to increase the Agriculture and Stock, so as to ensure the Certainty of a full supply of the inhabitants under all Circumstances.' Macquarie endeavoured to carry out these instructions, and in pursuance of a policy of increasing agriculture and stock, he encouraged exploration, and named several new towns (including one to honour Lord Castlereagh). His term of office was extended to 1822. The Macquarie River was discovered and named by George William Evans in 1813. The

Aboriginal name was Wammerawa, or Wambool; Lake Macquarie was Awaba, Level surface.

Macquarie Harbour T   Supposedly discovered by James Kelly in 1815. He circumnavigated Van Diemen's Land in a whale boat and anchored in the harbour on 24 December 1818. It was named after Governor Macquarie.

Macquarie Strait NT   When P. P. King set the *Mermaid's* course for Cape Arnhem in 1818, he passed through seas swarming with turtles, snakes, sharks, and dolphins, and anchored off Goulburn Island, naming the strait through which he had passed after Governor Macquarie.

Macrossan; Macrossan Range Q   After the Hon John Murtagh Macrossan, Minister of Mines. The Macrossan Range was named by John Moresby.

Maatsuyker Islands T   Named by Abel Tasman in 1642 after a member of the Dutch Council of India. The largest island is De Witt Island (or Big Witch). On Maatsuyker Island (or Little Witch) the most southerly lighthouse in Australia is located.

Macedon, Mount V   The mountain was sighted by Hume and Hovell in 1824, and climbed by T. L. Mitchell on 30 September 1836. Mitchell could see Port Phillip from the summit, and by recalling his ancient history named it Mount Macedon, apparently because Philip of Macedon, the father of Alexander the Great, happened to have the same name. The Aboriginal name was Geboor.

Macorna V   Aboriginal. Geese.

Madge's Hill SA   Named by W. G. Evans after his daughter Beatrice Madge Evans.

Madman's Track WA   This well-formed road in the Pilbara country was at one time described as a track that only a madman would use, for it traversed 1500 km of mulga and sandy wastes.

Maffra V   One of the early settlers, William Bradley, had served in the Peninsula War, and recollected a pleasant stay at the town of Mafra in Portugal. He gave the name to his property. When the town site was surveyed in 1865, Bradley's choice of name was adopted, but suffered in spelling.

Magnetic Island Q   'The East point I named Cape Cleveland,' wrote Cook on 6 June 1770, 'and the West, Magnetical Head or Island, as it had much the appearance of an Island; and the Compass did not traverse well when near it'. The phenomenon noted by Cook has not since been observed.

Maindample V   Aboriginal. Female breasts.

Maitland NSW   After James Maitland, Earl of Lauderdale. There have been changes and some confusion in the names given to this city on the Hunter River. The first settlement was formed by 'eleven well-behaved convicts' between 1818 and 1821. The part eventually known as West Maitland was known first as The Camp, then as Molly Morgan's Plains. Mary or Molly Jones married William Morgan and was transported to New South Wales in 1790 for stealing a few dollars' worth of yarn. She escaped and entered into a bigamous marriage in England. When transported a second time (for arson) she was settled at the place named after her, but the name was later changed to Wallis or Wallis's Plains after Captain James Wallis, the Commandant at Newcastle. She married for a third time in 1826 and died in 1833.

Wallis Plains were also known as Green Hills. The government town here, surveyed in 1829, was named Maitland, while the earlier settlement remained as Wallis Plains. But as Wallis Plains was also known as Maitland, some confusion arose and in 1855 the names East Maitland and West Maitland were officially adopted. The Aboriginal name of the former was Illulong and the latter Cooloogooloheit.

Maitland SA After Julia Maitland, daughter of the Earl of Lauderdale. The Aboriginal name was Madi-waltu, White flint.

Majorca V After the Mediterranean island.

Malakoff Q After a Russian sailor who established an inn hereabouts.

Malay Road NT This name recalls an interesting event in February 1803 when Matthew Flinders anchored in a roadstead south-west of Bramby's Islands and saw a number of prows from Macassar. The Malayans were searching for trepang (beche-de-mer). Flinders was visited by six Captains of the Malay prows, and presents were exchanged. The leader of the fishing expedition was Pobasso who had been one of the first of his people to come to Arnhem Land, some 26 years earlier. Flinders named one of the islands after him and the place of meeting, Malay Road.

Maldon V The name was given in 1856, after a port in Essex, meaning Hill surmounted by a monument or cross. It was first called by its Aboriginal name, Tarrangawer, Big Mountain.

Mallanganee V Aboriginal. Pine tree hill.

Mallee District V, SA This large expanse of country between the Wimmera and Murray Rivers, now largely cleared for wheat growing, was at one time covered by the dwarf eucalypt known as mallee.

Malmsbury V After the third Earl of Malmesbury, secretary of state for Foreign Affairs. Formerly Columbine.

Mandurah WA Aboriginal, from Mandjar, Trading place. It was one of the great sites where bartering took place between the tribes, tools, ornaments, weapons, shells, and other objects being exchanged in a trading system that had links across the continent. The name for the Peel Inlet here, was taken from an early settler, Thomas Peel, who adopted the Aboriginal name for his property.

Mandurama NSW Aboriginal. Water hole. It was the name adopted by Thomas Icely for his house.

Mandurang V Aboriginal. Cicada.

Mangalore V After Mangalore on the Malabar coast of India.

Mangana T Mangana was a leader of the Aborigines on Bruny Island.

Manilla; Manilla River NSW A corruption of the Aboriginal word Manellae, Muneela, or Munila, Winding river, or Round about river. The Manilla River formed an almost complete circle here. George Veness, who settled at the junction of the Namoi and Manilla Rivers, was responsible for the present spelling and pronunciation.

Manly NSW When Governor Arthur Phillip saw a number of Aborigines on 22 January 1788 and noted their proud bearing he gave the name Manly Cove; this name was therefore conferred even before that of Sydney Cove.

Mann Range NT, SA The range, which is an Aboriginal reserve, inhabited by the Pitjantjatjara tribe, was discovered by W. C. Gosse in 1873 and named after Charles Mann, a celebrated lawyer in South Australia.

Mannahill SA The name consists of two separate words, the first of which is supposedly from the food miraculously supplied to the Israelites after their flight from Egypt. It may have been coined by someone with good Biblical knowledge because the run had a good tucker shop, according to A. E. Martin.

Manning River NSW Possibly after Sir William Montagu Manning, politician and judge.

Mannum SA Aboriginal. Possibly a contraction of Manunph, the meaning of which is not known.

Manoora SA Aboriginal. A spring. A proposal to call it Chingford came to nothing.

Mansfield V After a village in Nottinghamshire, the name being given in the 1850s.

Mantung SA Aboriginal. White man's camp.

Maralinga SA Aboriginal. Thunder.

Marama SA Aboriginal. White duck.

Maranda Q Aboriginal. Hand, so called because the river and its tributaries had the appearance of a human hand. The name was adopted by T. L. Mitchell in 1846.

Marathon Q It seems likely that it was named from the famous place where the Greeks, outnumbered, successfully withstood an attack from the Persian army.

Marble Bar WA The quartz bar across the Coongan River, which gives its name to the mining town, is of red and blue jasper quartz. It lies like a dam across the wide river bed. Marble Bar is noted for its temperatures which in 1923 and 1924 never fell below 38°C for 160 days on end. It is reputed to be the hottest place in Australia. For a time it was known by its aborig.inal name of Nullagine, which is 130 km to the south.

Marburg Q   Named after a place in Saxony. It was first known as Sally Owen's Plains, after the wife of Robert Owen. Husband and wife were both shepherds. It was then called Rosewood Scrub, and finally Marburg.

Mardan V   Aboriginal. Scene of the tragedy or calamity.

Mareeba Q   Aboriginal. Meeting of the waters. Earlier names were Abbat Creek and Granite Creek.

Margaret, Mount SA   Named after Mrs Margaret Baker, the wife of A. J. Baker, the Superintendent of Fire Brigades in South Australia.

Maria Island NT   After Maria van Diemen, wife of the Governor-General of the Dutch East Indies. It was discovered and named by Abel Tasman, who honoured the same lady with the name Cape Maria van Diemen in New Zealand.

Maria Island T   Also named after Maria van Diemen by Tasman.

Maria, Lake T   After Lady Pedder. See under Lake Pedder.

Marion Bay T   After the French navigator and explorer, Marion du Fresne, who was killed by Maoris at the Bay of Islands, New Zealand. Du Fresne anchored in Marion Bay in 1772.

Marlee NSW   Aboriginal. Elderberry, a tree with small edible berries.

Marlo V   Aboriginal. Kangaroo.

Marnoo V   Aboriginal. Finger.

Marong V   Aboriginal. Murray pine.

Maroochy Q   The township and the river name are derived from the Aboriginal muru: bill; kutchi: red, so the name is that of the red bill or black swan.

Maroochydore Q   Aboriginal. Water where the black swan lives. See above.

Maroona V   Aboriginal. Pine trees.

Marrabel SA   After John Marrabel, a butcher of Adelaide who had property in the district.

Marrakai, Plains of NT   In a letter in *Walkabout*, June 1971, the writer states: 'The earliest white mapmakers asked a group of Aborigines for the native name of the area and the natives, knowing that the white man's name for a nearby river had been "Mary", and aiming to please, tried to say it was "the Mary River" area. It all came out as "Mary-kai" (the word kai being that of a river), and this was recorded for the future as "Marrakai".'

Marrar NSW   Aboriginal. Wolf spider, a ground-dwelling hunting spider about 2½ cm in length. The name may also mean Hand. It was first given to a station owned by J. P. Cox.

Marrawah T   Aboriginal. Gum trees.

Marree SA   Aboriginal. Place of possums. While the retention of Aboriginal names is an interesting and commendable feature of the Australian scene, it may be regretted that in this case the first European name was replaced during the ridiculous anti-German sentiment of the first World War. The first government township was named Hergott Springs in 1883. D. D. Herrgott (the correct spelling of his name) was a Bavarian artist and naturalist who discovered the springs together with J. McDouall Stuart in 1859. At the time of Herrgott's discovery there were 12 springs with a perennial water supply. The name Marree was chosen by G. W. Goyder.

Marsden NSW   After the Rev Samuel Marsden, Chaplain of New South Wales, who was also a magistrate and farmer and an eminent character both in Australia and New Zealand. The *Australian Dictionary of Biography* concludes a lengthy entry: '... his life, though often embittered by controversy, was relieved by substantial achievement and sustained by a confidence in the future of his adopted country.'

Martha, Mount V   After Martha Lonsdale (nee Smythe), wife of William Lonsdale, the first Administrator of Port Phillip.

Martin's Creek NSW   After an early settler.

Marulan NSW   An Aboriginal name which should be Murrawoollan, and may formerly have been spelt in this way.

Mary Kathleen Q   Named after Mary Kathleen McConachy, the wife of one of the discoverers of uranium in 1954. The prospectors Norman McConachy and his friends Clem Walton and son John were fossicking in the Mount Isa-Cloncurry district when McConachy's geiger counter indicated radio-active deposits. The friends sold the claim they established for $500,000 and a 9% shareholding in a company called Mary Kathleen Uranium Ltd, and the town was given the same name. Mrs McConachy died a few weeks after her husband's discovery. To locals the town is known as Mary K.

Mary River NT   Discovered by J. McDouall Stuart in 1862 and named after Mary Chambers.

Mary River Q   The river was discovered in 1842 by Andrew Petrie and Henry Russell, who had been sent to Moreton Bay to capture two escaped convicts who were living with an Aboriginal tribe. In 1847 it was explored by the surveyor J. C. Burnett and named for Lady Mary FitzRoy, the wife of the Governor, Sir Charles FitzRoy. Aboriginal names were Goodna, Monoboola, Morraboocoola, and Yaboon.

Maryborough Q   The town takes its name from the river. See above.

Maryborough V   Named after the birthplace in Ireland of the first Police Commissioner stationed on the goldfield in 1854. Before this the area had been settled by the Simson brothers who took up land in 1840. It was first named Simson's Plains, and Charlotte Plains after Mrs Charlotte Simson.

Maryvale NSW   So named because it was located on the banks of the Mary River.

Marysville V   After Mary Heales, daughter of Richard Heales.

Massacre, Lake SA   Named by John McKinlay in 1861, when he believed, mistakenly, that the local Aborigines had killed a number of Europeans at this place. It was here that McKinley and his party found the grave of Gray, a member of the Burke and Wills expedition. The Aboriginal name of the large water hole was Cadhi-baerri.

Mathinna T   The name of an Aboriginal girl who was befriended by Sir John and Lady Franklin.

Matong NSW   Aboriginal. Great, strong, or powerful. It was here that an Aboriginal displayed extraordinary strength on one occasion. The name was first applied to a pastoral holding.

Maxwelton Q   After Maxwelton in Scotland.

Mayday, Mount V   The mountain was climbed by Joseph Fossey on 1 May 1827.

Meadows SA   The name, which was probably descriptive, was given in 1839. The Aboriginal name was Battunga, Place of large trees.

Meatian V   Aboriginal. Moon.

Meeniyan V   Aboriginal. Moon.

Melbourne V   Although Hume and Hovell reached the western shore of Port Phillip at the conclusion of their 11 weeks overland journey (and believed they had reached Westernport), and an abortive settlement was located here to prevent French ambitions, it was not until John Batman came from Tasmania as agent for what was known as the Port Phillip Association, that a permanent settlement was located here. Batman 'purchased' 600,000 acres of land, and in the same year, 1835, John Pascoe Fawkner formed another independent settlement. Governor Bourke visited the locality in 1837, repudiated Batman's purchase, and in March of that year authorised the survey of a town site which he named after Lord Melbourne, the British Prime Minister. The site at the mouth of the Yarra was called Williamstown, after King William IV, Melbourne being reserved for another a little further inland. Names proliferated in those early days. The settlement was called Batmania and Glenelg (after the British Secretary of State for the Colonies, in Tasmania). Other names were Bearbrass, Bearport, Bearheap, and Bearbury, which were all variations of the Aboriginal Berrern or Bararing, and Doutigalla.

Melrose SA   Probably named after Melrose in Scotland; but there is a tradition that it was named by a surveyor who fell ill and was nursed back to health by the mother of George Melrose, a pastoral pioneer.

Melton V   After Melton Mowbray in Leicestershire.

Melville Island NT   Named by P. P. King during his north coast survey in 1818 in honour of Viscount Melville, First Lord of the Admiralty. The island had been sighted by Tasman in 1844, who thought it was part of the mainland. A settlement was formed by J. G. Bremer who took possession of the island on 26 February 1824. The Aboriginal name was Yermalner.

Memory Cove SA   It was here that Flinders set up a copper plate in February 1802 to commemorate the loss of several of his crew under tragic circumstances. The plate was replaced by a copy in 1897, the original now being kept in the Adelaide Museum. See under Cape Catastrophe and Thistle Island.

Menindee NSW   Aboriginal. Egg yolk. An earlier name was Laidley Ponds. A store was built here in 1859 and in 1862 it was chosen as the site of a town to be named Perry. Later it reverted to the Aboriginal name, first of Menindie, then Menindee. Another Aboriginal name for the locality was Williorara.

Meningie SA   Aboriginal. Mud.

Mentone V   After the Mediterranean health resort, the name being given by a development company. Formerly Dover Slopes.

Merbein V   Aboriginal. A corruption of Merebin, Sandhills. The town was first known as Whitecliffs.

Meribah SA   The name comes from the Book of Exodus, 17:7. It was the name of the rock that was struck by Moses, producing a stream of water for the thirsty Israelites, and was certainly an appropriate choice for an artesian bore.

Merimbula NSW   Aboriginal. Place of the big snake.

Merinda Q   Aboriginal. Beautiful woman.

Merino V   The Henty family were engaged in the breeding of merino sheep here.

Mernda V   Aboriginal. Earth.

Merredin WA   Aboriginal. The name was derived from Merret, the term for Timber. There is a bare mass of granite rock here, discovered by C. C. Hunt in 1864. It was near this rock that the Aborigines cut 'timber' for making spears.

Merrigum V   Aboriginal. Small plain.

Merrijig V   Aboriginal. Well done.

Merriton SA   Named after the president of a local cricket club, whose name was George Merrit.

Merriwa NSW   There have been several conjectures on the origin of this Aboriginal name. It seems that it was a favourite camping ground, and that the flat land at the junction of the Goulburn and Merriwa Creeks produced an abundance of grass. The seeds were gathered and ground to produce flour, while the name meant something like 'fertile place producing much grass seed'.

Merrygoen NSW   Aboriginal. Bleeding nose, or Blood of a dingo.

Merrywinebone NSW   Aboriginal. Great place for cockatoos.

Mersey River T   Discovered during a survey which had been organised by the Van Diemen's Land Company and named by Edwin Curr after the English river. As it was the second river encountered after leaving Launceston it was at first called Second Western River. The Aboriginal name was Paranaple.

Merton V   After Merton Place in Surrey.

Metcalfe V   After Baron Metcalfe, Governor of Jamaica and Governor-General of Canada.

Miandetta NSW   Aboriginal. Bend in the river.

Micabel or Mickabil NSW   Aboriginal. Tree struck by lightning.

Michaelmas Island WA   Discovered on Michaelmas Day, 29 September 1791 by Captain George Vancouver.

Mickibri NSW   Aboriginal. Place struck by lightning.

Middlesex Plains T   Discovered and named after the English county by Joseph Fossey when searching for an overland route to the north-western regions of Tasmania.

Midlands WA   The name was given in 1894 by the Midland Railway Company which had been granted land on the condition it linked up with the State railway line at Geraldton.

Miepoll V   The story is that an early police magistrate who seldom ventured to express his own opinion, prefaced his remarks by saying, 'My Poll says...'. So says Bill Beatty in *A Treasury of Australian Folk Tales and Traditions,* and adds that the name was coined by the surveyor J. G. Wilmot.

Mila NSW   Aboriginal. Eye. The syllable Mil is a component of many place names, and usually means Eye.

Milang SA   Aboriginal. A corruption of Milangk, Place of sorcerers.

Milbong Q   Aboriginal. One eye, or Eye gone away. In fact the place was originally known as One Eye, after a one-eyed sheep drover who lived here.

Mildura V   Aboriginal. Red earth. The Jamieson brothers of Murray Downs station conferred the name. The explanation given above seems more likely than another, derived from Dura: a fly, and Mil: eye, with the

151

meaning Place of sore eyes. Charles Sturt passed the site of the city in 1830, and there were several earlier settlers before the Jamiesons took up the run.

Miles Q   After William Miles, Colonial Secretary of Queensland in 1877.

Mill Brook V   The site of a mill at the time of settlement. The Aboriginal name was Moorabool, meaning Mussel.

Millicent SA   Named after Mrs Millicent Glen, wife of George Glen, at the request of Governor Fergusson. The town was built on the site of the Mayurra station, which was owned by Sir Samuel Davenport and George Glen. Mrs Glen, who was the daughter of Augustus Short, Bishop of Adelaide, was the only white woman (apart from her maids!) on the station in 1854. Mayurra was derived from the Aboriginal Maayera, Fern straws.

Millingimbi NT   The site of the Methodist Mission station takes its name from a large mythical snake which was supposed to inhabit the caverns at the Macassar well.

Millthorpe NSW   After the village in Lincolnshire, England. Meaning, Mill farm.

Milparinka NSW   Aboriginal. Water may be found here. It was near here that a terrible drought caused Charles Sturt to remain for a period of six months. See Mount Poole.

Mincha V   Aboriginal. Turkey.

Mindaribba NSW   Aboriginal. Hunter.

Minemoorong NSW   Aboriginal. Camping place.

Minineera V   Aboriginal. Mosquito.

Minlaton SA   A curious combination of an Aboriginal word with an Old English one. The Aborigines called a water hole here Minlacowie, Sweet water. The name can therefore be rendered Sweet water town. It was earlier known as Gum Tree Flat.

Minnamurra NSW   Aboriginal. Plenty of fish.

Minore NSW   Aboriginal. White flower. The name of a pastoral run.

Mintaro SA   This name comes from a Spanish word meaning Resting place, and was used appropriately by the Spanish mule drivers employed at the Burra mines.

Minyip V   Aboriginal. Ashes.

Miram V   Aboriginal. Branch of a tree.

Mirboo V   Aboriginal. Kidney.

Mirranpongapongunna, Lake NT   The lake, which is in the Simpson Desert, owes its inclusion here only to the fact that it is one of the longest Aboriginal names accepted for current use. The meaning is unknown.

Mirrool NSW   Aboriginal. Pipeclay, which was used for painting the body in preparation for initiation ceremonies.

Mission River Q   Earlier known as Myall Creek, the river finally took its name from the Presbyterian mission at Weipa.

Mitchell Q   After Sir Thomas Livingstone Mitchell.

Mitchell, Mount WA   After Sir Thomas Livingstone Mitchell, and named by Surgeon T. B. Wilson in 1838.

Mitchell River NSW, Q, V   The rivers in these three states were all named after T. L. Mitchell, a well-known explorer who conferred many place names and was Surveyor-General of New South Wales. The Mitchell River in New South Wales was also known as the Mann River. In Queensland the Mitchell was named by Leichhardt on 16 June 1845, and in Victoria by Angus McMillan in 1840.

Mitiamo V   Aboriginal. One man behind me.

Mitta Mitta; Mitta Mitta River V   Aboriginal, meaning either Thunder, or Little waters. Another explanation is that the name comes from Mida Modringa, Place of reeds. The river was discovered by Hume and Hovell in 1824.

Mittagong NSW   Aboriginal. Small mountain, High, rocky, scrubby hill, or Plenty of dingoes. The name did not take its present form officially until the railway came here in 1867. Governor Macquarie referred to it as Marragan and Minnikin in 1816, although by 1820 he spelt it Mittagong. The original Aboriginal name may have been Mirragong. In his autobiography Martin Cash, who lived here and later became a bushranger, called it Meadow Gang. In 1849 a small settlement called Fitzroy was established near the ironworks, and in 1862 Crown land was subdivided and named the 'Village of Fitzroy'. Another subdivision was named New Sheffield because of the association of the ironworks. The area was also known as Nattai.

Moama NSW   Earlier known as Maiden's Punt, after the man who operated the ferry. It was to this point that Captain W. R. Randell brought the steamship *Mary Ann,* and this proved to be the beginning of river trade on the Murray.

Mogongong NSW   Aboriginal. name of a nearby hill.

Molesworth V   After Sir William Molesworth, British Member of Parliament who was interested in colonisation.

Moleton NSW   This place takes its name from the adjacent Mole Creek.

Moliagul V   Aboriginal. A corruption of Moliaguli, Hill with trees.

Molle Islands; Port Molle Q   The islands were named by Lieut Charles

Jeffreys of the brig *Kangaroo* in 1815 after Colonel George Molle, the Lieut-Governor. West Molle was at one time advertised for tourist publicity purposes as Daydream Island.

Mologa V   Aboriginal. Red sandhill.

Molong NSW   Aboriginal. All rocks. Also the name of an estate in the vicinity.

Monaro; Monaro Plains; Monaro Range ACT   Aboriginal. Probably a corruption of Maneroo, Breasts or Navel. Olaf Ruhen states the meaning is most probably breasts, for the hills, particularly towards the southern end, are breast-shaped, and have outcrops of granite for nipples at their peaks. There have been several spellings — Maneroo, Monaroo, Manaroo, and Menaroo. They were discovered in 1823 by Captain Mark Currie, accompanied by John Ovens and Joseph Wild. They named the plains Brisbane Downs after Sir Thomas Brisbane.

Mongogarie NSW   Aboriginal. Spotted gum trees.

Monomeith V   Aboriginal. Planet Jupiter.

Montagu Island NSW   After George Montagu Dunk, Earl of Halifax. The island was seen by Captain Cook, but it was not recognised as an island until seen from the convict ship *Surprize* in 1790. Aboriginal name, Barunguba.

Montague Range; Montague Sound WA   After Admiral Robert Montague.

Monte Bello Islands WA   Named by Nicolas Baudin in *Le Geographe* in 1801 in honour of Marshal Lannes who was elevated to the title of Duke of Montebello by Napoleon. These uninhabited islands and rocky outcrops have a history that extends from 1622, when the British ship *Trial*, commanded by John Brooke, was wrecked at Tryal Rocks, q.v. to the 1950s, when atomic bomb tests were conducted here. As the Australian *Encyclopaedia* records, the outmoded practice of using names of British politicians was reverted to during the survey, and various features were named Attlee, Chamberlain, Disraeli, MacDonald, Palmerston, and Walpole. There were public protests, and it was then found that the Admiralty had overlooked the fact that the Australian hydrographic authorities had previously suggested descriptive names for these features.

Monteagle NSW   Probably named after Lord Monteagle, Secretary of State.

Monteith SA   After T. E. Monteith, a pioneer pastoralist.

Montrose V   After Montrose in Scotland.

Moody SA   After D. A. Moody, a South Australian Member of Parliament.

Moogerah Q   Aboriginal. Place of thunderstorms.

Moolap V   Aboriginal. Men going fishing.

Mooloolaba Q   Aboriginal. Place of snappers.

Moolooloo SA   Aboriginal. Slippery ridges.

Moolpa NSW   Aboriginal. Black duck.

Moombooldool NSW   Aboriginal. From Moom, Death.

Moonambel V   Aboriginal. Rock hole.

Moonan Brook; Moonan Flat NSW   Aboriginal. Difficult to accomplish.

Moondarra V   Aboriginal. Heavy rain, or Thunder.

Moonta SA   Aboriginal. A corruption of Moonterra, Place of impenetrable scrub. The name was confirmed by the Governor, Sir Dominick Daly, when the town was laid out in 1863.

Moorabool River V   Aboriginal. Curlew.

Moore, Lake WA   Discovered in 1864 by A. C. Gregory and named by him after George Fletcher Moore. See below.

Moore River WA   Discovered and named after George Fletcher Moore, who was an indefatigable explorer in this region in the 1830s. The river was first sighted in 1836. Moore was not only a pioneer settler but also became Advocate-General in Western Australia.

Moorlands SA   After Moorlands in Somerset.

Mooroobie Q   Aboriginal. Death adders.

Moorooduc V   Aboriginal. Dark.

Mooroopna V   Aboriginal. Deep water.

Moorunde SA   Aboriginal. Meeting place. The Moorunde Wild Life Reserve, where wombats have been established, is close to the place where E. J. Eyre set up his headquarters in 1841 on the banks of the Murray River as Protector of Aborigines.

Moppin NSW   Aboriginal. Thigh.

Morangarell NSW   Aboriginal. Nest of a waterfowl. The original Aboriginal word was Morangarel.

Morchard SA   After Morchard Bishop in North Devon, the birthplace of the father of Sir Samuel Way, Chief Justice of South Australia.

Moresby Range Q   Named by G. A. F. E. Dalrymple during his 1873 expedition, doubtless after John Moresby, Captain of the *Basilisk*.

Moreton Bay; Moreton, Cape; Moreton Island Q   Cook's Journal for 17 May 1770 reads: 'On the North side of this point [Point Lookout] the shore forms a wide open bay, which I have named Morton's Bay . . .' James, Earl of Morton, was President of the Royal Society in 1764, and one of the Commissioners of Longitude. A misspelling in Hawkesworth's edition of Cook's Journals has resulted in Cape Morton being perpetuated as Cape Moreton. Better known are Moreton Bay and Moreton Island, which should have preserved Cook's spelling. Moreton Island was named by Matthew Flinders in 1799, seven years after the publication of the Hawkesworth edition. In doing so Flinders recorded that the island 'would have received that name from Captain Cook had he known of its insularity'. Moreton Bay was explored by John Oxley in 1823. The Aboriginal name of Moreton Island was Gnoorganpin, or Tangalooma.

Morgan SA   The town was proclaimed in 1878 and named after Sir William Morgan, Chief Secretary of South Australia, and later Premier. Before 1878 it was known by several different names. In 1830 Sturt passed the site on his voyage down the Murray River and again on his return. When settlement began, and the overlanders on their way to Adelaide with stock left the river at this point, it was known as North-West Bend, the Great Bend, or the Great Elbow. About 1878 the township was connected by rail with Adelaide and for a while was known as Von Rieben's, after the proprietor of a public house at North-West Bend. The Aboriginal name was Coerabko, Meeting place of the tribes.

Morgan Island NT   Named by Flinders in 1803 after one of the crew of the *Investigator* who died of sunstroke.

Morgan, Mount Q   Although traces of gold were found by stockmen as early as 1870 it was not until 1881 and 1882 that the immense deposits of gold and copper were found. Edwin and Thomas Morgan, who owned the Callinngal run, were prospecting when they made their exciting discovery on a hill top. They were accompanied by Alexander Gordon, whose wife urged them to inspect the mountain. A third brother, Frederick, joined them in pegging out a claim. The Mount Morgan Gold Mining Company was formed in 1886. The 'mountain of gold' is now a deep chasm, and the town has been referred to as the town of the four gs — girls, goats, galahs, and glass bottles.

Moriac V   Aboriginal. Hill.

Morisset NSW   After Lieut-Colonel James Thomas Morisset, who was in command at Newcastle at one time.

Mornington; Mornington Peninsula V   After Mornington in Ireland.

Mornington Island Q   When Matthew Flinders discovered that Cape Van Diemen was an island on 7 December 1802, he named it after the second Earl of Mornington, Governor-General of India, after whom the Wellesley Islands were also named.

Mororo NSW   Aboriginal. Fighting place.

Morpeth NSW   After the colliery town of Morpeth, Northumberland, meaning Murder path. E. C. Close gave the name as 'The New Town of Morpeth' when he subdivided his property in 1834. Aboriginal name, Illulong.

Morphett Vale SA   After Sir John Morphett, who arrived in 1836.

Mortdale NSW   After Thomas Sutcliffe Mort, pioneer merchant, who had many business interests. His greatest claim to fame is the work he did to promote refrigeration.

Mortlake V   After Mortlake in Surrey, meaning Young salmon stream. The Aboriginal name was Boorook.

Morundah NSW   Aboriginal. Stuck in the mud.

Moruya; Moruya River NSW   Aboriginal. Place further south.

Morven NSW, Q   After a place in Argyllshire, Scotland, taken from an adjacent station.

Mosman NSW   After Archibald Mosman, ship owner and pastoralist. He established his shipping and whaling headquarters in the bay known as Mosman's Bay. Aboriginal name, Goran-Bullagong.

Moss Vale NSW   Jemmy Moss, an early settler, gave this name to his farm.

Mossiface V   A descriptive name which first took the form Mossy Face. The Aboriginal name was Martungdun, meaning Shellfish.

Mossman; Mossman River Q   Named after a member of Archibald Mosman's family, (see under Mosman) — probably Hugh Mosman, his son. The name seems to have been spelt both ways. Hugh Mosman was one of the discoverers of Charters Towers.

Moulamein NSW   Aboriginal, meaning not known.

Mount Gambier V   See Gambier, Mount.

Mount Isa Q   See Isa, Mount.

Mount Morgan Q   See Morgan, Mount.

Mourilyan Harbour Q   Discovered by Lieut Mourilyan of the *Basilisk* and named after him by Captain Moresby during the search for survivors of the *Maria* which was wrecked on Bramble Reef, Palm Island, on 26 February 1872.

Mowbullian, Mount Q   Aboriginal. Bald head.

Moyhu V   Aboriginal. Wind.

Muckatah V   Aboriginal. Small plain.

Mudamuckla SA   Aboriginal. Water supply.

Mudgee NSW   Aboriginal. Nest, Contented, or Sitting.

Mudgegong V   Aboriginal. Reverberations.

Mueller, Mount NT, T, WA   Named after the famous botanist and explorer Baron Sir Ferdinand Jakob Heinrich von Mueller. It is properly Muller, but was always spelt Mueller in Australia.

Mueller Range WA   Discovered by Alexander Forrest in 1879 and named in honour of Ferdinand von Mueller.

Muirhead, Mount SA   Named by Charles Bonney after one of the members of his expedition who was a stockman.

Mulligan, Mount; Mulligan River Q   Named after James Venture Mulligan, prospector and explorer. During a prospecting trip in May 1874 he discovered and named Mount Mulligan. The following year William Oswald Hodgkinson discovered and named the Mulligan River. Mulligan and Hodgkinson were responsible for naming rivers after each other.

Mullion Creek NSW   Aboriginal. Eagle-hawk. The Aboriginal word is sometimes spelt Mullian or Mulyan.

Mullumbimby NSW   Aboriginal word, possibly meaning Small round hill. The original name may have been Mullibumbi.

Mulwala NSW   Aboriginal. Rain.

Mumbil NSW   Aboriginal. Black wattle tree.

Mummulgum NSW   Aboriginal. Green pigeon.

Munbilla Q   Aboriginal. Plenty of water.

Mundoora SA   Aboriginal. Fishes, or Flood.

Mungeribar NSW   Aboriginal. Place of red earth — the name of an estate belonging to Thomas Bragg.

Mungindi Q   Aboriginal. Water hole by the river.

Munica V   Aboriginal. Fish.

Munro V   After a saw-miller who lived there.

Murchison V   An early settler, Captain Murchison, gave the name in honour of Sir Roderick Impey Murchison, the British geologist, to whom he was related.

Murchison River T   Discovered and named after Sir Roderick Murchison, the British Scientist, by Henry Hellyer in 1828.

Murchison River WA   Similarly named by George Grey during his heroic forced march from Shark Bay to the Swan River in 1839.

Murga NSW   Aboriginal. Cuckoo.

Murgon Q   Aboriginal. Water lily.

Murnpeowie SA   Aboriginal. Pigeon water. Bronze-wing pigeons were accustomed to resort to this water hole on the huge Murnpeowie station in large numbers.

Murphy's Range Q   Named by Leichhardt on 18 November 1844, during his first expedition, after 15-year-old John Murphy who had been included in the party.

Murrami NSW   Aboriginal. Crayfish.

Murray Bridge SA   The bridge across the Murray, after which the town was named, was opened for traffic in 1879, and for trains in 1886. The first settler, R. Edwards, came here in the early 1850s, and for some time the locality was known as Edwards Crossing, or The Turnoff, because drovers turned away from the river here when on their way to Adelaide. In 1860 the name was officially recognised as Mobilong, which was an Aboriginal name. The term Murray Bridge gradually came into use but did not receive official blessing until 1924.

Murray River NSW, SA, V   After Sir George Murray, Secretary of State for the Colonies. The river was discovered by Hume and Hovell near Albury in 1824, and named by them in honour of Hume's father. On his second expedition in 1829 Captain Charles Sturt set out with the intention of plotting the course of the southern rivers. By January 1830 he was travelling down the Murrumbidgee with his men in two boats when the torrent narrowed and they were swept out into what he described as a 'broad and noble river', and sailed as far as Lake Alexandrina. He was unaware that the upper reaches had already been named and was pleased to confer the name Murray 'in compliment to the distinguished officer, Sir George Murray, who then presided over the colonial department, not only in compliance with the known wishes of His Excellency General Darling, but also in accordance with my own feelings as a soldier'. Sturt considered that the Hume, Ovens, and Goulburn Rivers all contributed to the Murray. The *Australian Encyclopaedia* records that Murray was fortunate in having his name attached to the river in view of its earlier naming by Hume and Hovell, while the *Australian Junior Encyclopaedia* says the choice was unfortunate, for Murray was a 'totally inefficient' minister who tried to discourage British emigrants from coming to Australia.

Aboriginal names for various parts of the river include Goodwarra, Ingalta, Moorundie, Parriang-ka-perre, Tongwillum, and Yoorlooarra.

Murray Town SA   After the surveyor A. H. Murray.

Murrumba Q   Aboriginal. Good.

Murrumbidgee River NSW   Aboriginal. Big water. An unusual sequence occurred in connection with the name for it was known to white people before the river was discovered. In 1820 Charles Throsby, the explorer, informed the Governor that he was looking forward to finding 'a considerable river of salt water (except at very wet seasons), called by the natives Mur-rum-bid-gee'. He reached the river in April 1821. Brigade-Major Ovens and Captain Mark Currie also saw it in 1823. The river was more thoroughly explored by Charles Sturt in 1829.

Murrumburrah NSW   The proper Aboriginal name was Murrimboola, Two water-holes, and was used until 1882 when it was changed to Murrumburrah to avoid confusion with Merimbula. Murrumboolah was the name of an early pastoral holding.

Murrurundi NSW   A contraction of the Aboriginal name Murrum-doorandi, Place where the mists sit. Other meanings given are Mountain, and Five fingers.

Murtoa V   Aboriginal. Home of the lizard.

Murwillumbah NSW   An Aboriginal name for which two meanings have been given: Place of many possums, or Camping place. (Murray, big or many; Willum, possums; Bah, place of. Or, Murrie, men; Wollie, camp; Bah, place of.)

Musgrave Ranges NT, SA   The ranges were first sighted from the top of Ayers Rock by W. C. Gosse in 1873, and named by him after Sir Anthony Musgrave who was Colonial Administrator at the time, and who took office shortly afterwards as Governor of South Australia.

Muswellbrook NSW   So named because of the mussels found in the stream. The town was gazetted as Muscle Brook in 1833, and altered to Muswellbrook in 1838.

Muttama NSW   Aboriginal. Take it, the name of a local creek.

Myall, Lake NSW   Aboriginal. Myall tree, a small silver-grey wattle.

Myamyn V   Aboriginal. Meeting place.

Myponga SA   Aboriginal. A corruption of Malp-pinga, Cast-off wife.

Myrniong V   Aboriginal. Yam.

Myrtleford V   The name comes from the adjacent Myrtle Creek.

Mystic Park V   A whimsical name conferred by an Irishman, Paddy Bell.

Mywee V   Aboriginal. Deep water.

Nabiac NSW   Aboriginal. Fig tree.

Nackara SA   Aboriginal. Brother, or Looking eastwards.

Nadda SA   Aboriginal. Camp.

Nairne SA   After the maiden name of Mrs Matthew Smillie, whose husband laid out a township on his property where overlanders frequently grazed their cattle before taking them to Adelaide.

Nambour Q   Aboriginal. Red-flowering tea-tree.

Nambucca Heads; Nambucca River NSW   Aboriginal. Entrance to the waters, or Crooked river. Probably derived from Ngambugka.

Namoi River NSW   There are two possible derivations: a corruption of Nynamu, Breast, so called because the curve of the river resembled that of a woman's breast, or Ngnamai or Njamai, Place of the nyamai tree, a variety of acacia.

Nana Creek; Nana Glen NSW   Aboriginal. Small lizard.

Nanago Q   Aboriginal, meaning unknown. Formerly Goode's Inn.

Nandaly V   Aboriginal. Fire.

Nangwarry SA   Aboriginal. A corruption of Nrang-ware, Path to the cave.

Nantabibbie SA   Aboriginal. Black kangaroo.

Nantawarra SA   Aboriginal. Black kangaroo country, a corruption of Nurntowerrah.

Napier Broome Bay WA   Named after the Governor of Western Australia from 1882 to 1890, Sir Frederick Napier Broome. It was conferred by Staff Commander J. E. Coghlen who surveyed the coast between 1883 and 1886.

Narbethong V   Aboriginal. Merry.

Nar Nar Goon V   Aboriginal. Koala.

Narellan NSW   One account says that it comes from the name of a property belonging to Francis Mowatt; another that it was derived from Naralling, a property owned by William Hovell. In either case it is doubtless of Aboriginal origin.

Nargong NSW   Aboriginal. Light.

Nariah or Narriah NSW   Aboriginal. Bare place on a hill.

Narooma NSW   Aboriginal. A corruption of Noorooma, the name of a cattle station.

Narrabri NSW   Aboriginal. Forks, Forked sticks, or possibly, Large creek. Other forms of the name are Nurraburai, Nurraburi, and Nurruby, the latter being the name of the station taken up by Patrick Quinn and Cyrus M. Doyle in 1834.

Narracoorte SA   Aboriginal. A corruption of Gnage-kurt. Large water hole, or Running water. The name was adopted in 1869, but prior to this it had several names. It was first called Mosquito Plains at the time the first settler, George Ormerod, arrived. In 1845 a private town was surveyed and named Kincraig after the birthplace of its founder, William McIntosh. It did not develop until the Victorian gold rush in 1851, when gold escorts made it a staging post, and also a camp for Chinese immigrants who landed at Robe and were smuggled into Victoria. It was proclaimed a town in 1859, and then a second private town, Skytown, was developed. All names were finally dropped in favour of the Aboriginal word.

Narrandera NSW   Aboriginal. Place of lizards. It was the name of a pastoral holding and was gazetted a village in 1863.

Narrogin WA   Aboriginal. A corruption of Gnarajin or Gnargajin, Place of water, or Water hole.

Narromine NSW   Aboriginal. From Gnarrowmine, Place for honey, or Gnaroomine, Bony Aboriginal man. Narrowmine cattle station was established by Thomas Raine in 1840.

Narrung SA   Aboriginal. Place of large she-oaks.

Narrung V   Aboriginal. Moon.

Nash Spring (or Nash's Pond) NT   Named by J. McDouall Stuart in 1862 after Heath Nash, a member of his expedition.

Naturaliste Channel; Naturaliste, Cape WA   The cape and the bay were both named by Nicolas Baudin after his vessel which made a landfall here in 1801 when the French scientific expedition arrived on *Le Naturaliste* and *Le Geographe*.

Naturi SA   Aboriginal. Sandy soil.

Navarre V   After the European kingdom.

Nayook V   Aboriginal. Cockatoo.

Neales River (The Neales) SA   Named after John Bentham Neales, an auctioneer and Member of Parliament, who arrived in South Australia in 1838.

Nebo, Mount Q   In the Old Testament Moses surveyed the Promised Land from the summit of Mount Nebo. See Deuteronomy 34:1.

Neerim V   Aboriginal. Long.

Neeworra NSW   Aboriginal. Star.

Neilrex NSW   An inversion of the Christian name and surname of a local pioneer, Rex Neil, or McNeil.

Nelshaby SA   Aboriginal. A corruption of Nelcebee, Boiling spring.

Nelson; Nelson, Cape V   Named by Lieut James Grant on 4 December 1800, after his vessel, the *Lady Nelson*, during his survey of Bass Strait.

Nelson, Mount T   Also named after the *Lady Nelson*.

Nelungaloo NSW   Aboriginal. Lizard.

Nepean Bay SA   Discovered by Matthew Flinders and named by him on 21 March 1802 'in compliment to the first secretary'. Sir Evan Nepean was Under-Secretary for the Home Department, and Secretary to the Admiralty. Shortly afterwards Nicolas Baudin arrived at the bay and, unaware of Flinders's prior claim, called it Bougainville Bay 'in honour of the respected doyen of French explorers'.

Nepean, Point V   Named after Sir Evan Nepean by Lieut John Murray when he entered Port Phillip in 1800.

Nepean River NSW   After Sir Evan Nepean. The portion of the Hawkesbury River known as the Nepean was discovered by Captain Watkin Tench and his companions in 1789 and named by Governor Phillip.

Neptune Islands SA   Flinders named them after the god of the sea on 21 February 1802 because they were 'inaccessible to man'.

Neutral Bay NSW   So named because ships of foreign origin were required to anchor in the bay. In his diary entry of April 1789, Captain David Collins wrote: 'His Excellency inserted in the Port Orders, that all foreign ships coming into this harbour should anchor in this bay, which he named Neutral Bay.' The reason was to prevent convicts from escaping. Aboriginal name, Wirra-birra.

New Holland   The name New Holland was frequently used for the continent until the early part of the 19th century, when it was displaced by Flinders's Australia, q.v. The older name originated from Tasman, who called it Compagnis Nieu Nederland, which became anglicised as British interests increased. The name still survives in scientific nomenclature in the form novae-hollandiae.

New Norcia WA   After the birthplace of Saint Benedict in Italy. The mission settlement on the bank of the Moore River was founded by Dom Salvado, Dom Serra, two other Benedictines and an Irish catechist in 1846. The catechist was killed by the Aborigines and the other helpers left. When Dom Serra became coadjutor Bishop of Perth, Dom Rosendo Salvado struggled on alone at the lonely settlement.

New Norfolk T   So named because the first settlers came from Norfolk Island. The district was explored in 1805 and was known as The Hills. The Norfolk Island settlers, who had been granted land at Perth, not far from Hobart, were dissatisfied with the selection and moved southwards. In 1811 Governor Macquarie named the town site Elizabeth Town after his wife and hoped it might become the capital of Tasmania. The present name was approved in 1827.

New South Wales   The name New Wales was given to the whole of the eastern seaboard of Australia, i.e. present-day New South Wales and Queensland, by Captain James Cook in 1770, but he later altered the name to New South Wales. He gave no reason for his choice. There is a saying that the initials, which are now so well known, stand for Newcastle, Sydney, and Wollongong. There have been agitations for a change of name on a number of occasions.

The name was conferred by Cook on 22 August 1770. Having landed on Possession Island, he wrote: 'Having satisfied myself of the great Probability of a passage, thro' which I intend going with the Ship, and therefore may land no more upon this Eastern coast of New Holland, and on the Western side I can make no new discovery, the honour of which belongs to the Dutch Navigators, but the Eastern Coast from the Lat of 38° S. down to this place, I am confident, was never seen or Visited by an European before us; and notwithstanding I had in the Name of his Majesty taken possession of several places upon this Coast, I now once More hoisted English colours, and in the Name of His Majesty King George the Third took possession of the whole Eastern coast from the above Lat down to this place by the Name of New South Wales, together with all the Bays, Harbours, Rivers, and Islands, situated upon the said Coast; after which we fired 3 Volleys of Small Arms, which were answer'd by the like number from the Ship.'

It is to be noted that Cook took possession of 'The whole Eastern Coast', i.e. of the regions of what are now the coasts of New South Wales and Queensland. Possession of the whole of the eastern par of the Australian continent and Van Diemen's Land was not taken until Governor Phillip read the proclamation to members of the First Fleet on 7 February 1888. At that time New South Wales embraced the whole of the eastern half of Australia. Queensland was declared a separate state in 1859.

Newbridge NSW   The name came into being when a new bridge was built over the railway line.

Newcastle NSW   After the English coaling port of Newcastle-on-Tyne, which was so named when Henry II built a Norman castle between 1172 and 1177 on the site of an old Roman fortress. A small settlement was formed at 'Coal Harbour' in 1801 but later abandoned. Governor King appointed Lieutenant Charles Menzies commandant at the settlement he named Newcastle in 1804. Menzies attempted to honour the Governor by calling it King's Town. This name was used occasionally even on official documents, but by 1830 the Governor's choice had prevailed. Aboriginal name, Mulubinba, from an indigenous plant called mulubin.

Newcastle Waters NT   When J. McDouall Stuart discovered several water holes in this locality in 1861, he named them after the Duke of Newcastle, who was Secretary of State for the Colonies.

Newman, Mount WA   Discovered by H. S. Trotman in 1896 and named after his chief. The iron-ore township was built in 1967 when the iron deposits at Mount Whaleback were first developed.

Nhill V   Aboriginal. From Nyell, Place of spirits, or White mist on the water.

Niangala NSW   Aboriginal. Eclipse of the moon.

Nicholls Point WA   During his 1818 survey in the *Mermaid,* P. P. King sheltered in Cambridge Gulf and on Adolphus Island William Nicholls, one of his crew, was buried.

Nicholson, Mount Q   Named by Leichhardt in 1844, after Sir Charles Nicholson, the Speaker of the first Legislative Council of New South Wales.

Nicholson River Q   Also named by Leichhardt, in August 1845, but on this occasion after an English benefactor, William Nicholson.

Nicholson River V   Discovered by Angus McMillan on 18 January 1840, and named after Sir Charles Nicholson.

Nimbin NSW   Roland Robinson states that the Aboriginal Alexander

Vesper informed him that Nymbun is the name of a spirit in the form of a small man who lives inside the mountain. The Nymbun would be the barnyunbee, the totem of the place, and the mountain would be the jurraveel, or totemic site.

Nimmitabel NSW   Aboriginal. Meeting place of many waters. There can be few names that have taken so many forms over the years — Nimmitybelle, Nimitybell, Nimithyball, Nimity-Bell, Nimoitebool, Nimmittabel, etc.

Ninda V   Aboriginal. Cloud.

Ningana SA   Aboriginal. To rest.

Ninghi Creek Q   An Aboriginal tribal name (Ninghininghi).

Ninyenook V   Aboriginal. Beard.

Nivelle V   Named in 1836 by T. L. Mitchell, after a place in Spain where he had served during the Peninsula War.

Noarlunga SA   Aboriginal. Fishing place.

Nobby's Head NSW   Though sighted by Captain Cook, the island was first visited by Lieut-Colonel William Paterson, who called it Coal Island. In 1797 Lieut John Shortland named it Hacking's Island. Later it became known as Nobby's Island; the earliest mention of this name was in 1810. When connected to the mainland it became Nobby's Head. Aboriginal name Whibay-Garba.

Noltenius Lagoon NT   After J. L. Noltenius who was killed by Aborigines in September 1883 while at work on a copper lode near the Daly River.

Noojee V   Aboriginal. Contentment.

Noonbinna NSW   Aboriginal. Kangaroo.

Noora SA   Aboriginal. Camp.

Noorengong V   Magpie.

Noosa Heads Q   An Aboriginal name. First called Cape Bracefield, after James Bracefield, an escaped convict, who lived here together with James Davis among the Aborigines, and were known as the wild white men. Bracefield helped Mrs Fraser (see under Fraser Island) to reach civilization, and returned to the tribe, but six years later he was found by Andrew Petrie and pardoned.

Norman River Q   Named by J. L. Stokes after Captain Norman of the *Black Diamond*.

Normanby; Normanby River Q   Discovered in 1872 and named by William Hann after the Marquess of Normanby, then Governor of Queensland.

Normanton Q   The town is named after the river, q.v.

Normanville SA   After a dentist of this name, who arrived in 1847.

Norseman WA   Named after a horse that belonged to an early arrival on the gold field. It did not become a town until 1895. The gold field was once known as Dundas.

North Yathong NSW   Aboriginal. Tall sand hills.

Northam WA   Named by Governor Stirling after Northam in Devonshire in 1830, when Ensign Robert Dale led a party of colonists over the Darling Range into the valley of the Avon.

Northern Territory   When the territory was annexed to South Australia on 8 July 1863, it was described as comprising 'all the country to the northward of the 26th parallel S latitude and between the 129th and 138ths degrees of E longitude' – and so received its name. Before this it was part of New South Wales, and from 1911 has been administered by the Commonwealth. Early names for 'the Territory' were Alexandra Land and Prince Albert Land. During World War II there was a proposal to name it Churchill Land, and in 1954, when Queen Elizabeth II visited Australia, Elizabeth, but 'the Territory' has survived. Alexandra Land was suggested by J. McDouall Stuart in November 1864 in honour of Princess Alexandra, and was officially adopted for some time. Stuart's proposal was embodied in a paper sent to the Royal Geographical Society.

Northumberland, Cape SA   Named by Lieut James Grant while in command of the *Lady Nelson* on its voyage from England to Port Jackson. On 3 December 1880 Grant wrote: 'The first Cape I called Northumberland, after His Grace the Duke of Northumberland.'

Northumberland County NSW   After the English Northumberland, and named by Lieut Charles Menzies, commandant at Newcastle, about 1804.

Northumberland Islands Q   At the end of May 1770 the *Endeavour* threaded the Northumberland and Cumberland Islands. Cook made no reference to the 'Northumberland Isles' in his log, but entered the name on his charts, doubtless in honour of Hugh Percy, the first Duke of Northumberland.

North-West Cape WA   Named by P. P. King in 1818. The cape and the peninsula had been sighted by several Dutch vessels in the 17th century. In 1801 Baudin called it Cape Murat, after a brother-in-law of Napoleon, but the name was replaced by King's choice.

Nowa Nowa V   Aboriginal. Hill of black stones, or Rising sun.

Nowhere Else T   The name is a surprising contradiction, for there are two places of this name in Tasmania.

Nowra NSW   Aboriginal. Black cockatoo. Other translations are Two, or You and me.

Nubba NSW   Aboriginal. Young person.

Nullan V   Aboriginal. A contraction of Nullan Nullan, To blow.

Nullarbor Plain SA, WA   Although it has been speculated that this is an

Aboriginal word, it is unique (or almost so) in Australian nomenclature in that it comes from the Latin Nulla: no, arbor: tree, a descriptive name applied by Alfred Delisser who examined it at greater length than any other explorer. By a curious coincidence, Nulla also means None or Not any in an Aboriginal language. The area is not strictly defined, but extends about 300 km west and 220 km east of the border between Western Australia and South Australia, and about 200 km inland. It was first sighted by Pieter Niujts in 1627, and in 1802 by Matthew Flinders. E. J. Eyre traversed it from east to west on his epic journey in 1841. The plain was known at one time as the Bunda Plain.

Numurkah V   Aboriginal. War shield.

Nunga V   Aboriginal. Day.

Nunjikompita SA   Aboriginal. Water holes.

Nunkeri SA   Aboriginal. Beautiful.

Nuriootpa SA   This Aboriginal name has some connection with barter, for it was a famous trading centre for the tribes. The township laid out by William Coulthard in 1854 was first known as Gum Park, or Angas Park, for it was on property originally owned by George Fife Angas.

Nuyts Archipelago SA   Named by Flinders in 1802 after Pieter Nuyts or Nuijts, a member of the Council of India, who sailed with Francois Thijssen on the *Gulden Seepaard* (Golden Seahorse). The vessel sighted land on 26 January 1627 and skirted the south coast for about 1,600 kms between Cape Leeuwin and the Nuyts Archipelago. The *Australian Encyclopaedia* has an interesting note to the effect that when *Gulliver's Travels* was published in 1726, Jonathan Swift placed Lilliput and Blufescu in the latitude and longitude of Nuyts Archipelago. This may have been occasioned by a proposal made in 1717 by J. P. Purry that a Dutch Colony should be established here, because it provided the best climate in the world, and the only possible opposition could come from fortifications on the mainland — or giants! (See also under Shark Bay.)

Nuyts Point WA   It was at this point that land was sighted by the crew of the *Gulden Seepaard*. See above.

Nuytsland WA, SA   This early name for the Great Australian Bight was named after Pieter Nuijts, a member of the Council of the Indies.

Nyah V   Aboriginal. River bend.

Nyngan NSW   Aboriginal. Crayfish, Mussel, or Many creeks. T. L. Mitchell recorded the name in 1835 as Nyingan, and said that it meant Long pond of water.

Nyora V   Aboriginal. Cherry tree.

Nyrang Creek NSW   Aboriginal. Small. The name of an estate.

167

O.K. Q   This deserted copper mining township is said to have acquired its peculiar name from the miners when a jam tin of this brand was found beside the shaft.

Oaklands NSW   Named on account of its many oak trees, probably she-oaks.

Oaklands SA   Named for the same reason as in the preceding entry by R. D. Anderson.

Oakover River WA   Discovered and named by Frank T. Gregory in 1861.

Oatlands T   A descriptive name conferred by Governor Macquarie in 1821.

Oberon NSW   At first prosaically named Bullock Flat; a more romantic person later renamed it after the king of the fairies and husband of Titania in Shakespeare's *A Midsummer Night's Dream*.

Ogilvie, Mount Q   After W. H. Ogilvie, who was a Police Magistrate in the 1880s.

O'Halloran, Mount SA   After Major Thomas O'Halloran, a Commissioner of Police, who settled in the district in 1839.

Olary SA   Aboriginal. Creek.

Olga, Mount NT   Named by Ernest Giles in 1872. At first he wished to name it after his patron, the Baron von Mueller, but he persuaded the discoverer to name it after the Queen of Spain. Giles described the mountain graphically. 'I should think it's one of the most extraordinary mountains on the face of the earth. Most grotesque, like five or six enormous pink haystacks, all leaning against each other, or the backs of several elephants kneeling.' The mountain had earlier been seen by W. C. Gosse. The Aboriginal name was Katatjuta.

Olinda V   Named for Alice Olinda Hodgkinson, daughter of Clement Hodgkinson.

Olympic Highway NSW, V   Named at the time of the Olympic Games in Melbourne in 1956.

Olympus, Mount T   Named by George Frankland in 1835 when in a classical mood. Mount Ida, Lake Petrarch and other names of a similar character were chosen by him at this time.

Omeo V   Aboriginal. Mountains. The little settlement developed about 1835 when overlanders began to graze their stock on to the rich pasture lands.

One Tree Hill V   The surveyor Triggs left one tree standing in a clearing in the Dandenongs.

Onkaparinga River SA   Aboriginal. A common rendering of this name is Mother river plentiful, but it seems more likely that it comes from

Nganki-Parri, Woman's river, for when the Murray River tribes raided the local ochre mines, the Noarlunga men hid their women in a place then called Nganki-parri-unga, Place of the women's river, before going out to do battle. The river was discovered by Collet Barker in 1831. He used the Aboriginal name but transcribed it as Ponkepurringa. It was visited again in 1836 by Lieut W. G. Field in the *Rapid*. William Light renamed it Field's River, but later still Governor Gawler requested that the Aboriginal name be restored. In addition to the forms already recorded, it has been spelt Inangkiparri and Ungkeperringa.

Onslow WA   After Sir Alexander Campbell Onslow, Chief Justice of Western Australia. The settlement was transferred from its position near the mouth of the Ashburton River to Beadon Bay in 1926 after it had sustained damage from a cyclone.

Oodnadatta SA   Probably a corruption of Utnadata, Yellow blossom of the mulga. The town site was proclaimed by Lieut-Governor Sir Samuel Way in 1890.

Olldea (Ooldea Water) SA   Aboriginal. From Yooldil-Beena, Swamp where I stood to pour out water. The fascinating legend of the origin of this desert oasis is told in *The Passing of the Aborigines* by Daisy Bates*. Pumps used when the trans-continental railway line was being built reduced it to a dreary hollow.

Oondooroo Q   Aboriginal. A low prickly shrub.

Ootha NSW   Aboriginal. Ear.

Ophir; Ophir Bluff NSW   The scene of the first payable gold discovery in Australia, made by Edward Hargraves in February 1851. The Bathurst *Free Press* stated on 10 May 1851: 'Ophir is the name given to these diggings.' There are several references to Ophir, the land of gold, in the Old Testament, e.g. Job, 22-24: 'Then shalt thou lay up gold as dust, and the gold of Ophir as the stones of the brooks.'

Orange NSW   After the Prince of Orange, later King of the Netherlands. T. L. Mitchell, who doubtless gave the name, had served with the Prince in the Peninsula War. At an earlier date the future city was known as Blackman's Swamp, after John Blackman, the chief constable, who is said to have accompanied John Oxley when he led an expedition into the area in 1818.

Orara River NSW   Aboriginal. Place of the perch.

Orbost V   After Orbost in the Isle of Skye.

Ord, Mount WA   Discovered in 1903 by Frank H. Hann, probably after Sub-Inspector Ord who had accompanied him on his exploration of the tributaries of the Fitzroy River.

Ord, River WA   Discovered by Alexander Forrest in 1879 during his

* Heinemann and John Murray, 2nd edn., 1966.

journey from the De Grey River eastward to the Overland Telegraph Line. It was named after Sir Harry St George Ord, Governor of Western Australia. The Aboriginal name was Cununurra.

Ormerod NT   After George Ormerod.

Ororoo SA   Aboriginal, meaning unknown. In 1873 the township was proclaimed at Pekina, after the original run, but was renamed three years later. It is said that when Sir Charles Todd of Overland Telegraph fame was asked to site a Post Office there, he replied: 'Dear me, there are only two letters in Orroroo, so what do you want a post office for?'

Ossa, Mount T   Mount Ossa and Mount Pelion were included in the classical names chosen by George Frankland. See under Mount Olympus.

Otway, Cape V   On 7 December 1800 Lieut James Grant when in command of the *Lady Nelson* wrote: 'I named it Cape Albany Otway, in honour of William Albany Otway, Esq., Captain in the Royal Navy, and one of the Commissioners of the Transport Board.' The name was later shortened to its present form. The Otway Ranges have the same origin.

Oulnina SA   Aboriginal. Good water.

Ourimbah NSW   Aboriginal. Circle of the bora, the ceremonial ground where initial ceremonies were performed. At one time known as Blue Gum Flat.

Outtrim V   After Alfred Outtrim, Minister for Mines in Victoria.

Ouyen V   Aboriginal. Ghost water hole, or Wild duck.

Ovens River V   Named by Hume and Hovell in 1824 in honour of Major John Ovens, the soldier and explorer.

Owen Peak Q   Named by T. L. Mitchell in honour of Sir Richard Owen, the British naturalist.

Oxley; Oxley County; Oxley Creek; Oxley Highway; Oxley Island; Oxley's Peak; Oxley's Tableland NSW   After John Joseph William Molesworth Oxley, who is always referred to as John Oxley. It is proper that such a notable figure in the annals of early New South Wales exploration should be so fully commemorated. He was engaged in coastal survey work as early as 1802. His *Journals of Two Expeditions in the Interior of New South Wales,* published in 1820, prepared the way for later expeditions. He died at the early age of 42, 'Materially injured by the privations which he suffered during the Several Expeditions on which he was employed in exploring the Interior'. A grant of 5,000 acres of land was made to his sons in recognition of his services. Oxley in Victoria was also named after the explorer.

Oyster Bay T   A descriptive name. It is usually conceded that the discoverer was Matthew Weatherhead, captain of the whaler *Matilda,* who reported on 27 July 1791 that he had anchored here and named the bay after his ship; but it is also said that the brig *Mercury* was here in 1789, and that Cox Bight and Oyster Bay were named at that time. The area was first explored by Pierre Faure, a member of Baudin's expedition, in 1802. The name Fleurieu Bay, which still persists, was given at that time after the Comte de Fleurieu. The Aboriginal name was Poyanannupyalk.

Oyster Harbour WA Named by Captain George Vancouver on account of the number of oysters he found here in August 1791.

Pages, The SA Of this group of islets in Backstairs Passage, Flinders wrote in April 1802: 'There are three small, rocky islets near together, called The Pages.' In Aboriginal legend the two largest are the wives of Nurrunderi, the culture hero who created Kangaroo Island.

Painter, Mount SA J. M. Painter was a surveyor employed by W. G. Goyder to survey a portion of the North Flinders Ranges in 1857.

Pakenham V After Catherine Pakenham who became the Duchess of Wellington.

Palm Isles Q Named by Captain Cook on 7 June 1770 because of the cabbage palms growing there.

Palm Valley NT This noted beauty spot was discovered and named by Ernest Giles in 1872 on account of its luxuriant vegetation and tall palm trees, which are a survival from an earlier era when central Australia was covered with vegetation.

Palmer SA After Colonel George Palmer, a South Australian Colonisation Commissioner.

Palmer River Q Discovered by William Hann in 1872 and named after Sir Arthur Hunter Palmer, Premier of Queensland.

Palmerston; Palmerston Range Q Christie Palmerston, adventurer, explorer, and bushman, and discoverer of the Daintree Pass, is a legendary figure in northern Queensland. Stories are told of how he nursed the sick, protected settlers from hostile Aborigines, rescued lost prospectors, and was a superb bushman. He explored the headwaters of many Queensland rivers.

Pambula NSW Aboriginal. Two streams.

Pandora's Pass NSW Named by Allan Cunningham in 1823 when he was attempting to find a practical route between Bathurst and Liverpool Plains. He had difficulty in negotiating the Warrumbungle Mountains, and gave this hopeful name to the pass he discovered. The pass was negotiated successfully by John Oxley and himself two years later with a happier result than when Pandora, a character in Greek mythology, opened her box.

Panitya V Aboriginal. Piece of land.

Panmure V After Lord Panmure.

171

Panton Hill V   After Joseph Anderson Panton, artist, explorer, and Police Magistrate.

Parachilna SA   Aboriginal. River with steep banks.

Parattah T   Aboriginal. Ice.

Parilla SA   Aboriginal. Cold.

Paringa SA   Aboriginal. Whirlpool.

Parkes NSW   After Sir Henry Parkes, Premier of New South Wales. 1872-83 and 1887-91. The town was formerly Bushman's, from the mine named Bushman's Lead. It was changed to Parkes in 1873.

Parrakie SA   Aboriginal. Subterranean water.

Parramatta NSW   Aboriginal. Head of the river; Place where eels lie down or sleep; or Plenty of eels. When the land was cleared and a house erected for Governor Phillip, the area was named Rose Hill in honour of the Secretary of the British Treasury. The name was replaced by Parramatta by 1791, but was retained for the hill on which Government House had been built. John Macarthur's Elizabeth Farm estate was subdivided in the 1880s and formed into a township (now a suburb of Sydney) called Rosehill after the original Rose Hill. The parrots that frequented Parramatta were first called Rose Hill parrots, then Rose hillers, and finally Rosellas, a name that has become fully accepted.

Paruna SA   Aboriginal. Stopping place.

Parwan V   Aboriginal. Magpie.

Pascoe Q   After Lieut Pascoe, the son of Lord Nelson's Flag Lieutenant.

Paskeville SA   After General Paske, a brother-in-law of Governor Jervois.

Pasley, Cape; Pasley Island WA   Named by Flinders in January 1802 after his friend Captain T. S. Pasley, who assisted him to join the Royal Navy.

Pata SA   Aboriginal. Swamp gums.

Paterson; Paterson River NSW   After Lieut-Governor William Paterson, military officer, botanist, and explorer, who named the Grose Valley.

Patricks River NSW   The river was discovered on St Patrick's Day. This was in 1818. The discoverer was James Meehan. T. L. Mitchell was an advocate for the retention of the Aboriginal name and wished to change the name of the river, but was unable to do so because the Aboriginal name could not be discovered.

Patton's Cape V   Discovered and named by Lieut Grant in the *Lady Nelson* on 7 December 1800.

Peak Downs; Peak Range Q   Both features were named on 5 February 1844 by Leichhardt because of the appearance of the mountains. Outstanding among them is Wolfgang Peak which has been described as an 'immense natural obelisk nearly 1000 ft in height, rising out of a mountain that stands alone near the centre of a large expanse of undulating downs'.

Peake SA   After the Premier of South Australia, Archibald H. Peake.

Pearce, Point SA   Discovered and named by Flinders on 18 March 1802: 'We fetched to windward of the island-like point, to which I gave the name *Point Pearce,* in compliment to Mr Pearce of the Admiralty.'

Pedder, Lake T   The surveyor John Hilder Hedge wrote in his diary in 1835: 'On March 11 we reached two beautiful lakes which we named Lake Pedder and Lake Maria lying in the heart of the most romantic scenery and surrounded by lofty mountains.' Sir John Lowes Pedder was Chief Justice of Tasmania. His wife's name was Maria.

Pedra Blanca T   On 29 November 1642 Tasman wrote in his Journal: '... in the morning we were still by the rock which looks like the head of a Lion, had the wind westerly with topsail breeze; sailed along the coast which here stretches east and west, towards the midday passed two rocks, the westerly looked like a pedra branca, which lies on the coast of China ...' The name Pedra Branca was of Portuguese origin, meaning White Rock. The name for this guano-covered basalt rock has been retained in the form Pedra Blanca. Furneaux recorded the name Swilly on his chart, doubtless after his birthplace near Plymouth.

Peechelba V   Aboriginal. Behind.

Peel Island Q   Named after one of the discoverers of Port Denison. The Aboriginal name was Jeerkooroora.

Peel River NSW   Discovered in 1818 and named by John Oxley after Sir Robert Peel, the British Prime Minister.

Pelican Lagoon SA   When Flinders visited American River in 1802 he gave it this name because of the number of pelicans and pelican bones, forming the impression that it was a place where they assembled to die. It inspired him with solemn reflections: 'Alas, for the pelicans! Their golden age is past; but it has much exceeded in duration that of man.' An entry in the *Australian Encyclopaedia* notes that this passage inspired the English poet, James Montgomery to write a poem called 'Pelican Island'.

Pelsart Islands WA   This group of islands in the Houtman Abrolhos is a reminder of an early tragedy. In June 1629 the Dutch vessel *Batavia,* Commanded by Francois Pelsaert, was wrecked on a reef. The survivors took refuge on one of the islands while Pelsaert undertook the dangerous voyage to Batavia in an open boat. During his absence the supercargo, Jerome Cornelius, led a mutiny during which 125 of the castaways were murdered.

Pemberton WA   Named after Pemberton Walcott, son of an early settler at the Warren River.

Penguin; Penguin Creek T   So named by the botanist Ronald Campbell Gunn because of the number of small penguins found in the creek.

Penneshaw SA   This settlement on Kangaroo Island was first called Hog Bay (the bay on which it stands, so named because of the pigs that were brought here from Tasmania). Governor Jervois was not enamoured of the name and changed it to Penneshaw, probably after his Secretary Penne and a Miss Shaw who had been visiting his family.

Penola SA   Aboriginal. A corruption of Penaoorla, Big swamp.

Penrith NSW   After the town at the edge of the Lake District in Cumberland. Meaning, the Chief ford. The settlement was first called Evan.

Penshurst V   After a village in Kent. Meaning, Peven's hill.

Penwortham SA   John Horrocks laid out a township on his property, which he had settled on in 1839, and called it Penwortham after his birthplace, Penwortham Hall, Lancashire.

Pera Head Q   Named by Flinders on 9 November 1802 to commemorate the visit of the *Pera* which, in company with the *Arnhem*, sailed into the Gulf of Carpenteria 17 years after the visit of the *Duyfken* in 1606.

Percy Islands Q   Named by Flinders in 1802 after the Duke of Northumberland, whose family name was Percy.

Perponda SA   Aboriginal. Plains.

Perth WA   The site of Perth was chosen by Captain James Stirling in 1829, and the settlement named in honour of Sir George Murray, Secretary of State for War and the Colonies, who was born in Perthshire, Scotland.

Perth T   From Perth in Scotland.

Perthville NSW   At first named after Perth in Scotland, but later changed to Perthville to avoid confusion with Perth in Western Australia.

Peterborough SA   The town was formed in 1880 and named Petersburg in honour of Peter Doecke, one of the early settlers who took up land in the district. In 1917 when anti-German feeling was at its height, there was a proposal to substitute the Aboriginal name Mullya or Nelia, but compromise resulted in Petersburg being anglicised to Peterborough.

Petermann Range NT   Discovered by Ernest Giles in 1874 and named after Dr Augustus Petermann, a German geographer who had taken an interest in Australian exploration.

Petrie; Petrie, Mount; Petrie's Bight Q   Queensland owes much to the Petrie family, especially to Andrew, who arrived in 1831 and his son Tom, who was a skilled bushman, and blazed trails through the forest to open up the country for settlers. He also befriended the Aborigines and was held in great respect by them. One of them said to him, 'If all the whites were like you there would not have been so many killed'. Andrew climbed Mount Petrie in 1883 and carved his name and the date on a gum tree on the summit.

Pewsey Peak; Pewsey Vale SA   Named by Joseph Gilbert after his home town in Wiltshire. Before this he used the Aboriginal name Karrawatta, but changed it because of confusion with Tarrawatta.

Phillip Island T   After Governor Arthur Phillip.

Phillip Island V   First discovered in 1798 by George Bass, who described it as 'a high cape, like a snapper's head', and again by Lieut Grant in 1801 in the *Lady Nelson* who also noted the resemblance, hence the early name Snapper Island. After a short period when it was called Grant Island, after Lieut James Grant, it was named after Governor Phillip. Baudin's name, Ile des Anglais, did not survive.

Phillipson, Lake SA   After N. E. Phillipson who owned the Beltana station.

Piangil V   Aboriginal. Fish.

Pichi Richi Pass SA   Aboriginal. The name is derived from pituri, the plant used by the Aborigines as a mild intoxicant by chewing the leaves. The pass was discovered by William Pinkerton in 1843, and was first named Richman's Pass after John Richman, an early settler.

Picola V   Aboriginal. A corruption of Bigola, Whirlpool.

Picton NSW   Named by Major Antill after General Sir Thomas Picton, a British general who served in the Peninsula War and was killed at Waterloo. Governor Macquarie had called it Stonequarry, the village being on Stonequarry Creek. The new name came into use in the early 1820s.

Pieman River T   Named after a notorious character, 'Jimmy the Pieman', who escaped three times from the penal settlement at Macquarie Harbour. On his first escape he was captured near the mouth of the river named after him. The Aboriginal name was Corinna.

Pigeon House NSW   Captain Cook was the first to see the mountains. His Journal for 22 April 1770 read: 'A remarkable peak'd hill laying inland, the Top of which looked like a Pigeon house (dovecote), and occasioned my giving it that name.'

Pillar, Cape T   A descriptive name. Tasman called it De Zuyd Cap in 1642.

Pilliga NSW   Aboriginal. Place of swamp oaks; or from Biligha, Head of scrub oak.

Pimbaacla SA   Aboriginal. Many pine trees.

Pimpinio V   Aboriginal. Man squatting.

Pine Creek NT   The locality was discovered during the survey for the Overland Telegraph line, and was named on account of the many pine trees on the bank.

Pinjarra WA   Aboriginal. In the 1830s the settlement was known as Pinjarrup, but the meaning is not known.

175

Pinnaroo SA   Aboriginal. Tribal elder, or Important person.

Pioneer River Q   The river was discovered by the explorer John Mackay in 1860, but was later renamed after HMS *Pioneer,* commanded by Captain Burnett.

Piper, Point NSW   After Captain John Piper who was in receipt of considerable emoluments and who built an expensive house on what was first known as Point Eliza (after Mrs Macquarie). He was nicknamed the 'Prince of Australia'. He later purchased Vaucluse House (see Vaucluse) but was forced to sell it at a loss and was eventually ruined by his extravagances. Aboriginal name, Willara.

Piper, Cape; Piper Islands NT; Piper River T   All named after Captain Piper. See above.

Pisgah, Mount V   The mountain from which Moses viewed the Promised Land.

Pittsworth Q   The name came from the Pitt family which held the Goombungee station in 1854. The township was first called Beauaraba and changed to Pittsworth by Government proclamation in 1915.

Pittwater NSW   One of the earliest names bestowed in the colony. Governor Phillip named it Pittwater after William Pitt (the younger), the British Prime Minister, in 1788.

Plains of Promise, The Q   When Captain J. Lort Stokes first saw these open downs in Northern Queensland from the *Beagle,* when at the Albert River in 1841, his prophetic spirit rose to lyrical heights. In *Discoveries in Australia,* published in 1846, he prophesied that the horizons of the area he had named The Plains of Promise would some day be broken 'by a succession of tapering spires rising from many Christian hamlets that must ultimately stud this country, and pointing through the calm depths of the intensely blue and gloriously bright skies of Tropical Australia, to a still calmer and more glorious region beyond, to which all our sublimest aspirations tend, and where all our holiest desires may be satisfied'. The vision of a peaceful English countryside imposed on the Queensland terrain had little prospect of fulfilment, but doubtless the discoveries of uranium ore make a satisfactory substitute for the less romantic people of the 20th century.

Playfair Peak Q   Named by T. L. Mitchell in 1846 after Baron Lynd Playfair, a distinguished British scientist and politician.

Plenty River V   Named by J. T. Gellibrand because of the fertile country through which it flowed.

Plenty Salmon Ponds T   The first fish hatchery in the Southern Hemisphere was established here in 1864, when brown and rainbow trout ova were imported from England.

Pobasso Island NT   Named by Flinders in 1803. See under Malay Strait.

Poeppel Corner Q, SA, NT   Augustus Poeppel was the South Australian Government Surveyor who was sent in 1879 to survey the border between Queensland and South Australia along the 141st meridian from Cooper Creek northwards and along the 26th parallel of latitude to the 138th meridian, which forms the boundary between Queensland and the Northern Territory. The hardwood peg he drove into the ground to mark the junction of South Australia, Queensland, and Northern Territory became known as Poeppel's Peg. Further surveys were carried out by W. H. Cornish who discovered that Poeppel had placed the post 15 chains too far to the west, owing to an error in his chain. The 'peg' was therefore shifted to the new position. It has since been replaced by a concrete cylinder, but the traditional ceremony of hanging one's hat on the Poeppel Peg is still observed by the occasional passer-by at Poeppel Corner.

Point Hicks Hill V   On 19 April 1770, Captain Cook wrote: 'I have named it Point Hicks, because Lieut Hicks was the first who discover'd this Land.' The point of land named by Cook after Lieut Zacchary Hicks cannot be identified with certainty, but it is generally recognised as the granite promontory at the farthest east point of the coast of Victoria, now known as Cape Everard. Although Cook's name for the point disappeared from the maps, it was preserved in later years in Point Hicks Hill, some 8 km west of the cape. A monument to perpetuate the occasion of the first sighting of Australia by the *Endeavour* has been erected on Cape Everard. Midshipman Hicks was promoted to second Lieutenant prior to the departure of the expedition from England. Hicks Bay in New Zealand bears his name.

Pokataroo NSW   Aboriginal. Wide river.

Polly, Mount; Polly Springs SA   On 18 February 1861, J. McDouall Stuart wrote: 'At about 11 a.m. Polly slipped her foal. I could not think of leaving her behind, she has been such a faithful creature to me; has been with me on all my former journeys, and is now one of my best for enduring hardship and fatigue. I have never yet known her show the least symptoms of giving in; she and my other horse Jersey have endured more than any other horse in the colony.' Stuart's affection for his bay mare was also demonstrated in the naming of Mount Polly which he climbed on 25 April 1859.

Poole, Mount NSW   After James Poole who, with McDouall Stuart, then a young draughtsman, and sixteen other men, accompanied Charles Sturt in his expedition to the centre of the continent in 1844. This was one of the great feats of exploration in the history of Australia. Incredible hardships were suffered by the explorers. At Rocky Glen near Milparinka they were forced to remain for six months by a small waterhole. 'We were locked up in this desolate and heated region as effectively as if we were ice-bound at the Pole,' wrote Sturt. 'The thermometer reached 100 degrees and stayed there. Once it climbed up to 132°.' In the intense heat their fingernails split, and bolts and screws fell out of the wagons. Eventually the well dried up, but they were saved by a shower of rain — all except Poole. He had been affected by scurvy and Sturt had taken the desperate step of sending him home; on the second day out he died and was buried at the foot of the mountain that bears his name.

Pooraka NSW   Aboriginal. Turpentine or Tallow-wood tree.

Poowong V   Aboriginal. Carrion.

Porepunkah V   An Indian word that means Wind blowing. It is said that the town was christened during a storm.

Porongorup Range WA   Aboriginal. Discovered by Major Edmund Lockyer in December 1826.

Port Adelaide SA   After Queen Adelaide. See under Adelaide. The inlet was first discovered by Collet Barker, and later used as a base by William Light for his survey of the future capital. The Aboriginal name of the inlet was Yerta Boldinga.

Port Arthur T   The penal settlement was founded in 1830 by Lieut Governor George Arthur, and remained in use until 1877.

Port Augusta SA   Named after Lady Augusta Young, the wife of the Governor, Sir Henry Fox-Young, in 1852. The harbour was discovered by John Grainger and A. L. Elder in the *Yatala* on 24 May 1852. They wrote a letter to the Colonial Secretary telling of their discovery of 'the new Port (which we have taken the liberty of calling Port Augusta)...' The Aboriginal name was Kurdnatta, Place of drifitng sand.

Port Broughton SA   After Bishop Broughton, the first Bishop of New South Wales.

Port Campbell V   After Alexander Campbell, who built the cutter *Condor* and traded here at the beginning of settlement.

Port Clinton Q   Discovered by Matthew Flinders on 21 August 1802, and named by him after Captain James Bowen who was in command of naval vessels at Madeira when Flinders called there in the *Investigator* during his voyage to Australia. He named Cape Clinton at the same time, after Colonel Clinton, the commander of the land forces at Madeira. Clinton's name was substituted for Bowen's at a later date to avoid confusion with the town of Bowen, further to the north.

Port Curtis Q   Discovered by Flinders in August 1802 and named 'in honr of admiral Sir Roger Curtis, who had commanded at the Cape of Good Hope and had been so attentive to our wants, I gave to it the name Port Curtis...'

Port Dalrymple T   When Governor Hunter sent Bass and Flinders to circumnavigate Van Diemen's Land in 1798, the two adventurers entered the estuary of the Tamar River on 3 November and spent about three weeks exploring the harbour which they named after Alexander Dalrymple, the Admiralty hydrographer. Dalrymple was a firm believer in the non-existent great Southern Continent. When Cook disproved the theory he was annoyed, but he was a notable maker of charts which were held in great esteem by early navigators along the Australian coasts.

Port Darwin NT   J. L. Stokes, commander of the *Beagle*, found the harbour and named it in 1839. 'The other rocks,' he wrote, 'near it (Tall Head) were of a fine-grained sandstone:— a new feature in the geology of this part of the continent, which afforded us an appropriate opportunity of convincing an old shipmate and friend, that he still lived in our memory; and we accordingly named this sheet of water Port Darwin.' Charles Darwin had been on board the *Beagle* on an earlier voyage to several parts of the Southern Hemisphere. See also under Darwin.

Port Davey T   Named after the Lieut-Governor, Sir Thomas Davey. There are three claimants to the discovery of the harbour in 1816 — Dennis McCarty, an ex-convict (who did not actually claim to be the discoverer, but who may well have been the first), T. W. Birch, and James Kelly who circumnavigated the island in a whaleboat with four companions in 1815 and 1816.

Port Elliot SA   Named by Governor Young in 1850 after Sir Charles Elliot, Governor of Bermuda. A. E. Martin says that Sir Charles was Protector of Slaves in Guinea, Plenipotentiary in China, Charge d'Affaires in Texas, and successively Governor of Bermuda, Trinidad, and St Helens. The harbour was first sighted by Collet Barker in 1831. Governor Young hoped it would become a thriving port for the Murray River trade, but his hopes were disappointed.

Port Esperance T   Discovered and named by d'Entrecasteaux in 1792. The Aboriginal name was Raminea.

Port Essington NT   Discovered on 17 April 1818 by P. P. King, and named by him 'as a tribute of my respect for the memory of my lamented friend, Vice-Admiral Sir William Essington'. Sir J. G. Bremer took possession of the mainland on 20 September 1824, and founded the short-lived colony.

Port Fairy V   Named after the cutter *Fairy* (Captain J. Wishart) that was taken across the bar to avoid a storm, and entered the harbour. In 1835 the locality was called Belfast when James Atkinson of Sydney took up land in the vicinity, but eventually it reverted to its original name. The Aboriginal name was Pyipgil.

Port Germain SA   A misspelling of Germein. The port was discovered in June 1840 by Samuel Germein, captain of the government cutter *Waterwitch*, while engaged in conveying supplies to E. J. Eyre at the head of Spencer Gulf.

Port Hacking NSW   After Henry Hacking, explorer and first pilot at Port Jackson. It was Matthew Flinders who named the port that Hacking discovered. Aboriginal name, Goonamarra.

Port Hedland WA   When the town was laid out in 1863, the surveyor, L. C. Hunt, named it after Peter Hedland, a master pearler and captain of the cutter *Dolphin*, who had discovered the harbour in 1857.

Port Julia SA   Named after Mrs Julia Wurm, an early settler.

Port Jackson NSW   After Sir George Jackson, Judge-Advocate of the Fleet. Captain Cook's Journal of 6 May 1770 reads: '... at Noon, we were by observation in the Latitude of 33° 50 minutes S, about 2 or 3 miles from the Land, and abreast of the Bay, wherein there appear'd to be safe Anchorage which I called Port Jackson'. Jackson later changed his name to Duckett on account of a provision in the will of his second wife. He followed Cook's career with interest, probably because as a boy the navigator had worked as a stable boy for Jackson's sister at Ayton, Yorkshire. In a church at Bishop's Stortford, an inscription reads: 'To the memory of Sir Geo Jackson, Bart., afterwards Sir Geo. Duckett, Bart., who died Dec. 15, 1822, aged 97; for many years Secretary of the Admiralty and M. P. Capt. Cook, of whom he was a zealous friend and early patron, named after him Port Jackson in N. Zealand and Port Jackson in N. S. Wales.' It is perhaps unnecessary to say that Cook did not enter the harbour.

Port Kembla NSW   Aboriginal. Plenty of wildfowl. A jetty was built in this deep-water bay to ship coal brought from the mine at Mount Kembla, and this gave rise to the name of the bay.

Port Lincoln SA   Although whalers are reputed to have visited the harbour as early as 1800, Flinders made the formal discovery in 1802, and wrote: 'The port which formed the most interesting part of these discoveries I named Port Lincoln, in honour of my native province.' John Franklin was a midshipman on board the *Investigator* at the time. In 1841, when he was Sir John Franklin, and at the suggestion of Lady Franklin, he arranged for an obelisk to be erected to Flinders at the entrance to the port. The Aboriginal name of the harbour was Kallinyalla.

Port MacDonnell SA   Named by Benjamin Germein, a pilot and first lighthouse keeper at Cape Northumberland, who selected the bay as the site of a port. The town, surveyed in 1860, and port were named after Sir Richard MacDonnell, Governor of South Australia from 1855 to 1862. The Aboriginal name was Ngaranga.

Port Macquarie NSW   Discovered by John Oxley in 1818, and named by him in honour of Governor Macquarie.

Port Musgrave Q   Named after Governor Sir Anthony Musgrave.

Port Phillip V   Named after Captain Arthur Phillip, the first Governor of New South Wales. Lieut John Murray sailed into the harbour in the *Lady Nelson* on 14 February 1802 and anchored near the present site of Sorrento. After a careful survey, during which some of the crew were involved in a skirmish with the Aborigines, Murray had the British flag hoisted on 8 March and took formal possession of the territory, naming it Port King after the Governor, Philip Gidley King. Governor King subsequently changed it to Port Phillip in honour of the first governor. Matthew Flinders arrived at the harbour in the *Investigator* in April, and wrote: 'This place, as I afterwards learned at Port Jackson, had been discovered ten weeks before by Lieutenant John Murray, who had succeeded Captain Grant in command of the *Lady Nelson.*'

Until the separation of Victoria from New South Wales in 1851 the colony was known as the Port Phillip district. The Aboriginal name was Geelong, q.v.

Port Pirie SA   Named after the vessel *John Pirie* which was the first to sail into the river, bringing early settlers from Britain. The town was surveyed in 1871. The Aboriginal name was Tarparrie, Muddy creek.

Port Stephens NSW   After naming Port Jackson, Captain Cook named the next harbour after the second Secretary to the Admiralty, Sir Philip Stephens. Journal, 11 May 1770: 'At 4 P.M. past at the distance of one mile, a low rocky point which I named Point Stephens... on the N. side of this point is an inlet which I called Port Stephens (Lat 32° 40 minutes; Long 207° 51 minutes), that appear'd to me from the Masthead to be shelter'd from all Winds.'

Port Usborne WA   J. L. Stokes of the *Beagle* recorded on 21 March 1838: 'On our return to the ship, we found Mr Usborne had discovered good anchorage in the cove we had seen from the hill, which in commemoration of his providential recovery was called after him Port Usborne.'

Port Wakefield SA   After Edward Gibbon Wakefield. The harbour was discovered by a lighterman named Buck, and called Henry, possibly after Sir Henry Ayers who was then Secretary of the Burra Copper Mining Company. A suggestion that it should be renamed Port Young was firmly resisted by Governor Young. Finally, when the town was surveyed in 1850 it took its name from the Wakefield River, q.v.

Port Welshpool V   See Welshpool.

Portland NSW   So named because of the cement works, which were a reminder of the famous stone quarried at Portland, Dorset.

Portland; Portland Bay V   On his first passage through Bass Strait in 1800 in the *Lady Nelson*, Lieut James Grant passed the bay. On 7 December he wrote: 'I also distinguished the Bay by the name of Portland Bay, in honour of his Grace the Duke of Portland' — who had given Grant his official orders. The bay was known to whalers before this. In 1802 Baudin examined it and called it Tourville Bay, but the name has not survived. The first settlement was pioneered by E. Henry and his brother in 1834 or 1835.

Possession Island Q   On 22 August 1770 Captain Cook formally took possession of what was then called New South Wales q.v., on this island. The ceremony of taking possession was commemorated in 1925 by the erection of an obelisk.

181

Potts Point NSW   After J. H. Potts, a clerk in the Bank of NSW. Aboriginal name, Yarranabbe.

Powelltown V   So named because the Powell Company's wood processing works were located here.

Pozieres NT   The name commemorates the Battle of Pozieres in France on 25 July 1916, in which Australian troops took part.

Prahran V   Aboriginal. Almost surrounded by water.

Preservation Island T   The scene of the wreck of the *Sydney Cove* in 1797. The ship was bound for Port Jackson from Calcutta and was beached here, after springing a leak, on 8 February. Seventeen members of her crew attempted to reach Sydney in the ship's boat, but it was capsized near Cape Everard. A journey overland, notable for the hardships endured, followed as Hugh Thompson, the chief officer, and W. Clarke led their party to the young settlement at Port Jackson. They made notable discoveries on the way, but only three of them survived. A rescue expedition was dispatched — and history continued to be made then and later when a number of convicts escaped and went south with the intention of refloating the vessel and leaving Australia.

Preston River WA   Named in 1829 by Captain Stirling of the *Sulphur*, after its discoverer, Lieut William Preston, who was accompanied by the ship's surgeon, Alexander Collie.

Price SA   After the Premier of South Australia, Thomas Price.

Prince of Wales Islands Q   Named by Captain Cook on 22 August 1770 in honour of King George III's eight-year-old son. The Prince of Wales Island had been skirted by the *Duyfken* in 1606, and named 't Hooghe Eijlandt — the High Island.

Princes Highway   The name given after the visit of Edward, Prince of Wales (later King Edward VIII), in 1920.

Princess Charlotte Bay Q   Discovered in May 1815 by Lieut Charles Jeffreys of the brig *Kangaroo*. He named it in honour of Princess Charlotte, daughter of King George IV.

Princess Royal Harbour WA   Captain George Vancouver in the *Discovery* and Lieut W. R. Broughton in the *Chatham* entered and named King George Sound in 1791, and on 29 August named this part of the sound in honour of the Princess, as it was her birthday.

Proserpine Q   George A. F. E. Dalrymple, who explored this region, conferred on it a name derived from the Roman goddess of fertility, Proserpina (Persephone to the Greeks) because of the productive nature of the soil. This has been borne out by the success of sugar cane and banana plantations in the district.

Prospect NSW   It was from this hill in April 1788 that Governor Phillip viewed the western mountains in the hope that there might be more land for settlement. He named the eastern side of the hill Bellevue. The hill itself was called Tench's Prospect Hill, q.v., in 1789 when Captain Tench climbed to the top and saw the Blue Mountains.

Providential Channel Q   On 17 August 1770 the *Endeavour* began to drift toward the breakers, and was towed clear by the ship's boats with some difficulty. 'In this truly terrible situation,' wrote Cook, 'not one man ceased to do his utmost, and that with as much calmness as if no danger had been near.' Saved by a light breeze, the ship sailed through the channel. 'It is but a few days ago,' Cook continued, 'that I rejoiced at having got without the Reef, but that was nothing compared to what I now felt at being safe at an Anchor within it.'

Pucawan NSW   Aboriginal. Koala.

Puddingpan Hill Q   A descriptive name given by Captain Bligh when on his way to Timor after the *Bounty* mutiny.

Pullabooka NSW   Aboriginal. Head.

Pullut V   Aboriginal. Boxwood tree.

Pungonda SA   Aboriginal. Fight.

Pyrenees V   A descriptive name given by T. L. Mitchell in 1836 because the hills reminded him of those he had seen in the lower Pyrenees in the Peninsula War. The Aboriginal name was Peerick.

Quaama NSW   Aboriginal. Shallow water.

Quaker's Hill NSW   A family of Quakers lived here at one time.

Quamby Q   Aboriginal. Stop!

Quandary NSW   Said to be the name of a homestead which took its name from an English parish.

Quandialla NSW   Aboriginal. Porcupine.

Quantong V   Aboriginal. Plum tree.

Quart Pot Creek; Quart Pot Range Q   The creek was so named because a drinking vessel was discovered here in the early days. The name was applied also to the township of Stanthorpe, but was changed in 1870 – in spite of protests by local residents.

Queanbeyan; Queanbeyan River NSW   Aboriginal. Clear water. The first pastoral holding 1828 was called Queen Bean, and the town gazetted as Queanbeyan in 1838. The Surveyor-General endorsed the original application for a land grant with the comment: 'Quinbean is a hackneyed native name for part of the country not yet surveyed.'

Queenscliff V   The fishing village which sprang up about 1846 was known at first as Whale Head or Shortland Bluff, but was finally christened Queenscliff in honour of Queen Victoria.

Queensland   The state was named in honour of Queen Victoria at her own request. Before its separation from New South Wales it was usually known as the Moreton Bay district. At the time of separation several names were suggested — Cooksland, Flinders, and Flindersland.

Queenstown T   Also named for Queen Victoria, in 1897.

Quipolly NSW   Aboriginal. Creek with small waterholes containing fish.

Quirindi NSW   Aboriginal. The meaning is not clear. It is thought to be a corruption of Giyer warinda or Giyer warindi, variously rendered as Dead wood, Dead trees on a mountain top, and Waters fall together. The following variations have been recorded at different periods: Cuerindi, Cuerindie, Kuwerhindi.

Quorn SA   Named by Governor Jervois after Quorndon in Leicestershire, the home of his secretary J. H. B. Warner.

Radium Hill SA   So named because it was a field for mining ore with radium content. The venture failed, but it has grown in importance since 1952 when davidite was discovered here.

Radstock, Cape SA   On 9 February 1802 Flinders wrote: '. . . at six, a bold cliffy head, which I named Cape Radstock, in honour of admiral Lord Radstock . . .'

Raglan NSW   After a village in Monmouth, England.

Raglan V   Named after Lord Raglan, a veteran of the Crimean War. The Aboriginal name was Gerup Gerup.

Rainbow Beach; Rainbow Reach Q   Rainbow Reach is named after HMS *Rainbow* which anchored here in 1827. By a curious coincidence there was an Aboriginal legend about a man who fell in love with the rainbow that formed over Noosa Heads every evening.

Raine Island; Raine Passage Q   Named after the discoverer, Thomas Raine, a seaman who became a pastoralist. In 1815 he set sail for China in the *Surry,* and explored parts of the Great Barrier Reef.

Ramco SA   Aboriginal. An abbreviation of Dogorampko, a race of men who were believed to have the power of making themselves invisible.

Ramhead NSW   Named by Captain Cook on 19 April 1770: 'This land rises to a round hillock very much like the Ramhead going into Plymouth sound on which account I called it by the same name.' Cook recorded it as Ram Head; it also appears in the form Rame Head.

Rand NSW   Named after Robert Rand, an early settler.

Rapid Bay SA   Named by Colonel William Light after his vessel, the *Rapid,* when he visited the bay in 1836. Collet Barker probably visited the bay in 1831 before his crossing of the Murray Mouth and subsequent death. The Aboriginal name was Patpungga.

Ravenshoe Q   A. E. Martin notes that when the locality was first surveyed, a tattered copy of Charles Kingsley's *Ravenshoe* was found in a tree.

Ravenswood V   A local inn bore this name which was taken from Sir Walter Scott's *The Bride of Lammermoor.*

Rawlinson Range WA   In 1873 Ernest Giles and his party camped on the western slopes of the Tompkinson Range, not daring to shift camp until rain came to replenish their supply of water. Eventually Giles became impatient and travelled 80 km across the desert to a distant range, where he found a permanent water supply at a spot he named Fort McKellar. He named the hills after the President of the Royal Geographic Society.

Rawnsley Bluff SA   A curious fact emerges from the naming of the bluff south of Wilpena Pound. It was visited by the somewhat turbulent surveyor H. C. Rawnsley, but he claimed that the bluff already bore his name, conferred on it by settlers, before his arrival.

Recherche Archipelago WA   Admiral d'Entrecasteaux traversed the islands and shoals of the archipelago in *La Recherche* in 1792, and named them the D'Entrecasteaux Islands, the name being changed later. The Admiral gave French names to a number of the islands, and these were anglicised by Flinders in 1802, and others added. The first visitor was Pieter Niujts in 1627. Vancouver was also there in 1791.

Recherche Bay T   In April of the same year that d'Entrecasteaux was in the Recherche Archipelago in Western Australia, he entered and named Recherche Bay to effect repairs to his ships.

Red Point NSW   Named by Captain Cook. The Journal entry for 25 April 1770 reads: '. . . a point that I call'd Red Point; some part of the Land about it appeared of that colour'.

Redcliffe Q   This was the first site chosen for the Brisbane (q.v.) penal settlement by John Oxley in November 1823. The settlement was founded on 24 September 1824. Water was scarce and it proved necessary to move the settlement. When this happened, the Aborigines called the deserted cluster of buildings Oompiebong, meaning Dead huts, and so originated the name Humpybong.

Redfern NSW   After William Redfern, assistant surgeon, who was placed in charge of the hospital at Norfolk Island.

Redhead NSW   The name was given because of the reddish coloration of a nearby headland.

185

Redland Bay Q   The Aboriginal name was Talwurrapin, Hibiscus tree.

Reefton NSW   A name transported from the West Coast of the South Island of New Zealand. This was a rich goldmining area, and the person who bestowed the name was a 'West Coaster'.

Reid SA   After Sir George Houston Reid, Prime Minister of Australia from 1904 to 1905.

Remarkable, Mount SA   Although the hill was sighted from Spencer Gulf by Flinders in 1802, it was not named until 1840, when E. J. Eyre was on his third expedition. He wrote in his Journal: 'From our present encampment a very high pointed hill was visible far to the north-northwest. This, from the lofty way it towered above the surrounding hills, I named Mount Remarkable.' The Aboriginal names were Willowie and Wong-yarra.

Rendelsham SA   Named after the parish of Rendlesham in Sussex, meaning Rendle's Village.

Renmark SA   Aboriginal. Red mud.

Repose, Lake V   T. L. Mitchell formed a rest camp here for his men for a fortnight in 1836.

Repulse Bay Q   According to the *Australian Encyclopaedia*, Cook probably gave the name because, in spite of the favourable aspect of the bay, he was unable to find a suitable place to careen the *Endeavour*. Dr J. C. Beaglehole, however, refers to the sentence: '. . . low land, quite a Cross what we took for an opening between the Main and the Islands', this having 'repulsed' Cook, forcing him to haul his wind to the eastward. The name was given on 3 June 1770.

Research V   A lead of gold was found here, but it petered out, and was discovered once more after a 're-search'.

Resolution Creek T   A commemorative cairn marks the spot where Cook, having anchored the *Resolution* and the *Discovery* in the bay on Bruny Island on 24 January 1777, obtained water, as also did Bligh at a later date.

Restoration Island Q   While on his famous journey by boat to Timor after the mutiny on the *Bounty*, Lieut William Bligh landed on this small island on 29 May 1789. 'This day being the anniversary of the restoration of King Charles II,' he wrote, 'and the name not being inapplicable to our present position (for we were restored to health and strength), I named this Restoration Island.' Bligh and his men were able to regale themselves on turtle meat and the tips of palm leaves while they were here.

Reynella SA   Named after John Reynell who arrived in South Australia in 1838, obtained vine cuttings from Sir William Macarthur in New South Wales, and established his famous vineyards and vinery. He called his property Reynella and used the same name for the township founded in 1854.

Riana T   Aboriginal. Corroboree dance.

Richmond NSW   After the Duke of Richmond, Master-General of Ordnance. This was one of the five townships formed as a refuge from floods in 1810, and named by Governor Macquarie.

Richmond T   Named by Governor Sorell in 1824 when he purchased part of David Long's estate, Richmond Downs. In 1803 Lieut John Bowen explored the district, and discovered coal, which led to its being called Coal River. A settlement was formed in 1815, and renamed in 1824.

Richmond River NSW   The river was discovered, explored, and named by Captain H. Rous of HMS *Rainbow* in 1828.

Riley, Point SA   On 15 March 1802 Flinders wrote: '. . . a cliffy projection, named Point Riley after the gentleman of that name in the Admiralty'.

Risdon; Risdon Cove T   Risdon Cove was named by Captain John Hayes in February 1792. The *Australian Encyclopaedia* has several speculations in this connection: that Risdon was a friend or an official of the East India Company, or that he was second officer of his ship, the *Duke of Clarence*. Risdon was the first European settlement in Tasmania.

River Lett NSW   As the *Australian Encyclopaedia* says, it is of interest more for its name than its nature. Assistant Surveyor G. W. Evans recorded a 'Riverlett' in his notebook in November 1813. It may be presumed that he intended to write 'Rivulet', but the entry was taken at face value, and became River Lett or Lett River. Aboriginal name, Tarrapalet.

River Peak NT   In October 1839 J. L. Stokes recorded that 'The high land south of M Adam Range was found to terminate in a remarkable peak, which in the certainty of our search proving successful, we named River Peak.'

Riverina NSW   Several of the largest rivers flow through this extensive area in southern New South Wales. They include the Murray, Murrumbidgee, Lachlan, and Edward.

Riverstone NSW   After Riverston in Ireland. Lieutenant-Colonel M. C. O'Connell was given a land grant by Governor Macquarie, and named it Riverston, after his birthplace in Ireland. The name, in the slightly amended form, was adopted for the town that was formed in 1878.

Riverton SA   So named by James Masters because it was on the Gilbert River. Masters had taken up a sheep run in 1840, which was cut up and sold in 1854. Masters bought one of the sections and laid out a town which he named in 1855.

Rivoli Bay SA   The bay was discovered by Nicolas Baudin in 1802. He named it after the Duke of Rivoli, whom Napoleon had nicknamed 'the favoured child of Victory'. The Aboriginal name of the northern portion of the bay was Mirmal-Ngrang, the southern Wilichum.

Rob Roy NSW   After Sir Walter Scott's novel, first published in 1817.

Robbins Island T   The insularity of Robbins Island was established by Charles Robbins in the *Buffalo* in 1804.

Robe SA   Named after the Governor, Lieut-Colonel F. H. Robe, who arrived at Guichen Bay in the Government Schooner *Lapwing* in January 1846, and selected the site of the town.

Robertstown SA   After the first postmaster stationed here. It was earlier called Emu Flats.

Robinson Ranges WA   After William Frederick Cleaver Robinson. He was successively Governor of the Falkland Islands, Prince Edward Isle, Western Australia, the Straits Settlements, South Australia, and Victoria. He was a brother of Sir Hercules Robinson.

Robinson River Q   Named by Leichhardt during his first expedition, on 18 November 1844, probably after one of the men of his party.

Robinvale V   After Robin Cuttle, son of a local farmer.

Rochester V   A name that has suffered a curious change. The town was called Rowechester, after Dr Rowe, the first squatter to take up land in the district. In the 1860s the Lands Department must have thought it a corruption of Rochester in Kent, and with the best of intentions, changed the spelling. The Aboriginal name was Watneel.

Rockbank V   A descriptive name, taken from the first hotel in the locality.

Rockhampton Q   The name of 'the beef town of Australia' was suggested in 1857 by W. H. Wiseman, Commissioner of Crown Lands, partly on account of the many rocky outcrops in the river, and also because he came from Hampton in England. Charles and William Archer discovered the Fitzroy River in 1855 and established the Gracemere station there. The town was laid out by Wiseman at the time of the gold discoveries at Canoona.

Rockingham WA   Named after the tea-clipper which broke its moorings and was wrecked here in 1830.

Rockingham Bay Q   Named by Cook on 8 June 1770 after the Marquis of Rockingham, Prime Minister of England in 1765 and 1766. The present Halifax Bay was first named Rockingham Bay in the Journal, and subsequently the position of the two names was reversed.

Rockley NSW   After a place in England. Taken from Rockley Manor, the New South Wales home of Captain Steele.

Rocks, The NSW   The name was given at an early date, probably about 1800, to the high sandstone area to the west of Sydney Cove because of its broken nature. P. R. Stephensen says that 'many a stranded sailor has found himself financially as well as physically "on the rocks" because of the waterfront pubs and harpies' dens that formerly flourished on that ridge'.

Roe, Mount WA Named by Surgeon T. B. Wilson after J. S. Roe, Surveyor-General of Western Australia.

Roebourne WA Also named after J. S. Roe, when the town was proclaimed in 1866.

Roebuck Bay; Roebuck Plains WA When William Dampier visited Australia, this time on the *Roebuck,* in 1699, he made a landing about 80 km from the present Roebuck Bay, obtained some brackish water, and saw a few Aborigines. The bay was not named, but when P. P. King, on his last survey, in the *Bathurst,* skirted the coast as far as Cambridge Gulf, he conferred the name.

Rokeby V The name came from Sir Walter Scott's narrative poem *Rokeby.*

Rolland; Roland, Mount T Named after Captain John Rolland, who attempted to discover a route to the west coast from the Macquarie River in 1823. He was forced to turn back at Mount Roland. For a long time it was known as Rolland's Repulse, and when renamed the spelling was mistakenly altered.

Rolleston Q After Rolleston in Nottinghamshire or Leicestershire.

Roma Q Named after Lady Diamantina Roma Bowen, wife of the first Governor of Queensland, and daughter of Count Roma, a Venetian noble.

Romsey V After Romsey in Hampshire, meaning Rum's Island.

Roper River NT Named by Leichhardt on 19 October 1845 for the first member of his party to sight the river, 24-year-old John Roper. The expedition was on its way from Darling Downs to Port Essington. Roper was wounded by Aborigines during the journey. Roper's Lake was also named after him.

Rose Bay NSW Named by Governor Phillip after George Rose, Secretary to the Treasury. Aboriginal name, Goud-joul-gang, Home or Camp (or Ginnagulla).

Rosebery T The gold field was discovered by J. McDonald who called the company he floated the Rosebery Prospecting Association after the Earl of Rosebery (Archibald Philip Primrose), who became British Prime Minister in 1894 and 1895. He spent two years in Australia in 1883 and 1884. Gold was discovered at Rosebery in 1893.

Rosebery V Also named after the Earl of Rosebery. See above.

Rosebud V Named after the schooner *Rosebud,* a Greek vessel wrecked off the coast about 1844.

Rosedale V   After Mrs Rose Okeden, wife of an early settler.

Rosetta Head SA   Named after Mrs Rosetta Angas, the wife of George Fife Angas. The whalers, who used it as a look-out, called it The Bluff. In 1837 Captain Richard Crozier named it Cape Victor, after the vessel used in his survey of Encounter Bay. A tablet on the head commemorates the meeting in 1802 of Flinders and Baudin in Encounter Bay, q.v.

Rosevale Q   A corruption of Ross, the name of an early settler.

Roseworth SA   Land was taken up in this district by W. H. Gartrell in 1855. When a townsite was chosen his widow selected the name of her home village in Cornwall for the town.

Roslyn NSW   Probably from Roslin or Rosslyn, the village near Edinburgh, made famous in Scott's *Lay of the Last Minstrel*. It was the name given by Dr Mitchell to his estate.

Ross T   In 1821 Governor Macquarie gave the name to the guard station, established in 1812 for the protection of travellers between Hobart and Launceston, after the birthplace in Scotland of his friend H. M. Buchanan. The town site was surveyed in 1844.

Rottnest Island WA   The Dutch word means Rats' Nest, and was given in December 1696 by Willem de Vlamingh because of the numerous quakkas, a small wallaby that he thought to be a rat, that swarmed over the island. Rottnest Island was first explored by Dutch sailors in 1658. Vlamingh commanded a flotilla that was searching for *De Riderschap van Holland*, that had been lost two years before.

Rous Channel Q   After Captain H. J. Rous, who visited Moreton Bay in 1827.

Rudall SA   After S. B. Rudall, a Member of Parliament.

Rufus River NSW   Amusingly named by Charles Sturt after Sir George Macleay, who, as a young man, accompanied him on his 1830 expedition down the Murray River. Macleay had red hair, hence the nickname Rufus. There is also a legend that the river ran red after the 'Battle of the Rufus' when a punitive expedition was sent against Aborigines who had molested overlanders travelling with their stock to South Australia.

Ruined Castle Valley Q   So named by Leichhardt on 2 December 1844, as he skirted the Carnarvon Range, and found that the surface was 'fissured and broken like pillars and walls and the high gates of the ruined castles of Germany'.

Ruined City of Arnhem Land NT   This sandstone region north of the Roper River has seldom been visited by Europeans, but has been described by an eye-witness as one of the wonders of the world. Apparently the sandstone formation has weathered to such an extent that the outcrops have the appearance of streets of houses and buildings, their caves and recesses containing brightly coloured Aboriginal paintings. The latter 'buildings' cluster thickly together, giving the impression of a city, with less densely crowded dwellings in the 'suburbs', and surrounded with more distant outlying 'settlements'.

Rum Jungle NT   Many stories are told of the origin of this quaint name, most of them relating to prospectors who indulged in an orgy of drinking, or to teamsters who broached the casks on their wagons for the same purpose. Apparently it was a recognised stopping place for waggoners. The term Jungle is a misnomer because the land is covered with rocky outcrops. The place came into prominence in 1949 when it was developed as Australia's first large uranium project.

Rupanyup V   Aboriginal. Tree growing by a swamp.

Rushcutters Bay NSW   In the earliest days of settlement convicts came here to cut rushes for various purposes. In 1788 two convicts who were cutting rushes were killed by Aborigines. The Aboriginal name was Koggerah, Where rushes grow.

Rushworth V   When gold was discovered here in 1853 the young township was known as the Wet Diggings. It was later changed to Rushworth, reputedly from the remark of a gold fields warden who said it was 'a gold rush worth while'.

Russell River Q   After the maiden name of the wife of the Marquess of Normanby.

Rutherglen V   From the birthplace in Scotland of John Wallace, a notable figure in the days of the gold fields.

Ryde NSW   After the town of Ryde in the Isle of Wight, England. Meaning, a Stream. An early resident came from this town. It is said that he was G. M. Pope, owner of the 'Ryde Store'. Once known as Kissing Point, q.v., then Eastern Farms, and then Field of Mars. Members of the famous or infamous New South Wales Corps occupied a large portion of this area, thus giving rise to this martial name. The unit was raised in England in 1789 for service in New South Wales, and is referred to frequently as the 'Rum Corps', Though the suburb is now known as Ryde, Field of Mars is retained for the cemetery.

Saddleworth SA   After Saddleworth Lodge in England, the birthplace of James Masters.

St Andrews V   After St Andrews in Fifeshire, Scotland.

St Albans V   Saint Alban was the British saint and martyr of the fourth century.

St Arnaud V   Named after Jacques Leroy de St Arnaud, the French commander in the Crimean War. The gold field was first called New Bendigo.

St Clair, Lake T   Named by the Surveyor-General, George Frankland, in 1835 after the St Clair family of Loch Lomond, Scotland. The previous Surveyor-General, W. S. Sharland, claimed to have been the discoverer in 1832, but there is some reason to believe that the lake was found by Jorgen Jorgensen in 1826. The Aboriginal name was Leeawulena.

St Francis Island SA   The island has the distinction of being named both by Pieter Niujts in 1627 and Matthew Flinders in 1802. The islands St Pierre and St Francois were so called after the patron saints of Nuijts and of Francois Thijssen, captain of the *Gulden Zeepaard*, and are the largest islands in the Nuijts Archipelago. It was Flinders who named the archipelago and confirmed the names bestowed by Nuijts but in an anglicised form.

St George Q   T. L. Mitchell crossed the Balonne River on a bridge of rocks at this spot on St George's Day, 23 April 1846.

St George, Cape NSW   Seen by Captain Cook on 24 April 1770. The Journal entry reads: 'A point of land which I named Cape St George, we having discovered it on that Saint's day.' St George's Day is on 23 April; Cook's entry was made by ship's time, in which each day begins at midday of the preceding day. However, when crossing the 180th meridian of longitude, he made no adjustment to the dates in the log and journal.

St George River Q   Named after Howard St George, Gold Commissioner, by J. V. Mulligan when leading an expedition from Cooktown in 1874.

St Germaine's V   A fourth century duke who was Governor of Gaul. The Aboriginal name was Underra or Tandarrah.

St Helena Island Q   Two imaginative theories, both connected with Napoleon's exile on St Helena Island, have been put forward. One, as related by Bill Beatty, is that the island was once a prison. A Brisbane judge, in passing sentence on an Aboriginal, whose name was given as Bonypart, said: 'Well, here's the penal settlement and here's its first occupant — Bonaparte. Let's call the island St Helena.'

The other account, by A. E. Martin, is that Captain Logan marooned an Aboriginal who was supposed to resemble Napoleon, on the island. The Aboriginal name was Noogoon, Yam; or Nugoon, Nephew.

St Kilda V   Named by Superintendent Lonsdale after the yacht *Lady of St Kilda* that belonged to Colonel Acland. The Aboriginal name was Euro-yroke, Stone used for sharpening knives and spear heads.

St Mary's NSW   After the name of the parish church of St Mary Magdalene, consecrated in 1840. It was earlier known as South Creek.

St Mary's Peak SA   The appropriateness of the name of the mountain, which was sighted by E. J. Eyre in 1840 and named by B. H. Babbage in 1856, has been disputed. C. H. Harris says, 'The appropriateness of the apellation is obvious to anyone acquainted with its appearance and surroundings, for the white mantle of snow by which it is more frequently invested than any other hill in South Australia conveys an irresistible impression of saintliness' — a reference to Mary, the mother of our Lord. However, snow is rarely seen on the mountain. William Jessop, who was in the area in 1859, thought it 'an inconceivably strange name'. Hans Minchan in *The Story of the Flinders Range** draws attention to the fact that Babbage named St Mary's Pool in the MacDonnell Creek, and lived at St Mary's, Adelaide, both of which may have some significance in relation to his naming of the peak.

St Peter Island SA   Named by Pieter Nuijts and Matthew Flinders. See under St Francis Island.

St Valentine's Peak T   Discovered on 14 February 1827 and, being St Valentine's Day, was so named by Henry Hellyer.

St Vincent Gulf SA   Named by Matthew Flinders in March 1802 'In honour of the noble admiral who presided at the Board of Admiralty when I sailed from England, and had continued to the voyage that countenance and protection of which Earl Spencer had set the example, I named this new inlet the Gulph of St. Vincent.' Nicolas Baudin arrived in the Gulf shortly after Flinders and named it Golfe Josephine 'in honour of our august Empress', but Flinders's name took precedence. The Aboriginal name was Wongayerlo meaning Western sea or lake, or Overwhelming water where the sun sets.

Sale V   Named after Sir Robert Henry Sale (Fighting Bob), who saw much army service in India and Afghanistan, and was killed at the Battle of Moodkee in 1845. The first settler was Archibald McIntosh who arrived in the early 1840s. His property suffered through a flood and was then known as Flooding Creek. The township was first called The Heart by Governor La Trobe, because it was in the heart of Gippsland.

Salisbury SA   Named by John Harvey after the birthplace of his wife, in Wiltshire.

Salisbury V   After Lord Salisbury, Lord Privy Seal.

Salvator Peak Q   Named in 1846 by T. L. Mitchell after Salvator Rosa, the Italian poet and painter who lived in the 17th century.

Sandford V   This was an estate belonging to the Henty family, named after the book *Sandford and Merton,* by Thomas Day. The Aboriginal name was Watchropat, meaning Place of bream.

Sandgate Q   The Aboriginal name was Warra.

Sandwich Bay Q   Named on 8 June 1770 by Cook in honour of George Dunk, Earl of Halifax and Earl of Sandwich. See also under Halifax Bay.

Sandy Bagots SA   An amusing example of the corruption of a name by mispronunciation. A water hole found by Samuel Parry was called Saint a'Becket's Pool, and has evolved, or degenerated, to its present form.

* Rigby, 1964.

Sandy Cape Q   The northern point of Fraser Island was named by Cook on 20 May 1770 '...on account of 2 very large white Patches of Sand upon it'.

Sarina Q   The name was bestowed by a Greek surveyor.

Savernake NSW   After Savernake Forest in Wiltshire. It is probably a river name identical with Severn.

Sawtell NSW   After O. C. Sawtell, a local resident.

Schanck, Cape V; **Schanck, Mount** SA   Both the cape and the mountain were named by Lieut James Grant when on the *Lady Nelson* in 1802, in honour of Captain John Schank (who thus spelt his name). Schank was later promoted to admiral. He had designed the *Lady Nelson* and was the inventor of the sliding keel with which it was equipped.

Schouten Island T   Named by Tasman in 1642 after William Schouten, a member of the Dutch East India Company. The Aboriginal name was Tiggana Maraboona.

Scone NSW   After the village in Perthshire, where the ancient kings of Scotland were crowned. In 1831 an early settler, Hugh Cameron, presented a petition asking that the name Strathearn should be used, mentioning that the valley of Strathearn was close to the 'Ancient Palace and Abbey of Scoone'. The village was gazetted as Invermein in 1837, but this was later changed, under the instructions from the Colonial Secretary, to Scone.

Scoresby V   Named after Rev W. S. Scoresby, FRS, who came to Australia in 1856 to make observations in terrestrial magnetism.

Scott Bay; **Scott Creek**; **Scott, Mount** SA   Named by E. J. Eyre on his 1840 expedition in honour of his second-in-command, eighteen-year-old Edward B. Scott, of whom the leader wrote: 'As a companion I could not have a better selection. Young, active and cheerful, I found him ready to render me all the assistance in his power.' The Aboriginal name of Mount Scott was Bilparoo.

Scottsdale T   In the 1850s Assistant-Surveyor James Scott made an extensive exploration of the Ringarooma-Scottsdale area, then covered in dense forest. Early known as Ellesmere, the name Scottsdale was conferred in 1893.

Sea Lake V   A. E. Martin says that a bullock driver drove into the lake and on underestimating its depth, exclaimed, 'It's a blinking sea'.

Seabrook, Lake WA   The lake was discovered in 1864 by C. C. Hunt and named after a member of his survey party, John Seabrook.

Sebastian V   A gold lead was found here by Sebastian Smith.

Sebastopol V   Named after Sebastapol when blasting operations reminded old soldiers of gunfire in the Crimea.

Sedan SA   Named after the Battle of Sedan between the French and Germans in 1870, by the surveyor G. Pfeiffer.

Sedgwick V; **Sedgwick, Mount** T   Named by Charles Gould after the British geologist, Adam Sedgwick.

Separation Creek SA   A name that perpetuates an incident in the search for C. C. Dutton who had abandoned the Port Lincoln settlement, and while driving his stock back to the settled areas of South Australia, became overdue. Police and volunteers set out in search of him, but disagreements arose. The Police then returned leaving the volunteers to continue the search at Separation Creek.

Seppeltsfield SA   At the site of the largest family-owned winery in the world, Joseph Seppelt planted his first vines, near Nuriootpa, in 1851.

Serocold Creek, Serocold, Mount Q   Named after the pioneer pastoralist in the upper reaches of the Dawson River, George Pierce Serocold.

Serviceton V   After James Service, Premier of Victoria.

Settlement Island T   A penal settlement was established here in Macquarie Harbour in 1821. It was first named Sarah Island by its discoverer, James Kelly.

Seventeen-Seventy Q   This unusual name comes from the fact that Captain Cook landed in the area in that year. The name was given official approval in 1953.

Seventy Mile Range Q   The mountains were 70 miles from the nearest town, Ravenswood.

Severn River NSW, Q   After the Severn River, which flows through several English counties. The river is on the border of the two states.

Seville V   After Miss Seville Smith, an early resident.

Seymour V   The first settlers arrived here in 1837. When the town site was surveyed in 1843, it was named after Lord Seymour, son of the eleventh Duke of Somerset, and a Minister in Lord Melbourne's Cabinet.

Shannon River T   Named by Governor Sorell.

Shark Bay WA   When William Dampier, then in command of the *Roebuck*, entered the bay in 1699 he called it Shark's Bay 'for it was full of sharks and turtles and its shores swarming with kangaroo rats and iguanos'. It seems certain that Jonathan Swift placed the locale of the 'country of the Houyhnhms' here. His map was copied from Dampier's chart, and Gulliver was supposed to be a cousin of the author of *A Voyage to New Holland Etc. in the year 1699*. See also under Nuyts Archipelago.

Shelbourne V   After the Irish village of Shelburne.

Shepparton V   Named after Sherbourne Sheppard who took over the Tallygaroopna station from the first settler Edward Khull in 1843. In the early 1850s a man named Macguire built an inn by the crossing and commenced a ferry service over the river, thus giving the name Macguire's Punt which was in use for some time; but when the town was surveyed in

1855 the present name was well established. The Aboriginal name was Tallygaroopna (adopted also for the sheep run), meaning River of big fish.

Sheringa SA   Aboriginal. Yams, which grew plentifully here.

Sherlock SA   Named by Governor Buxton after a friend in 1907.

Shoalhaven River NSW   Named by George Bass on his epoch-making 600-mile voyage in an open whaleboat in search of the survivors of the wreck of the *Sydney Cove*. It was on this voyage that he finally established the existence of Bass Strait. He gave the name Shoals Haven on 7 December 1797.

Silver Valley Q   J. V. Mulligan found silver here in 1880 — the first such discovery in Queensland.

Silverton NSW   So named when a rich silver-lead seam was discovered and mining began, about 1880. Previously the place was known as Umberumberka, the Aboriginal which meant Meeting of two creeks.

Simpson Desert NT, SA   This vast stretch of arid land was first entered by Charles Sturt in 1845, but was not named until 1929. It was named by Dr C. T. Madigan, for A. A. Simpson, President of the South Australian branch of the Royal Geographical Society. Simpson was largely instrumental in raising the funds for an exhaustive aerial survey which Dr Madigan conducted, the results being published in his book *Crossing the Dead Heart*.

Singleton NSW   Benjamin Singleton was a member of a party led by John Howe, chief constable of Windsor, when he reached (possibly for the second time) this area and named St Patrick's Plains in 1820. In 1822 Singleton settled there. Twelve years later his property was subdivided and the town of Singleton had its beginning.

Sinnett Peak SA   Named after Frederick Sinnett who undertook extensive surveys of the Northern Flinders.

Sir Charles Hardy Islands Q   Named by Cook on 19 August 1770 after Admiral Sir Charles Hardy who was second-in-command in Hawke's great action in Quiberon Bay in 1759.

Sir Colin MacKenzie Wild Life Sanctuary V   After the eminent surgeon and scientist, Director of the National Museum.

Sir Edward Pellew Group NT   Named by Flinders in 1802 'in compliment to a distinguished officer of the British Navy'.

Sir Isaac Point SA   Named by Flinders on 16 February 1802 in gratitude to the Resident Commissioner, Sir Isaac Coffin.

Sir James Smith Group Q   An interesting play on words has been given in the names Bellows, Coppersmith, Goldsmith, Anvil, Hammer, Tinsmith Islands, and Forge Rock.

Sir Joseph Banks Group SA   When Flinders named these islands on

25 February 1802, he wrote: 'This was called Sir Joseph Banks Group, in compliment to the Right Honourable president of the Royal Society, to whose exertion and favour the voyage was so much indebted.'

Sir William Grant's Cape V   Named by Lieut James Grant in the *Lady Nelson* on 5 December 1900.

Sir William Thomson Range Q   Named after Sir William Thomson (Lord Kelvin).

Skipton V   After a place of this name in Yorkshire, meaning Sheep farm. The Aboriginal name was Woran.

Skirmish Point Q   Named by Flinders when in the *Norfolk* in 1799. He landed on Bubie Island with some of his men and was attacked by a number of Aborigines.

Slopen Island T   First sighted and named by Tasman in 1642.

Smith River WA   The name commemorates a sad event when George Grey returned from his expedition to Shark Bay. As his men were suffering severely from hunger and other privations, Grey went on ahead to Perth and returned with a rescue party. The only fatality was that of an 18-year-old boy named Smith. His body was found among the sand hills and was buried there. Grey named the nearby river in his memory.

Smithton T   Named after the prospector James Smith, who discovered the Bischoff tin mine, and who was nicknamed Philosopher Smith because of his ability to work out in his mind promising locations of mineral deposits. The settlement was located on the Dusk River, discovered in 1826, and went by this name from its foundation until the end of the century. The Aboriginal name for the Smithton-Stanley district was Martula.

Smoky Bay SA   Discovered by Flinders in January 1802, and so named because 'there was so dense a haze that the true horizon could not be distinguished from several false ones.'

Smoky Cape NSW   Seen by Captain Cook on 13 May 1770. His Journal entry reads: '... a point or head land, on which were fires that Caused a great Quantity of smoke, which occasioned my giving it the name of Smoky Cape.' A hill, rising to more than 300 metres, about a mile north of the cape, was subsequently named Big Smoky. The Aboriginal name was Gooung, which also means Smoky.

Smythesdale V   After Captain John James Barlow Smythe. The Aboriginal name was Naringook.

Snowtown SA   Named by Governor Jervois when the town was proclaimed in 1878 after Thomas Snow, his aide-de-camp and his brother Sebastian Snow, who was the Governor's private secretary.

Snowy Mountains; Snowy River NSW, V   A popular descriptive name which has supplanted the Aboriginal name, which was Muniong (or

Munyang), and was bestowed on the range by the Rev W. B. Clarke who made a geological exploration in 1851-52; The mountains had been described (though not named) as 'snowy' by Captain Mark Currie in 1823 and by Hamilton Hume in 1825.

Snuggery SA   This unusual name, says A. E. Martin, was bestowed 'because of a cheerful valley that brightens the locality'.

Sodwalls NSW   The name first given to a house built with sod walls for Andrew Loftus.

Solander, Point NSW   After Dr Daniel Carl Solander, one of the scientific observers and an assistant to Joseph Banks on the *Endeavour*. The headland at Botany Bay was named in his honour by Captain Cook on 29 April 1770. The Swedish community erected an obelisk to his memory in 1914.

Soldier's Point NSW   After Sergeant John Andrews, an early settler.

Solitary Islands NSW   In his Journal for 15 May 1770 Captain Cook wrote: 'Between 2 and 4 we had some small rocky Islands between us and the land...' He recorded the name on his chart. In the Hakluyt edition of the Journal, Dr J. C. Beaglehole quotes from *Historical Records of New South Wales:* 'The complete isolation of these islands from themselves as well as from the mainland was doubtless heightened by the fact that night was fast closing in when they were sighted.' He comments that 'the Australian night was not fast closing in between 2 and 4 p.m., but the weather would perhaps have an even more gloomy effect. Flinders, who added two or three to the group, thought they were miserable as well as solitary.'

Somerset Q   Sir George Bowen, the first Governor of Queensland, selected the site of the settlement in 1862 and named it after the Duke of Somerset, First Lord of the Admiralty. William Jardine, the father of Frank and Alexander Jardine, was the first Resident Commissioner.

Somerville V   After the Somerville family of Ireland.

Sorrell T   The name was given in 1821 by Governor Macquarie for Lieut-Governor William Sorell when he visited the site. He had overridden Governor Davey's proposal to situate it elsewhere in 1816. Lake Sorrell and Mount Sorrell were also named after the Lieut-Governor of Tasmania.

Sorrento V   When Charles Gavan Duffy arrived in the 1860s he built a large house here and named it Sorrento because the landscape was reminiscent of the Italian Sorrento. It was the site of the first settlement in October 1803.

South Australia   Before the official designation of the state was determined in 1836, several alternative suggestions were discussed. Dr John Dunmore Lang advocated Williamsland in honour of King William IV, and D. I. Gordon wished to call it Central State. For some time the whole area was known as Flinders Land, Baudin's map had shown it as Terre Napoleon.

Southern Cross WA   The township was so named because two prospectors,

T. R. Risely and M. Toomey, were directed to the hills they were seeking by being told that they should travel slightly to the east of the Southern Cross. They did so and were rewarded by finding a promising gold field which they named on account of their experience. When the township was laid out the streets were named after various constellations, such as Altair, Antares, Sirius, Spica, etc.

Southport Q   At the time the town was surveyed it was named by Thomas Blacket Stephens, Minister of Lands, after his birthplace in Lancashire. It was earlier known as Nerang Heads. The Aboriginal name was Goo-en.

Spec, Mount Q   The name originated in 1896 when tin and wolfram were being discovered in the locality, thus raising much speculation as to the mineral wealth of the area.

Spencer Gulf SA   Early in 1802 Matthew Flinders hoped that the extensive inlet was the commencement of a channel leading northwards as far as the northern coast, thus providing a route to the centre of the continent. On 20 March 1802, when he realised that his hopes were not fulfilled, he named it Spencer's Gulphe 'in honour of the respectable nobleman who presided at the Board of Admiralty when the voyage was planned and ship put into commission. I named it Spencer's Gulphe'. He also named Cape Spencer. Nicolas Baudin attempted to call it Golphe Bonaparte.

Speult River NT   See Liverpool River.

Spilsby Island SA   Named by Matthew Flinders on 21 February 1802 After a village in Lincolnshire, the birthplace of John Franklin who was midshipman on the *Investigator* at the time.

Spring of Hope, The SA   One of the few poetic names given by J. McDouall Stuart. In May 1839 he wrote: '...came upon a beautiful spring in the bed of the creek (Davenport), for which I am truly thankful. I have named this "The Spring of Hope". It is a little brackish, not from salt, but soda, and runs a good stream of water.'

Springsure Q   The town, which was laid out in 1854, takes its name from the fact that water from perennial springs ran down the rocks.

Springwood NSW   Governor Macquarie's Journal entry of 26 April 1815, written on his way to Bathurst, reads: 'Halted at three o'clock in a very pretty wooded Plain near a Spring of very good fresh water...I have named it Spring-Wood.' This is the oldest named town in the Blue Mountains.

Standley Chasm NT   Named after an early woman teacher in the school at Alice Springs.

Stanley T   This town, which was the first headquarters of the Van Diemen's Land Company, was probably named after Lord Stanley, who became Colonial Secretary in 1833.

Stanmore NSW After Stanmore House, owned by John Jones, who named it after his birthplace in Middlesex, England.

Stannary Q A stannary is a tin-mine, the place in Queensland being so named for obvious reasons.

Stansbury SA The name was chosen by Governor Musgrave; originally Oyster Bay.

Stanthorpe Q Known as a tin-mining area from 1872 to 1900, the name coming from Stannum, the Latin word from which Stannary is derived. See also under Quart Pot.

Staten (or Staaten) River Q During his investigation of Torres Strait in the *Pera* in 1623, Jan Carstensz sailed down the west coast of Cape York Peninsula and anchored at the estuary of the river. He recorded that 'since according to resolution it was agreed to make the return journey from here, we have had a wooden column, in the absence of stone, nailed to a tree, there being carved thereon the following words "In the year 1623 on 24 April there came two ships sent by the High and Mighty States General". Accordingly the aforenamed river is entitled in the newly made chart the Staten River'. The second ship mentioned was *Arnhem,* under the command of Dirck Meliszoon.

Frank and Alexander Jardine reached the river by land in 1864, and called it the Ferguson after the Governor of Queensland, Sir George Ferguson Bowen.

Stawell V Named after Sir William Foster Stawell, Chief Justice of Victoria, in 1857, when the big gold rush commenced. 20,000 miners were then working on the field. It was earlier known as Pleasant Creek, while the Aboriginal name was Kobram.

Steel's Creek V After an early settler, Matthew Steel.

Steizglitz; Steiglitz Mount V Named after Robert William von Steiglitz, an early pastoralist.

Stewarts SA After a squatter, D. Stewart.

Stickney Island SA Named by Flinders in February 1802 after a village in Lincolnshire, meaning Stick island.

Stirling, Mount; Stirling Range WA The names commemorate Captain James Stirling who surveyed the Swan River in 1827 and in 1829 established the settlement of Perth. He later became Governor of Western Australia and was knighted. In 1835 Stirling, accompanied by J. S. Roe, travelled to Albany and the Stirling Range, which had first been sighted (but not named) by Flinders on 5 January 1802. Mount Stirling was named by Robert Dale in 1830.

Stockwell SA After Samuel Stockwell, a local identity.

Stokes Bay SA After the first mate of the ship *Hartley.*

Stokes Bay WA On 14 March 1838 J. L. Stokes of the *Beagle* noted

'. . . this extensive bay which Captain Wickham, out of compliment, named after myself'.

Stokes, Mount Q   After Francis Stokes, manager of the Coonatto run.

Stone Hut SA   The name came from a hut on the property of H. Walter.

Stonehenge Q   After Stonehenge on Salisbury Plain, meaning Horizontal stones resting on stone pillars.

Stony Desert SA   See Sturt's Stony Desert.

Storm Bay T   Named Stormbaij by Tasman in November 1642. The *Heemskirk* and *Zeehaen* were about to enter the bay when they were driven out to sea by a storm. It was three days before they were able to return. Two boatloads of men went ashore to gather fresh greens, and landed near the present site of Hobart.

Stradbroke Island Q   The nomenclature of Moreton Bay centres round Captain the Hon Henry John Rous, commander of HMS *Rainbow,* which conveyed Governor Darling there in June 1827. Stradbroke Island was named after Rous's father, Viscount Dunwich, Earl of Stradbroke. Rainbow Reach is where the *Rainbow* anchored. The channel between Stradbroke Island and Moreton Island was named for Captain Rous, and his father was remembered in Dunwich Point.

Strahan T   After the Governor from 1881 to 1886, Sir George Cumine Strahan.

Strangways River; Strangways Springs NT   Discovered and named by J. McDouall Stuart in 1862 'after the Hon H. B. Templar Strangways, Commissioner of Crown Lands, South Australia, and who, since his taking office, has done all in his power to promote exploration of the interior'. Strangways was also instrumental in persuading the South Australian Government to embark on the Overland Telegraph Line project.

Stratford NSW   After the London suburb, meaning Ford by which a Roman road crosses the river.

Stratford V   Because the settlement was on the River Avon, Angus McMillan named it Stratford.

Strathalbyn SA   Named by William and Dr John Rankine in 1839 after their home territory in Scotland, Strath is Gaelic for a wide valley, Albyn a variant of Albion.

Strathallan V   After the birthplace in Scotland of William Campbell. The Aboriginal name was Konela. The first recognised name of the settlement was Cornelia Creek, a corruption of Konela.

Strathdowie V   The name was given by a Scotsman, G. MacKillop.

Strathewin V   Named after Ewin Cameron, a Parliamentarian.

Strathfieldsaye V   After the estate of the Duke of Wellington, in Hampshire.

Strathkellar V   After a Mr Kellar, a local property holder.

Streaky Bay SA   So named by Matthew Flinders in January 1802 because of the discoloured streaks he noticed in the wake of the *Investigator*. The earliest European contact went back to 1627, when Nuijts and Thijssen sailed along the south coast in the *Gulden Zeepaard*, and turned back at this point. The Aboriginal name was Cooeyanna.

Streatham V   After the London suburb.

Stroud Road NSW   After Stroud, a market town in Gloucestershire. Meaning, Marshy land overgrown with brushwood.

Struck Oil Q   A name that is redolent of the 1960s and 1970s, but in fact comes from a melodrama called *Struck Oil*. According to Bill Beatty, some prospectors who were visiting Mount Morgan to register a claim on the Dee River saw the play and decided to adopt the name. They met the leading lady, Maggie Moore. A. E. Martin adds the following information — that Maggie's real name was Margaret Virginia Sullivan, who married J. C. Williamson in 1874 and helped her husband in his theatrical enterprises.

Strzelecki Creek SA   Discovered by Charles Sturt on 18 August 1845 and named after the explorer Sir Paul Edmund de Strzelecki.

Strzelecki; Strzelecki Ranges V   The redoubtable explorer (see above) was born in Poland. The *Australian Encyclopaedia* states that the usual Australian pronunciation is 'Strezlecki', but in Polish it is nearer to 'Stcheletzki'.

Stuart Creek; Stuart, Mount; Stuart Pass; Stuart Range SA   It is appropriate that John McDouall Stuart, who undertook such strenuous journeys in his trans-continental journeys and conferred so many place names, should himself be remembered in similar fashion. The creek was named Chambers Creek by the explorer in 1858, after John Chambers, but renamed by B. H. Babbage. It is not known whether Stuart named the mountain after himself while working in the Oratunga district about 1855, or whether by local settlers. The pass was named by Winnecke, who wrote: 'I have called the several gorges and gaps through which the Hugh takes its course in this part of the MacDonnell Ranges Stuart Pass.' Stuart skirted the Stuart Range in 1858, and it was named in his honour by the Governor, Sir Richard MacDonnell.

Stuart, Point; Stuart Swamp NT   J. McDouall Stuart found the water holes at Daly Waters in May 1862 and named the swamp after himself. It also seems likely that Point Stuart was self-named, for it is near the terminal of his successful crossing of the continent in 1861 and 1862.

Sturt Creek WA   Named after Charles Sturt, the celebrated explorer.

Sturt, Mount NSW   Named for Charles Sturt, who named both the Darling and the Murray Rivers. The Sturt Highway also bears his name.

Sturt, Mount NT   See Central Mount Sturt.

Sturt Plains NT   In 1861 J. McDouall Stuart named the Plains of Sturtia after the venerable commander of the expedition of 1845, but later referred to them as Sturt's Plains.

Sturt's Stony Desert SA   'That iron region' was crossed by Sturt in 1845. He said that the gibbers reminded him of shingle on a beach. Sturt River in South Australia is also named after him.

Sullivan Cove T   After John Sullivan, Under-secretary of the Colonial Office.

Sunbury V   The name came from the Sunbury Inn on Jackson's Creek, and this in turn from Sunbury on Thames in Middlesex and so named by Samuel and William Jackson, the first settlers. The town was surveyed in 1851. The Aboriginal name was Koora Kooracup.

Sunday Island Q   Named by Captain Bligh on a Sunday in 1792. See under Thursday Island.

Sunraysia V   A name given to the district largely devoted to dried fruit production, embracing Mildura, Red Cliffs, Merbein, and Irymple. The trade name Sun-Raysed was used by C. J. de Garis in the 1920s, and the term adopted for the whole region.

Surat Q   From Surat in the East Indies.

Surfers Paradise Q   The name comes from a hotel built in the 1920s by J. F. Cavill on the sandspit between the Nerang River and the surfing beaches. About 1876 J. H. C. Meyer operated a ferry on the Nerang River and the place was known as Meyer's Ferry. For some time the beach was called simply Main Beach. See also City of Gold Coast.

Sutherlands SA   After William Sutherland, a local resident.

Sutton Grange V   From Sutton-Manners, Viscount Canterbury.

Suttor River Q   Discovered on 5 March 1845 by Leichhardt and named after William Henry Suttor who had donated four bullocks to the expedition, and had helped in other ways. Suttor was a member of a distinguished Queensland family noted for its contribution to the progress of the pastoral work of the state.

Swan Hill V   The name arose from the fact that while camped here in 1836, T. L. Mitchell's sleep was disturbed during the night by swans and other wild fowl on a nearby lagoon. The Aboriginal name was Martiragnir.

Swan Point T   In his Journal for 10 November 1798, Matthew Flinders wrote: 'In running from Egg Island to the opposite point we observed a flock of swans at the back of the shoal which lays off it, and as their numbers far exceeded any we had met before, I called this low sandy projection Swan Point.'

Swan Pond V   In describing Flinders's return from an expedition ashore in May 1802, Samuel Smith of the *Investigator* wrote: '... our boat and crew came on board. Brought with them 2 swanns and a number of native spears.'

Swan River WA   The naming of the river goes back to 1696 when Willem de Vlamingh of the *Geelvink* made his first inland exploration of the west coast of Australia. He was amazed to see the many black swans, which had not been known up to that time. He promptly gave the name Black Swan or Swan River. It was first seen by the British when Captain James Stirling of the *Success* explored the river for about 80 km during his 1827 survey which ultimately led to the establishment of the Swan River settlement.

Swansea NSW, T   Probably named after the seaport in Glamorganshire, Wales. Before 1887 the settlement in New South Wales was known as Pelican Flat. The Tasmanian Swansea was named by George Meredith, a Welshman.

Sweers Island Q   Matthew Flinders visited the island in the *Investigator* in 1802 and obtained fresh supplies of water. As Dutch explorers had been the first Europeans to explore the head of the Gulf of Carpentaria, he named the island after Salamon Sweers, a member of the Batavia Council which had arranged Tasman's voyage of 1842.

The 'Investigator Tree' on this island was one of the most famous trees in Australia. Dutch and Chinese navigators had left inscriptions on it at various times. Flinders had the name of his vessel cut into the trunk together with that of his first lieutenant, Robert Devine. In succeeding years others continued the practice. One of them, J. Lort Stokes, named the spot Point Inscription. The tree was blown down in 1887, but portion of the trunk, still bearing the *Investigator* inscription, was placed in the Queensland Museum.

Sydney NSW   After Thomas Townshend, first Viscount Sydney, Secretary of the Home Department, who submitted the plan for a convict settlement at Botany Bay to the Treasury. When Captain Arthur Phillip transferred the settlement from Botany Bay to Port Jackson, he named the bay where he landed Sydney Cove. Phillip's first thought was to call it Albion, but he abandoned this in favour of the British minister and thus 'gave immortality to an obscure minister', as Lord Rosebery once said. The following extract from the Governor's first dispatch is authority for the origin of the name: 'The different coves were examined with all possible expedition. I fixed on the one that had the best spring of water, and in which the ships can anchor so close to the shore that at a very small expense quays can be made at which the largest ships may unload. This cove, which I honoured with the name of Sydney, is about a quarter of a mile across at the entrance, and half a mile in length.' The dispatches were headed Sydney Cove until 1790, when it was abbreviated to Sydney – the portion of the capital city that now includes Circular Quay.

It is thought that Townshend believed that New South Wales would be 'a very proper place' for a convict settlement. As Secretary of State for the Home Department, he was responsible for arranging for the dispatch of the First Fleet and the appointment of Captain Phillip as leader of the expedition. In view of the fact that he reprimanded Phillip for seeking a new site when Botany Bay proved unsuitable, it is ironic that his name should be perpetuated in the largest city in Australia.

The settlement was also known as Sydney Town at one time. The Aboriginal name was Warrane.

Table Cape T   The cape was sighted by Bass and Flinders in 1798. On 5 December Flinders wrote in his Journal: 'It is moderately high and level, whence I called it Table Cape.'

Table Top NSW   The name was taken from the estate of a Mr Mitchell, and originated in the shape of the nearby mountain.

Tabulam NSW   In *Aboriginal Myths and Legends** Roland Robinson records an account by the Aboriginal, Alexander Vesper, of an attack on the Aborigines at Tabulam by the settler Edward Ogilvie. When the Aborigines were attacked they called out, 'We Jabilum,' meaning 'we are the originals'.

Taggerty V   Aboriginal. Blue clay, used in body painting.

Tahmoor NSW   Aboriginal. Bronzewing pigeon. The name given to his residence by James Crispe.

Tailem Bend SA   Probably Aboriginal. Tailem may be a corruption of Thelim. Donald Gollen, an early settler, first called his run 'Pine Camp, then Taleam. It has been suggested that as stock were herded or 'tailed' here when being driven overland from New South Wales to Victoria and South Australia, this may have been the origin of the name. The town was proclaimed in 1887.

Talbot V   After Lord Talbot. Formerly Black Creek.

Talc Head NT   In September 1839, J. L. Stokes described it as a point 'where some talc slate, pieces of which measured four inches in length, was found embedded in quartz. The point was called in consequence, Talc Head'.

Taldra SA   Aboriginal. Kangaroo.

Talgarno V   Aboriginal. Dry country.

Tallangatta V   Aboriginal. Many trees. When the town was transferred in 1955-1956, more than a hundred years after its foundation, on account of an extension of the Hume Weir, the Governor-General, Sir William Slim, remarked at the official opening that he approved of the retention of the name, for it sounded 'like the ring of a blacksmith's hammer'.

Tallawang NSW   Aboriginal. Place of native apple trees.

Tallimba NSW   Aboriginal. Young man.

* Sun Books

Tallong NSW   Aboriginal. Spring of water, or Tongue of land.

Tallygaroopna V   Aboriginal. Tall trees.

Tamar River T   The Tamar River was navigated as far as Shoal Point by Bass and Flinders in 1798. William Collins, whose investigations were continued up to the north Esk, called it the Dalrymple, but in 1804 Col William Paterson renamed it the Tamar after the river that flows between Devon and Cornwall.

Tamban NSW   Aboriginal. Place of wiry grass.

Tambo Q   Aboriginal. Yam, or Fish.

Tambo River V   Aboriginal. Fish.

Tamborine; Tamborine Mountain Q   Aboriginal. A corruption of a word that has been spelt in several ways — Dumberin, Jambooin, Tamborine, and Tchambreen, all of which mean Place or Cliff of lime trees or yams.

Tamworth NSW   After the town in Staffordshire and Warwickshire represented in the British Parliament by Sir Robert Peel, British Prime Minister. It was probably named by John Oxley who also named the Peel River. The name means Homestead on the River Tame.

Tandara V   Aboriginal. Camping place.

Tandarook V   Aboriginal. Green vegetable.

Tangambalanga V   Aboriginal. Crayfish.

Tantanoola SA   The name is said to come either from the Aboriginal Tanta-noorla, Brushwood shelter, or is a Malay word meaning Boggy. The place is remembered on account of the fabulous 'Tantanoola Tiger' which still figures in local folklore. The phrase has attained some circulation through an apparently inexplicable or incredible fact. The story is that one morning in 1889 a young man saw a tiger leap over a fence with a sheep in its mouth. A tiger-hunt ensued, and eventually a large dingo was discovered. But, perhaps coincidentally, one of the residents was convicted of sheep-stealing shortly afterwards. At one time the town was called Lucieton.

Tanunda SA   Aboriginal. Plenty of wild fowl in the creek.

Taplan SA   Aboriginal. Grass tree.

Tara River V   See Tarra River.

Taradale V   After Taradale in Ross-shire.

Tarago NSW   Aboriginal. Country.

Taragoro SA   Aboriginal. Small black cormorant.

Taralga NSW   Aboriginal. Native companion.

Tarana NSW   Aboriginal. Large waterhole.

Tarcowie SA   Aboriginal. Washaway water.

Tarcutta NSW   Aboriginal. Grass-seed flour. The name was first given to the home of a settler named Mate.

Taree NSW   Aboriginal. A contraction of Tarrabit or Tareebin, Native fig tree.

Taripta V   Aboriginal. Small trees in swamp.

Taroom Q   Aboriginal. Lime tree.

Taronga Park NSW   Aboriginal. Taronga means Good view.

Tarra River; Tarra Valley V   Aboriginal. A party led by W. A. Brodribb reached here on 13 February 1841, and named the Albert and Tarra Rivers.

Tarrangower, Mount V   Aboriginal. Big mountain.

Tarranyurk V   Aboriginal. Water vessel.

Tarrawingee V   Aboriginal. Emu.

Tarrington V   When the three sons of Thomas Henty went to Australia in 1829 they wre accompanied by labourers from West Tarring.

Tarwin V   Aboriginal. Thirsty.

Tasman Peninsula T; **Tasman Sea**   After Abel Janszoon Tasman. The name Tasman Sea was recommended in 1890 by the Australian and New Zealand Association for the Advancement of Science. It is usually referred to as 'the Tasman'.

Tasmania   It was many years before Tasmania was proved to be an island. After sighting the coast on 24 November 1642, Tasman wrote on the following day: 'This land being the first land we have met with in the South Sea, and not known to any European nation, we have conferred on it the name *Anthoony van Diemenslandt*, in honour of the Hon. Governor-General, our illustrious master, who sent us to make this discovery; the islands circumjacent, so far as known to us, we have named after the Hon. Councillors of India, as may be seen from the little chart that has been made of them.' On 3 December Tasman took formal possession of the land he had discovered. The anglicised form, Van Diemen's Land, remained in use until 1855 in official documents, but by the middle of the 1820s the modern name Tasmania (in honour of the discoverer) was beginning to become into general use.

Tasman's Eylandt T   Named by Tasman.

Tate River Q   Discovered on an expedition to the north-east coast, led by William Hann and his brother Frank H. Hann. The river was named after the botanist of the party, Dr Thomas Tate, on 7 July 1872.

Tatham NSW   Aboriginal. Young child, or Woman with child. A large gum tree growing here had a small diameter trunk at the base, a large middle barrel, and a small top. The local Aborigines said that it represented a pregnant woman. The original name may have been Chargem, Baby.

Tathra NSW   Aboriginal. Place of wild cats, or Beautiful country.

Tatura V   Aboriginal. Small lagoon.

Taylor Islands SA   Matthew Flinders was greatly distressed at the loss of some of his crew near Cape Catastrophe, q.v. On 28 February 1802 he wrote: 'These I called *Taylor's Isles*, in memory of the young gentleman who was in the cutter with Mr Thistle.'

Teddywaddy V   Aboriginal. Dirty water.

Telford SA   Named after Thomas Telford, a civil engineer, in 1858.

Temora NSW   After Temora Castle, in a poem by Ossian. The name was given by J. D. Macanash in 1848. The township was formed at the time of the gold rush in 1880. It was proposed to call it Watsonford, but the miners insisted on retaining the name of Macanash's property.

Tempe NSW   After a valley in Thessaly in Greece, celebrated for its beauty, cool shade, and singing birds. Tempe House on this site was owned by A. B. Sparke, who was a merchant in the early days of settlement.

Tempy V   A peculiar contraction of 'Temporary', to show that supplies were left here temporarily for railway construction workers.

Tench's Prospect Hill NSW   After Watkin Tench, who accompanied Governor Phillip on an expedition in 1789 to try to determine whether the Nepean and Hawkesbury were the same river. They climbed a hill to see whether they were above or below Richmond Hill, and this gave the Governor occasion to bestow Tench's name on it.

Tennant Creek NT   Discovered by J. McDouall Stuart on 6 June 1860, and named after John Tennant, a settler in the Port Lincoln district.

Tenterfield NSW   After the family estate of Stuart Alexander Donaldson, first Premier of New South Wales under responsible government. He gave the name to his property in the 1840s. This was taken for the town that was gazetted in 1851.

Terang V   Aboriginal. Bare twig.

Termination Island WA   This was the last point seen by Vancouver and Broughton when they sailed eastward along the southern coast in the *Discovery* and *Chatham* in 1791.

Terowie SA   The Aboriginal name of a creek in the vicinity.

Thalia V   One of the Muses in Greek mythology.

Thallon Q   After J. F. Thallon, Commissioner of Railways.

Tharbogang NSW   Aboriginal. Old woman.

Thargomundah Q   Aboriginal. Porcupine.

Theodore Q   After Edward Granville Theodore, a prominent Labor Parliamentarian in Queensland.

Thevenard SA   Flinders took the name from an old map drawn by the French Minister of Marine whose name was Thevenard.

Thirsty Sound Q   'This inlet,' wrote Cook on 30 May 1770, 'which I have named Thirsty Sound, by reason we could find no fresh water...'

Thirlmere NSW   After a lake in Cumberland that supplies water to Manchester. Formerly known as Picton Lakes.

Thirroul NSW   Aboriginal. Valley or hollow.

Thistle Island SA   The tragedy in February 1802 when John Thistle, master of the *Investigator*, and several of the crew were drowned affected Matthew Flinders deeply. Thistle had been with Bass when he discovered Westernport and with Bass and Flinders during their circumnavigation of Van Diemen's Land. Flinders wrote to his wife on his return to Sydney: 'It will grieve thee, as it has me, to understand that poor Thistle was lost on the south coast. Thou knowest how I valued him...' The story of the tragedy is related briefly in the entry Cape Catastrophe, q.v. 'I satisfied myself of the insularity of this land,' Flinders wrote on 21 February, 'and gave to it, shortly after, the name of Thistle's Island, from the master who accompanied me.'

Thomson River Q   Discovered by E. B. C. Kennedy in 1847 and named after the Colonial Secretary of New South Wales, E. Deas Thomson.

Thoona V   Aboriginal. Hill.

Thornton V   After Dr Thornton who came here in 1848.

Thorny Passage SA   The channel between the islands and the mainland was named by Flinders on 21 February 1802 because of the difficulty he experienced in navigating it.

Thorpdale V   After the English Thorpdale, meaning Village in a valley. The Aboriginal name was Narracan, which was adopted by the first settlers, then changed to Wallington, after Captain Wallington, the Governor's A.D.C., and finally to Thorpdale.

Three Brothers, The NSW   On 12 May 1770, Captain Cook wrote in his Journal: '3 remarkable large high hills lying Contigious to each other, and not far from the shore, bore N.N.W. As these Hills bore some resemblance to each other we called them the 3 Brothers.'

Three Points, Cape NSW   A Cook Journal entry of 7 May 1770: 'Some pretty high land which projected out in 3 bluff Points, and occasioned my calling it Cape 3 Points.'

Three Sisters, The NSW   Aboriginal names for these three remarkable formations in the Blue Mountains were Meeni, Wimlah, and Gunedoo.

Thring Creek NT   Named by J. McDouall Stuart after the third in command of his 1862 expedition. F. W. Thring was in charge of the horses. Stuart gave the name 'in token of my appreciation of his conduct throughout the expedition'.

Thuddungra NSW   Aboriginal. Water running down.

Thursday Island Q   The islands in the vicinity of Cape York named after the days of the week provide some problems for those who are interested in nomenclature. Wednesday Island was named by Captain Bligh in 1789 and probably Sunday Island. Monday, Tuesday, Wednesday, Thursday, and Sunday Islands have all been named. Thursday Island first appeared on an Admiralty chart in 1850, and it was declared a Queensland municipality in 1912. The Aboriginal name was Waiben.

Tibarri Q   Aboriginal. Eye.

Tibbuc NSW   Aboriginal. Vine.

Tiberias, Lake T   See under Jerusalem.

Tichbourne NSW   L. A. Unger, Research Officer of the Parkes and District Historical Society states that a butcher from Wagga named Orton claimed to be the long-lost heir of the Tichbourne estates. One of the gold leads was named the Wapping Butcher after him.

Tiega V   Aboriginal. Sister.

Tilba Tilba NSW   Aboriginal. Many waters.

Tilbuster NSW   The name was first given by the Dumaresq family to a pastoral holding.

Timboon V   Aboriginal shell used as a cutting implement.

Timmering V   Aboriginal. Kangaroo on the plain.

Timor NSW   The name of the estate of James White.

Tinamba V   Aboriginal. Pull my toe.

Tinaroo Creek Q   John Atherton, while prospecting with James Robson for tin in the ranges near Emerald End in June 1879, found the metal at the creek and shouted: 'Tin! Hurroo!'

Tingha NSW   Aboriginal. Flat.

Tinline, Mount SA   Named after a banker, George Tinline.

Tinonee NSW   Aboriginal. A corruption of Tinobah, Shark.

Tintinara SA   The poetic Aboriginal name was given by the mother of the novelist Guy Boothby. Tinjinlara, the correct form, is the constellation of Orion's Belt. The stars were believed to be young men hunting emus and kangaroos.

Tocumwal NSW   Aboriginal. Deep hole. The local Aborigines believed that the hole in the river extended from here to The Rock, seven miles to the north-east.

Tod River SA   Discovered by Robert Tod, who was employed by the South Australian Company, in 1839. It is the only river of any size over a range of 1,600 km from Albany to Port Augusta.

Todd River NT   A survey party from the Overland Telegraph Line discovered the river and named it after the Postmaster-General, Sir Charles Todd, who was responsible for the construction of the line. The dry bed of the stream, which loses itself in the Simpson Desert at Alice Springs is the scene of the famous annual 'boat race', in which the 'boats' are carried by runners. At certain seasons the river becomes a rushing torrent.

Tom Price, Mount WA   After Thomas Price, Vice-President of a U.S. Steel Corporation.

Tom Ugly's Point NSW   There has been some controversy over the origin of the name. One account says that Tom Huxley was an early settler, and that as the Aborigines were unable to pronounce his name correctly, he was known as Tom Huckley. The point then came to be known as Tom Huckley's Point, and eventually Tom Ugly's Point. Alternatively there may have been a white man (or an Aboriginal) with only one leg and one arm who was known as Tom Wogul or Wogully. Wogul is an Aboriginal name meaning one, or one eye. The name was eventually corrupted to Tom Ugly.

Tomingley NSW   Aboriginal. Blind ears (Death adder).

Toobeah Q   Aboriginal. To point, so named because of the pointing finger sign installed here at one time.

Tongala V   Aboriginal. The first station established here took its name from an Aboriginal term for the Murray River.

Toogoolawah Q   Aboriginal. A corruption of the name of the Tugulawa tribe.

Toolondo V   Aboriginal. Muddy swamp.

Tooloom NSW   Aboriginal. Head-louse, or Place of lice and ticks. In the first myth of Dirrangun in *The Man Who Sold his Dreaming** Roland Robinson states the original form of the name was Dooloomi, meaning Louse.

Toongabbie V   Aboriginal. Near water.

Toongi   Aboriginal. Scrub turkey.

Toora V   Aboriginal. Woman.

Tooradin V   Aboriginal. A term for the fabulous bunyip.

Toorak V   Aboriginal. Tea-tree springs.

Tooraweenah NSW   Aboriginal. Plenty of brown snakes.

Tootool NSW   Aboriginal. A now extinct bird. The name of a nearby estate.

Toowong Head Q   Aboriginal. Note of the cuckoo.

Toowoomba Q   Aboriginal (?). No final answer can be provided to

* Currawong Publications

questions on the origin of the name of the city located at what was once known as The Swamp, or The Swamps. One theory is that in attempting to pronounce the name the Aborigines called it Tchwampa, which became modified to Toowoomba. Another is that it was Choowoom or Toowoomba, Place where melons grow, or Water sit down — referring to underground water. A. E. Martin adds the interesting information that the Archdeacon Glennie preached at The Swamp in 1848. Disliking the name of the young settlement he entered the place of the birth of babies as Toowoomba in the Parish Register. At a sports meeting held on New Year's Day 1858, the word was displayed in white letters on a sheet of red calico and erected at the winning post. Thomas Alford settled here in 1852 and at that time named his house Toowoomba. The town was proclaimed a city in 1904.

Torment, Point WA   An entry in J. L. Stokes's Journal in February 1838 reads: 'A name was soon found for our new territory, upon which we with rueful unanimity conferred that of Point Torment, from the incessant and vindictive attacks of swarms of mosquitoes, by whom it had evidently been resolved to give the new comers a warm welcome.'

Toronto NSW   After Toronto in Canada. The name was given in honour of Edward Hanlan, world champion sculler, who came from Toronto in Canada.

Torrens Creek Q   Discovered by William Landsborough and Nathaniel Buchanan in 1860 and probably named after Sir Robert Richard Torrens, Premier of South Australia.

Torrens, Lake; Torrens River SA   The lake was discovered by E. J. Eyre in 1839 and later named by him after Colonel Robert Torrens, Chairman of the South Australia Colonization Commission, and father of Sir Robert Richard Torrens (see above). The river was discovered by G. S. Kingston in November 1836, but named by the Surveyor-General, William Light after Colonel Torrens. The river had several Aboriginal names. Where it flowed through Adelaide it was Karran-wirra-parri, River of the red gum forest, and when in flood Yertala.

Torres Strait Q   Named by Alexander Dalrymple, the British hydrographer, in 1767 in honour of the Spaniard Luis Vaez de Torres who was the first European to sail through it. The Spanish fleet that sailed from Peru in 1605 was under the command of de Quiros, with Torres as second-in-command. At the New Hebrides there was a mutiny. Quiros returned, but Torres went on, sighted Cape York (which he believed to be a chain of islands), and threaded his way through the reefs and islands.

Torrington NSW   After Great Torrington in Devonshire. Meaning, town on the River Torridge. Formerly called The Mole.

Tostaree V   After a place in Denmark, by a Dane who named his home Tostaree House. Formerly Hospital Creek.

Tottenham NSW   Doubtless from the urban district which is part of Greater London. Meaning, Tota's village.

Townsend, Mount NSW   After Thomas S. Townsend, who was responsible for the first systematic survey of the area in 1846. For a long time there was confusion between this mountain and Kosciusko. The Survey Departments of New South Wales and Victoria had different ideas on the subject, which is treated briefly in the *Australian Encyclopaedia*, Volume 5, page 213.

Townshend, Cape Q   Named on 28 May 1770 by Captain Cook after Charles Townshend, who was known as 'Spanish Charles' because of his diplomatic service in Spain, to distinguish him from his cousin of the same name who was Chancellor of the Exchequer in 1767 and the uncle of Thomas Townshend who became Viscount Sydney.

Townsville Q   Named in honour of Robert Towns, who was responsible for its founding. Towns commissioned John Melton Black to select a port that would serve the agricultural regions of northern Queensland. Black did so and named his choice Castleton, after a town of that name on the Isle of Man in 1864; but when the Governor, Sir George Bowen, visited it a year later he rechristened it Townsville. Towns was a man of progressive ideas. He pioneered cotton-growing in Australia and later turned to sugar cane production. He visited the town named after him only once, in 1866.

Towrang NSW   Aboriginal. Shield.

Tozer, Mount Q   After Sir Horace Tozer, Agent-General for Queensland.

Trafalgar; Trafalgar, Mount V   The mountain was named by T. L. Mitchell in 1836 after the famous naval battle.

Trangie NSW   Aboriginal. Quick intercourse.

Traralgon V   Aboriginal. Heron or crane feeding on frogs.

Trawalla V   Aboriginal. Wild water.

Trentham V   After a village in Staffordshire, meaning Village on the River Trent.

Triabunna T   Aboriginal, meaning unknown. It was first called Port Monthazin by Nicolas Baudin after one of his men, and then Spring Bay, so called by George Meredith after his dog.

Tribulation, Cape Q   On 10 June 1770, the day before the *Endeavour* grounded on a reef, Cook named the northern point he had in sight 'Cape Tribulation, because here began all our Troubles'.

Trinity Bay Q   On the same day that Cook named Cape Tribulation he also gave the name Trinity Bay because it was discovered on the eve of Trinity Sunday.

Troubridge Hill SA   Named by Flinders on 25 March 1802 — 'A hummock upon this low part was named Troubridge Hill' — possibly after

213

an officer named Troubridge who served in the *Culloden* under Earl St. Vincent.

Truro SA After Truro in Cornwall, meaning Village on a hill.

Tryal Rocks WA The British ship *Tryal*, commanded by John Brooks, was wrecked here as early as 1622, so the name is one of the first given in Australia by an Englishman. The ship struck the rocks on 25 May 1622. 92 of the 128 passengers and crew were lost. Thomas Bright, the first mate, wrote: '128 souls were left to God's mercy, whereof 36 were saved.' They eventually reached Batavia.

Tubbul Road NSW Aboriginal. Bone.

Tuggerah NSW Aboriginal. Cold, or Where two waters meet.

Tullamarine V Aboriginal. A corruption of Tullamareena, the name of an Aboriginal boy.

Tullamore NSW After a town of Offaly in Ireland. Formerly known as Bullock Creek.

Tullibigeal NSW Aboriginal. Place where yarran spears are split.

Tully; Tully River Q Named after William Alcock Tully, the Surveyor-General. He had been a member of G. A. F. E. Dalrymple's expedition in 1864.

Tumbarumba NSW Aboriginal. Sounding ground. The name is onomatopaeic, for the ground here gives a hollow sound when stamped on. An early pastoral holding here was named Tombrumba Creek.

Tumby Bay SA After a parish in Lincolnshire, meaning Fenced village.

Tumut NSW Aboriginal. Camping by the river. Spelt Doomat or Doomut in the early days of settlement.

Turnagain, Cape Q See Cape Keer-weer.

Tungamah V Aboriginal. Bustard turkey.

Turon River NSW The word is undoubtedly of Aboriginal origin. In 1821 George Cox recorded it as Choorun, and William Lawson as Yooran in 1822.

Turrawan NSW Aboriginal. Grey magpie.

Turriff V After the manager of a pastoral run.

Tutye V Aboriginal. Rest.

Tweed Heads; Tweed River NSW, Q Named by John Oxley in 1823 after the Tweed River which, in part, divides England from Scotland. In 1828 Captain Rous came upon Oxley's discovery and, believing himself to be the discoverer, named it the Clarence. When the mistake was revealed, the name Clarence was transferred to what was then known as Big River.

Twin Island Q Originally named Double Island by Captain Bligh.

Twin Peaks Islands WA A descriptive name given by Flinders in January 1802.

Twin Towns NSW, Q The towns of Tweed Heads on the south side of the Tweed River (on the Queensland-New South Wales border) and Coolangatta on the north side are together known as the Twin Towns.

Two People Bay WA A French and an American naval vessel happened to take shelter in the bay simultaneously.

Two Wells SA So named because two small adjacent wells were there.

Tyabb V Aboriginal. Worm.

Tyagarrah NSW Aboriginal. Open grass country. Probably from the word Tyagurah.

Tyers V After the surveyor Charles James Tyers.

Tylden V After an officer who served in the Crimean War.

Tynong V Aboriginal. Plenty of fish.

Tyrrell, Lake V Discovered by E. J. Eyre in 1838 and named by him after a squatter in the Port Phillip district.

Tyson, Mount Q James Tyson's name has become a legend in Queensland. He established a large sugar cane plantation in the 1870s, but subsequently became a pastoralist when restrictions on the employment of kanakas caused labour shortages.

Uardry NSW Aboriginal. Yellow box tree. The name was first given to a sheep station.

Ulamambri NSW Aboriginal. Breeding place of possums. The name of a pastoral holding established by E. K. Cox.

Ulladulla NSW Aboriginal. Safe harbour. One record states that the original Aboriginal name was Wooladoorh. The common name in the earliest days was Holey Dollar. The Aboriginal Percy Mumbulla told Roland Robinson that the place was called Ole Dollar. No doubt he meant Hole Dollar. According to Mumbulla, the white people wanted to make it sound Aboriginal, so they called it Ulladulla, which is not a genuine Aboriginal name. A Holey Dollar was a coin from which a small circular piece was struck from the centre. The small coin was worth 1s. 3d., and was termed a dump; the larger ring-shaped portion, a 'holey' dollar, worth 5 shillings. These coins were issued in January 1814 and were in circulation in New South Wales until the early 1830s.

Ulmarra NSW Aboriginal. River Bend. A bend in the Clarence River. At one time known as The Sandspit.

Ulooloo SA   Aboriginal. Water by two hills. The name was given to the creek by E. C. Frome. It was known at one time as Hell's Gates.

Ultima V   A contraction of Ultima thule, the creek being first named U.T.

Ulverstone T   After Ulverston in the Lakes district of England. Earlier known as The Leven.

Umbango Creek NSW   Aboriginal. From Umbanga, To gape, or to Look closely.

Unanderra NSW   Aboriginal. Meeting place of two creeks. The original form seems to have been Unundurra.

Undera V   Aboriginal. Fat.

Underbool V   Aboriginal. Ear and Water.

Ungarie NSW   Aboriginal. Thigh. The name of a pastoral station.

Unumgar NSW   Aboriginal. Tall ironbark trees, or Infested with lizards.

Uppingham NSW   After a town in Rutlandshire. Meaning, Village of people on the hill.

Upright, Point NSW   Captain Cook's Journal of 23 April 1770 reads: 'At 5, we were abreast of a point of land which, on account of its perpendicular Cliffs, I call'd Point Upright.'

Uralla NSW   Aboriginal. In a little while, Big hill, or Red wood.

Urana NSW   Aboriginal. A word that imitated the sound of quail rising. Several attempts have been made to reduce it to writing — Wahrinah and Wirrinah.

Urangeline NSW   Aboriginal. After the name of the pastoral station of Robert Rand.

Uranquinty NSW   Aboriginal. Plenty of rain, or Sheltering from the rain. Formerly spelt Uranquintry.

Urunga NSW   Aboriginal. Long beach.

Van Diemen Gulf Q   The name dates back to 1636. After the discoveries made by *Pera* and the *Arnhem* along the northern coast in 1823 the yachts *Klen-Amsterdam* and *Wesel*, commanded by Gerrit Thomaszoon Pool were dispatched to undertake further explorations. They named a stretch of coast about 120 km in length Van Diemen's Landt after the Governor-General of the East Indies. Although the name has disappeared in this form it has survived in Van Diemen Gulf.

Van Diemen's Landt   See Tasmania.

Vanderlin Island NT   Probably named by Tasman in 1644.

Vasse WA   The name of a member of Baudin's expedition who was lost, probably killed by Aborigines, in 1801.

Vaucluse Bay; Vaucluse Heights; Vaucluse Point NSW   After the estate and house Vaucluse, which in turn was named after the Valley of the Rhone in Vaucluse, a department in South East France. Vaucluse is the French form of the Latin *vallis clausa*, an enclosed valley. Vaucluse House was built by an eccentric Irishman, Sir Henry Brown Hayes, who had been sentenced to death for abducting an heiress, but the sentence was changed to transportation. When he was freed he built the house and gave the name 'because it (the district) reminded him of the beautiful closed-up valley in France known as Vaucluse which he had often visited'. The story has often been told of how he imported soil from Ireland in order to banish snakes from his property because of the efficacy of St Patrick! The story must not be received with scepticism, for the bill of lading for the shipment was preserved until the end of last century. Captain John Piper and William Charles Wentworth subsequently bought the house, which is sometimes known as Wentworth House. One Aboriginal name for the point was Moring, or Morung, another Koo-e-lung, Porpoises, which were frequently seen from the point.

Vectis East V   Major Firebrace, who settled here, chose the name because he was born on the Isle of Wight, the Roman name of which was Vectis. The Aboriginal name was Yawnbul.

Veitch SA   After a local resident.

Verran SA   After John Verran, Premier of South Australia.

Victor Harbour SA   Named after HMS *Victor* in which Captain Richard Crozier surveyed Encounter Bay in 1837.

Victor, Mount SA   Named by the Surveyor-General E. C. Frome when he saw it from a distance.

Victoria   On separation from New South Wales in 1851, the new Colony was named after Queen Victoria. Prior to this the area was usually referred to as the Port Phillip district, q.v. In 1836 T. L. Mitchell led a party along the Lachlan River to the Murray and went south. He named the fertile land Australia Felix.

Victoria, Lake V   Discovered by Charles Bonney and Joseph Hawdon, while travelling from New South Wales to South Australia in 1838, and named after the Queen.

Victoria, Mount V   Named by T. L. Mitchell in 1835 after Princess, later Queen Victoria. The Aboriginal name was Boreang.

Victoria Ranges V, WA   Similarly named for Queen Victoria, the Victoria range by T. L. Mitchell in 1836, the Western Australia range by George Grey in 1840.

Victoria River NT   Discovered and named by Captain J. C. Wickham in 1839. The *Beagle* was taken up the river for about 80 km, and ship's boats a further 150 km. J. L. Stokes wrote at the time: '..."This is indeed a noble river!" burst from several lips at the same moment; "and worth," continued I, "of being honoured with the name of her most gracious majesty the Queen:" which Captain Wickham fully concurred in, by at once bestowing upon it the name of Victoria River.'

Victoria Spring WA   This oasis in the desert was discovered by Ernest Giles in 1875, sixteen days after leaving the previous supply of water, during his crossing of the Nullarbor Plain. 'We have no Victoria or Albert Nyanza,' he wrote, 'no Tanganyika or Zambesi, like the great African travellers, to honour with Her Majesty's name, but the humble offering of a little spring in the hideous desert.'

Violet Town V   Named Violet Ponds by T. L. Mitchell on 10 October 1835 because of the violets he found growing there.

Virginia SA   After Virginia in County Cavan, Ireland.

Vite Vite V   Aboriginal. Wading birds.

Von Doussa NT   After the Attorney-General of South Australia, Louis von Doussa.

W Tree V   A peculiar name which originated when a tree was broken in a gale, the remaining portion being in the shape of the letter W.

Wagerup WA   Aboriginal. Place of emus. Many place names in Western Australia end in -up, which has the related meanings of Water (indicating a water hole) and Camp.

Wagga Wagga NSW   Aboriginal. Many crows, the word being an imitation of their call. The name comes from the station first owned by Robert Holt Best.

Wagin WA   Aboriginal. Place of emus.

Wahgonga NSW   Aboriginal. Place of nettles.

Wahgunyah V   Aboriginal. Beware!

Wahratta NSW   Aboriginal. Camp.

Waikerie SA   Aboriginal. Wings, or Anything that flies — referring particularly to the fact that wildfowl were plentiful. Charles Sturt passed the site coming and going on his expedition down the Murray River in 1830. A station was established here by T. Shepherd in 1882, and was known as Round Flat because the river looped round the station buildings, but Shepherd, who knew the meaning of the Aboriginal term, preferred to retain it.

Wail V   Aboriginal. Curlew.

Waitchie V   Aboriginal. Crow.

Wakefield River SA   The river was discovered in 1838 by William Hill, who named it after Edward Gibbon Wakefield.

Walcha NSW   Aboriginal. Sun. The name was taken from a pastoral holding.

Walgett NSW.   Aboriginal. Many meanings have been given: Meeting of the waters; Long waterhole; High hill (from Wolgar); Point of land; River; Plenty of swamp; Plenty of water.

Walhalla V   An old gold mining town which was first called Stringer's Creek, after Ned Stringer, a prospector.

Walker Creek Q   Named after Frederick 'Filibuster' Walker, who commanded a corps of black trackers as a Police force. He was noted for the ruthlessness of his methods and on dismissal in 1855 he formed a private force in the service of the squatters. He was ordered to disband his unofficial force and then undertook some valuable exploratory work. The name was bestowed by William Landsborough.

Walla Walla NSW   Aboriginal. Plenty of rain. From a pastoral holding.

Wallabadah NSW   Aboriginal. Stone.

Wallace V   After an early settler, J. Wallace. The Aboriginal name was Connadoyen.

Wallacia NSW   Said to be of Welsh origin.

Wallan V   Aboriginal. Flood.

Wallarobba NSW   Aboriginal. Rainy gully.

Wallaroo SA   Aboriginal. A corruption of Wadla-waru, meaning unknown. The first run established here was named Wallawaroo, shortened to Wallaroo because it saved time when branding wool bales.

Wallendbeen NSW   Aboriginal. Stony place, or Stony hill. The name of a pastoral holding.

Wallerberdina SA   Aboriginal. Place of the willy wagtail. The original spelling was Wallelberdina.

Wallerawang NSW   Aboriginal. Plenty of water. From the estate of James Walker.

Wallis, Lake NSW   After Captain James Wallis, military commandant at Newcastle. The lake was seen by Oxley in 1815.

Walloway SA   Aboriginal. Plain of bustard turkeys.

Wallum Q   Aboriginal. *Banksia aemula*, a tall shrub.

Walpeup V   Aboriginal. Big smoke. Early known as Consolation Plain.

Walsh Island NSW   After Henry Deane Walsh, at one time district engineer at Newcastle.

219

Walsh River Q   Named by William Hann when he reached the river on 9 July 1872 during his northern expedition, after W. H. Walsh, Minister for Public Works and Goldfields. Hann did not claim to be the discoverer for he said that he had 'no desire to pluck a single bay from the chaplet that surrounds the memory of their first discoverer, the courageous but unfortunate E. B. Kennedy'.

Wanalta V   A. E. Martin says that though it has the appearance of an Aboriginal name, it is a corruption of a settler's 'One Halter Plain'.

Wanbi SA   Aboriginal. Wild dog.

Wandilo SA   Aboriginal. Swamp of native companions.

Wandin V   Aboriginal. A contraction of Wandin Yallock, Swift-running stream.

Wandong V   Aboriginal. Spirit.

Wangaratta V   Aboriginal. Nesting place of cormorants, or Meeting of the waters. The district was first seen here by Hume and Hovell in 1824, and then by T. L. Mitchell in 1836. The first settler, George Faithfull, arrived in 1837. The name may be a misspelling of Wangaralta.

Wangara SA   Aboriginal. Crows, or Talk.

Wangianna SA   Aboriginal. Hill on the plain.

Wantabadgery NSW   Aboriginal. Place where a fight occurred. The first arrival here was Charles Sturt, in December 1829. He said the place was called Pondebadgery. At a later date he referred to the name as Pontebadgery. When James Thorne took up land he called his estate Wantebadgery, but by 1866 it had taken its present form.

Waranga Reservoir V   Aboriginal. To sing.

Waratah T   Named after the flower.

Waratah Bay V   Named after a ship, the *Waratah*, that sheltered in the bay in 1854.

Warburton V   When the town was established in 1864 at the time of the gold rush it was named after Charles Warburton Carr, the district magistrate.

Warburton Range SA; **Warburton River** WA   After Peter Egerton Warburton, Police Commissioner and explorer.

Wardang Island SA   Aboriginal. Bandicoot Island. The Aborigines were accustomed to swim 2 km from the mainland to take the bandicoots on the island.

Wardell NSW   After an early doctor who was resident here.

Ward's River NSW   After a family of early settlers.

Wargambegal NSW   Aboriginal. Crow come along.

220

Warialda NSW   Aboriginal. Place of wild honey.

Warner's Gully Q   William Hann gave the name when leading the Northern Expedition Party in 1872 after his surveyor, Frederick H. Warner, who discovered gold near the Palmer River. The following year prospectors flocked to the Palmer Valley in great numbers.

Warnertown SA   Named by Governor Jervois after his secretary, J. H. B. Warner.

Warning, Mount NSW   Named by Captain Cook, who gives the reason for the name in his Journal entry of 16 May 1770: 'We now saw the breakers again within us, which we past at the distance of 1 League; they...stretch off East 2 Leagues from a point under which is a small Island, there situation may always be found by the peaked mountain beforementioned, which bears SWBW from them, and on this account I have named [it] *Mount Warning.*'

Warooka SA   Aboriginal. Brightly coloured parrot.

Warracknabeal V   Aboriginal. Large gum trees. E. J. Eyre was here in 1884, and in 1885 the Scott brothers established the Warracknabeal station.

Warragul V   Aboriginal. Wild. The settlement was first known as Brandy Creek.

Warrah NSW   Aboriginal. Rain, or Left hand.

Warral NSW   Aboriginal. Bee, or Honey.

Warralillialillialillia SA   Claimed by some to be the longest place name in Australia, but see below. It was listed as a spring in the South Australian Gazetteer of 1869.

Warrawarrapiraliliullamalulacoupalunya NT   Rev John Flynn of the Australian Inland Mission collected this name in the 1930s. As a matter of interest, the name of record length must surely be held by the New Zealand title holder, Taumatawhakatangihangikoauauotamateapokaiwhenuakitanatahu. The Maori name means Brow of the hill where Tamatea who sailed all round the land played his nose flute to his lady love — whereas no meaning has yet been given to the Australian contender.

Warrego Range; Warrego River Q   Both the river and the range were explored by T. L. Mitchell in 1845 and 1846, the Aboriginal name being retained.

Warren NSW   Aboriginal. Strong, or Large root. The latter meaning has a physiological significance.

Warrigal NSW   Aboriginal. Dingo. It was the name of a pastoral holding and the trademark of the Nyngan Refrigerating Company.

Warrigal Q   Aboriginal. Wild. The term was applied to outlawed Aborigines and dingoes.

221

Warrior Island Q   Named after a warship that was attacked by Aborigines in the early days. The Aboriginal name was Tute.

Warrnambool V   Aboriginal. Running swamps, Plenty of water, or Place of plenty. The name was originally spelt Warnimble.

Warrong V   Aboriginal. Dew.

Warrumbungle Range NSW   Aboriginal. Small mountains. A descriptive name, as this spur of the Great Dividing Range is broken up into small hills and jagged peaks. John Oxley, who explored the mountains in 1818, called them the Arbuthnot Range, but the name did not survive.

Warwick Q   Probably comes from the English name, meaning Weir or Dam. The Aboriginal name was Gooragoody.

Wasleys SA   After the first settler, Joseph Wasleys.

Watchem V   Aboriginal. Place of hops.

Waterhouse Range NT   Named by J. McDouall Stuart after the naturalist in his expedition.

Watson SA   This station on the Transcontinental Railway was named after John Christian Watson, the first Labour Prime Minister in the Australian Government, who was in office from April until August 1904.

Wattamolla NSW   Aboriginal. Place close to running water. Bass and Flinders named it Providential Cove. They were forced to take refuge here when their boat was nearly swamped in 1796. Flinders stated that the Aboriginal name was Watta Mowlee.

Wauchope NSW   It is said that Wauchope was named after Captain Wauch or Wauche, who came to New South Wales in 1836 and was given a grant of land which he named Wauchope, to express his hopes for the future prosperity of his estate.

Waugoola NSW   Aboriginal. To dig. The name of a pastoral holding.

Waygara V   Aboriginal. Crow.

Wean NSW   Aboriginal. Fire.

Weary Bay Q   Named by Captain Cook on 14 June 1770.

Wedderburn V   After a Scottish stream, probably given by W. J. Willis. Formerly Mount Korong.

Weddin Mountain; Weddin Range NSW   Aboriginal. Wait. This was a place where young men remained to prepare themselves for the ordeal of the initiation ceremonies.

Wedge Island SA   Named by Flinders on 24 February 1802 'from its shape'.

Wedge, Mount SA   Named by the explorer John Charles Darke in 1844 after the name of his uncle, John Hilder Wedge, who had come from England to Tasmania with Darke's mother and father.

Wednesday Island Q   See under Thursday Island.

Wee Waa NSW   Aboriginal. Fire thrown away. The first cattle station here was called Weeawaa.

Weeaproinah V   Aboriginal. Large trees.

Weemelah NSW   Aboriginal. Good view, or High look-out point.

Weerite V   Aboriginal. Swamp.

Weetaliba NSW   Aboriginal. Scarcity of wood, or Place where the fire went out.

Welcome Hill T   During his 1827 expedition Henry Hellyer was in great difficulties owing to shortage of food and inclement weather and feared that he and his men would not survive. On 24 February he sighted the sea from this hill, and bestowed the name in recognition of his relief.

Welcome Hill WA   'It's a welcome sight!' exclaimed Mrs John Withell when her husband showed her the camping place for the night. The courageous pioneer settlers had landed at Cossack in 1863 and were on their way to their holding at Roeburn Pool.

Weld WA   Named after Sir F. A. Weld, Governor of Western Australia from 1869 to 1874.

Wellesley Islands Q   Named by Flinders in December 1802 after the first Marquis Wellesley (second Earl of Mornington), Governor-General of India.

Wellington NSW   Named Wellington Valley by John Oxley in August 1817 on his journey in search of the Macquarie River, doubtless after the first Duke of Wellington. The *Australian Encyclopaedia* quotes a protest by the French zoologist, R. P. Lesson, in 1824: 'How can a nation so civilized as the English degrade its trophies with tinsel that denotes poverty and bad taste? A crowd of places in New South Wales bear the names "Waterloo" and "Wellington". On the day when the Russians attack India and attain an uncontestable predominance in Europe, the English, chased from their vast possessions, will discover how little the battle of Waterloo was really worth to them.'

Wellington SA   Also named after the Duke. The Aboriginal name was Wirrum Wirrum.

Wellington, Mount T   The mountain has suffered many changes of name. The present one was probably conferred by Lieut Governor Sorell in the early 1820s, after the Duke of Wellington, and confirmed as the official name by Lieut Governor Franklin in 1839. It was first sighted and named Table Hill by Bligh in 1788. In 1793 J. B. P. Willoumez, a member of d'Entrecasteaux's expedition called it Montagne du Plateau, and in the same year Lieut John Hayes had a preference for Skiddaw. Bass and

Flinders were there with a preference for Mount Table, while Lieut Governor Collins preferred Table Mountain. The only exception, up to this time, to a reference to its flat topped appearance was a short-lived designation as Mount Collins. The Aboriginal name was Urganyaletta.

Welshpool V   Named after P. W. Welsh, a merchant of Melbourne, who had an ambitious scheme to use the port (for it was also known as Port Welshpool) as an outlet for produce from Gippsland.

Wemyss River NSW   Named in 1822 by William Lawson, probably after Deputy Commissary-General William Wemyss.

Wendouree, Lake V   Now an artificial lake that preserves the Aboriginal name, it was known as Black Swamp when W. C. Yuille and Henry Anderson arrived there with a flock of sheep in 1839.

Wenlock River Q   In the past there was much confusion between the names Wenlock and Batavia. It was not until 1939 when an aerodrome was established in the vicinity and became confused with Batavia in Java that Wenlock was finally confirmed. Early British explorers assumed that the river was that discovered by William Jansz of the *Duyfken* in 1606, when a boat party went up an estuary. More recent research shows that the boat navigated the estuary of the Dulhunty and Ducie Rivers which flow into Port Musgrave where the *Duyfken* was anchored. Jan Carstensz named the estuary Rivier Carpentier in 1623, but the name Rivier Batavia was substituted by the Dutch East India Company. When the Jardine party were in the vicinity in 1864-65 it was assumed that the headwaters of a river they had encountered were those of the Batavia, but they were in fact the Wenlock. The origin of the name appears to be obscure.

Werribee V   The Werribee River has been given many names — Peel, Tweed, Exe, and Arndell, the latter by W. H. Hovell who wrote in 1825 '...in compliment to the late Dr Arndell, and to my son Arndell Hovell'. Dr Arndell was Hovell's father-in-law. It seems apparent that Werribee is an Aboriginal name, for Captain King of the *Rattlesnake* referred to it as Weariby Yalook or Exe.

Wentworth; Wentworth Falls; Wentworthville NSW   After William Charles Wentworth, the noted politician and explorer who crossed the Blue Mountains in 1813 and who, it has been said, has possibly had more streets, parks, and places named after him than any other pioneer. Wentworth Falls were first known as The Weatherboard. It did not receive its present name until 1867, when the station was renamed Wentworth Falls. Wentworth claimed to have given the colony 'the liberty of the press, trial by jury, and the constitutional right of electing their own representatives'.

Werrington NSW   Takes its name from the estate which belonged to Sir Henry Parkes. Formerly known as Parkes Platform.

Wessel Islands NT   Named after the *Wesel* or *Wessel* which was accompanied by the *Klem-Amsterdam* in 1637 to investigate the northern coast. The *Arnhem* had been there in 1623 and the group Speult Islands had been named in honour of the Governor of Amboine. However, the name Wessel later appeared on Dutch charts and was used by Flinders in 1803. Two intriguing names of capes on the main Wessel Island were applied by the skipper of the *Arnhem*. De Caep guade Hoop and Het gat de goede Hoop — The Cape of Bad Hope and the Cape of Good Hope.

West Cape Howe WA Discovered in 1791 by Captain Vancouver, who named it Cape Howe after Admiral Earl Howe. It was renamed West Cape Howe by Flinders in December 1801 to avoid confusion with Cook's Cape Howe on the south-east coast.

West Point WA This cape on Dirk Hartog Island is the most westerly point of Australia.

West Wyalong NSW Doubtless an Aboriginal name. The town of Wyalong which was established in 1893 when gold was discovered was named after an old sheep station. Wyalong Village was laid out in 1894 and a year later another township, previously known as Main Camp, was called West Wyalong.

Westall, Mount Q, SA; Westall Point SA Named by Flinders in January (SA) and August (Q) 1802 after William Westall, the artist on the *Investigator*.

Western Australia As with the states that separated from New South Wales, there was controversy over the name. The first Governor, Sir James Stirling, wanted to call it Hesperia — Land looking west, and in modern times Churchill has been proposed. It is a long name but has become so firmly entrenched that future change is unlikely. When cable messages were confined to words of ten letters, Westralia was coined as an abbreviation.

Westernport V Originally discovered and named and spelt Western Port, by George Bass on 5 January 1798 because it was the most westerly of the harbours at that time.

Westonia WA Named after a Mr Weston. The streets bear the names of minerals, ranging from Diorite to Scheelite.

Whetstone Q It has been said that the name came from the fact that large stones in the vicinity were used by the Aborigines for sharpening their axes, but the explanation is scarcely convincing.

Whidbey Islands; Whidbey Point SA On 17 February 1802 Flinders wrote: 'I named Whidbey's Isles, after my worthy friend the former master-attendant at Sheerness.' Whidbey had a large part in the fitting out of the *Investigator*.

Whidporie NSW Aboriginal. Fine weather.

Whirlpool Channel WA On 24 March 1839, J. L. Stokes of the *Beagle* wrote: 'A rapid tide soon carried us...into a very winding channel scarcely half a mile wide, and more than 20 fathoms deep. in this we experienced violent whirlpools, the first of which, from want of experience, suddenly wrenching the oars out of the men's hands, and whirling the boat round with alarming rapidity; after several round turns of this kind we shot out of the channel (which from the above circumstances we called Whirlpool Channel).'

White Cliffs NSW   So named because of the outcrops of white shale in which opals were found.

Whitelaw V   After a surveyor named Whitelaw.

Whitsunday Island Q   The passage, the island, and its highest peak were all named by Captain Cook on Whitsunday, 4 June 1770.

Whittlesea V   After a Whittlesey in Cambridgeshire meaning Wittel's island and sea.

Whitton NSW   After the Chief Engineer of the New South Wales Railways.

Whyalla SA   Aboriginal. Deep water, an appropriate name for the port from which iron ore was first shipped in 1915. Up until then it was known as Hummock Hill (popularly called Hummocky), a descriptive name probably given by Flinders in March 1802.

Wiangaree NSW   Aboriginal. Pine ridge.

Wickham, Mount; Wickham River NT   After Captain T. C. Wickham, who was in command of the *Beagle* when it departed from England to survey the northern coast. Leichhardt named the river in 1845.

Wide Bay Q   Named by Captain Cook on 18 May 1770.

Widgiewa NSW   Aboriginal. What do you want?

Widgelli NSW   Aboriginal. To drink.

Wight's Land V   Lieut James Grant wrote on 7 December 1800 aboard the Lady Nelson: 'It resembles the Isle of Wight as near as possible in its appearance from the water; I therefore called this part of the coast... Wights, in honour of Captain Wight of the Royal Navy, son-in-law to Commissioner Schank.'

Wilberforce NSW; **Wilberforce, Cape** NT   Named after William Wilberforce, who worked so long and successfully to abolish slavery. Cape Wilberforce was so named by Flinders on 17 February 1803.

Wilcannia NSW   Aboriginal. Gap in a bank where flood waters escape.

Wild Horse Plains SA   Named by Thomas Day and J. Hewitt because wild horses were found there.

Wild River Q   A descriptive name given by J. V. Mulligan on his fifth expedition.

Wiles, Cape SA   Named on 19 February 1802 by Flinders: 'This projection I named Cape Wiles, after a worthy friend at Liguanea, in Jamaica.'

Wilkawatt SA   Aboriginal. Wild dog. An earlier name for the locality was Cotton.

Willamulka SA   Aboriginal. Bright green stones.

Willi Willi NSW   Aboriginal. Plenty of possums.

William Creek SA   Named by J. McDouall Stuart for William Chambers, a son of John Chambers.

William, Mount V   T. L. Mitchell climbed the mountain and named it after William IV.

Williamstown SA   Named after an early settler, William Symonds.

Williamstown V   The Melbourne suburb was named after William IV.

Willochra SA   Aboriginal. Flooded creek by the polygonum bushes.

Willowie SA   The Aboriginal name for Mount Remarkable.

Wills Creek Q   After William John Wills, the explorer and companion of Burke on the 1860-1861 Expedition.

Willunga SA   Aboriginal. A corruption of Will-ngga, Place of green trees.

Wilmington SA   It seems probable that the name comes from Wilmington in North Delaware, USA. The fact that Lady Musgrave, the wife of the Governor-General in 1876, was an American, may have had some bearing on the choice. An earlier name was Beautiful Valley. The residents did not approve of the change.

Wilmot T   After Sir John Eardley-Wilmot, who was appointed Governor of Tasmania in 1843.

Wilpena Pound SA   A mixture of Aboriginal and English words. Wilpena means Place of bent fingers. One theory is that it is so cold here at times that the Aborigines were unable to bend their fingers, but a more likely explanation is that the area resembles a hand with the fingers, which represent the mountain peaks, bent upwards. Pound is used in the same sense — a small enclosure such as those in which cattle are kept.

Wilson Inlet WA   Probably named after T. B. Wilson, a Naval surgeon, who discovered and named the Denmark River in 1839.

Wilson Promontory V   Named by Governor Hunter after Thomas Wilson, a merchant of London who traded with New South Wales, and was a friend of Matthew Flinders. George Bass was the discoverer in 1798. He named it Furneaux Land in the mistaken belief that it was the peninsula seen by Furneaux in 1773.

Wiluna WA   Aboriginal. A corruption of Weeluna, Call of the bush curlew. The Aborigines gave the name to the lake now known as Lake Violet.

Wimbledon NSW   After Wimbledon in Surrey, the birthplace of Allan Cunningham, and now the headquarters of the All-England Lawn Tennis Club.

Wimmera District; Wimmera River V   Aboriginal. Boomerang or Throwing stick. The district was discovered by T. L. Mitchell in 1836.

Winchelsea V   After George William Finch-Hatton, Earl of Winchelsea.

Winchester WA   After Winchester in England, the Castle of pleasure.

Windang NSW   Aboriginal. Place where a fight took place.

Windeyer NSW   After a Mr Windeyer who was engaged in a number of philanthropic and social projects.

Windsor NSW   After Windsor in Berkshire, famous for its royal castle. Meaning, Landing place with a windlass. The name was given by Governor Macquarie 'from the similarity of this situation to that of the same name in England', when he appointed it as a flood refuge in 1810. The history of the locality, however, goes back as far as 1794, when Lieut-Governor Francis Grose was responsible for placing settlers along the banks of the Hawkesbury River. By 1798 the settlement was known as Green Hills, and was so called until Macquarie renamed it.

Windsor SA   A. E. Martin records the fact that in an advertisement Nathaniel Hailes states that the district merited an imposing name and pointed out that the quarry contained sufficient stone to build a South Australian Windsor Castle.

Wingello NSW   Aboriginal. To burn.

Wingen NSW   See Burning Mountain.

Winnap V   Aboriginal. Fire.

Winninnie SA   Aboriginal. Many, or Meeting place. A sheep station in this locality was so named in 1856.

Winton Q   Named by the postmaster, Robert Allen, after his birthplace — a suburb of Bournemouth, in 1879. The *Australian Encyclopaedia* has an interesting note to the effect that *Waltzing Matilda* was composed and sung in public at Winton for the first time in May 1895, and that the town was the birthplace of Qantas in November 1920.

Winton V   The birthplace in Westmoreland of the surveyor J. G. Wilmot.

Wirega NSW   Aboriginal. Cleared ground.

Wirilya SA   Aboriginal. Home of the native ground lark.

Wirrabara SA   Aboriginal. Gum trees by a stream.

Wirraminna SA   Aboriginal. Gum tree water.

Wirrawilla SA   Aboriginal. Green trees.

Wirrega   Aboriginal. Forest dwellers.

Wirrinya NSW   Aboriginal. Sleep.

Wiseman's Ferry NSW   After Solomon Wiseman, an ex-convict who established a ferry service across the Hawkesbury River when the road to the Hunter Ferry commenced in 1827. He was known to many as King of the Hawkesbury.

Wittenoom Gorge WA   After Sir Edward Horne Wittenoom, a pastoralist and politician. It was first called simply Wittenoom, and the word Gorge added at the request of the residents in 1951.

Wodonga V   Aboriginal. Edible nut. The first settlers were Paul and Charles Huon, who took up the Wodonga run, and C. H. Ebden in 1836. When the town was gazetted in 1852 it was called Belvoir, but changed to Wodonga in 1876. As it was so much smaller than the neighbouring city of Albury across the border it was nicknamed Struggletown for a while.

Wollar NSW   Aboriginal. Rocks, or Small flat by a creek.

Wollombi; Wollombi Creek; Wollombi Falls; Wollombi River NSW   Aboriginal. Meeting of the waters. The creek, which was discovered by Chandler (see Beardy Waters), was at one time known as Cockfighters Creek.

Wollongong NSW   Aboriginal. Many contradictory meanings have been given, the most popular being that it was an expression of surprise and fear when the Aborigines first saw a ship in full sail. This has been rendered as 'See! the monster comes'. One authority who agrees with this version says that the word was pronounced Nywoolyarngungh. Other suggestions include: hard ground near water, and song of the sea. Other versions of the spellings are Wollonya, Wollonga, and Woolyunyal.

Wolumbla NSW   Aboriginal. A corruption of Wolumba, Big waterhole.

Wombat NSW   The Aboriginal name was first recorded when John Price and James Wilson crossed the Nepean, and on 26 January 1798, near the present village of Bargo, saw 'several sorts of dung of different animals, one of which Wilson called a Whom-batt...'

Womboyn, Mount NSW   Aboriginal. Kangaroo.

Wongarbon NSW   Aboriginal. Tribal name.

Wongoni NSW   Aboriginal. Cod.

Wonthaggi V   Aboriginal. To drag or pull along.

Woodbridge T   Named by George Miles, a settler who arrived in 1847, after his birthplace in Sussex.

Woodenbong NSW   Several explanations have been offered. Aboriginal. Lagoon, or a corruption of Noyamboon, Platypus. The Aboriginal Eustan Williams told Roland Robinson that it was a corruption of Nguthunbung, the name of the ancestral being who came out of the rocks in the sea at Byron Bay and travelled over the New England Range, created a cave at Woodenbong, and slept there. He continued his journey across the continent to the 'Borrgoor', the sea in the west.

Woodend V   The place where the track from Melbourne to the Castlemaine and Bendigo gold fields emerged from the forests of Mount Macedon.

Woodford NSW   After Woodford House, the residence of Alfred Fairfax. At one time it was called Buss's.

Woodforde Creek NT   Discovered by J. McDouall Stuart on 4 April 1861, and named after Dr Woodforde, the father of John Woodforde, a member of his expedition. Dr Woodforde was Colonial Surgeon of South Australia.

Woodhouse Lee NSW   After an early settler named Woodhouse.

Woodroffe, Mount SA   When W. C. Gosse sighted the mountain from the summit of Ayers Rock at a distance of 130 km in 1873, he named it after George Woodroffe Goyer, the Surveyor-General of South Australia.

Woods Point V   This ghost town was a thriving centre with a population of 20,000 in the 1860s. One of the first storekeepers was Henry (Mabelle?) Woods, after whom the locality was named.

Woodside SA   After a village in Scotland.

Woodstock NSW   An early resident named Wood gave his name to Wood's Flat, later changed to Woodstock.

Woodstock Q   From Sir Walter Scott's novel.

Woolbrook NSW   The name was conferred when a wool-scouring firm was established here.

Wooli NSW   Aboriginal. From Woolli, Cedar tree.

Woollahra NSW   Aboriginal. Look-out, from Woolara. In some early records it was spelt Wilarra.

Woolloomooloo NSW   Aboriginal. Possibly from Wullaoomullah, Young kangaroo, though it is also said that it is an attempt by Aborigines to say Windmill, or Whirling round. There have been many spellings — Woolomoola, Wullaoomullah, Walomolo, Wallamulla, Wallamullah, and Wallabahmulla. The name was adopted by John Palmer, Commissary-General, in 1793 for his estate. The locality was also known as Garden Cove and Palmer's Cove.

Woolloongabba Q   Aboriginal. Whirling round. As pronounced by the Aborigines the accent was placed on the second syllable. Locally this Brisbane suburb is often contracted to The Gabba.

Wooltanna SA   A hybrid name, coming from the Aboriginal Ana or Tana, meaning Place, and the English Wool, thus meaning Place where wool comes from.

Woomelang V   Aboriginal. Poor.

Woomera SA   Aboriginal. Throwing stick — an appropriate term for the site of the rocket range project.

Woonona NSW   Aboriginal. Place of young wallabies, or else derived from Wunona, Sleep.

Woorak V   Aboriginal. Honeysuckle.

Woori Yallock V   Aboriginal. Swift running creek.

Woronora; Woronora River NSW   Aboriginal. Black rock.

Woy Woy NSW   Aboriginal. Deep water, Much water, or Porpoise.

Wreck Bay NSW   Named on account of the many wrecks that occurred here.

Wreck Island Q   The *America* was wrecked on the island in June 1831, the survivors being rescued by the *Nelson*.

Wreck Reef Q   Matthew Flinders left Port Jackson on 10 August 1803 in the *Porpoise*, accompanied by the *Cato* and *Bridgewater*, on his way to England to procure another ship for coastal exploration, the *Investigator* having been proved unseaworthy. On 17 August both the *Porpoise* and the *Cato* went aground on the reef, and were deserted by the captain of the *Bridgewater*. On 26 August Flinders, having seen to the comfort of the crews on the reef, left in the ship's cutter, returned to Sydney, and came back to their rescue. He then continued his voyage in the *Cumberland,* but was arrested at Mauritius and kept prisoner there for six years, and died shortly after his return to England.

Wudina SA   Aboriginal. Granite rocks.

Wumbulgal NSW   Aboriginal. Black duck.

Wunghnu V   Aboriginal. Boomerang.

Wunnamurra NSW   Aboriginal. Eagle hawk.

Wyalong NSW   See West Wyalong.

Wyan NSW   Aboriginal. Hip, or Tree root.

Wyanga NSW   Aboriginal. Mother.

Wybalena NSW   Aboriginal. The settlement located on Flinders Island as a last refuge for Tasmanian Aborigines, about 1840. The settlement was given the name Wybalene meaning literally 'Aborigines, sit down here', with the significance of a refuge.

Wycheproof V   Aboriginal. Witchie plant growing on a hilltop.

Wychitella V   Aboriginal. This name also refers to the witchie plant.

Wyee NSW   Aboriginal. Fire.

Wynarka SA   Aboriginal. Strayed.

Wyndham WA   Named by Sir John Forrest after the son of Lady Barker, wife of the Governor, Sir Napier Broome. The site was earlier known as Anthon's Landing after the captain of a small vessel that entered the gulf in 1885.

Wynnum Q   Aboriginal. Breadfruit tree.

Wynyard NSW, T   After Major-General Edward Buckley Wynyard. He was a military officer in New South Wales. Wynyard visited Tasmania in 1850 and 1851. The township was earlier known as Table Cape and Ramsay. Table Cape was named by Bass and Flinders in 1798, but the first settlers did not arrive until the early 1840s.

Wyong NSW   Aboriginal. Place of running water.

Wyuna V   Aboriginal. Sparkling water.

Yaamba Q   Aboriginal. Camping ground.

Yaapeet V   Aboriginal, meaning unknown. Formerly Turkey Bottom.

Yabba North V   Aboriginal. Plenty talk.

Yacka SA   Aboriginal. A contraction of Yackamoorundie, Sister to the big river.

Yackandandah V   Aboriginal. Mother and Hill.

Yallingup NSW   Aboriginal. A corruption of Yalleroi, Lagoon.

Yallourn V   Aboriginal. Yellow fire.

Yamba NSW   The well-known Aboriginal athlete and sculler Rocky Laurie informed Roland Robinson that Yamba was so called after the yams that grew there. Another conjecture is that it is an Aboriginal name meaning Headland.

Yambuk V   Aboriginal. Moon.

Yampi Sound WA   Aboriginal. J. L. Stokes of the *Beagle* conferred the name in 1838 when he found fresh water supplies here, for the word means Fresh water.

Yan Yean V   Aboriginal. Unmarried man.

Yanac V   Aboriginal. Bats flying in the night.

Yanco NSW   Aboriginal. A corruption of Yanko, Sound of running water.

Yandiah SA   Aboriginal. Camp of lively gossip.

Yandina Q   Aboriginal. Small watering place.

Yankalilla SA   Aboriginal. A name for which no meaning has been discovered, and which has taken various forms. Colonel Light recorded it as Yanky Lilla, which led to a conjecture that an American lived there with his daughter Lily.

Yannathan V   Aboriginal. Walkabout.

232

Yannergee NSW   Aboriginal. To walk.

Yarck V   Aboriginal. Long river.

Yarra NSW   Aboriginal. Red gum tree.

Yarra River V   Aboriginal. The present name was first used by Europeans when J. H. Wedge surveyed the region for John Batman in September 1835. Of the several Aboriginal names for the river he preferred Yarra Yarra, which he thought they used for a waterfall (which would have been Yarram-Yarram). The actual meaning may be either Running water, or Red gum trees. The river was discovered by the Surveyor-General of New South Wales, Charles Grimes, on 2 February 1803, and was named by James Flemming, a member of the survey party, Freshwater River. Another Aboriginal name for the river, used occasionally, by white settlers, was Berrern or Birra-rang.

Yarragon V   Aboriginal. Hair of the head.

Yarram V   Aboriginal. A contraction of Yarram Yarram, Waterfalls or Plenty water.

Yarramalong NSW   Aboriginal. Place of white horses.

Yarraman NSW   Aboriginal. Horse.

Yarrawonga V   Aboriginal. Cormorants' nesting place. The Shire was created in 1891.

Yarroweyah V   Aboriginal. Gale of wind.

Yass NSW   Aboriginal. A corruption of Yarh or Yahr, meaning Running water. Hamilton Hume and William Hovell reached the plains and called them McDougall's Plains. An apocryphal story says that when Hume asked one of his scouts if the country was suitable for travelling, he replied 'Ya-ass, plains.'

Yea V   Named after Colonel Lacy Yea.

Yelarbon Q   Aboriginal. Water lily.

Yeltukka SA   Aboriginal. New camp.

Yerong Creek NSW   Aboriginal. Initiation ground.

Yethera NSW   Aboriginal. Three tracks.

Yiddah NSW   Aboriginal. Recovering from sickness.

Yinnar V   Aboriginal. Woman.

Yoongarilup WA   Aboriginal. Place where kangaroos scrape holes in the ground.

York WA   The first settlers arrived here in 1830 and on 13 March 1831 Governor James Stirling announced that he had 'opened up the district for location under the name of Yorkshire which it was thought in some respects to resemble'. The name was contracted to York.

York, Cape Q   On 21 August 1770 Captain Cook wrote: 'The point of the Main, which forms one side of the Passage...and which is the Northern Promontory of this Country, I have named York Cape, in honour of his late Royal Highness, the Duke of York.' This was Edward Augustus, Duke of York and Albany, a brother of King George III. The Aboriginal name of the cape was Goodangarkagi.

Yorke Peninsula SA   In May 1802 Flinders recorded in his Journal that 'to the peninsula...I have affixed the name of Yorke's Peninsula, in honour of the Right Honourable Charles Philip Yorke, who followed the steps of his above mentioned predecessors at the Admiralty [Earl St Vincent and Earl Spencer]'. Nicolas Baudin called it Cambaceres, after the Duc de Cambaceres.

Yorketown SA   The town took its name from the peninsula. There was a proposal to rename it Salt Lake City when production of salt from the salt lakes began.

You Yangs V   Aboriginal, meaning unknown.

Young NSW   Named after Sir John Young (later Baron Lisgar), Governor of New South Wales, in 1861 during his term of office. An earlier name was Lambing Flat, a small plain used as a lambing place. Aboriginal name, Burrangong. A sheep run first occupied by James White.

Yuluma NSW   Aboriginal. Wallaroo.

Yunderup WA   Aboriginal. Water hole.

Yungaburra Q   Aboriginal. Place of spirits. At first called Alumba, it was changed to avoid confusion with Aloomba.

Yunta SA   Aboriginal. Part of the female anatomy.

Yuranigh Creek NSW   After an Aboriginal of this name, known also as Jacky, who accompanied T. L. Mitchell on his northern expedition in 1845-46, and proved invaluable. Mitchell wrote of him: 'Guide, companion, counsellor, and friend.' He died in 1850, and a memorial was erected to his memory by the Government of New South Wales in 1900.

Yuraraba Q   Aboriginal. Round mountain.

Yurgo SA   Aboriginal. A long way.

Zeehan; Zeehan, Mount T The mountain was sighted by Tasman in 1642, and named after one of his vessels by Flinders during the voyage of the *Norfolk* in 1798 and 1799. The township was named after the mountain. The Aboriginal name was Weiawenena.

Zeil, Mount NT The mountain was discovered by Ernest Giles in 1872 and named by von Mueller while editing Giles's *Geographic Travels in Central Australia*. The origin of the name may be Ernest Zeil, a horticultural editor at Leipzig.

Zero, Mount V Named by T. L. Mitchell on 17 July 1835, during bitterly cold weather.

Zetland NSW After the Earl of Zetland, and named by Sir Hercules Robinson, Governor of New South Wales.

INDEX OF PEOPLE
MENTIONED IN THE TEXT

Names followed by an asterisk are those actually named after the persons listed. Where no asterisk appears they may be the discoverers, or their names appear in the text of the entry. Names in brackets are those no longer in use. Reference to these will be found in the entry that precedes the bracket. Where a name is followed by a question mark e.g. Bandianna (*?), there is some doubt whether the place was named for the person concerned.

a'Beckett, Thomas: Sandy Bagots*
Aberdeen, Lord: Aberdeen
Acland, Colonel: St Kilda
Adelaide, Queen: Adelaide*; Adelaide River*
Ainslie: Mount Ainslie*
Ainsworth, James: Ballina
Airey, G. S.: Airey's Inlet*
Airly, Duke of: Airly*
Alban, Saint: St Albans*
Albany, Duke of: Leopold*
Albert: Albert*
Albert, Prince: Lake Albert*; Albert River*; Alberton*
Alexander the Great: Mount Macedon
Alexandra, Princess: Northern Territory (Alexandra Land*)
Alexandra, Queen: Alexandra*
Alexandrina, Princess: See Queen Victoria
Alford, Henry: Alford*
Alford, Thomas: Toowoomba
Alfred, Duke of Edinburgh: Alfred and Marie Range*
Allen, John: Allen Island*
Allen, Robert: Winton
Althorpe: Althorpe Islands*
Amadeus, King: Lake Amadeus*
Anderson: Galah (Anderson's Plains*)
Anderson, Henry: Lake Wendouree
Anderson, R. D.: Oaklands
Andrews, John: Soldier's Point
Angas, George Fife: Angaston*; Greenock; Kingscote (Angas*); Nuriootpa (Angas Park*); Rosetta Head
Angas, Mrs Rosetta: Rosetta Head*
Anna: Bandianna (*?)
Anson, Lord George: Anson Bay*
Anthon, Captain: Wyndham (Anthon's Landing)

Antill, Major: Blackheath; Picton
Apsley, Baron (Lord Bathurst): Apsley*; Apsley Strait*
Archer, Charles and William: Fitzroy River; Gracemere; Rockhampton
Archer, Thomas: Archer River*
Aristotle: Artarmon
Arndell, Dr: Werribee (Arndell River*)
Artemon: Artarmon*
Arthur, Lieut-Governor Sir George: Mount Arthur*; Arthur River*; Port Arthur*; Arthur's Creek
Arthur, Henry: Arthur's Creek*
Ash, George: Ashville*
Ashburton, Lord: Ashburton River*
Atherton: Chillagoe
Atherton, John: Atherton*; Atherton Tableland*; Tinnaroo Creek
Atkinson, James: Port Fairy
Attlee, Clement: Monte Bello Islands
Auckland, Baron: Eden*
Auld, William Patrick: Auld's Chain of Ponds*
Austin, Robert: Lake Austin*; Cowcowing Lakes
Ayers, Sir Henry: Ayers Rock*; Port Wakefield (Port Henry*)

Babbage, Benjamin Herschell: Mount Babbage*; Blanchewater Plains; Lake Dutton; Lake Gregory; St Mary's Peak; Stuart Creek
Bacchus, Captain W. H.: Bacchus Marsh*
Backhouse, James: Carrington
Bacon, Lady Charlotte: Charlotte Waters*
Baillie, Governor Charles Wallace: See Baron Lamington
Baines, Thomas: Mount Baines*; Baines River*
Baker, A. J.: Mount Margaret

237

Baker, Mrs Margaret: Mount Margaret*
Balfour, J. O.: Gunyah
Ball, Lieut Lidgbird: Lord Howe Island (Mount Lidgbird*)
Ball, R. T.: Balldale*
Ballendella: Ballendella*
Balliang: Balliang*
Balloo, Billy: Billy Blue's Point*
Balmain, William: Balmain*
Banks, Sir Joseph: Australia; Cape Banks*; Banks Strait*; Botany Bay; Mount Dryander; English Company's Islands; Grose River; Mount King George (Mount Banks*); Kurnell; Sir Joseph Banks Group*; Point Solander
Barangaroo: Bennelong Point
Barker, Lady: Wyndham
Barker, Collet: Mount Barker*; Onkaparinga River; Port Adelaide; Rapid Bay
Barker, Dr Edward: Barker's Creek*
Barker, Wyndham: Wyndham*
Barkly, Sir Henry: Barkly Tableland*
Barlow, Captain Maurice: Fort Dundas
Barney, Lieut-Colonel George: Gladstone
Barrallier, Francis: Barrallier*
Barron, Sir Harry: Lady Barron
Barron, Lady: Lady Barron*
Barron, T. H.: Barron River*
Barrow, John: Barrow Island*
Barrow, John Henry: Barrow Creek*
Barton, Sir Edmund: Barton*
Barwite: Barwite*
Bass, George: Bass Hill*; Bass Point*; Bass Strait*; Circular Head; Coal Cliff; Corner Inlet; George's River; Hunter Group; Illawarra; Lake Illawarra; Phillip Island; Port Dalrymple; Shoalhaven River; Table Cape; Tamar River; Thistle Island; Wattamolla; Mount Wellington; Westernport; Wilson Promontory (Furneaux Land); Wynyard (Table Cape)
Bateman, Captain Nathaniel: Bateman Bay*
Bates, Daisy: Ooldea
Bathurst, Henry, third Earl of: Bathurst*; Bathurst Harbour*; Bathurst Island*; Lake Bathurst*; Brisbane
Bathurst, Lord: See Baron Apsley
Bateman, John: Bateman's Hill*; Bungaree; Geelong; Melbourne (Batmania*); Yarra River
Baudin, Nicolas: American River; Cape Borda; Busselton; Busselton River; Ceduna; Discovery Bay; Encounter Bay; Freycinet Peninsula; Geographe Bay; Guichen Bay; Investigator Strait; Cape Jaffa; Joseph Bonaparte Gulf; Lacepede Bay; Cape Leveque; Monte Bello Islands; Naturaliste Channel; Cape Naturaliste; Nepean Bay (Bougainville Bay); Oyster Bay; Phillip Island; Portland Bay (Tourville Bay); Rivoli Bay; Rosetta Head; St Vincent Gulf (Golfe Josephine); South Australia; Spencer Gulf; Triabunna (Port Monthazine); Vasse; Yorke Peninsula (Cambaceres)
Bauer, Ferdinand: Cape Bauer*; Mount Brown
Baxter: Baxter*
Baxter, John: Baxter Range*
Beaconsfield, Earl of (Benjamin Disraeli): Beaconsfield*; Monte Bello Islands
Beaglehole, Dr J. C.: Broken Bay; Repulse Bay; Solitary Islands
Beale, Lindsay: Kinglake
Beames, Walter: Beames Brook*
Beatty, Bill: Canberra; Cape Clear; Dead Man Crossing; Dee Why; Fisher's Ghost Creek; Humpty Doo; Katamatite; Miepoll; St Helena Island; Struck Oil
Beaufort, Rear-Admiral Sir Francis: Beaufort*
Beeac: Beeac*
Bell, Archibald: Bell*
Bell, Hugh: Bell Point*
Bell, Joshua Peter: Bell*
Bell, Patrick: Mystic Park
Bellender-Ker, John: Bellender-Ker Range*
Benedict, Saint: New Norcia
Bennelong: Binalong*
Bennelong: Bennelong Point*
Benson, E. W.: Belgrave
Bent, Judge-Advocate Ellis: Bringelly
Bent, Thomas: Darnum
Bentinck, Lord: Bentinck Island*
Berry, Alexander: Berry*; Clyde River; Coolangatta
Bessonet, James: Donnybrook
Best, Robert Holt: Wagga Wagga
Beveridge Peter: Beveridge*
Bicheno, James Ebenezer: Bicheno*

Biggs, Frederick: Lake Cargellico
Billiatt, John W.: Billiatt Springs*
Birch, T. W.: Port Davey
Birnie, Captain James: Kurnell
Bischoff, James: Mount Bischoff*
Black, Captain John: King Island
Black, John Melton: Townsville
Blackall, Samuel Wensley: Blackall*
Blackman, John: Orange (Blackman's Swamp*)
Blackwood, Captain Henry: Blackwood*; Blackwood River*
Blaxland, Gregory: Blaxland*; Mount Blaxland*; Blaxland's River*; Blue Mountains; Fish River; Lawson
Bleesdale, Dr: Gembrook
Bligh, Captain William: Adventure Bay; Annandale; Booby Island; Derwent River; Puddingpan Hill; Resolution Creek; Restoration Island; Sunday Island; Thursday Island; Twin Island (Double Island); Mount Wellington
Blinman, 'Pegleg' Robert: Blinman*
Blue, Billy: Blue's Point*; Lavender Bay
Blunden: Gawler River
Blyth, Sir Arthur: Blyth*
Bonapart, Joseph: Joseph Bonapart Gulf*
Bonapart, Napoleon: See Napoleon Bonapart
Bonney, Charles: Lake Bonney*; Mount Muirhead; Lake Victoria
Bonypart: St Helena Island
Boothby, Guy: Tintinara
Boothby, Mrs: Tintinara
Borda, Jean Charles: Cape Borda*
Bougainville: See de Bougainville
Boulter, Mrs Beatrice: Beatrice River*
Boulter, C. C.: Beatrice River
Bourke, Governor Sir Richard: Bourke*; Melbourne
Bowden: Bowden*
Bowden, John: Kersbrook
Bowen, Lady Diamantina Roma: Diamantina River*; Roma*
Bowen, Governor Sir George Ferguson: Bowen*; Bowenvale*; Diamantina River; Roma; Somerset; Staten River (Ferguson River*); Townsville
Bowen, G. M. C.: Bowenfels*
Bowen, Captain James: Bowen Strait*; Port Clinton (Port Bowen*)
Bowen, Lieut John: Coal River; Hobart; Richmond
Bowen, Lieut Richard: Jervis Bay

Bower: Bower*
Bowman, E. and C.: Bowmans*
Boyd: Boyd River*
Boyd, Benjamin: Boyd Town*; Condobolin; Deniliquin
Bracefield, James: Noosa Heads (Cape Bracefield*)
Bradfield, John Job Crew: Bradfield*
Bradley, Lieut William: Bradley's Head*; Maffra
Bragg, Thomas: Mungeribar
Braidwood, Dr Thomas: Braidwood*
Bremer, Sir James Gordon: Bremer Range*; Mount Gordon*; Melville Island; Port Essington
Bribie: Bribie Island*
Bridgewater, Duke of: Cape Bridgewater*
Bright, John: Tryal Rocks
Bright, John: Bright*
Brinkworth, George: Brinkworth*
Brisbane, Governor Sir Thomas Macdougall: Brisbane*; Brisbane Water*; Ipswich; Lockyer Valley; Monaro Plains (Brisbane Downs*)
Brock: Brock's Creek
Brockman, F. S.: King Edward River
Brodribb, William Adams: Albert River; Brodribb River*; Latrobe River; Yarra River
Brooke, Captain John: Monte Bello Islands; Tryal Rocks
Brookman, Sir George: Boulder City
Brookman, W. G.: Boulder City
Broome: Lucky Bay
Broome, Governor Sir Frederick Napier: Broome*; Napier Broome Bay*; Wyndham
Broughton, Bishop: Broughton River*; Port Broughton*
Broughton, Captain W. R.: Broughton Islands*; King George Sound; Princess Royal Harbour; Termination Island
Brown, Mrs Ellen: Ellendale*
Brown, Nicholas: Ellendale
Brown, Robert: Mount Brown*; Kingston (Browns Bay*)
Brown, W. C.: Croydon; Curlewis
Browne: Mount Browne*
Browne, Captain Sylvester: Enmore
Browne, Dr W. J.: Bottle Hill
Bruce, Lieut-Colonel John: Mount Bruce
Bryan, Guy: Mount Bryan*
Bryant: Coleraine

239

Buache, Jean Nicolas: Garden Island
   (Isle Buache*)
Buccleuch, Duke of: Buccleuch*
Buchanan, H. M.: Ross
Buchanan, Nathaniel: Buchanan Hills*;
   Buchanan's Creek*; Landsborough;
   Torrens Creek
Buck: Port Wakefield
Buck, Robert: Lasseter
Buckinghamshire, Earl of: See Robert
   Hobart
Buckland, William: Buckland Tableland*
Buffon, Comte: Cape Buffon*
Bullen, Ben: Ben Bullen*
Buller: Mount Buller*
Bunbury, Lieut Henry William St
   Pierre: Bunbury*
Bungaree: Bungaree*
Burdekin, Mrs Mary Ann: Burdekin
   River*
Burdekin, Thomas: Burdekin River
Burges: Mount Burges*
Burke, Robert O'Hara: Barkly Tableland;
   Burketown*; Cloncurry; Diamentina
   River; Georgina River; Hodgkinson
   River; Julia Creek; Landsborough;
   Lake Massacre; Wills Creek
Burnett, Captain, Mackay: Pioneer River
Burnett, James Charles: Burnett River*;
   Mary River
Burnie, William: Burnie*
Burr, Thomas: Burr Creek*
Burrowes, C. A.: Drysdale River
Bussell, Grace: Busselton
Bussell, John Garrett: Busselton*
Butler, Sir Richard: Butler*; Butler Dome*
Buxton, Governor: Algebuckina;
   Sherlock
Bynoe: Bynoe Harbour*; Bynoe Range*;
   Bynoe River*
Byron, Captain John: Byron Bay*; Cape
   Byron*
Byron, Lord: Byron*; Charlotte Waters

Cadell, Francis: Cadell*
Cairns, Governor William Wellington:
   Cairns*
Caledon, Governor: Caledon Bay*;
   Mount Caledon*
Caley, George: Caley Hill*; Caley's
   Repulse*; Mount King George
Calvert: Gilbert Range
Cambridge, Duke of: Cambridge Gulf*
Camden, Lord: Camden*

Cameron, Alexander: Alectown*
Cameron, Bessie: Bessibelle*
Cameron, Donald Charles: Barcaldine
Cameron, Ewan: Lochiel
Cameron, Ewin: Strathewin*
Cameron, Hugh: Scone
Cameron, R.: Black Stump
Campbell, Alexander: Port Campbell*
Campbell, Alexander: Glenorchy
Campbell, Sir Colin (Lord Clyde): Coal
   and Candle Creek (*?)
Campbell, John: Cessnock
Campbell, Robert: Duntroon
Campbell, Thomas: Lochiel
Campbell, William: Strathallan
Campbell, William: Campbell's Creek*;
   Clunes
Canning, George: Canning River*
Canning, Alfred Wernham: Canning
   Stock Route*
Canterbury, Viscount: See Sutton-
   Manners
Cape, Captain: Cape River*
Cardwell, Viscount: Cardwell*
Carlingford, Lord: Fortescue River*
Carmarthen, Marquess of: Blue
   Mountains (Carmarthen Hills*)
Carnarvon, Lord: Carnarvon*
Carr, Charles Warburton: Warburton*
Carrington, Lord: Carrington*
Carron: Kennedy Bay
Carstensz, Jan: Archer River; Arnhem
   Land; Gulf of Carpentaria; Staten
   River; Wenlock River (Batavia River)
Casey, Gavin: Boulder City
Cash, Martin: Mittagong
Castlemaine, Viscount: Castlemaine*
Castlereagh, Lord: Castlereagh*;
   Castlereagh Bay*; Castlereagh River*;
   Macquarie Fields
Cathcart, Major: Cathcart*
Caulfield, John: Caulfield*
Cavendish, Lord Ferderick: Cavendish*
Cavill, J. F.: Surfers Paradise
Chace, William: Chace Range*
Chamberlain, Joseph Neville (?): Monte
   Bellow Islands
Chambers, Anna: Anna's Reservoir*
Chambers, Charles: Charles Creek*
Chambers, Elizabeth: Chambers Bay*
Chambers, James: Anna's Reservoir;
   Central Mount Stuart; Chambers Bay;
   Mount Chambers*; Chambers Pillar*;
   Katherine River

Chambers, John: Mount Chambers*; Charles Creek; Stuart Creek (Chambers Creek*); William Creek
Chambers, Katherine: Chambers Bay; Katherine River*
Chambers, Mary: Mary River*
Chambers, William: William Creek*
'Champagne Charlie': See Lord Carrington
Champion, Canon: Canberra
Chandler: Beardy Plains*; Chandler River*; Chandler Peak*; Wollambi Creek
Charles II, King: Restoration Island
Charlotte, Princess: Princess Charlotte Bay*
Chermside, Governor Herbert Charles: Chermside*
Cheyne, George McCartney: Cheyne Island*
Chifley, Joseph Benedict: Chifley*
Childers, Hugh Culling Eardley: Childers*
Churchill, Thomas: Churchill Island*
Clarence, Duke of: See William IV
Clarendon, Earl of: Clarendon*
Clarke: Clarke Island*
Clarke: Clarke River*
Clarke, W.: Preservation Island
Clarke, Rev W. B.: Snowy Mountains
Clay: Casino
Cleland: Cleland Hills*
Cleveland, Duke of: Cleveland*; Cape Cleveland(*?)
Cleveland, John: Cleveland Bay*; Cape Cleveland(*?)
Clinton, Colonel: Cape Clinton*; Port Clinton*
Cloncurry, Lady Elizabeth: Cloncurry*
Close, E. C.: Morpeth
Clyde, Lord: See Sir Colin Campbell
Cobden, Richard: Cobden*
Cockburn, Vice-Admiral Sir John: Cockburn*; Cockburn Sound*
Codrington, Captain: Codrington*
Coen, Governor-General: Archer River (Coen River*)
Coffin: Mount Coffin
Coffin, Vice-Admiral Sir Isaac: Coffin Bay*; Greenly Islands; Mount Greenly; Sir Isaac Point*
Coghlen, Staff-Commander J. E.: Napier Broome Bay
Colbert, Dr E. H.: Dinosaur Point
Coleridge, Samuel Taylor: Greta

Colless, George and William: Come-by-Chance
Collie, Sir Alexander: Collie*; Collie River*; Preston River
Collins, Charles: Collinsville*
Collins, Lieut-Governor David: Blue Mountains; Hobart; Launceston; Neutral Bay; Mount Wellington (Mount Collins*)
Collins, William: Launceston; Tamar River
Colton, Sir John: Colton*
Compton: Compton*
Connell, John: Cronulla (*?); Kurnell (*?)
Conner, M. L.: Mount Conner*
Connor, Daniel: Connors Range*
Constantin, King: Dunkeld
Conway, Henry Seymour: Cape Conway*
Cook, Archibald: Cooke's Plains*
Cook, Captain James: Adventure Bay; Cape Banks; Bass Strait; Bateman Bay; Booby Island; Botany Bay; Breaksea Spit; Broken Bay; Broughton Islands; Bustard Bay; Byron Bay; Cape Capricorn; Cleveland Bay; Cape Cleveland; Mount Cook*; Cook's Passage*; Cook's River*; Cooktown*; Cumberland Islands; Point Danger; Cape Dromedary; Mount Dromedary; Dunk Island; Eddystone; Edgcumbe Bay; Endeavour Reef; Endeavour River; Endeavour Strait; Fitzroy Island; Fraser Island; Furneaux Group; Gerringong; Glasshouse Mountains; Gloucester Island; Great Sandy Island; Cape Hawke; Hervey Bay; Point Hicks; Hinchinbrook Island; Hope Islands; Cape Howe; Jervis Bay; Keppel Bay; Keppel Islands; Kurnell; Lizard Island; Long Nose Point; Lookout Point; Magnetic Island; Montagu Island; Cape Moreton; New South Wales; Nobby's Head; Northumberland Islands; Palm Isles; Pigeon House; Point Hicks Hill; Port Dalrymple; Port Jackson; Port Stephens; Possession Island; Prince of Wales Islands; Providential Channel; Ramhead; Red Point; Repulse Bay; Resolution Creek; Rockingham Bay; Cape St George; Sandwich Bay; Sandy Cape; Seventeen-seventy; Sir Charles Hardy Islands; Smoky Cape; Point Solander; Solitary Islands;

Thirsty Sound; The Three Brothers;
  Cape Three Points; Cape Tribulation;
  Trinity Bay; Point Upright; Mount
  Warning; Whitsunday Island; Wide
  Bay; Cape York
Cook, Mrs James: Kurnell
Cook, Sir Joseph: Cook*
Cooke, John M.: Point Cook*
Coombe, E. H.: Coombe*
Cooper, H. M.: Mount Attunga
Copley, John Singleton: See Baron
  Lyndhurst
Cordeaux, William: Cordeaux*; Mount
  Cordeaux*
Cornelius, Jerome: Pelsart Islands.
Cornish, W. H.: Poeppel Corner
Cosgrove, P.: Admiraby; Cosgrove*
Coster: Costerfield*
Cotton: Cotton*
Coulthard, William: Nuriootpa
Cowan, John: Lake Cowan*
Coward, Thomas: Coward Springs*
Cowley, Frank: Bethungra
Cowper: Cowper*
Cowper, Dean: Cowper*
Cowper, William: Cowper*
Cox, E. K.: Ulamambri
Cox, George: Turon River
Cox, J. P.: Marrar
Cox, William: Cox's Pass*; Cox's River*
Cranbourne, Viscount: Cranbourne*
Creswick, Henry: Creswick*
Creswick, John: Creswick*
Crispe, James: Tahmoor
Croker, S.: Buchanan's Creek
Cropper, Charles: Brocklesby
Crozier, Captain Richard: Rosetta Head;
  Victor Harbour
Cue, Thomas: Cue*
Cumberland (Ernest Augustus), Duke of:
  Cumberland*
Cumberland (Henry Frederick), Duke of:
  Cumberland Islands*
Cummins, W. P.: Cummins*
Cunningham, Allan: Mount Alford; Allan
  Cunningham*; Bellender-Ker Range;
  Blaxland's River; Mount Castle;
  Cunningham*; Cunningham's Gap*;
  Darling Downs; Dumaresq River;
  Gwydir; Mount Lindesay; Macintyre
  River; McPherson Range; Pandora's
  Pass; Wimbledon
Cunningham, Captain Charles:
  Cunningham Islands*

Cunningham, Hastings: Mount Gambier
Cunningham, Richard: Allan Cunningham
Curlewis: Curlewis*
Curr, Edwin: Mersey River
Currie, Captain Mark: Monaro;
  Murrumbidgee River; Snowy
  Mountains
Curtis, Admiral Sir Rover: Curtis Island*;
  Port Curtis*
Custon: Custon*
Cuttle, Robin: Robinvale*

D'Aguilar, Sir George S.: Daguilar Range*
Dale, Ensign Robert: Mount Caroline;
  Northam; Mount Stirling
Dalhunty, Mrs: Cullen Bullen
Dalrymple, Alexander: Cape Hawke;
  Port Dalrymple*; Torres Strait
Dalrymple, George Augustus Frederick
  Elphinstone: Bartle Frere; Bowen;
  Cardwell; Daintree River; Dalrymple*;
  Mount Dalrymple*; Elphinstone
  Creek*; Herbert River; Herbert
  Range; Johnstone River; Mount
  Jukes; Moresby Range; Proserpine;
  Tully; Tully River
Daintree, Richard: Mount Daintree*;
  Daintree River*
Daly, Governor Sir Dominick: Clifton
  Centre; Daly River*; Daly Waters*;
  Moonta
Dampier, William: Buccaneer
  Archipelago*; Cygnet Bay; Dampier
  Archipelago*; Dampier Bay*;
  Roebuck Bay; Shark Bay
Darke, John Charles: Darke Peak*;
  Mount Wedge
Darling, Lady (nee Dumaresq): Dumaresq
  River*
Darling, Governor Sir Ralph: Albany;
  Black Stump; Darling Downs*;
  Darling Range*; Darling River*;
  Dumaresq River; Logan River;
  Murray River
Darlot, James Monckton: Horsham
Darwin, Charles: Darwin*; Mount
  Darwin*; Port Darwin*
Davenport, Sir Samuel: Millicent
Davey, Lieut-Governor Sir Thomas:
  Hobart; Port Davey*; Sorell
Davis, James: Noosa Heads
Davis, Pamela: Doo Town
Dawson, Robert Barrington: Bentley;
  Dawson Range*; Dawson River*

242

Day, Thomas: Wild Horse Plains
de Blemont, William: Bloomsbury
de Bougainville, Louis Antoine: Nepean Bay (Bougainville Bay*)
de Cambaceres, Duc: Yorke Peninsula (Cambaceres)
de Carpentier, Governor-General Pieter: Gulf of Carpentaria
de Castella, Mrs Lily: Lilydale*
de Castella, Paul: Lilydale
de Cretin, Lieut.: D'Entrecasteaux Channel
de Fleurieu, Comte: Oyster Bay (Fleurieu Bay*)
de Freycinet, Louis Claude de Saulces: Freycinet Peninsula; Geographe Bay; Leschenault Estuary
de Garis, C. J.: Sunraysia
de Grey, Earl: De Grey River*
de Houtman, Frederick: Houtman Abrolhos Islands*
de Kermadec, Huon: Esperance; Huon Peninsula*; Huon River*; Huonville*
de Lacepede, Count B. G. E. Delaville: Lacepede Bay
de Quiros, Pedro Fernandez: Australia; Torres Strait
de Rose, Charles: Boulder City
de Saint-Aigan, Lieut: D'Entrecasteaux Channel
de St Arnaud, Jacques Leroy: St Arnaud*
de Satge, Oscar: Clermont
de Strzelecki, Paul Edmund: Gippsland; Mount Kosciusko; Strzelecki*; Strzelecki Creek*; Strzelecki Ranges*
de Torres, Luis Vaez: Torres Strait*
de Vlamingh, Willem: Geelvink Bay; Cape Inscription; Rottnest Island; Swan River
de Witt, Gerrit Frederickszoon: De Witt Island*; De Witt's Land*
Deakin, Alfred: Deakin*; Holder
d'Edel, Jacob: Edel Land
Delisser, Alfred: Nullarbor Plain
Denison, Sir William: Denison*
Denmark, Surgeon: Denmark*
D'Entrecasteaux, Admiral Joseph Antoine Bruni: Adventure Bay; Blackman Bay; Bruny Island*; Cygnet Bay; D'Entrecasteaux Channel*; D'Entrecasteaux Point*; d'Entrecasteaux Reef*; Derwent River; Esperance; Great Australian Bight; Huon River; Huon Peninsula;

Port Esperance; Recherche Archipelago; Recherche Bay; Mount Wellington
Derby, Lord: Derby*
Devine, Lieut Robert: Sweers Island
Devlin, Hugh: Hughenden*
Devlin, N.: Ganmain
D'Foigny, Gabriel: Australia
Dickie: Bowden
Dickson: Cairns (Dickson*)
Diggory: Diggora*
Dillon, Captain Peter: La Perouse
Discombe, Reece: La Perouse
Disraeli, Benjamin: See Earl of Beaconsfield
Docker, Rev Joseph: Benalla; Docker*
Doecke, Peter: Peterborough*
Donald, W.: Donald*
Donaldson, Stuart Alexander: Tenterfield
Douglas, A.: Barron River
Dowling, Mrs: Dowlingville*
Doyle, Cyrus M.: Narrabri
Drouin: Drouin*
Drummond, James: Drummond*
Dryander, Jonas: Mount Dryander*
Drysdale: Drysdale River*
Drysdale, Miss: Drysdale*
du Fresne, Captain Marion: Marion Bay*
Duffy, Charles Gavan: Sorrento
Dulhunty, John: Dulhunty*; Dulhunty Plains*; Dulhunty River*
Dulhunty, Robert V.: Dubbo; Dulhunty
Dumaresq family: Tilbuster
Dumaresq, Henry: Dumaresq River
Dumaresq, Colonel William J.: Armadale; Beardy Plains
Duncan, Lord: Camperdown (Duncan*)
Dundas, Henry (Viscount Melville): Dundas Strait*; Fort Dundas*
Dunk, George Montagu (Earl of Halifax and Sandwich): Dunk Island*; Halifax Bay*; Halifax Island*; Montagu Island*; Sandwich Bay*
Dunlea, Father T. V.: Boys Town
Dunn, John: Bridgewater
Dunstan, John: Australia
Dunwich, Viscount: See Earl of Stradbroke
Durack family: Durack River*
Dutton, Charles Christian: Callanna; Lake Dutton*; Separation Creek
Duval: Beardy Plains*; Mount Duval*
Duverney: Cressy

243

Eardley-Wilmot, Sir John: Wilmot*
Ebden, Charles H.: Carlsruhe; Wodonga
Eddington, Captain John: Eddington
Eddy, C. M. G.: Clyde
Edgcumbe, Lord: Edgcumbe Bay*
Edinburgh, Duke of: Cobourg*
Edinburgh, Duke and Duchess of: See Alfred, and Marie
Edkins, R. E.: Edkins Range*
Edward VII, King: Alexandra; King Edward River*
Edward VIII, King: Princes Highway*
Edwards, R.: Murray Bridge (Edwards Crossing*)
Elder, Alexander Lang: Mount Aleck*; Elder Range*; Port Augusta
Elizabeth II, Queen: Elizabeth*
Ellery, R. L. J.: Mount Ellery*
Elliot, Sir Charles: Port Elliot*
Elphinstone, Montstuart: Elphinestone*
Elsey, Joseph Ravenscroft: Elsey Creek*
Embley, J. T.: Embley Range*; Embley River*
Engel, Philip: Kalbar (Engelsburg*)
Essington, Vice-Admiral Sir William: Port Essington*
Etheridge, Donald: Etheridge Goldfield*; Etheridge River*
Evans, Beatrice Madge: Beatrice Hill*; Madge's Hill*
Evans, George William: Bathurst; Mount Blaxland; Castlereagh; Fish River; Mount Evans*; Lachlan River; Macquarie River; River Lett
Evans, Thomas: Evans Island*
Evans, William Greig: Beatrice Hill; Madge's Hill
Everard, William: Lake Everard*; Everard Range*; Mount Everard*
Exmouth, Viscount: Exmouth Gulf*
Eyre, Edward John: Mount Babbage; Baxter Range; Beltana; Lake Blanche; Broughton River; Burr Creek; Clare; Mount Deception; Eucla; Eyre Creek* Lake Eyre*; Mount Eyre*; Eyre Peninsula*; Flinders Ranges; Frome Creek; Lake Frome; Gawler Ranges; Lake Hindmarsh; Mount Hopeless; Leigh Creek; Moorunde; Port Germain; Mount Remarkable; St Mary's Peak; Scott Bay; Scott Creek; Mount Scott; Lake Torrens; Lake Tyrell; Warracknabeal

Fairfax, Alfred: Woodford
Faithfull, George: Wangaratta
Faraday, Sir Michael: Mount Faraday*
Farley, John: Fisher's Ghost Creek
Farrell, Dean: Farrell Flat*
Faure, Pierre: Freycinet Peninsula; Oyster Bay (Fleurieu Bay)
Fawkner, John Pascoe: Fawkner*; Melbourne
Fergusson, Governor Sir James: Ardrossan; Edith; Frances; Jamestown*; Kilkerran; Millicent
Fergusson, Lady Edith: Edithburg*
Field: Costerfield*
Field, Judge Barron: Field Island*
Field, Lieut W. G.: Onkaparinga River
Finch-Hatton, George: Finch Hatton
Fine, Oronce: Australia
Finke, William: Mount Finke*; Finke River*
Finley, F. G.: Finley*
Finnerty, John Michael: Coolgardie
Finniss, Colonel Boyle Travers: Ashbourne (Finnis*); Daly River; Escape Cliffs; Finnis*; Finniss River*; Finniss Springs*
Firebrace, Major: Vectis East
Fisher, Andrew: Fisher*
Fisher, Fred: Fisher's Ghost Creek*
Fisher, George: Georgetown*
Fitzgerald, Lord: See John F. Foster
FitzGerald, Governor Sir Charles: Geraldton*
Fitzgerald, Thomas Henry: Innisfail (Geraldton*)
Fitzmaurice, L. R.: Adelaide River; Fitzmaurice River*
Fitzroy, Augustus Henry: Fitzroy Island*; Grafton*; Cape Grafton*
FitzRoy, Sir Charles: Fitzroy Downs*; Fitzroy Gardens*; Fitzroy River*; Mary River
FitzRoy, Lady Mary: Mary River*; Maryborough*
FitzRoy, Captain Robert: Fitzroy River*
Flaxman, C.: Angaston
Fleming, Robert: Flemington
Flemming, James: Yarra River (Freshwater River)
Flinders, Mrs Annette (nee Chappelle): Mount Chappell*
Flinders, Matthew: Albatross Island; Allen Island; Althorpe Islands; Anxious Bay; Arnhem Land;

244

Australia; Avoid Bay; Backstairs Passage; Cape Banks; Barn Hill; Bass Hill; Bass Point; Bass Strait; Cape Bauer; Bay of Rest; Bell Point; Ben Lomond; Bentinck Island; Blackman Bay; Bountiful Island; Bribie Island; Broken Bay; Mount Brown; Caledon Bay; Cape Catastrophe; Mount Chappell; Cape Chatham; Circular Head; Clarence River; Coffin Bay; Corner Inlet; Corny Point; Cunningham Islands; Curtis Island; Denial Bay; Duyfken Point; Encounter Bay; English Company's Islands; Evans Island; Eyre Peninsula; Flinders*; Flinders Bay; Flinders Chase*; Flinders Island*; Flinders Passage*; Flinders Peak*; Flinders Ranges*; Flinders River*; Fowler Bay; Fowler Point; Franklin Island; Gambier Islands; George's River; Good Island; Goose Island; Great Australian Bight; Greenly Islands; Mount Greenly; Horn Island; Hunter Islands; Illawarra; Lake Illawarra; Investigator Group; Investigator Strait; Judgment Rock; Kangaroo Island; Cape Keer-Weer; Kent Group; Cape Leeuwin; Mount Lofty; Point Lowly; Lucky Bay; Malay Road; Memory Cove; Moreton Island; Morgan Island; Mornington Island; Nepean Bay; Neptune Islands; New Holland; Nullarbor Plain; Nuyts Archipelago; The Pages; Cape Pasley; Pasley Island; Point Pearce; Pelican Lagoon; Pera Head; Percy Islands; Pobasso Island; Port Clinton (Port Bowen); Port Curtis; Port Dalrymple; Port Hacking; Port Lincoln; Port Phillip; Cape Radstock; Recherche Archipelago; Mount Remarkable; Point Riley; Rosetta Head; St Francis Island; St Peter Island; St Vincent Gulf; Sir Edward Pellew Group; Sir Isaac Point; Sir Joseph Banks Group; Skirmish Point; Smoky Bay; Solitary Islands; South Australia (Flinders Land*); Spencer Gulf; Spilsby Island; Stickney Island; Stirling Range; Streaky Bay; Swan Point; Swan Ponds; Sweers Island; Table Cape; Tamar River; Taylor Islands; Thevenard; Thistle Island; Thorny Passage; Troubridge Hill; Twin Peaks Island; Wattamolla; Wedge Island; Wellesley Islands; Mount Wellington; Wessel Islands; West Cape Howe; Mount Westall; Westall Point; Whidbey Islands; Whidbey Point; Whyalla (Hummock Hill); Cape Wilberforce; Wilson Promontory; Wreck Reef; Wynyard (Table Cape); Yorke Peninsula; Mount Zeehan

Flinders, Samuel Ward: Flinders Group*; Flinders Island*; Cape Jervis

Flynn, Constable: Flynn*

Forbes, Sir Francis: Forbes*

Forrest, Alexander: Forrest; King Leopold Range; Mount Lennard; Lennard River; Mueller Range

Forrest, Sir John: Lake Barlee; Forrest*; Forrest Lakes*; Mount Forrest*; Forrest River*; Wyndham

Forrest, Mrs Mary Barrett (nee Lennard): Mount Lennard; Lennard River*

Forster, A.: Angaston

Fortescue, C. S. P.: Fortescue River*

Fossey, Joseph: Arthur River; Mount Block; Mount Mayday; Middlesex Plains

Foster, John F.: Foster*

Fowler, Robert: Fowler Bay*; Fowler Point*

Frankland, George: Mount Anne; Bellerine; Frankland*; Frankland Beach*; Mount Frankland*; Frankland River*; Mount Hugel; Mount Ida; Mount Olympus; Mount Ossa; Lake St Clair

Franklin, Harry: Lake Harry*

Franklin, Governor Sir John: Franklin*; Franklin Harbour*; Franklin Island*; Franklin River*; Mathinna; Port Lincoln; Spilsby Island; Mount Wellington

Franklin, Lady: Mathinna; Port Lincoln

Fraser, Captain James: Fraser Island*

Fraser, Mrs James: Fraser Island; Noosa Heads

Frederick, Duke of York and Albany: Albany*

Freeling, Sir A. H.: Freeling*

Fremantle, Sir Charles How: Fremantle*

French, James: French's Forest*

Frere, Sir Henry Bartle: Bartle Frere*

Frew, James: Frew River*; Frew's Ironstone Pond*

245

Frew, Robert: Birdsville
Freycinet: See de Freycinet
Frome, E. C.: Mount Chambers; Frome Creek*; Lake Frome*; Ulooloo; Mount Victor
Fulton, Rev Henry: Cowra
Furneaux, Captain Tobias: Adventure Bay; Bass Strait; D'Entrecasteaux Channel; Eddystone; Furneaux Group*; Pedra Blanca (Swilly*); Wilson Promontory (Furneaux Land*)
Furner, Luke: Furner*; Mount Furner*
Fyan, Foster: Fyansford*

Gairdner, Gordon: Lake Gairdner*
Gambier, Lord: Gambier Islands*; Mount Gambier*
Gardiner, John: Gardiner's Creek*
Garfield, James Abram: Garfield
Garland, Charles: Garland*
Gartrell, W. H. and Mrs Gartrell: Roseworthy
Gascoyne, Captain J.: Gascoyne River*
Gawler, Governor George: Lake Albert; Mount Eyre; Eyre Peninsula; Flinders Ranges; Gawler*; Gawler Ranges*; Gawler River*; Lyndoch; Onkaparinga River
Geeves, William: Geevestown*
Gellibrand, Joseph Tice: Gellibrand*; Plenty River
Gellions, John: Agnes
Gellions, Agnes: Agnes*
George III, King: Bennelong Point; Cambridge Gulf; Cumberland; George's River; Gloucester Island; King George's Sound*; New South Wales; Prince of Wales Islands; Cape York
George IV, King: Albany; Lake Cargellico (Regent's Lake*); Lake George*; Mount King George; Princess Charlotte Bay
George V, King: Alexandra
Germain, Saint: St Germain's*
Germaine, Hugh: Jericho
Germain, Benjamin: Port Macdonnell
Germein, Captain Samuel: Port Germain*
Gerritz, Hessel: Cape Leeuwin
Gibson, Alfred: Gibson Desert*
Gibson, F. F.: Caragabal
Gibson, T. F.: Burrumbuttock
Gilbert, John: Gilbert Range*; Gilbert River*; Gilberton*

Gilbert, Joseph: Pewsey Peak; Pewsey Vale
Giles, Ernest: Alfred and Marie Range; Lake Amadeus; Ayers Rock; Mount Destruction; Ehrenberg Range; Ernabella; George Gill Range; Gibson Desert; Lake Giles*; Great Victoria Desert; Great Victoria Spring; Mount Olga; Palm Valley; Petermann Range; Rawlinson Range; Victoria Spring; Mount Zeil.
Gill, George: George Gill Range*
Gill, S. T.: Lake Dutton (Lake Gill*)
Gilles, Osmond: Gilles Plain*; Glen Osmond*
Gillies: Gillies Highway*
Gipps, Governor Sir George: Blayney; Gippsland*; Gosford
Gisborne, Henry Fyshe: Gisborne*
Gladstone, William Ewart: Gladstone* (Q); Gladstone* (SA)
Gleeson, Edward B.: Clare
Glen, George: Millicent
Glen, Mrs Millicent (nee Short): Millicent*
Glenelg, Lord: Glenelg River* (V); Glenelg River* (WA); Melbourne (Glenelg*)
Glennie, James: Glennies Creek*
Gloucester, Duke of: Gloucester Island*
Goddard: Kennedy Bay
Goddard, W.P.: Mount Goddard*
Goldie: Arthur River
Gollen, David: Tailem
Gooroobarrooboollo: Bennelong Point
Gordon, Alexander, and Mrs Gordon: Mount Morgan
Gordon, D.I.: South Australia
Gordon, James: Gordon River*
Gordon, John: Gordonvale*
Gore, St George: Gore*
Gore, William: Artarmon
Gormanston, Viscount: Gormanston*
Gosford, Earl of: Gosford*
Gosse, William Christie: Ayers Rock; Mount Conner; Everard Range; Gosse Range*; Musgrave Ranges; Mount Olga; Mount Woodroffe
Goulburn, Frederick: Goulburn; Goulburn River*
Goulburn Henry: Goulburn*; Goulburn Islands*; Goulburn Plains*; Goulburn River*; Goulburn Valley*

Gould, Charles: Mount Darwin; Mount Huxley; Mount Jukes; Mount Lyell; Mount Sedgwick
Gould, John: Gould*
Goyder, George Woodroffe: Auld's Chain of Ponds; Mount Babbage; Darwin; Lake Ayre; Goyder Lagoon*; Lake Harry; Mount Painter; Mount Woodroffe*
Grafton, Duke of: Fitzroy Island*; Grafton*; Cape Grafton*
Graham, Thomas (Baron Lyndoch): Barossa Valley
Grainger, John: Port Augusta
Grant, Captain Charles: Grant Island*
Grant, Lieut James: Banks Strait; Cape Bridgewater; Churchill Island; Discovery Bay; Mount Gambier; Grantville*; Lady Julia Percy Island; Lady Nelson's Point; Lady Nelson's Reef; Nelson; Cape Nelson; Cape Northumberland; Cape Otway. Phillip Island (Grant Island*); Port Phillip; Portland Bay; Cape Schanck; Mount Schanck; Sir William Grant's Cape; Wight's Land
Grant, James MacPherson: Alvie
Grant, Sir William: Sir William Grant's Cape*
Gray: Lake Massacre
Gray, William: Graysholme*
Green: Greensborough*
Greene, G. H.: Greenthorpe*
Greenly, Miss: Greenly Islands*; Mount Greenly*
Greenough, George Bellas: Greenough River*
Gregory, Sir Augustus Charles: Mount Augustus*; Lake Blanche; Lake Callabonna; Clermont; Cooper Creek; Elsey Creek; Fortescue River; Geraldton; Gregory River*; Herbert River; Herbert Range
Gregory, Frank Thomas; Ashburton River; Mount Augustus; Mount Baines; Baines River; Mount Bruce; De Grey River; Fortescue River; Hamersley Range; Oakover River
Grenfell, T. G.: Grenfell*
Grey, Lady Eliza: Lake Eliza*
Grey, Sir George: Arrowsmith River; Buller River; Lake Eliza; Gascoyne River; Lake George; Glenelg River; Greenough River; Irwin River; Murchison River; Smith River; Victoria Range
Griffin, Walter Burley: Lake Burley Griffin*; Griffith
Griffith, Arthur: Griffith*
Grimes, Charles: Yarra River
Grose, Lieut-Governor Francis: Grose River*; Grose Vale*; Grose Wold*; Windsor
Guichen, Admiral: Guichen Bay*
Gullifer: Lilliput
Gunn, Ronald Campbell: Penguin; Penguin Creek
Gunson, Dr: Mount Gunson*
Gwydir, Lord: Gwydir*

Hack, Stephen: Lake Gairdner; Gawler Ranges
Hacking, Henry: Port Hacking*
Hahn, Captain D. N.: Hahndorf*
Hailes, Nathaniel: Windsor
Haley, C. R.: Kingaroy
Halifax, Earl of: See George Montagu Dunk
Hall, George: Halbury*
Hallett: Hallett*
Hall, Charles: Hall's Creek*
Hamelin, Captain: Garden Island; Cape Inscription
Hamersley, Edward: Hamersley Range*
Hamilton, A. G.: Figtree
Hamilton-Gordon, George: Aberdeen
Hamley, Lieut-Colonel: Hamley Bridge*
Hanlon, Edward: Toronto
Hann, Mrs Elizabeth: Mount Elizabeth*
Hann, Frank H.: Adcock River; Caroline Range; Charnley River; Mount Daintree; Lake Disappointment; Edkins Range; Mount Elizabeth; Mount Hann*; Hann Range*; Hann River*; Hann Tabletop*; Isdell River; Mount Ord; Tate River
Hann, William: Mount Daintree; Normanby; Normanby River; Tate River; Walsh River; Warner's Gully
Hannah, William: Hannah's Bridge*
Hannan, Patrick (Paddy): Kalgoorlie (Hannan's Find*)
Hanson, Sir Richard: Hanson*
Harcourt, Sir William: Harcourt*
Hardy, Mrs Ellen: Ellin*
Hardy, John: Ellin
Hardy, Admiral Sir Charles: Sir Charles Hardy Islands*

247

Hargraves, Edward Hammond: Hargraves*; Ophir
Harnett, Richard: Chatswood
Harnett, Mrs Richard (Chatty): Chatswood*
Harrington, Earl of: Harrington*
Harris, C. H.: St Mary's Peak
Harris, John: Five Dock
Harris, Peter: Mount Harris*
Harrison, Samuel: Ariah Park
Hart, Captain John: Hart
Hartnell, F. A.: Birdsville
Hartog, Dirck (Hartoge, Theodoric): Dirk Hartog Island*; Eendracht Land; Cape Inscription
Harvey, Major: Harvey*; Harvey River*
Harvey, John: Salisbury
Hassall: Ashley
Hastings, Warren: Daylesford; Hastings Point*; Hastings River*
Hawdon, Joseph: Black Dog Creek; Lake Bonney; Victoria Range
Hawke, Sir Edward; Cape Hawke*
Hawker, George Charles: Hawker*
Hawkesbury, Baron: See Charles Jenkinson
Hawkesworth, Dr John: Cape Moreton
Hawkins, Edward: Beaudesert
Hay, Sir John: Hay*
Hayes, Sir Henry Brown: Vaucluse Bay; Vaucluse Heights
Hayes, Commodore Sir John: Bruny Island; Derwent River; Mount Hayes*; Risdon Cove; Mount Wellington
Head, Benjamin: Mount Ben*; Head Range*
Heales, Sir Richard: Healesville*; Marysville
Heales, Lady Mary: Marysville*
Hedland, Captain Peter: Port Hedland*
Hedley, Dr: Hedley*
Hellyer, Henry: Arthur River; Mount Block; Burnie; Cam River; Mount Dipwood; Hellyer River*; Murchison River; St Valentine's Peak; Welcome Hill
Henry, Ernest: Argylla; Hughenden
Henry II, King: Newcastle
Henty family: Merino; Sandford; Tarrington
Henty, E. and brother: Portland
Henty, Henry: Henty*
Henty, S. G.: Blue Lake
Henty, Thomas: Tarrington
Hepburn, Captain: Hepburn
Herbert, Sir Wyndham: Herbert River*; Herbert Range*; Herberton*
Herrgott, D. D.: Marree (Hergott Springs*)
Herschell, Sir William: Brisbane
Hervey, Admiral Augustus John: Hervey Bay*
Hewitt, J.: Wild Horse Plains
Hey, Rev Nicholas: Hey River*
Hicks, Lieut Zacchary: Point Hicks Hill*
Hicks-Beach, Sir M. E.: Beachport*
Hill, William: Hillston*
Hill, William: Wakefield River
Hindmarsh, Governor Sir John: Hindmarsh*; Lake Hindmarsh*
Hobart, Robert: Hobart*
Hobson, Captain William: Point Cook
Hodkinson, Miss Alice Olinda: Olinda*
Hodgkinson, Clement: Olinda
Hodgkinson, William Oswald: Hodgkinson River*; Mulligan River
Hodgson, Christopher Pemberton: Hodgson*
Holbrook, Lieut Norman: Holbrook*
Holder, Sir Frederick: Holder*
Home, Colonel: Home Hill*
Hooker, Sir Joseph Dalton: Mount Lindesay (Mount Hooker*)
Hooker: Mount Brown
Hopkins, Sir John Paul: Hopkins River*
Hopwood, Henry: Echuca (Hopwood's Ferry*)
Horner, O.: Gladstone
Horrocks, John Ainsworth: Gulnare; Lake Dutton; Mount Horrocks*; Penwortham
Hotham, Governor Sir Charles: Mount Hotham*; Dennington
Houtman, Frederick de: See de Houtman
Hovell, Arndell: Werribee (Arndell River*)
Hovell, William Henry: Mount Buffalo; Mount Disappointment; Goulburn River (Hovell River*); Hume Dam; Hume Highway; Hume Reservoir; Mount Macedon; Melbourne; Mitta Mitta River; Murray River; Narallen; Ovens River; Wangaratta; Werribee (Arndell River); Yass
Hovell, Mrs W. H.: Werribee
Howe, Lord: Lord Howe Island*
Howe, John: Singleton

Howe, Admiral Richard (Earl): Cape Howe*; West Cape Howe*
Hughes, H. B.: Gladstone; Laura
Hughes, Herbert: Herbert*
Hughes, John Bristow: Bundaleer; Laura
Hughes, William Morris: Hughes*
Hume, Andrew Hamilton: Lake Bathurst; Bogan Gate; Mount Buffalo; Mount Disappointment; Goulburn Plains; Goulburn River; Hume Dam*; Hume Highway*; Mitta Mitta River; Murray River (Hume River*); Ovens River; Snowy Mountains; Wangaratta; Yass
Hunt, Charles C.: Lake Cowan; Mount Hunt*; Lake Lefroy; Mount Lefroy; Merredin; Port Hedland; Lake Seabrook
Hunter, Governor John: Coalcliff; Hunter Group*; Hunter River*; Kent Group; Kissing Point; Wilson Promontory
Huon, Charles and Paul: Huon*; Wodonga
Hurley, John: Cootamundra
Hurst: Hurst Bridge*
Hutchinson, Y. B.: Hindmarsh
Hutt, Sir William: Hutt River*
Huxley, Thomas Henry: Mount Huxley*
Huxley, Tom: Tom Ugly's Point*

Icely, Thomas: Mandurama
Idriess, Ion L.: Lasseter Country
Imlay, Alexander: Mount Imlay*
Imlay, Dr George: Bega; Dr George Mountain*; Mount Imlay*
Imlay, Peter: Mount Imlay*
Ingham, William Bairstow: Ingham*
Innes, Major Archibald Clunes: Clunes*; Glen Innes*
Irving, Clarke: Casino
Irwin, Frederick Chidley: Irwin River*
Isaac, Frederick Neville: Isaac River*

Jack, R. Logan: Lockhart River
Jackson, Sir George: Port Jackson*
Jackson, Samuel and William: Sunbury
Jacky Jacky: Jacky Jacky*; Kennedy Bay
Jamieson brothers: Mildura
Jamieson family: Jamieson*
Jamison, Sir John: Capertee
Jansz, Willem: Gulf of Carpentaria; Duyfken Point; Cape Keer-Weer; Wenlock River (Batavia River)

Jardine, Alexander: Jardine River; Somerset; Staten River; Wenlock River
Jardine, Francis Lascelles: Archer River; Jardine River*; Somerset; Staten River; Wenlock River
Jardine, John: Jardine River
Jardine, William: Somerset
Jarvis, Thomas: Jarvisfield*
Jeffreys, Lieut Charles: Molle Islands; Princess Charlotte Bay
Jenkinson, Charles: Hawkesbury River*
Jervis, Admiral Sir John (Earl St Vincent): Jervis Bay*; Cape Jervis*; St Vincent Gulf*; Troubridge Hill; Yorke Peninsula
Jervois, Carrie: Carrieton*
Jervois, Gordon: Gordon*
Jervois, Hammond: Hammond*
Jervois, Governor Sir William Francis Drummond: Carrieton; Cleve; Custon; Farina; Gordon; Hammond; Jervois Range*; Paskeville; Quorn; Snowtown; Warnertown
Jessop, William: St Mary's Peak
Jimmy the Pieman: Pieman River*
Johnson, Carl W. R.: Carlwood*
Johnston, David: Adelong
Johnston, George: Annandale; Grose River
Johnston, Lieut Robert: Clyde River
Johnstone, Richard Arthur: Barron River; Johnstone River*
Jones, D. O.: Frances
Jones, Mrs Frances: Frances*
Jones, John: Stanmore
Jorgensen, Jorgen: Lake St Clair
Josephine, Empress: St Vincent Gulf (Golfe Josephine*)
Joskins, J.: Barraba
Jukes, Dr: Direction Hill
Jukes, Joseph Beete: Mount Jukes*

Kable, Henry: Annandale
Kavell, Augustus: Klemzig
Kellar: Strathkellar*
Kelly, Captain James: Bathurst Harbour; Gordon River; Kelly Bay*; Kelly Island*; Macquarie Harbour; Port Davey; Settlement Island
Kelly, Ned: Kelly Country*
Kelvin, Lord: See Sir William Thomson
Kemp, Anthony Fern: Kempton*

Kempe: Hermannsburg
Kendall, Henry: Kendall (*?)
Kendall, Captain Joseph (*?)
Kennedy, Governor Sir Arthur: Georgina River
Kennedy, E. B. C.: Barcoo River; Carron River; Cooper Creek; Jacky Jacky; Kennedy Bay*; Kennedy River*; Thomson River; Walsh River
Kennedy, Georgina: Georgina River*
Kent, Captain William: Kent Group*
Kentish, Nathaniel Lipscombe: Kentish*
Keppel, Viscount: Keppel Bay*; Keppel Islands*
Kermadec, Huon de: See de Kermadec
Kernot: Kernot*
Keyneton, Joseph: Keyneton*
Keys, C.: Adelaide River
Khull, Edward: Shepparton
Kidman, Sir Sidney: Kidman Country*
Kidston, William: Kidston*
Kimberley, Earl of: Kimberley Range*
Kinchela, John: Kinchela*
King, Governor Philip Gidley: Gidley*; King Island*; Newcastle (King's Town*); Port Phillip (Port King*)
King, Captain Philip Parker: Alligator River; Apsley Strait; Barrallier; Bathurst Island; Bay of Rest; Bellender-Ker Range; Bowen Strait; Buccaneer Archipelago; Cambridge Gulf; Claremont Isles; Clarence Strait; Coburg Peninsula; Mount Cook; Dampier Archipelago; Mount Dryander; Exmouth Gulf; Goulburn Islands; Grant Island; Hinchinbrook Island; Joseph Bonapart Gulf; King Sound*; Liverpool River; Macquarie Strait; Melville Island; Nicholls Point; North-West Cape; Port Essington; Roebuck Bay; Werribee
King, Stephen: Billiatt Springs
Kinglake, Alexander William: Kinglake*
Kingscote, Henry: Kingscote*
Kingsley, Charles: Ravenshoe
Kingston, Sir George Strickland: Kingston*; Torrens River
Kitchener, Field-Marshall Horatio Herbert: Kitchener*
Knuckey, R. B.: Charlotte Waters; Mount Knuckey*
Korff, John: Coff's Harbour*
Kosciusko, Tadewsz; Mount Kosciusko*

La Trobe, Governor Charles Joseph: Camperdown; Gisborne; Latrobe*; Latrobe River*; Sale
Laing, Edward: Grose River
Lakeland, Claud: Claudie River*
Lakeland, William: Bowden; Claudie River
Lamb, E. W.: Lamb Range
Lamington, Baron: Lamington*; Lamington Plateau*; Lamington National Park*
La Perouse, The Chevalier: D'Entrecasteaux Point; La Perouse* ; Mount La Perouse*
Landsborough, William: Aramac; Barkly Tableland; Diamantina River; Georgina River; Gregory River; Landsborough*; Torrens Creek; Walker Creek
Lang: Lang Lang*
Lang, Rev John Dunmore: Goulburn; South Australia
Langhorne, Alfred: Langhorne Creek*
Langtree: Langtree*
Lannes, Marshall: See Duke of Montebello
Lansdowne, Marquess of: Blue Mountains (Lansdowne Hills*)
Lascelles, E.: Lascelles*
Lasseter, Lewis Harold Bell (Harry or Possum): Lasseter Country*
Lauderdale, Earl of: See James Maitland
Laurie, Rocky: Yamba
Lavender, George: Lavender Bay*
Lavender, Susannah (nee Blue): Lavender Bay
Laver, Dr: Laverton*
Lawley, Sir Arthur: Mount Lawley*
Lawson, Henry: Ben Bullen
Lawson, William: Mount Blaxland; Blue Mountains; Goulburn River; Lawson*; Turon River; Wemyss River
Le Hunte, Governor: Loxton
Leakes, Edward and Robert: Glencoe
Learmonth, Charles: Learmonth*
Learmonth, Thomas Livingstone: Mount Buninyong; Groongal; Learmonth*; Lake Learmonth*
Lee: Larras Lee*
Lee, Charles Alfred: Leeton*
Lee, William: Condobolin
Lefroy, Henry Maxwell: Mount Burges; Lake Lefroy*; Mount Lefroy*
Lefroy, Sir John: Lefroy*

Leichhardt, Friedrich Wilhelm Ludwig:
  Alligator River; Beames Brook; Lake
  Blanche; Boyd River; Burdekin River;
  Cape River; Clarke River; Comet;
  Comet River; Dawson Range; Elsey
  Creek; Exhibition Range; Gilbert
  Range; Gilbert River; Hodgson; Isaac
  River; Katherine River; Mount
  Leichhardt*; Leichhardt Range*;
  Leichhardt River*; Lynd Range;
  Lynd River; McArthur River;
  McKenzie River; Mitchell River;
  Murphy's Range; Mount Nicholson;
  Nicholson River; Peak Downs; Peak
  Range; Roper River; Roper's Lakes;
  Ruined Castle Valley; Sutton River;
  Wickham River
Leigh, Harry: Leigh Creek*
Leisler, Louis: Mount Leisler*
Leopold II, King: King Leopold Range*
Leopold, Prince of Saxe-Cobourg:
  Cobourg*
Leslie, Patrick: Leslie Peak*
Leschenault: Leschenault Estuary*
Lesson, R. P.: Wellington
Lethbridge: Lethbridge*
Liddell, Professor Henry: Liddell (*?)
Light, Colonel William: Barossa Valley;
  Finniss; Gawler; Goolwa; Light
  River*; Onkaparinga River; Port
  Adelaide; Rapid Bay; Torrens River
Lillico, Andrew: Lillico
Lindesay, Sir Patrick: Lindesday River*;
  Mount Lindesay*
Lipson, Captain: Lipson*
Lisgar, Baron: See Sir John Young
Lithgow, William: Lithgow*
Liverpool, Earl of: See also Charles
  Jenkinson; Liverpool*; Liverpool
  Plains*; Liverpool Range*
Loch, Baron (Henry Brougham): Loch*
Lockhart, C. G. N.: Lockhart*
Lockhart, Hugh: Lockhart River*
Lockyer, Major Edmund: Albany;
  Lockyer Valley*; Porongorup
  Range
Loftus, Andrew: Sodwalls
Logan, Captain Patrick: Ipswich; Logan
  River*
Long, David: Richmond
Long, W. J.: Longlea*
Longford, Lord: Longford*
Lonsdale: St Kilda

Lonsdale, Mrs Martha (nee Smythe):
  Mount Martha*
Lonsdale, Captain William: Mount
  Martha; Point Lonsdale*
Loutit, Captain: Lorne (Loutit Bay*)
Loxton, S. C.: Loxton*
Luther, Martin: Lobethal
Lyell, Sir Charles: Mount Lyell*
Lynd, Robert: Lynd Range*; Lynd
  River*
Lyndhurst, Baron: Lyndhurst*
Lyndoch, Baron: See Thomas Graham
Lyndoch, General: Lyndoch*
Lyons, Joseph Aloysuis: Lyons*

Macalister, Lachlan: Macalister*;
  Macalister River*
Macanash, J. D.: Temora
Macarthur, James: McArthur River*
Macarthur, John: Camden; The
  Cowpastures: Macarthur River;
  Parramatta
Macarthur, Sir William: McArthur River;
  Reynell
McCarty, Dennis; Port Davey
McConachy, Mrs Mary Kathleen; Mary
  Kathleen*
McConachy, Norman: Kathleen
McDonald, A. C.: Lake Macdonald*
MacDonald, G. J.: Armadale
McDonald, J.: Rosebery
MacDonald, Ramsay: Monte Bello
  Islands
MacDonnell, Governor Sir Richard
  Graves: Lake Blanche; Blanche Town;
  Blancheport; Blanchewater Plains;
  Blue Lake; Lake Eyre; Lake Gregory;
  Kadina; Kingston; MacDonnell Bay*;
  MacDonnell Creek*; MacDonnell
  Range*; Port MacDonnell*; Stuart
  Range
MacDonnell, Lady Blanche Skurray: Lake
  Lake Blanche*; Blanche Town*;
  Blancheport*; Blanchewater Plains*;
  Blue Lake (Lady Blanche Lake*)
McDougall, Archibald C.: Dunolly
Macguire: Shepparton
McIlwraith, Sir Thomas: Ayr; McIlwraith
  Range*
McIntosh, Archibald: Sale
McIntosh, William: Narracoorte
Macintyre, Peter: Macintyre River*
Mackay, Donald: Lake Mackay*

251

Mackay, Captain John: Mackay*;
    Pioneer River (Mackay River*)
McKee, John: Braefield
McKenzie: Kergunyah
Mackenzie, Sir Colin: Sir Colin
    Mackenzie Wild Life Sanctuary
McKenzie, Sir Evan: Kilcoy; McKenzie
    River*
Mackenzie, Sir Robert Ramsay: Aramac*
McKeown (or McEwan): Jenolan Caves
    (McKeown's Caves*)
MacKillop, G.: Strathdowie
McKinlay, John: Diamantina River;
    Hodgkinson River; Lake Massacre
Maclean: Maclean*
Macleay, Alexander: Macleay Islands*;
    Macleay Point*; Macleay Range*;
    Macleay River*
Macleay, Sir George: Rufus River*
McMillan, Angus: Avon River; Bowman
    River; Gippsland; Mount Haystack;
    Latrobe River; Macalister River
McPherson, Major Duncan: McPherson
    Range*
Macquarie, Governor Lachlan: Australia;
    Bathurst; Bellevue Hill; Blackheath;
    Blacktown; Blue Mountains; Bothwell;
    Brisbane; Caley Hill; Campbell Town;
    Castlereagh; Cox's Pass; Cox's River;
    Elizabeth Town; Emu Plains;
    Fish River; Lake George; Hartley;
    Illawarra; Jarvisfield; Karuah;
    Lachlan River*; Liverpool; Macquarie
    Fields*; Macquarie Harbour*; Lake
    Macquarie*; Macquarie Pass*;
    Macquarie River*; Macquarie Strait*;
    Mittagong; New Norfolk; Oatlands;
    Picton; Port Macquarie*; Richmond;
    Riverstone; Ross; Sorell; Springwood;
    Windsor
Macquarie, Lady Henrietta Elizabeth (nee
    Campbell; Governor Macquarie's
    second wife): Campbell Town*;
    Campbelltown*; New Norfolk
    (Elizabeth Town*); Point Piper
    (Point Eliza*)
Macquarie, Lady Jane (nee Jarvis,
    Governor Macquarie's first wife):
    Blacktown; Jarvisfield*
McQueen, T. P.: Botany Bay
Macrossan, John Murtagh: Macrossan*;
    Macrossan Passage*
Maatsuyker: Maatsuyker Islands*
Maiden: Moama (Maiden's Punt*)

Madigan, Dr Cecil Thomas: Simpson
    Desert
Maitland, James (Earl of Lauderdale):
    Maitland
Maitland, Julia: Maitland*
Malakoff: Malakoff*
Malmesbury, Earl of: Malmsbury*
Manifold, John and Peter: Camperdown
Mann, Charles: Mann Range*
Marhadour, Jean-Marie: D'Entrecasteaux
    Point
Marie, Duchess of Edinburgh: Alfred and
    Marie Range*
Marrabel, John: Marrabel*
Marsden, Rev Samuel: Marsden*
Marsh, Charles W.: Guyra
Martin: Martin's Creek*
Martin, A. E.: Bandiana; Chillingollah;
    Cape Cape: Innisfail; Jardine River;
    Learmonth; Lilliput; Mannahill; Port
    Elliot; Ravenshoe; St Helena
    Island; Sea Lake; Snuggery;
    Toowoomba; Wanalta; Windsor
Martin, William: Lake Illawarra
Masters, James: Saddleworth
Masters, John: Riverton
Mate: Tarcutta
Mathinna: Mathinna*
Matthews, Julia: Julia Creek*
Mayman, Edward: Boulder City
Maynard, John: Clare
Meehan, James: Lake Bathurst; Dee Why;
    Goulburn Plains; Patrick's Plain
Melbourne, Lord: Melbourne*; Seymour
Meliszoon, Jan: Staten River
Melrose Mrs: Melrose*
Melrose, George: Melrose
Melville, Viscount (Henry Dundas):
    Dundas Strait*; Melville Island*
Menge, Johann: Barossa Valley
Menzies, Lieut Charles: Newcastle;
    Northumberland County
Mercator: Australia
Meredith, George: Swansea; Triabunna
    (Spring Bay)
Merrilees, Duncan: Dinosaur Point
Merrit, George: Merriton*
Messell, Professor: Blue Mountains
Metcalfe, Baron: Metcalfe*
Meyer, J. H. C.: Surfers Paradise
    (Meyer's Ferry*)
Miles, George: Woodbridge
Miles, Isabella: Mount Isa*
Miles, William: Miles*

252

Miller, Lieut: Brisbane
Miller, J. J.: Bayswater
Minchan, Hans: St Mary's Peak
Mitchell: Table Top
Mitchell, Dr: Roslyn
Mitchell, Sir Thomas Livingstone: Mount Abundance; Aquarius Peak; Mount Arapiles; Avoca River; Ballendena; Balonne River; Barcoo River; Benalla; Lake Boga; Bourke; Bowral; Broke; Buckland Tableland; Mount Buller; Burnett River; Burning Mountain; Lake Cargellico; Castlemaine; Chetwynd; Collector; Cooper Creek; Currabubula; Discovery Bay; Mount Faraday; Fitzroy Downs; Mount Frankland (Mount Mitchell*); Glenelg River; Goulburn River; The Grampians; Grange Burn; Hamilton; Hopkins River; Kaputar; Loddon River; Mount Macedon; Mount Lindesay; Maranoa; Mitchell*; Mount Mitchell*; Mitchell River* (NSW, Q, V); Nivelle; Nyngan; Orange; Patrick's River; Playfair Peak; Pyranees; Mount Repose; St George; Salvator Peak; Swan Hill; Trafalgar; Mount Trafalgar; Victoria (Australia Felix); Mount Victoria; Victoria Range; Violet Town; Wangaratta; Warrego Range; Warrego River; Wimmera District; Yuranigh Creek; Mount Zero
Molesworth, Sir William: Molesworth*
Molle, Colonel George: Molle Islands*; Port Molle*
Montague, Admiral Robert: Montague Range*; Montague Sound*
Monteagle, Lord: Monteagle*
Montebello, Duke of (Marshall Lannes): Monte Bello Islands*
Monteith, T. E.: Monteith*
Montgomery, James: Pelican Lagoon
Monthazin: Triabunna (Port Monthazin*)
Moody, D. A.: Moody*
Moore, George Fletcher: Lake Moore*; Moore River*
Moore, Sir John: Corunna
Moore, Maggie: See Mrs T. C. Williamson
Moore, Thomas: Ashbourne; Avon River
Moorhouse, W.: Gladstone
Moresby, Captain John: Johnstone River; McIlwraith Range; Moresby Range*; Mourilyan Harbour

Morgan: Morgan Island*
Morgan, Edwin, Frederick, and Thomas: Mount Morgan*
Morgan, Molly (or Mary, nee Jones): Maitland (Molly Morgan's Plains*)
Morgan, Sir William: Morgan*
Morgan, William: Maitland
Morison, Mrs Grace Lindsay: Gracemere*
Morisset, Lieut-Colonel James Thomas: Morisset*
Mornington, Earl of (Marquis Wellesley): Mornington Island*; Wellesley Islands*
Morphett, Sir John: Clarendon; Morphett*
Morris, Edward E.: Billabong
Morris, James: Balladoran
Mort, Thomas Sutcliffe: Mortdale*
Morton, Earl of: Moreton Bay*; Cape Moreton*; Moreton Island*
Moses; Mount Horeb; Mount Pisgah
Mosman, Archibald: Mosman*; Mossman
Mosman, Hugh: Mossman*; Mossman River*
Moss, Jemmy: Moss Vale*
Mourilyan, Lieut: Mourilyan Harbour*
Mowatt, Francis: Narellan
Mueller, Ferdinand von: See von Mueller
Muirhead: Mount Muirhead*
Mulligan, James Venture: Barron River; Hodgkinson River; Mount Mulligan*; Mulligan River*; St George River; Silver Valley; Wild River
Mumbulla, Percy: Ulladulla
Munro: Munro*
Murat: North-West Cape (Cape Murat*)
Murchison, Sir Roderick: Murchison River* (T, WA)
Murchison, Captain: Murchison
Murchison, Roderick Impey: Murchison*
Murphy, John: Murphy's Range
Murray, A. H.: Murray Town*
Murray, Sir George: Murray River*; Perth
Murray, Lieut John: Flinders Passage; Point Nepean; Port Phillip
Musgrave, Governor Sir Anthony: Lucinda; Musgrave Ranges*; Port Musgrave*; Stansbury; Wilmington
Musgrave, Lady Lucinda: Lucinda*; Wilmington
Mynors, Captain William: Christmas Island

253

Napoleon Bonapart: Bonapart Archipelago*; Joseph Napoleon Gulf; Longwood; Monte Bello Islands; St Helena Island; South Australia (Terre Napoleon*); Spencer Gulf (Golfe Napoleon*)
Nash, George: Donnybrook
Nash, Heath: Nash Spring*
Nash, James: Gympie (Nashville*)
Neales, John Bentham: Neales River*
Neil, Rex: Neilrex*
Nelson, Lord Horatio: Blackwood; Pascoe
Nepean, Sir Evan: Nepean Bay*; Point Nepean*; Nepean River*
Newcastle, Duke of: Newcastle Waters*
Newman: Mount Newman*
Nicholls, William: Nicholls Point*
Nicholson, Sir Charles: Mount Nicholson*; Nicholson River*
Nicholson, William: Nicholson River*
Nind, P. N.: Innisfail (Nind's Camp*)
Nixon, Thomas: Bonnie Doon
Noltenius, J. L.: Noltenius Lagoon*
Norman: Normanville*
Norman, Captain: Norman River*
Normanby, Marquess of: Normanby*; Normanby River*; Russell
Normanby, Marchioness of (nee Russell): Russell*
Northumberland, first Duke of (Hugh Percy): Northumberland Isles*
Northumberland, second Duke of: Cape Northumberland*; Percy Islands*
Norton: Gayndah (Norton's Camp*)
Nuijts, Pieter: Fowler Bay; Great Australian Bight; Nullarbor Plain; Nuyts Archipelago*; Nuyts Point*; Nuytsland*; St Francis Island (St Francois); St Peter Island (St Pierre); Streaky Bay

Oakes, Francis: Lake Cargellico
O'Connell, Sir Maurice C.: Hillgrove; Riverstone
O'Connor, Roderic: Longford
Ogilvie, Edward: Tabulum
Ogilvie, W. H.: Mount Ogilvie*
O'Halloran, Major Thomas: Mount O'Halloran*
Okeden, Mrs Rose: Rosedale*
Olga, Queen: Lake Amadeus; Mount Olga*

Oliver, Mrs: Church Point
Oliver, Rev William: Church Point
Onslow, Sir Alexander Campbell: Onslow*
Orange, Prince of: Orange*
Ord, Sub-Inspector: Mount Ord*
Ord, Governor Sir Harry St George: Ord River*
Ormerod, George: Narracoorte, Ormerod*
Ortelius: Australia
Orton: Tichbourne
Ossian: Temora
O'Sullivan, D. and S.: Lake Cargellico
Otway, Captain Albany: Cape Otway*; Otway Ranges*
Outtrim, Alfred: Outtrim*
Ovens, Brigade-Major John: Canberra; Monaro; Murrumbidgee River; Ovens River*
Owen, Sir Richard Owen Peak*
Owen, Robert: Marburg
Owen, Mrs Sally: Marburg (Sally Owen's Plain*)
Oxford, Earl of: Charlotte Waters
Oxley, John Joseph William Molesworth: Allan Cunningham; Mount Arthur; Bowral; Boyne River; Brisbane; Lake Cargellico; Castlereagh; Clarence River; Forbes; Harrington; Hastings Point; Hastings River; Lachlan River; Liverpool Plains; Liverpool Range; Moreton Bay; Orange; Oxley*; Oxley County*; Oxley Creek*; Oxley's Tableland*; Pandora's Pass; Port Macquarie; Redcliffe; Tamworth; Tweed Heads; Tweed River; Lake Wallis; Warrumbungle Range; Wellington
Oxley, Mrs. John: Hastings Point; Hastings River

Pabst, John: Holbrook
Painter, J. M.: Mount Painter*
Pakenham, Alice (Duchess of Wellington): Pakenham*
Palmer, Sir Arthur Hunter: Palmer River*
Palmer, Colonel George: Palmer*
Palmer, John: Grose River; Wooloomooloo (Palmer's Cove*)
Palmerston, Christie: Palmerston*; Palmerston Range*

Palmerston, Viscount (Henry John Temple): Darwin (Palmerston*); Monte Bello Islands
Panmure, Lord: Panmure*
Panton, Joseph Anderson: Panton*
Parkes, Sir Henry: Parkes*; Werrington
Parry, Samuel: Aroona; Mount Desire; Lyndhurst; Sandy Bagots
Pascoe: Pascoe*
Paske, General: Paskeville*
Pasley, Captain T. S.: Cape Pasley*; Pasley Island*
Paterson, Banjo: Come-by-Chance; Coolabah
Paterson, Lieut-Colonel William: Beaconsfield; Ben Lomond; Blue Mountains; Grose River; Kissing Point; Launceston (Patersonia*); Nobby's Head; Paterson*; Paterson River*; Tamar River

Patton: Patton's Cape*
Patton, Alexander: Alectown*
Peake, Archibald H.: Peake*
Pearce: Point Pearce*
Pearce, Nathaniel: Pearcedale*
Pearce, Samuel: Boulder City
Pedder, Sir John Lowes: Lake Pedder*
Pedder, Lady Maria: Lake Maria*
Peel: Peel Island*
Peel, Sir Robert: Peel River*; Tamworth
Peel, Thomas: Mandurah (Peel Inlet*)
Pellew, Sir Edward: Sir Edward Pellew Group*
Pelsaert, Francois: Pelsart Islands*
Pendleton, Captain: American River
Penne: Penneshaw*
Percy, Hugh: See Duke of Northumberland
Percy, Lady Julia: Lady Julia Percy Island*
Peron: Kangaroo Island
Perry, Mrs J. (nee Alston): Alston*
Perry, Hon. J.: Alston
Petermann, Dr Augustus: Petermann Range*
Petrie, Andrew: Mary River; Noosa Heads; Petrie*; Mount Petrie*; Petrie's Bight*

Petrie, Thomas: Petrie*; Mount Petrie*; Petrie*s Bight*
Pfeiffer, G.: Seddon
Philip of Macedon: Mount Macedon*

Phillip, Governor Arthur: Albion; Bennelong Point; Blue Mountains; The Cowpastures; Cumberland; Grose River; Hawkesbury River; Mount Macedon; Manly; Nepean River; Parramatta; Phillip Island*; Pittwater; Port Phillip*; Prospect; Rose Bay; Sydney; Tench's Prospect Hill
Phillipson, N. E.: Lake Phillipson*
Pinkerton, William: Pichi Richi Pass
Picton, General Sir Thomas: Picton*
Piper, Captain John: Point Piper*; Cape Piper*; Piper Island*; Piper River*; Vaucluse
Pitt: Pittsworth*
Pitt, William: Bruny Island; Pittwater*
Playfair, Baron Lyon: Playfair Peak*
Pobasso: English Company's Islands; Malay Road; Pobasso Island*
Poeppel, Augustus: Poeppel Corner*
Pool, Gerrit Thomaszoon: Van Diemen Gulf (Van Diemen's Landt)
Poole, James: Mount Poole*
Pope, G. M.: Ryde
Portland, Duke of: Portland*; Portland Bay*
Potts, J. H.: Potts Point*
Power, Mrs David: Blue Lake (Lake Power*)
Preston, Governor Jenico William Joseph (Viscount Gormanston): Gormanston*
Preston, Lieut William: Collie; Preston River*
Price, John: Wombat
Price, Thomas: Mount Tom*
Price, Thomas: Price*
Primrose, Archibald Phillip: See Earl of Rosebery
Proserpina: Proserpine*
Pullan, Vice-Admiral William J. S.: Lake Albert
Pullen, Captain: Goolwa (Port Pullen*)
Purry, J. P.: Nuyts Archipelago

Quin, Patrick: Narrabri
Quiros: See de Quiros

Radstock, Admiral Lord: Cape Radstock*
Raglan, Lord: Raglan*
Raine, Thomas: Narromine; Raine Island*; Raines Passage*

255

Rand, Robert: Rand*; Urangeline
Randell, Captain W. R.: Cadell; Moama
Rankine, Dr John and William: Strathalbyn
Rawlinson: Rawlinson Range*
Rawnsley, H. C.: Rawnsley Bluff (*?)
Rayleigh: Blue Mountains
Redfern, William: Redfern*
Reid, Captain: King Island
Reid, Sir George Houston: Reid*
Reynell, John: Reynella*
Richman, John: Pichi Pichi Pass (Richman's Pass*)
Richmond, Duke of: Richmond*
Riley, Point: Point Riley*
Risdon: Risdon*; Risdon Cove*
Risely, T. R.: Southern Cross
Rivoli, Duke of: Rivoli Bay*
Robbins, Charles: Robbins Island*
Robe, Governor Lieut-Colonel Frederick Holt: Robe*
Robert, John: Doncaster
Roberts: Robertstown*
Robinson: Robinson River*
Robinson, Governor, Sir Hercules: Robinson Ranges; Zetland
Robinson, Roland: Lake Cargellico; Nimbin; Tabulum; Yooloom; Ulladulla; Woodenbong; Yamba
Robinson, William Frederick Cleaver: Robinson Range*
Robson, James: Tinaroo
Rockingham, Marquis of: Rockingham Bay*
Roe, James S.: Mount Augustus; Brewer Range; Mount Frankland (Mount Roe*); Mount Gordon; Mount Roe*; Roebourne*; Stirling Range
Rolland, Captain John: Mount Roland (Rolland's Repulse*); Rolland*
Roma, Count: Roma
Roper, John: Gilbert Range; Roper River*; Roper's Lakes*
Rosa, Salvator: Salvator Peak*
Rose: Parramatta (Rose Hill*); Rose Bay*
Rosebery, Earl of (Archibald Philip Primrose): Rosebery*; Sydney
Ross: Rosevale
Ross, John: Alice Springs
Rous, Captain the Hon. Harry John: Clarence River; Richmond River; Rous Channel*; Stradbroke Island; Tweed River

Rowan brothers: Glenrowan*
Rouse, Dr: Rochester* (Rowechester)
Rowe, Captain Edward: Christmas Island
Rudall, S. B.: Rudall*
Rudder, E. W.: Kempsey
Ruhen, Olaf: Breadalbane; Monaro
Ruse, James: Annandale
Russell, Henry: Mary River
Ryrie, William: Lilydale

St Clair family: Lake St Clair*
St George, Howard: Georgetown*; St George River
St Vincent, Earl: See Sir John Jervis
Sale, Sir Robert Henry: Sale*
Salisbury, Lord: Cranbourne; Salisbury*
Salvado, Dom Rosendo: New Norcia
Sandwich, Earl of: See George Montagu Dunk
Sawtell, O. C.: Sawtell*
Schank, Admiral John: Cape Schanck*; Mount Schanck*; Wight's Land
Schouten, William: Schouten Island*
Schwarz: Hermannsburg
Scoresby, Rev W. S.: Scoresby*
Scott, Alexander: Esk
Scott brothers: Warracknabeal
Scott, Edward B.: Scott Bay*; Scott Creek*; Mount Scott*
Scott, Gideon: Esk
Scott, James: Legerwood; Scottsdale*
Scott, Thomas: Deloraine
Scott, Sir Walter: Deloraine; Ivanhoe; Kenilworth; Lochinvar; Ravenswood; Rob Roy; Rokeby; Roslyn; Woodstock
Seabrook, John: Lake Seabrook*
Sedgwick, Adam: Sedgwick*; Mount Sedgwick*
Seppelt, Joseph: Seppeltsfield*
Serocold, George Pierce: Serocold Creek*; Mount Serocold*
Serra, Dom: New Norcia
Serventy, Vincent: Dinosaur Point
Service, James: Serviceton*
Seymour, Lord: Seymour*
Shakespeare, William: Oberon
Sharland, W. C.: Lake St Clair
Shaw, Miss: Penneshaw*
Shaw, George: Australia
Shaw, Norton: Baines River
Sheppard, Sherbourne: Shepparton*
Shepherd, W. T.: Waikerie

256

Sherlock: Sherlock*
Sherrard, Charles: See Charles Sherratt
Sherratt, Charles: Bendigo
Short, Bishop Augustus: Millicent
Shortland, Lieut John: Nobby's Head
Shortland, Lieut T. G.: Hunter River
Simpson, A. A.: Simpson Desert*
Simpson, John: Dead Heart
Simson brothers: Maryborough (Simson's Plains*)
Simson, Mrs Charlotte: Maryborough (Charlotte Plains*)
Sinclair, Colin: Black Stump
Singleton, Benjamin: Singleton*
Sinnett, Frederick: Mount Desire; Sinnett Peak*
Slattery, Jack: Hall's Creek
Slim, Sir William: Tallangatta
Smillie, Mrs (nee Nairne): Nairne*
Smillie, Matthew: Nairne
Smith: Smith River*
Smith, Rear-Admiral Isaac: Kurnell
Smith, James: Angaston; Greenock
Smith, James ('Philosopher Smith'): Smithton*
Smith, James Edward: Australia
Smith, Mrs Leslie: Euchareena
Smith, Samuel: Swan Pond
Smith, Sebastian: Sebastian*
Smith, Miss Seville: Seville*
Smith, Lieut Sydney: Johnstone River
Smith, William: Cairns
Smythe, Captain John James Barolow: Smythesdale*
Snow, Sebastian: Snowtown*
Solander, Dr Daniel Carl: Botany Bay; Kurnell; Point Solander*
Somerset, Duke of: Seymour; Somerset*
Somerset, Sir Henry: Chalkerup
Somerville family: Somerville*
Sorell, Lieut-Governor: Shannon River; Sorell*; Mount Wellington
Southey, Robert: Greta
Sparke, A. B.: Tempe
Spencer, Earl: Althorpe Islands; St Vincent Gulf; Spencer Gulf*; York Peninsula
Speult, Governor: Wessel Islands (Speult Islands*)
Standley, Miss: Standley Chasm*
Stanley, Lord: Stanley*
Stapleton: Casino
Stapylton, G. Chetwynd: Chetwynd*

Stawell, Sir William Foster: Stawell*
Steel, Matthew: Steel's Creek*
Steele, Captain: Rockley
Stephens, Alfred: Glenbrook
Stephens, Sir Philip: Port Stephens*
Stephens, Thomas Blacket: Southport
Stephensen, P. R.: Chiswick; The Rocks
Stevens, Mrs E. J.: Adavale*
Stewart, Major: Bendinck Murrell
Stewart, D.: Stewarts*
Stirling, Lieut-Governor Sir James: Beverley; Blackwood; Bunbury; Canning River; Darling Range; Fremantle; Garden Island; Northam; Perth; Preston River; Mount Stirling*; Stirling Range*; Swan River; Western Australia; York
Stirling, Keith: Keith*
Stirling, Sir Lancelot: Keith
Stockwell, Samuel: Stockwell*
Stokes: Stokes Bay*
Stokes, Francis: Mount Stokes*
Stokes, Captain John Lort: Albert River; Beagle Bay; Bynoe River; Cascade Bay; Fitzmaurice River; Fitzroy River; King Sound; Port Darwin; River Peak; Stokes Bay*; Sweers Island; Talc Head; Victoria River; Whirlpool River; Yampi Sound
Straborn: Cumnock
Stradbroke, Earl of and Viscount Dunwich: Stradbroke Island* (Dunwich Point*)
Strahan, Sir George Cumine: Strahan*
Strangways, H. B. Templar: Gawler River; Hindmarsh; Strangways River*; Strangways Springs*
Strehlow, T. G. H.: Hermannsburg
Strehlow, Rev C.: Hermannsburg
Stringer, Ned: Walhalla (Stringer's Creek*)
Strzelecki: See de Strzelecki
Stuart, John McDouall: Alice Springs; Anna's Reservoir; Attack Creek; Auld's Chain of Ponds; Barrow Creek; Mount Ben; Billiatt Springs; Central Mount Stuart*; Chambers Bay; Mount Chambers; Chambers Pillar; Charles Creek; Mount Coffin; Daly Waters; Mount Finke; Finke River; Freeling; Frew River; Mount Harris; Head Range; Katherine River; MacDonnell Range; Hergott Springs;

257

Mary River; Nash Springs; Newcastle Waters; Mount Polly; Polly Springs; Mount Poole; The Spring of Hope; Strangways River; Strangways Springs; Stuart Creek*; Mount Stuart*; Stuart Pass*; Point Stuart*; Stuart Pass*; Stuart Range*; Stuart Swamp*; Sturt Plains; Tennant Creek; Thring Creek; Waterhouse Range; William Creek; Woodforde Creek

Sturt, Charles: Lake Alexandrina; Mount Barker; Barrier Range; Lake Blanche; Blanche Town; Bogan River; Central Mount Stuart (Central Mount Sturt*); Cooper Creek; Darling River; Eyre Creek; Hindmarsh; Lindesay River; Mildura; Milparinka; Morgan; Murray River; Murrumbidgee River; Mount Poole; Rufus River; Strzelecki Creek; Sturt Creek*; Sturt Highway*; Mount Sturt*; Sturt Plains; Sturt River*; Sturt's Stony Desert*; Waikerie; Wantabadgery

Sullivan: Mount Harris (Mount Sullivan*)

Sullivan, John: Sullivan Cove*

Sullivan, Margaret Virginia: See Mrs T. C. Williamson

Sutherland, William: Sutherlands*

Sutton-Manners (Viscount Canterbury): Sutton Grange*

Swan, Captain: Buccaneer Archipelago

Sweers, Salamon: Sweers Island*

Swift, Dean Jonathan: Lilliput; Nuyts Archipelago; Shark Bay

Sydney, Viscount: See Viscount Townshend

Symonds, William: Williamstown*

Talbot, Lord: Talbot*

Tasman, Abel Janszoon: Adventure Bay; Blackman Bay; Maatsuyker Islands; Maria Island (T, NT); Pedra Blanca; Tasmania*; Tasman's Eylandt*; Vanderlin Island; Mount Zeehan

Tate, Dr Thomas: Tate River*

Taylor, William: Cape Catastrophe

Telford, Thomas: Telford*

Tench, Captain Watkin: Emu Plain; Hawkesbury River; Nepean River; Prospect; Tench's Prospect Hill*

Tennant, John: Tennant Creek*

Tennyson, Lord Alfred: Elaine; Locksley

Thallon, J. F.: Thallon*

Theodore, Edward Granville: Theodore*

Thevenard: Thevenard*

Thijssen, Francois: Nuyts Archipelago; St Francis Island; Streaky Bay

Thistle, John: Cape Catastrophe; Lucky Bay; Thistle Island*

Thompson, Hugh: Preservation Island

Thompson, William 'Abednego': Bendigo*

Thomson, E. Deas: Thomson River*

Thomson, Sir William (Lord Kelvin): William Thomson Range*

Thorne, James: Wantabadgery

Thornton: Cairns (Thornton*)

Thornton, Dr: Thornton*

Thring, F. W.: Thring Creek*

Throsby, Charles: Murrumbidgee River

Tietkins, Henry: Lake Macdonald

Tod, Robert: Tod River*

Todd, Lady Alice: Alice Springs*

Todd, Sir Charles Heavitree: Alice Springs; Heavitree Gap*; Orroroo, Todd River*

Tolmer, Alexander: Bordertown

Toomey, M: Southern Cross

Torrens, Colonel Robert: Lake Torrens*; Torrens River*

Torrens, Sir Robert Richard: Torrens Creek*

Torres: See de Torres

Towns, Robert: Etheridge; Townsville*

Townsend, Thomas S.: Mount Townsend*

Townshend, Charles: Cape Townshend

Townshend, Charles ('Spanish Charles'): Cape Townshend*

Townshend, Thomas (Viscount Sydney): Sydney*; Cape Townshend

Townson, John: Kogarah (Townson's Bay*)

Tozer, Sir Horace: Mount Tozer*

Trickett, Ted: Chiswick

Trigg: One Tree Hill

Trotman, H. S.: Canning Stock Route; Mount Newman

Troubridge: Troubridge Hill*

Tullamarine: Tullamarine*

Tully, William Alcock: Charleville; Tully*; Tully River*

Turriff: Turriff*

Tyers, Charles James: Tyers*

Tyrrell: Lake Tyrrell*

Tyrrell: Burragorang

Tyson, James: Mount Tyson*

258

Unger, L. A.: Tichbourne
Usborne: Port Usborne*

Van Diemen, Anthony: Maria Island; Tasmania (Van Diemen's Land*); Van Diemen's Gulf* (Van Diemen's Landt*)
Van Diemen, Maria: Maria Island*
Vancouver, Captain George: Albany; Breaksea Island; Cape Chatham; Eclipse Islands; King George Sound; Michaelmas Island; Oyster Harbour; Princess Royal Harbour; Recherche Archipelago; Termination Island; West Cape Howe
Vasse: Busselton River (Vasse River*); Vasse*
Veitch: Veitch*
Veness, George: Manilla
Venn, Harry Whittall: Cave River
Vere, Sir Charles Broke: Broke*
Verran, John: Verran*
Vesper, Alexander: Nimbin; Tabulum*
Victoria, Queen: Albert River; Lake Albert; Lake Alexandrina*; Barcoo River; Coburg Peninsula; Great Victoria Desert*; Great Victoria Spring*; Kingscote (Queenscliffe*); Leopold; Queenscliffe*; Queensland*; Queenstown*; Victoria*; Lake Victoria*; Mount Victoria*; Victoria Ranges*, Victoria River*, Victoria Spring*
Visscher, Pilot-Major: Blackman Bay
Vlamingh, Willem de: See de Vlamingh
Von Doussa, Louis: Von Doussa*
Von Mueller, Baron Ferdinand Jakob Heinrich: Diamantina River (Mueller's Creek*); Ernabella (Ferdinand Creek*); Mount Hotham; Mount Mueller*; Mueller Range*; Mount Olga; Mount Zeil
Von Rieben: Morgan (Von Rieben's*)
Von Steiglitz, Robert William: Ballan, Steiglitz*; Mount Steiglitz*

Wakefield, Edward Gibbon: Port Wakefield*; Wakefield River*
Walcott, Pemberton: Pemberton*
Wales, Prince of (son of George III): Prince of Wales Islands*
Wales, Prince of (later Edward VIII): Princes Highway*

Walker, Frederick: Walker Creek*
Walker, James: Coonamble; Kameruka; Wallerwang
Walker, W.: Kameruka
Wallace, John: Rutherglen; Wallace*
Wallace, R. D.: Antiene
Wallington, Captain: Thorpdale (Wallington*)
Wallis, Captain James: Maitland (Wallis Plains*); Lake Wallis*
Walpole, Robert: Monte Bello Islands
Walsh, Henry Deane: Walsh Island*
Walsh, W. H.: Walsh River*
Walter, H.: Stone Hut
Walton, Clem and John: Mary Kathleen
Warburton, Major Peter Egerton: Central Mount Wedge; Coward Springs; Finniss Springs; Lake Gairdner; Gawler Ranges; Warburton Range*; Warburton River*
Ward family: Ward's River*
Wardell, Dr: Wardell*
Warner, Frederick H.: Warner's Gully
Warner, J. H. B.: Quorn; Warnertown*
Warrall: Fisher's Ghost Creek
Wascoe, John Outrim: Blaxland (Wascoe's*)
Wasleys, Joseph: Wasleys*
Waterhouse: Waterhouse Range*
Watson, John Christian: Watson*
Wauba Debar: Bicheno (Wauba Debar*)
Wauch, Captain (or Wauche): Wauchope*
Way, Sir Samuel: Beachport; Morchard; Oodnadatta
Weatherhead, Captain Matthew: Oyster Bay
Wedge, John Hilder: Lake Pedder; Mount Wedge*; Yarra River
Weld, Sir Frederick Aloysius: Beaconsfield; Weld*
Wellesley, Arthur: See Duke of Wellington
Wellesley, Marquis: See Earl of Mornington
Wellington, Duchess of: See Alice Pakenham
Wellington, Duke of (Arthur Wellesley): Apsley; Mount Arapiles; Mount Arthur*; Pakenham; Strathfieldsaye; Wellington*; Mount Wellington*
Wellman, Mrs (nee Beckham): Beckom*
Wells, L. A.: Butler Dome; Lake Disappointment

Welsh, P. W.: Welshpool* (Port Welshpool*)
Wemyss, William: Wemyss River*
Wentworth, William Charles: Mount Blaxland; Lawson; Vaucluse; Wentworth*; Wentworth Falls*; Wentworthville*
Westall, William: Mount Brown; Mount Westall*; Westall Point*
Weston: Westonia*
Weston, James: Coonabarabran
Whalan, Charles and James: Jenolan Caves
Whidbey: Whidbey Islands*; Point Whidbey*
Whitaker, G. P. D. and J. T.: Dowlingville
White: Jenolan Caves
White: Timor
White, Isaac: Echuca
White, James: Young
Whitelaw, Alexander: Alectown*
Whitton: Whitton*
Wickham, Captain John Clements: Beagle Bay; Bynoe Harbour; Bynoe River; Darwin; Fitzroy River; Stokes Bay; Victoria River; Mount Wickham*; Wickham River*
Wight, Captain: Wight's Land*
Wilberforce, William: Wilberforce*; Cape Wilberforce*
Wild: Kergunyah
Wild, Joseph: Lake George; Monaro
Willaumez, J. B. P.: Mount Wellington
William IV, King: Adelaide; Clarence River*; Clarence Strait*; Coburg Peninsula*; Melbourne (Williamstown*); South Australia; Mount William*; Williamstown*
Williams, Eustan: Woodenbong
Williamson, Mrs T. C. (nee Margaret Virginia Sullivan): Struck Oil
Wills, Horatio Spencer: Ararat
Wills, William John: Barkly Tableland; Cloncurry; Diamantina River; Georgina River; Hodgkinson River; Landsborough; Lake Massacre; Wedderburn; Wills Creek*
Wilmot, J. G.: Baddaginnie; Bessiebelle; Dimboola; Dookie; Miepoll; Winton

Wilson, Braidwood: Braidwood (*?)
Wilson, J. S.: Baines River
Wilson, James: Wombat
Wilson, Surgeon T. B.: Mount Barker; Denmark; Mount Frankland; Mount Mitchell; Mount Roe; Wilson Inlet*
Wilson, Thomas: Wilson Promontory*
Wilson, William: Lismore
Winchelsea, Earl of (George William): Finch Hatton*; Winchelsea*
Windeyer: Windeyer*
Wiseman, W. H.: Rockhampton
Wiseman, Solomon: Wiseman's Ferry*
Wishart, Captain J.: Port Fairy
Withell, John and Mrs: Welcome Hill
Wogul, Tom: Tom Ugly's Point (*?)
Wollstonecraft, Edward: Berry; Crows Nest
Wood: Woodstock*
Wood, Richard: Hopping Dick Creek* (Limpinwood*)
Woodforde, Dr: Woodforde Creek*
Woodforde, John: Woodforde Creek*
Woods, Henry (Mabelle?): Woods Point*
Wright, Captain W.: Castlemaine
Wurm, Mrs Julia: Port Julia*
Wynn-Carrington, Charles Robert (Earl Carrington): Carrington*
Wynyard, Major-General Edward Buckley: Wynyard*

Yea, Colonel Lacy: Yea*
York: Adminaby
York, Lieut: Albany Island
York and Albany, Duke of (Edward Augustus): Cape York*
Yorke, Rt Hon Charles Philip: Yorke Peninsula*; Yorketown*
Young, Lady Augusta: Port Augusta*
Young, Governor Sir Henry Fox: Port Augusta; Port Elliot; Port Wakefield
Young, Sir John (Baron Lisgar): Young*
Yuille, William Cross: Lake Mendouree
Yuranigh (Jacky): Yuranigh Creek*

Zeil, Ernst: Mount Zeil (*?)
Zetland, Earl of: Zetland*

SUPERSEDED PLACE NAMES

The present day name follows the earlier name. An asterisk indicates that the origin of the older name is given in the main entry.

Abbot Creek: Mareeba
Ada's Veil: Adavale
Airds: Campbelltown*
Albany Otway, Cape: Cape Otway*
Aldbury: Albury
Alec's Flat: Alectown
Alexander, Mount: Castlemaine
Alexandra Land: Northern Territory*
Alumba: Yungaburra
Anthony Van Diemen's Landt: Tasmania*
Ambleside: Hahndorf
Anderson's Plains: Galah*
Angas: Kingscote*
Angas Park: Nuriootpa*
Anthon's Landing: Wyndham*
Arbuthnot Range: Warrumbungle Range
Arndell River: Werribee*
Arrowsmith River: Coomera River
Auralia: Kalgoorlie
Australia Felix: Victoria*
Avoca River: Avon River*
Avon River: Avoca River*

Back Creek: Talbot
Baie du Nord: Blackman Bay*
Banks Island: Cockatoo Island
Banks, Mount: Mount King George
Bar Swamp: Ettalong
Barron Falls: Biboohra
Batavia River: Wenlock River*
Batmania: Melbourne*
Bayley's Find: Coolgardie*
Bearbrass: Melbourne*
Beauaraba: Pittsworth
Beautiful Valley: Wilmington
Belfast: Port Fairy
Bell's Line: Bell
Belvoir: Wodonga
Bennelong: Binalong*
Bernisdale: Bairnsdale
Big River: Shoal Bay
Big Tom's Lagoon: Lake Illawarra*
Biggah: Bega*
Bilacote Hills: Barrington Heights*
Billy Blue's Point: Blue's Point*
Black Swamp: Lake Wendouree
Black Swan River: Swan River*

Blackman's Swamp: Orange*
Blanche, Lake: Blue Lake*
Blaney: Blayney
Blue Mountains: Lawson
Bluegum Flat: Ourimbah
Bluff, The: Rosetta Head
Blumbergville: Boonah*
Boat Alley: Bodalla
Bonaparte, Golfe: Spencer Gulf*
Bougainville Bay: Nepean Bay*
Bowden's Point: Birriegurra
Bowen Falls: Bowenfels
Bracefield, Cape: Noosa Heads*
Brandy Creek: Warragul; Beaconsfield
Brisbane Downs: Monaro Plains*
Brookdale: Glenrbook
Brown's Bay: Kingston*
Brown's Inn: Inglewood*
Buache, Isle: Garden Island*
Bulldog Creek: Illabrook
Bullock Creek: Tullamore
Bullock Flat: Oberon
Bunda Plain: Nullarbor
Buntingdale: Birriegurra
Bushman's: Parkes*
Bussell Town: Busselton*
Buss's: Woodford
By Goo: Kamarah
Byerock: Byrock*

Cabbage Tree Hill: Beaconsfield
Caledonia Australis: Gippsland*
Cambaceres: Yorke Peninsula*
Camp, The: West Maitland
Candos: Kandos*
Cara: Killgrove
Careening Point: Cremorne Point
Caribean: Carrington*
Carmarthen Hills: Blue Mountains*
Carpentier River: Wenlock River*
Castleton: Bendigo; Townsville*
Cattle Chosen: Busselton*
Central Mount Sturt: Central Mount Stuart*
Chambers Creek: Stuart Creek*
Charlotte's Plains: Maryborough*
Charters Tors: Charters Towers*
Clyde: Karuah

261

Coal Harbour: Newcastle*
Coal Island: Nobby's Head
Coal River Settlement: Richmond*
Coaldale: Coledale*
Cob o' Corn: Afterlea
Cockfighter's Creek: Wollombi Creek
Collins, Mount: Mount Wellington*
Columbine: Malmsbury
Consolation Plain: Walpeup
Cooerwull: Lithgow
Coraiya: Geelong
Cornelia Creek: Strathallan
Cotton: Wilkawatt
Cox's Creek: Bridgewater
Crown Hill: Mount Desire
Crushers (Crushings): Katoomba

Dalrymple River: Tamar River*
Darling River: Logan River*
Daydream Island: Molle Islands*
De Zuyd Gap: Cape Pillar
Deception, Mount: Beltana*
Decre's, L'Isle: Kangaroo Island*
D'Entrecasteaux Islands: Recherche Archipelago*
Devil's Inkbottle: Blue Lake
Diamantina Crossing: Birdsville
Dickson: Cairns*
Dirty Swamp: Locksley
Don River: Hellyer River
Double Island: Twin Island
Doughboy Hollow: Ardglen
Doutigalla: Melbourne
Dover Slopes: Mentone
Duck Creek Mountain: Alston
Duck Ponds: Lara
Duck River: Smithton
Dundas Goldfield: Norseman

Eastern Farms: Ryde
Edinglassie: Brisbane
Edwards Crossing: Murray Bridge*
Eliza, Point: Point Piper*
Elizabeth Town: New Norfolk*
Ellesmere: Scottsdale*
Emu Bay: Burnie
Emu Flats: Robertstown
Emu Island: Emu Plains
Emu River: Cam River*
Engelsburg: Kalbar*
Evan: Penrith
Exe River: Werribee

Farris Lagoon: Gracemere
Fat Doe River: Bothwell
Ferdinand Creek: Ernabella*
Ferguson River: Staten River*
Field of Mars: Ryde*
Field's River: Onkaparinga River*
Fiery Creek: Beaufort*
Fish River Caves: Jenolan Caves
Five Islands: Illawarra*
Flinders Land: South Australia*
Flindersland: Queensland*
Flooding Creek: Sale*
Fly Flat: Coolgardie
Forest Hill: Castlemaine
Fort Bourke: Bourke*
Frederick Henricz Bay: Blackman Bay*
Frederickstown: Albany*
Freshwater River: Yarra River*
Frenchman's Bay: La Perouse
Frome's Eagle Nest Hill: Mount Chambers*
Furneaux Land: Wilson Promontory*

Gambier Town: Mount Gambier*
Garden Cove: Wooloomooloo
Geraldton: Innisfail*
German Pass: Angaston
Germanton: Holbrook*
Gibraltar: Bowral
Gill Lake: Lake Dutton
Gittins Lagoon: Ettalong
Gladys River: Johnstone River
Glenelg: Melbourne*
Glengarrie River: Latrobe River
Good Dog: Cambewarra
Goode Island: Good Island*
Goode's Inn: Nanago
Government Gums: Farina*
Grange, The: Hamilton*
Granite Creek: Mareeba
Grant Island: Phillip Island*
Great Bend (or Elbow): Morgan*
Green Hills: Windsor; Maitland
Green Park: Juriootpa
Gum Tree Flat: Minlaton

Hacking's Island: Nobby's Head
Hannans: Kalgoorlie*
Heart, The: Sale*
Hell's Gates: Ulooloo
Herbert River: Georgina River*
Hergott Springs: Maree*
Hills, The: New Norfolk

Hog Bay: Penneshaw*
Hollandia, De Caep: Cape Arnhem*
Hooker, Mount: Mount Lindesay
Hopeful, Mount: Mount Babbage*
Hopetown: Innamincka
Hopwood's Ferry: Echuca*
Hospital Creek: Tostaree
Hovell River: Goulburn River*
Hovell's Creek: Lara
Howe, Cape: West Cape Howe*
Hulk Bay: Lavender Bay*
Hummock Hill (Hummocky): Wyalla*
Humpbybong (Umpic Bong): Redcliffe*

Iles des Anglais: Phillip Island*
Isis Scrub: Childers

Jones, Lake: Lake Echo
Jerusalem: Colebrook*
Jewnee: Junee
Jillong: Geelong*
Jim Crow Diggings: Daylesford*
Johnston's Bush: Annandale*
Josephine, Golfe: St Vincent Gulf*
Jump Up: Bungulla

Kiama (Kiamma): Crookwell
Kingcraig: Narracoorte*
King River: Franklin River*
King's Town: Newcastle
Kissing Point: Ryde*
Korong, Mount: Wedderburn

Lady Blanche Lake: Blue Lake*
Laidley Ponds: Merindee
Lambing Flat: Young*
Lansdowne Hills: Blue Mountains
Latour: Longford
Leven, The: Ulverstone
Liffey River: Callipe River
Lightwood Bottom: Geeveston
Limestone: Ipswich*
Limestone Plains: Canberra*
Locke's Platform: Locksley
Loftus: Junee
Lower Herbert: Ingham
Loxton's Hut: Loxton*
Lucieton: Tantanoola

McDougall's Plains: Yass
Macguire's Punt: Shepparton*
McIvor Diggings: Heathcote
Mackay River: Pioneer River*

McKeown's Caves: Jenolan Caves
McLeod, Mount: Haystack
Maiden's Punt: Moama
Main Beach: Surfers Paradise*
Main Camp: West Wyalong
Maria Creek: Kingston*
Matilda Bay: Oyster Bay
May Day Hills: Beechworth
Meyer's Ferry: Surfers Paradise*
Mobilong: Murray Bridge
Moent: Crab Island
Mole, The: Torrington
Molly Morgan's Plains: West Maitland*
Montague du Plateau: Mount Wellington*
Monto's Marsh: Ellendale
Moorabool: Millbrook*
Mosquito Plains: Narracoorte
Mount Rose Township: Eidsvol
Muddy Waterholes: Leithbridge
Mueller's Creek: Diamantina River*
Mulgrave: Gordonvale
Mulligan, Lake: Lake Callabonna*
Murat Bay: Ceduna*
Murat, Cape: North-West Cape*
Muscle Brook: Muswellbrook
Myall Creek: Mission River; Dalby

Narracan: Thorpdale
Nashville: Gympie*
Nelson: Gordonvale
Nerang Heads: Southport
New Ballarat: Chiltern
New Bendigo: St Arnaud
New Chicago: Echuca*
New Holland: Australia*
New South Caledonia: Gippsland*
New Year's Creek: Bogan Gate*
Nind's Camp: Innisfail*
Nine Mile Springs: Lefroy
Ninety Mile Desert: Coonalpyn Downs
Nobby's Island: Nobby's Head
Norfolk Plains: Longford*
North East Arm: Brisbane Water
North-West Bend: Morgan*
Norton's Camp: Gayndah*
Nullagine: Marble Bar

Ohllsen-Bagge, Mount: Mount John*
Old Diggings: Coolgardie
One Eye: Milbong*
One Tree Hill: Mount Coot-tha
Ovens Diggings: Beechworth
Oyster Bay: Stansbury

Palmer's Cove: Wooloomooloo*
Palmerston: Darwin*; Escape Cliffs*
Parkes Platform: Werrington*
Patersonia: Launceston*
Peel River: Werribee
Pekina: Orroroo
Pelican Flat: Swansea
Pentridge: Coburg
Petersburg: Petersborough*
Phillips River: Hann River*
Picton: Jarvisfield
Picton Lakes: Thirlmere
Plateau, Le: Mount Wellington*
Pleasant Creek: Stawell
Port Bowen: Port Clinton*
Port Caroline: Lacepede Bay*; Kingston
Port Henry: Port Wakefield*
Port King: Port Phillip*
Port Monthazin: Triabunna
Port Pullen: Goolwa*
Power, Lake: Blue Lake*
Prince Albert Land: Northern Territory*
Providential Cove: Wattamolla*

Quart Pot: Quart Pot Range*
Queen's Cross: King's Cross
Queenscliffe: Kingscote*

Ramsay: Wynyard*
Red Banks: Caltowie
Red Gate: Alexandra
Redbank: Hillston
Regent's Lake: Lake Cargellico
Richman's Pass: Pichi Richi Pass*
Riviere du Nord: Derwent River*
Robertson's Point: Cremorne Point
Rocky Mouth: Maclean
Rolland's Repulse: Mount Roland*
Rose: Eidsvol
Rosewood Scrub: Marburg
Rose Hill: Parramatta*
Round Flat: Waikerie*
Rowechester: Rochester*

Saint a'Becket's Pool: Sandy Bagots*
Sally Owen's Plains: Marburg*
Sandhills, The: Deniliquin
Sandhurst: Bendigo*
Sandspit, The: Ulmarra
Sawpit Gully: Elphinstone
Sarah Island: Settlement Island*
Second Western River: Mersey River*
Seymour: Adaminaby

Shoal Bay: Clarence River
Shortland Bluff: Queenscliff
Simson's Plains: Maryborough*
Skiddaw, Mount: Mount Wellington*
Skyetown: Narracoorte
Snapper Island: Phillip Island*
South Coast Town: City of Gold Coast
South Creek: St Mary's
Speult Islands: Wessel Islands*
Speult Bay: Triabunna
Springs, The: Drayton; Dripstone
Stockyard Creek: Foster
Stonequarry: Picton
Strathallen: Goulburn
Stringer's Creek: Walhalla*
Stuart: Alice Springs*
Swamp, The: Toowoomba*
Swilly: Pedra Blanca*

Table Cape: Wynyard
Table Hill: Mount Wellington*
Table, Mount: Mount Wellington*
Tarrangower: Maldon*
Ten Mile Creek: Holbrook
Terre Napoleon: South Australia*
Thornton: Cairns*
t'Hooge Eijlandt: Prince of Wales Island*
t'Landt van der Leeuwin: Cape Leeuwin*
Tom Thumb's Lagoon: Illawarra*
Toowong: Antiene
Tourville Bay: Portland Bay*
Townson's Bay: Kogarah*
Turnoff, The: Murray Bridge*
Tweed River: Werribee
Tweedvale: Lobethal*

U.T.: Ultimo*

Van Diemen's Land: Tasmania*
Vanderlyn Island: Freycinet Peninsula
Vasse River: Busselton River*
Vasse, The: Busselton*
Victor, Cape: Rosetta Head*
Victoria River: Barcoo River*
Village of Cootamundry: Cootamundra
Vinegar Hill: Bellevue Hill*
Vliege Bay: Albatross Bay
Von Rieben's: Morgan*

Wallaby Ground: Broadwater
Wallington: Thorpdale
Wallis Plains: Maitland*
Wascoes: Blaxland*
Wascoe' Siding: Glenbrook

Watertank: Glenbrook
Wauba Debar: Bicheno*
Weatherboard, The: Wentworth Falls
Wet Diggings: Rushworth*
Whale Head: Queenscliff
Whisky Creek: Drouin West*
Whitecliffs: Merbein
Wild Cattle Run, The: Korumburra
William, Mount: Mount Hann*
William Pitt's Island: Bruny Island*

Williamsland: South Australia*
Wirreander Siding: Gordon
Wittenoom: Wittenoom Gorge
Woodlands: Landsborough
Wooroonooran Range: Bellender-Ker Range

Yarrayne River: Loddon River
Yarrowie: Appila
Yering: Lilydale*

INDEX OF ABORIGINAL NAMES

The present day name follows the Aboriginal name. An asterisk indicates that the meaning of the Aboriginal name is given in the main entry.

Alcaroona: Aroona
Appila-Yarrowie: Appila
Artula: Mount Conner*
Awaba: Lake Macquarie*

Barunguba: Montagu Island
Battunga: Meadows*
Bayunga: Goulburn River
Belalie: Jamestown
Benhennie: Camden*
Beri-beri: Berri
Berrern: Yarra River; Melbourne
Bilparoo: Mount Scott
Bindoo: Clyde River
Binoomea (or Benomera): Jenolan Caves*
Birrabirra: Burnett River
Birra-rang (or Berrern): Yarra River; Melbourne
Bitup: Cressy
Bongamila (or Bongam bilor): Horsham*
Bonyi: Blackall Range*
Boogarah Boogarah: Mount Barney*
Boolool Nahl: Blue Nob*
Booroogarra-bowyra-neyand: Clarence River*
Boorook: Mortlake
Boortheboorthanna: Boorthanna*
Booyooarto: Mount Herbert
Budiu: Lipson Cove
Bukartilla: Hahndorf*
Bunda Bund: Nullarbor Plain
Bungambrewatha: Albury
Bungung: Currency Creek
Burbong: Goulburn
Burra-gy (or Burroggy): Bradley's Head
Burrangong: Young
Butcha: Mount Castle*
Butingitch: Ararat

Cadhi-baerri: Lake Massacre
Cappoong: Cunningham's Gap
Carawatha: Finley*
Carrappee: Dark Peak
Chiniala: Eucla
Coerabko: Morgan*
Cognon: Hunter River
Collum-been: Creswick
Connadoyen: Wallace

Cooeyanna: Streaky Bay
Cooloogoolooheit: West Maitland
Coonanbarra: Hunter River
Coonanglebah: Dunk Island
Cununurra: Ord River
Coraiya: Geelong
Corinna: Pieman River
Cowa: The Grampians
Cussrunghi: Jerseyville*

Daarangurt: Balmoral
Deerabubbin: Hawkesbury River
Dhinmar: Lady Julia Percy Island
Doma Mungi: Chiltern
Dulgambone: Deepwater*
Dundeppa: Garden Island*

Erengbalam: Mount Gambier*
Etikaura (or Idracowie): Chambers Pillar
Euro-Yroke: St Kilda*

Gabi-Kylie: Esperance*
Geboor: Mount Macedon
Geelong: Port Phillip
Gerup Gerup: Raglan
Gilladin: Mount Alford
Ginnagulla (or Goud-joul-gang): Rose Bay*
Gnoorganpin: Moreton Island
Goodangarkagi: Cape York
Goodna: Mary River
Goodwarra: Murray River
Goo-en: Southport
Goonamarra: Port Hacking
Goon-gerah: Mount Ellery*
Gooragoody: Warwick
Gooro: Lake Hindmarsh
Gooung: Smoky Cape*
Gorambeep Barak: Mount Ararat
Goran-Bullagong: Mosman
Goud-joul-gang (or Ginagulla): Rose Bay*
Gunnamatta: Cronulla

267

Idracowra (or Etikaura): Chambers Pillar
Illulong: East Maitland; Morpeth
Ingalta: Murray River

Jabbribillum: Burleigh Heads
Jalgumbun: Mount Lindesay
Janukin: Glenorchy
Jeerkooroora: Peel Island
Jellurgul: Burleigh Heads
Jillong: Geelong*

Kaleeya (or Kaleteeya): Gawler
Kallinyalla: Port Lincoln
Karaula: Barwon River; Macintyre River
Karlk: Camperdown
Karran-wirra-parri (or Karra-wirra-parri): Torrens River
Karrawatta: Pewsey Vale
Karta: Kangaroo Island*
Katatjuta: Mount Olga
Katitanda: Lake Eyre
Kayinga: Lake Alexandrina
Keirbarban: Broadwater*
Kindaitchin: Glen Innes*
Kobram: Stawell
Koggerah: Rushcutters Bay
Kolaan Kandahl: Coal and Candle Creek*
Konela: Strathallan
Koo-e-lung: Vaucluse Point*
Koora Korracup: Sunbury
Kooringa: Burra
Korijekup: Harvey
Korra-oondungga: Hindmarsh
Kumarangk: Hindmarsh
Kurdnatta: Port Augusta*
Kyneetchya: Clare

Larapinta (or Lirambenda): Finke River*
Lecawulena: Lake St Clair
Lunawanna-alonna: Bruny Island

Maayera: Millicent*
Madi-waltu: Maitland*
Marrang: Mount Buller
Martiragnir: Swan Hill
Martula: Smithton and Stanley district
Martungdun: Mossiface*
Melnunni: Hillston*
Minlacowie: Minlaton
Minni Minni: Alum Mountains
Monoboola: Mary River
Moonbil: Aberdeen*

Mooraboocoola: Mary River
Moorekyle: Helpburn
Moormurn: Lindenowe
Moorundie: Murray River
Moring (or Morung): Vaucluse
Morone (or Murroon): Birregurra
Mullachan: Callabonna
Mulleraterong: Hamilton
Mulubinba: Newcastle
Mungungboora (or Mungungcoora): Fine Flower
Mungkooli: Lake Alexandrina
Muniong (or Munyong): Mount Kosciusko
Murroon (or Morone): Birregurra

Nadia: Denial Bay
Nandeebie: Cleveland Point
Naringook: Smythesdale
Narracan: Thorpdale
Narram Narram: The Grampians
Narupai: Horn Islands
Nelia (or Nullya): Peterborough
Nganki-Parri: Onkaparinga River
Ngaranga: Port MacDonnell
Niambooyoo: Mount Cordeaux
Noogoon (or Nugoon): St Helena Island
Nookamka: Lake Bonney
Nugoon (or Noogoon): St Helena Island
Nullya (or Nelia): Peterborough
Nulta Nulta: Bourke
Nundewar: Mount Lindesay
Nyarritch: Eddington

Oolra: Ayers Rock

Paranaple: Mersey River
Parnka: Lake Alexandrina
Parriang-ka-perre: Murray River
Parrieagana: Inglewood*
Pater-Purrer: Escape Cliffs
Patpungga: Rapid Bay
Peerick: Pyrenees
Pokar: Dartmoor*
Ponkepurringa: Onkaparinga River
Poyanannupyal: Oyster Bay
Putpa (or Putrayerta): Lyndoch
Pwooyam: Lismore South*
Pyipgil: Port Fairy

Quiberee: Lavender Bay

Taengarrah Warrawarildi: Barraba
Talcumbin: Mount Lindesay
Tallygaroopna: Shepparton*
Talwurrapin: Redland Bay*
Tandarnya (or Tandarynga): Adelaide
Tandarrah (or Undera): St Germain's
Tangalooma: Moreton Island
Tarparrie: Port Pirie*
Tarrapalet: River Lett
Teemtoommelememennye: Derwent River
Thelim: Tailem Bend*
Tiggana Maraboona: Schouten Island
Tipa: Beveridge
Tjauritji: Alice Springs
Togranong: Cathcart
Tongwillum: Murray River
Tooma-thoo-gamie: Diamantina River
Toorbunna: Ben Lomond
Toowong: Antiene
Tuckerimbah (or Tuckerimbah): Lismore*
Tulmur: Ipswich

Uluru: Ayers Rock
Undera (or Tandarrah): St Germain's
Urganyaletta: Mount Wellington

Waaor (or Waawor): Blue Lake
Waiben: Thursday Island
Walar Walar: Gellibrand
Wambool: Macquarie River
Wammerawa: Macquarie River
Warkowodli-wodli: Klemzig
Waroojra: Landsborough
Warra: Sandgate
Warrane: Sydney
Warrieubah: Cockatoo Island
Watchropat: Sandford*
Watneel: Rochester
Weiawenena: Mount Zeehan
Werriwa: Lake George
Wertie Mertie: Bourke*
Wetiarto: Mount Brown

Whibay-Garba: Nobby's Head
Wilichum: Rivoli Bay
Willara: Point Piper
Williorara: Menindee
Willogoleeche: Hallett
Willowie: Mount Remarkable
Willyama: Broken Hill*
Wingen: Burning Mountain
Wirmal-Ngrang: Rivoli Bay; Beachport
Wirra-Birra: Neutral Bay
Wirramatya: Laura*
Wirrembirchip: Birchip
Wirrum-Wirrum: Wellington
Wobbumarjoo: Benleigh*
Woma-mu-kurta (or Womma-mu-kurta): Mount Barker
Wongayerlo: Gulf St Vincent*
Wong-Yarra: Mount Remarkable
Woodnawolpena: Elder Range
Woolpal: Emu Park
Woran: Skipton
Wran Wran: Sebastapol
Wulworra-jeung: Cremorne Point
Wurtamurtah: Bourke*
Wy Yung: Bairnsdale

Yaboon: Mary River
Yaktanga: Mount Barker
Yalata: Fowlers Bay*
Yamamillah: Argylla
Yarkiamba: Lindeman Island*
Yarralinka: Light River
Yarram Yarram: Beaufort
Yarranabbe: Potts Point
Yarrandabby: Macleay Point
Yarrowie: Appila
Yawmbul: Vectis East
Yermalner: Melville Island*
Yerroulbine: Long Nose Point*
Yerta Boldinga: Port Adelaide
Yertala: Torrens River
Yoolooarra: Murray River
Yure Idla: Mount Lofty*

BIBLIOGRAPHY

Aboriginal Place Names of Australia. A. W. Reed. A. H. & A. W. Reed, 1967
Australian Dictionary of Biography 1788 - 1850, 2 volumes. Melbourne University Press, 1967
Australian Encyclopaedia, 10 volumes. Grolier Society, 1963.
Captain Cook in Australia. Ed. A. W. Reed. A. H. & A. W. Reed, 1969
Discovery of Australia, The. Andrew Sharp. Clarendon Press, 1963
Encyclopaedia of Australia. T. A. and M. Learmonth. Warne, 1966
Fatal Impact, The. Alan Moorehead. Hamish Hamilton, 1966
Guide to Australia. Osmar White. Heinemann, 1968
Heroic Journey of John McDouall Stuart, The. Ian Mudie. Angus and Robertson, 1968
Names of Railway Stations in New South Wales and their Meaning. C. A. Irish, 1927
Nomenclature of South Australia. R. Cockburn, 1908
One Thousand and More Place Names in New South Wales. A. E. Martin. NSW Bookstall Company, 1943
Place Names in Queensland, New Zealand, and the Pacific. A. E. Martin. NSW Bookstall Company, 1944
Place Names in Victoria and Tasmania. A. E. Martin. NSW Bookstall Company, 1944
Place Names of New South Wales. A. W. Reed. A. H. & A. W. Reed, 1969
Story of the Flinders Ranges, The. Hans Mincham. Rigby, 1964
Treasury of Australian Folk Tales and Traditions. Bill Beatty. Ure Smith, 1960
Twelve Hundred and More Place Names in South Australia, Western Australia, and the Northern Territory. A. E. Martin. NSW Bookstall Company, 1943.
Victoria Place Names. J. G. Saxton, 1907.
Voyage of the Investigator 1801 - 1803. K. A. Austin. Rigby, 1964
Various periodicals, with particular reference to *Walkabout,* and early issues of *Science of Man.*

OTHER REED BOOKS

Aboriginal Place Names compiled by A. W. Reed. A comprehensive collection of names and their derivations from all parts of Australia. The book also includes a section giving English words and their Aboriginal translations, as well as an appendix of present day names with earlier Aboriginal names. 184 mm x 114 mm, 144 pages, limp.

Aboriginal Words of Australia by A. W. Reed. Words used by Aboriginal tribes with their meanings, as well as an English-Aboriginal section which is useful for those who wish to choose names for houses, boats, etc. 184 mm x 114 mm, 144 pages, illustrated, limp.

Aboriginal Fables by A. W. Reed. A varied collection of Aboriginal folk tales and legends that gives imaginative explanations of animal life and natural things. Included are myths about the creation of the world. 184 mm x 114 mm, 144 pages, illustrated, limp.

Aboriginal Myths by A. W. Reed. This book is divided into three parts, dealing first with acts of creation by the Great Spirit or All father, second with totemic ancestors and third with the origin of natural phenomena and specific features of animal life. 184 mm x 114 mm, 142 pages, limp.

Aboriginal Legends by A. W. Reed. A large selection of Aboriginal legends dealing mainly with the origin of different forms of animal life. The legends come from a variety of tribes from all parts of the continent. 184 mm x 114 mm, 142 pages, limp.

The Australian Aboriginal by Roland Robinson and Douglass Baglin. A fascinating record of the Aboriginals' traditional way of life, with chapters on myths, legends, food gathering, weapons and implements. The book also traces the impact of white society on the Aboriginal since 1770. 279 mm x 215 mm, 128 pages, 86 colour plates, cased, jacketed.

Aboriginals of Australia by Barbara Mullins and Douglass Baglin. A record in words and pictures of the Australian Aboriginal's fast-disappearing way of life, showing food preparation, social behaviour, entertainment and tribal rites. 241 mm x 184 mm, 32 pages, illustrated, limp.

Aboriginal Art of Australia by Barbara Mullins and Douglass Baglin. The art of Australia's Aboriginals reflects their traditional way of life, and this book discusses the best-known forms of Aboriginal art, what they mean, how they were done and where they can be found. 241 mm x 184 mm, 32 pages, illustrated, limp.